WOMEN AND RELIGION IN AMERICA

Women and Religion in America

Volume 1: The Nineteenth Century

ROSEMARY RADFORD RUETHER

ROSEMARY SKINNER KELLER

1817

Harper & Row, Publishers, San Francisco

Cambridge, Hagerstown, New York, Philadelphia
London, Mexico City, Saõ Paulo, Sydney

To the women of the Garrett-Evangelical Theological
Seminary Community:

"S A R A H ' S   C I R C L E ,"

past, present, future

FIRST EDITION

Designed by Jim Mennick

Library of Congress Cataloging in Publication Data

Main entry under title:
    WOMEN AND RELIGION IN AMERICA: THE NINETEENTH CENTURY.

    1. Women in Christianity—United States—History—19th century—Addresses, essays,
lectures. 2. Women in Judaism—United States—History—19th century—Addresses, essays, lectures. 3. United States—Religion—Addresses, essays, lectures. I. Ruether, Rosemary Radford. II. Keller, Rosemary Skinner.
BR515.W648 1981   280'.088042   80–8346
ISBN 0–06–066829–6

---

81 82 83 84 85 10 9 8 7 6 5 4 3 2 1

Contents

63374

Acknowledgments

This volume grew out of a vision that the history of women in religion in nineteenth century America should be written by a group of female historians working in collegial relationship. Our deepest appreciation goes to those five women who have begun to explore with us the vast world of women's ministries in the nineteenth century by contributing analytical articles and primary source documents to this study.

Among us, we discovered archival resources that had been unknown and unused in contemporary times. We are especially grateful for the rich holdings in the library of Garrett-Evangelical Theological Seminary and for the new dimensions of history they have opened up to us. Our particular thanks to Alva Caldwell, librarian, Leo Constantino, formerly of the library staff, and other members of the library staff who have helped us so much. "Remembering Women's History," a bibliography developed by Martha Scott and David Himrod, revealed significant new material, employed throughout this collection.

Special thanks also to Albert Hurd, librarian of the Hammond Library at the Chicago Theological Seminary, and to librarians at the Chicago Historical Society, the Newberry Library, the American Jewish Historical Society at Waltham, Massachusetts, the Chicago Jewish Historical Society at Spertus College of Judaica, and the Special Collections Department of the Rutgers University Library.

Of the many individuals who have helped us recover valuable resources, we particularly thank James Stein, Frederick Norwood, Lois Boyd, Martha Scott, and Joann Brown. Jualynne Dodson, Sylvia Jacobs, and David Wills made possible the inclusion of materials on women in the African Methodist Episcopal Church by sharing their sources and analysis with us. Bob Keller provided discerning criticism and strong support and Naomi Janowitz, Jocelyn Brodie, and Liza Braude also gave valuable help on this project.

Photographer Arch McLean added much to the interest of this volume with his excellent reproduction of pictures. Our typists, Kathi Douglas, Sue Johnson, and Delores Roessler, were much a part of our production team, and we appreciate their involvement and contribution.

Finally, our sincere appreciation to our editor at Harper & Row, Marie Cantlon, for her perceptive evaluation of the strengths and needs of this project and for her guidance in refining the volume.

ROSEMARY RADFORD RUETHER
ROSEMARY SKINNER KELLER

Evanston, Illinois
July, 1980

Grateful acknowledgment is made to the following archives and publishers for permission to reprint material:

"Revelations on the Eternity of the Marriage Covenant, Including Plurality of Wives," Joseph Smith, *Doctrine and Covenants of the Church of Jesus Christ of Latter Day Saints,* Salt Lake City, Utah, 1883, reprinted by permission of Greenwood Press, 1971 reprint edition.

Ellen G. White, *Early Writings,* Review and Herald Press, pp. 11–13 and 32–33. Copyright 1945, reprinted by permission of the Ellen G. White Estate.

"Sophia Hymns," nos. 343, 362, 394, 397, 398, Hilda A. Kring, *The Harmonists: A Folk Cultural Approach,* copyright © 1973, reprinted by permission of Hilda A. Kring and the Scarecrow Press.

Mary Baker Eddy, *Science and Health* (1894, 86th edition, p. 510, lines 1–21; *Science and Health* (1917 edition, p. 560, lines 6–15 and 561, lines 8–29, 32–41 ("The Woman in the Apocalypse"), and *Church Manual* (1906, 53rd edition, article XXII, "Relation and Duties of Members to Pastor Emeritus," reprinted by permission of the Manager, Committees on Publication, The First Church of Christ Scientist, Boston, Massachusetts.

Letter of Archbishop John Carroll to Mother Elizabeth Seton, Sept. 11, 1811, copyright © 1976, The John Carroll Papers, Notre Dame University Press, reprinted by permission of the Archives of the University of Notre Dame.

"Sister Blandina's Adventures in the Southwest," from *At the End of the Santa Fe Trail,* Bruce Publishing Company, reprinted by permission of the Archives of the Sisters of Charity, Mount St. Joseph, Ohio.

Anna Marie Smith, "Diary," 1827–1828, reprinted by permission of the Special Collections Department, Rutgers University.

"1492," "The New Colossus," and sections of "Epistles to the Hebrews," from *Emma Lazarus: Selections from Her Poetry and Prose,* edited by Morris U. Schappes (1978 edition), reprinted by permission of Morris U. Schappes and The Emma Lazarus Federation of Jewish Women's Clubs.

Excerpt from *The Fabric of My Life: The Autobiography of Hannah G. Solomon,* reprinted by permission of Bloch Publishing Company.

Letters of Rebecca Gratz, edited by Rabbi David Philipson, D.D., pp. 73–76, 141–144, 256, 274–275, copyright © 1929, reprinted by permission of The Jewish Publication Society of America.

Introduction

"The time will come," wrote Frances Willard near the end of the nineteenth century, "when these gates of Gospel Grace shall stand open night and day, while woman's heavenly ministries shall find their central home within God's house." As the first president of the Woman's Christian Temperance Union and an active Methodist Episcopal laywoman, Frances Willard was one of the most influential social reformers and strongest advocates for the rights of women in church and society in her age. Her words sum up much of the vision of women in religion in nineteenth century America.

Woman's religious role had been defined primarily as a domestic one prior to this era. Her spiritual power was supposedly best exerted as a quiet influence on her husband and children within their home. The nineteenth century, however, witnessed an explosion of woman's religious involvement as females sought to extend their "heavenly ministries" to a wider "central home within God's house," seeking leadership in churches and synagogues. Women were so bold as to claim that the world was their home as they carried their spiritual impulse into every social reform movement across the land, and even founded new religious movements.

Women and Religion in America: The Nineteenth Century recovers the fascinating story of women's leadership and participation in religious institutions during this formative century. It is a colorful history of the diverse streams of female religious experience. In seven chapters, each including an analytical essay and illustrative documents, experiences of racial and ethnic minority women are examined in relation to the participation of Anglo-Saxon women. The story begins with the leadership of women in evangelicalism and in utopian movements in the early nineteenth century and continues with contrasting pictures of women in the Catholic, Jewish, and Protestant traditions. It examines the struggle of females to be ordained, to gain professional lay status, and to create voluntary societies "for women only" in mainstream Protestantism, concluding with the contributions women made to broad areas of social reform.

This documentary history has been compiled in response to two specific needs. First, participation of women has been virtually unknown in the history of Judaism and Christianity; the focus has been largely on the leadership of men, particularly ordained clergy and rabbis, in religious institutions. Further, though many collections of writings by American women in the nineteenth century have been published, they contain little or nothing of the religious aspect of women's lives. Religious history has often gone unnoticed, or at least been minimized, by historians of secular culture, because of the academic split between secular and church history.

Lack of representation of women's religious views and roles is a serious omission. The fullness of religious and secular history cannot be understood without including women's participation. Equally important, the contributions of women help establish the essential unity of these two streams of history.

Religion in America was being reshaped and redefined during the nineteenth century. Changing definitions of maleness and femaleness were an important part of that reshaping. The location of religion and the definition of women in relation to it were shifting within the dominant Protestant ethos of American society. With the disestablishment of mainline Protestant denominations after the revolutionary war, religion officially became a private concern, plural, personal, and voluntary. All religions were potentially included, although Catholics and Jews experienced the American religious scene as very much molded by Anglo-Saxon Protestantism.

Secularization of society meant that the religious leader lost something of his official standing as a public figure. The old Puritan union of minister and magistrate was broken. Ministers now exerted their influence primarily in voluntary assemblies. The church became an extension of the home rather than the right hand of government. Predominantly female congregations, which already had characterized Protestantism, continued to increase.

The many-faceted story that emerges in these pages reveals the complex role religion played in the lives of women in nineteenth century America. The repressive, isolating, and negative influence of religion is a part of the history which cannot be denied. Location of religion in the domestic or personal side of life reinforced a tendency to see religion as a particularly feminine sphere, to view women as normatively religious and men as preoccupied with the secular concerns of the "real world." Key Christian categories—sacrificial love, servanthood, altruism, and even redemptive grace—came to be identified as characteristically feminine. Piety, domesticity, and submissiveness were also seen as essential to woman's nature and contrary to man's.

In one sense, the feminization of religion strengthened the dominant social ideology and roles of women. Religion was a means of enculturating women to their domestic maternal role, to acceptance of powerlessness and dependency on men. When biblical texts were taken out of the context of larger biblical understandings, they often became powerful tools with which to limit rather than liberate women's spiritual gifts.

On the other hand, religion enabled women to expand their self-understandings and to break out of the traditional roles society had long prescribed for them. The Bible itself provided the strongest justification for human liberation that nineteenth century feminists could employ. Throughout every movement considered in *Women and Religion in America,* one sees religion as an infinitely variable instrument for "enlarging women's sphere" through utopian movements, evangelism, ordination, missionary work, and social reform. The gains made by women through the sanction of faith should be examined within the context of their times, as this volume attempts to do, rather than evaluated from a viewpoint of the late twentieth century. From this proper perspective, the liberating rather than the repressive power of religion predominates.

Each of the seven sections of this documentary history tells its own story; each develops a major theme that distinguishes women's roles in a particular segment of history.

Revivals were the scene of the earliest organized participation of women in religious movements of the nineteenth century. Thus, Martha Blauvelt's chapter on "Women and Revivalism" provides the proper starting point for this volume. The perfectionist view of femininity, which suggests that the woman uplifts "mankind" and directs her husband and children toward virtue, was the impetus for women's participation in revivalism, both as subjects and as promoters of evangelicalism. Because women were understood to be more religious than men, they were seen as the natural subjects of revivalism and as more effective evangelists in their homes and immediate communities. As revivalism flourished, women increasingly sought avenues of expression within the movement; they were no longer simply the *objects* of evangelization. Once converted, they sought to share their religious experiences. First leading female prayer meetings, women began to encroach on mixed prayer meetings and to claim the right to active ministry. From there it was but a short step for women to preach in more public assemblies, setting the stage for their efforts, later in the century, to be ordained.

The perfectionist view of female nature was central not only to revivalism but to much of nineteenth century American religion. Among its most pronounced expressions were the early nineteenth century utopian and millennialist sects, as demonstrated by Rosemary Radford Ruether in her chapter on "Women in Utopian Movements." These sects saw themselves as the avante-garde of a dawning age of human perfection. Many of them viewed the reunion of masculine and feminine elements, or the recovery of a human androgyny in the image of divine androgyny, as the key to redemption. Two female-founded sects, the Shakers and Christian Scientists, explicitly linked the perfection of humanity with the feminine as the higher element representing divine wisdom and love. The Shakers, however, were the only utopian community to develop a consistent system of equal empowerment of women with men. Though elements of feminism are found in utopian communities, their beliefs did not consistently imply the leadership of females alongside men in the structures of community life.

In her discussion of "The Leadership of Nuns in Immigrant Catholicism," Mary Ewens demonstrates a more liberated view of Catholic nuns than has heretofore been cited. Nuns had a mobility, autonomy, and control over their own organizations that could be claimed by few other American women at that time. Yet they were indoctrinated with the traditional view, linked to their separate and celibate female orders, of femininity as subservient to male clerical authority. In a predominantly Protestant society that linked female piety closely to marriage and maternity, the celibate woman was an object of superstitious fear; nuns therefore often received the brunt of anti-Catholic bigotry. They played a major role in introducing Catholicism to America and in gaining greater public acceptance for Catholicism through their devoted service to the church and to civic and military institutions, especially through nursing and teaching. Nuns were not so much drawn to reflect on their role as women as to see themselves as representatives of Catholicism. While Protestant women who nursed in the Civil War thought of their activity as gaining new roles for women, nuns saw their purpose as gaining acceptance for Catholics.

Mainstream Christianity identified women within the home as the bearers of piety and religiosity. This was not true, however, of the heritage that immigrant Eastern European Jews brought to America. Ann Braude describes the traditional role of Jewish women and the adaptations created through Americanization in her chapter on "The Jewish Woman's Encounter with American Culture." Godliness had long been defined as preeminently a male responsibility. Women supported this male godliness by freeing men for piety through female economic activity. In Judaism, in a certain sense, the male was religious and the female secular. The woman's work within the home was understood primarily as a secular activity that allowed her husband to withdraw into religious study and contemplation. One of the particular strains on Jewish communities, as they went through successive attempts to adapt to American middle-class society, was a cultural dissidence with their earlier traditions. The traditional rabbinic male was not sufficiently secular and "masculine," while the traditional Jewish female needed to be more religious and "feminine," by American standards. Developments within Reform Juda-

ism in America encouraged and enhanced the woman's role in the synagogue, and in the process served to expand her whole identification as
a woman.

In mainstream Protestantism, vigorous debate over the right of wom-
en to preach and to be ordained set the stage for the development of
"ordination movements" in the twentieth century. This debate is docu-
mented by Barbara Zikmund in her chapter on "The Struggle for the
Right to Preach." Questions of female propriety were introduced as
women took an increased leadership role in revivals during the early
nineteenth century. After the Civil War, however, scattered individual
women began to seek licenses to preach and to be ordained. The proper
role of women in the church—be it singing, teaching, prayer, or preaching—became an issue of intense debate. Many of the arguments, which
sought to reinterpret biblical authority and social prescriptions of limits
and liberation of women, are as prominent today as they were 100 years
ago.

Though denied ordination and leadership in mainline Protestantism,
women created parallel female societies and sent deaconesses and female
missionaries to home and foreign mission stations throughout the world.
These involvements, which characterized the major functions of women
outside the home in post–Civil War America, are analyzed by Rosemary
Skinner Keller in her chapter on "Lay Women in the Protestant Tradition." The development of separate spheres of service for women had a
dual potential: it could contain and isolate women's work from the major
service of clergymen or it could enable women to develop autonomous
power and self-conscious sisterhood. In fact, women's separatist organizations produced both results. In addition, these associations became the
first training stations for women, enabling them to move into wider fields
of service in the church and in secular society by the end of the nineteenth
century.

Social reform became a religious calling to a large and active segment
of women in nineteenth century America, as demonstrated by Carolyn
Gifford in her concluding chapter on "Women in Social Reform Movements." Female reformers not only worked for the rights of women but
entered all areas of social reform, including abolitionism, education,
peace and arbitration, antilynching, and professional social work. The
question of how women should pursue social reform—within their
homes or in the public arena—was central to their efforts, as in other
areas of their religious involvement. By the end of the century, they had
demonstrated that women could serve wherever their minds, bodies, and
wills took them. Women responded to the increasing secular needs of
society at the turn of the century, but many continued to act out of the
strong theological motivations that had led their sisters into social reform
throughout the preceding era.

A highly utilitarian motivation—that women should extend their "fields of usefulness" beyond the home into active service of the institutional church and society—pervades the literature of women in the preaching tradition, lay work, and social reform. It was an extension of the perfectionist doctrine that women had a special uplifting, even purifying, work that only they could contribute. By establishing their own usefulness, middle-class women justified their worth to themselves and to others in a day when society increasingly viewed females of their class as ornamental appendages to men to enhance the careers of their husbands and sons.

In contrast to the Victorian doctrine of feminist perfectionism, liberalism espoused an egalitarian doctrine of human nature. Associated with a secular or nonreligious view of humanity, it ascribed to all persons the same capacity for reason and conscience. Through this liberal doctrine, on which the Declaration of Independence was based, all persons were assigned equal human rights. Inconsistently, however, proponents failed to apply the theory to blacks, women, and propertyless people.

The utopian and perfectionist strain in American religious thought gravitated toward the complementary view with its suggestion of a redemptive uplift of the "carnal masculine" through the "spiritual feminine." Even militant feminists found it hard to be content with mere claims of equality when they might also suggest that they were superior, that through womanhood would come the redemption of the race! The attitudes of most nineteenth century female leaders, whether of secular or religious persuasion, reflect mingled elements of both the egalitarian and the "higher feminine" traditions in their thought and action.

We do not expect to settle in the volume the question of whether the nineteenth century women's movement did itself a disservice by espousing a complementary rather than consistently egalitarian doctrine of human nature. Our evidence shows that the doctrine of the "higher feminine," so deeply rooted in religious thought, was a complex and pervasive view in nineteenth century America. Through use of this doctrine, women opened up more and more fields of competence for themselves in religion and society while still maintaining an idealistic and redemptive model of women's normative activity.

Although black women's religious movements and roles during this period could easily become the subject of an entire documentary history, we have chosen to show the ethnic diversity of religious roles for women by inclusion rather than separation. Since black women shared many of the same roles as white women—revival subjects and leaders, preachers, deaconesses, missionaries, social reformers—we have included examples of such women in several of the chapters. Such important figures as Sojourner Truth (revival leader), Jarena Lee (preacher), Amanda Berry Smith (evangelist and missionary), and Ida B. Wells-Barnett (reformer) are part of this volume. Black women were also active in utopian movements, especially among the Shakers, who espoused equality of sexes and races from the beginning. There were also "colored" Catholic religious sisterhoods. While black women were seen by white society as a distinct group, their activities paralleled the range of white women's roles in religion.

Although this study is a pioneer effort, a first step in the recovery of the history of women and religion in nineteenth century America, there are many fields of research still to be opened up. For example, religious activities of women in some minority communities, including Hispanic, Oriental, Indian, Eastern, and Southern European, are largely unrepresented in this volume. We hope, however, that our collective assessment will stimulate women and men to deeper understanding and further research and analysis in the many areas of women and religion.

Women and Revivalism

MARTHA TOMHAVE BLAUVELT*

"Revivals of religion," Calvin Colton wrote in 1832, "have been gradually multiplying, until they have become the grand absorbing theme and aim of the American religious World. . . ."[1] Historians have since affirmed the importance of revivalism in nineteenth century American culture and have investigated the origins of religious concern in great detail. But despite their numerous studies of the Second Great Awakening, the "Burned-Over District," and the urban campaigns of Moody, Sankey, and Billy Sunday, scholars have largely neglected the role of women in nineteenth century evangelicalism. Their studies have noted female participation in revivals, but their interpretations of the origins of mass religious fervor have characteristically concentrated on men.

Yet church membership records show that women—mainly women under age thirty—comprised about two-thirds of those joining New Jersey Presbyterian, New England Congregationalist, and Southern evangelical churches during the Second Awakening (1795–1830).[2] Moreover, revival accounts, religious magazines, and clerical correspondence reveal that females often acted as evangelists within their homes and communities and helped instigate the century's frequent revivals. Women's prominence as both revival subjects and promoters invites further investigation. Why were females more susceptible to the evangelical message than males? What methods did women use to foster religious interest in others? An examination of women's role in early nineteenth century revivalism suggests some answers.

WOMEN AS REVIVAL MEMBERS

Women's greater religiosity during the nineteenth century must partly be imputed to cultural expectations. The prescriptive literature of

*MARTHA TOMHAVE BLAUVELT is Assistant Professor of History at Northwestern University. She was formerly a lecturer in history at the University of California at Berkeley and holds M.A. and Ph.D. degrees in American history from Princeton University. She is presently writing a book on Presbyterian evangelicalism from 1730 to 1830.

Victorian America insisted that the "true woman's" very nature was pious; religiosity, it declared, was synonymous with femininity. For a woman to be irreligious was somehow to be unsexed. This association of piety and gender had first appeared in American thought during the last quarter of the eighteenth century, the generation just preceding the Second Awakening in which women were to be so prominent. In articulating these concepts of womenhood, Americans had borrowed heavily from British sex-role literature. Such works as Doctor Gregory's *Letters to His Daughters* and James Fordyce's *Sermons to Young Women* were widely read and reprinted in revolutionary America. (Document 1.) Yet if Americans often used British phrases to express their ideas on women, those ideas themselves had developed in response to peculiarly American conditions.

The late eighteenth century insistence that women were naturally pious reflected both religious reality and a fear that that reality was deceptive. On the one hand, it ratified what Americans had long known: that women were in fact more likely to be religious than men. For female church members had vastly outnumbered males during most of the colonial period. Even during revivals, which were particularly effective in recruiting male converts, men had not always equaled the number of women joining. During the First Great Awakening (1739–1743), for example, the proportion of women admitted to Connecticut churches averaged about 56 percent.[3] The proportion of women joining during nonrevival years was much higher. Americans' late eighteenth century declaration that women were naturally religious was, in one sense, a factual observation.

On the other hand, there is considerable evidence that this belief reflected not so much a confidence in women's natural religiosity as a fear for their impiety. The literature of revolutionary America is filled with condemnations of females who were frivolous, immoral, and selfish. Oblivious to women's greater religiosity, virtually every issue of such journals as the *American Moral and Sentimental Magazine* contained an essay or poem castigating the woman

> Who pants beneath the weight
> Of irksome jewels and afflicting state:
> Whose glass and pillow do her time divide,
> At once oppress'd with sickness and with pride.[4]

These anxieties over women's behavior seem to have been inspired by the revolutionary generation's fear for the Republic. Whig ideology stressed that liberty depended upon popular virtue; the American people must be pious, disinterested, and unworldly if the Republic were to survive. This belief made *everyone's* behavior politically relevant—women's as well as men's—and created an exaggerated awareness of vice. Fearing especially that women would corrupt their sons, whose upbring-

ing was in maternal hands, Americans formulated a feminine ideal that
would threaten neither republican ideals nor male authority. By telling
women that it was natural for them to be pious, men hoped that women
would, in James Fordyce's words, "act up to the best standard of [their]
sex."[5] Convinced that piety was "the only effectual means of insuring
[women's] good behaviour," men marshalled every argument that might
ensure female religiosity. In the process, they formulated an eighteenth
century version of what historian Barbara Welter has called "True Womanhood."[6] It was the woman possessed of modesty and domesticity, but
above all of sensibility and piety, who fulfilled her nature and who would
preserve the Republic.

Development of the belief that, as Benjamin Rush put it, "the female
breast is the natural soil of Christianity," simultaneously calmed patriot
nerves and exhorted women to fulfill their natural destiny.[7] It also assured that the feminization of church membership would intensify. An
ideology which insisted that religion was natural to women implied that
it was somehow unnatural in men. It subtly encouraged men to relegate
religion to their mothers, wives, and sisters; at the same time, it counseled
women to regard religion as their duty. As a result, women participated
in nineteenth century revivals in even greater proportions than they had
during the colonial period.

The immediate circumstances of women's lives encouraged female
religiosity as much as did cultural expectations. Reality had to intersect
with ideology to create the religious need that manifested itself in revivals. What those circumstances were, however, varied from region to
region and class to class; no one interpretation of the place of piety in
women's lives will suffice. Instead, several different explanations must be
considered.

One historian, Nancy F. Cott, has suggested that the peculiar nature
of New England's economy during the early nineteenth century led
women to embrace religion.[8] She has theorized that the region's growing
commercial and market orientation "unsettled" single females by reducing their economic significance within the household and compelling
them to seek outside employment. This often meant geographical mobility, substitution of peer-group ties for family authority, and the decline
of parents in arranging marriages. In short, the modernization of New
England's economy decreased women's power at the same time that it
increased the unpredictability of their lives. In response, Cott maintains,
women turned to religion, the one area in which they could bypass male
authority by voluntarily "coming" to Christ, and entered a world of
sympathetic sisterhood.

Diaries, letters, and conversion accounts from the mid-Atlantic states
suggest yet another interpretation. There the contrast between women's
single and married lives may have made young women especially prone
to conversion. As foreign observers often remarked, nineteenth century

American culture allowed single women much more independence than
their married sisters: they could attend mixed "Frolicks," spend time
alone with men, pay calls, visit neighboring towns, and enjoy other light-
hearted pastimes. It was also acceptable for single women to be irreligious. Indeed, both male and female youth were often openly impious
and derided those who "got" religion. While men could continue to be
independent and irreligious after marriage, however, women could not.
As de Tocqueville noted, "in America the independence of women is
irrevocably lost in the bonds of matrimony. . . . [The unmarried woman]
makes her father's house an abode of freedom and of pleasure; the [wife]
lives in the home of her husband as if it were a cloister."[9]

The marital home was indeed a cloister, and conversion helped wom-
en take their vows. As women approached maturity and marriage, the
frivolity of their youth no longer seemed appropriate, but sinful, and
they became particularly susceptible to the revival's evangelical message.
Like Anna Maria Smith of New Jersey, they quickly succumbed to the
belief that they were "consigned to an everlasting Hell." (Document 2.)
Conversion offered a resolution to such religious anxieties. It also prepared women for the radical change in life that accompanied marriage.
The renunciation of past sinfulness, recognition of one's powerlessness
in matters of salvation, and acceptance of God's sovereignty that characterized the Calvinist conversion paralleled the renunciation of youthful
frivolities, acceptance of a drastic loss in independence, and recognition
of man's superior authority which women experienced as they made the
transition from carefree single girl to stolid matron. In this regard,
conversion was the means through which women adapted to their culture's demands that they submit to both God and man.

While there is ample information on the place of conversion in the
lives of Northern women, discussion of Southern women's religiosity
must be severely limited. Compared to their Yankee sisters, few Southern
women kept diaries or penned conversion accounts. It is therefore difficult to determine the place of conversion in Southern life patterns with
any precision. What evidence remains, however, suggests several distinct
themes. Because Southern religion was closely connected to the camp
meeting, Southern women's conversions were much more spontaneous
and emotional than those of Northern Calvinists. Women acted out their
conversion experiences—rolled convulsively on the floor and shouted
hallelujah—in a manner far different from the labored internal struggles
of Anna Maria Smith.

Camp meetings were also a prominent part of black religion, and
black women, whether slave or free, Southern or Northern, underwent
highly emotional conversions. Amanda Berry Smith, a freed black who
lived in rural Pennsylvania during the 1850s, had determined never to
answer an altar call, but her resolve disappeared in the face of communal
pressure and the revival's high drama. To her amazement, she found

herself rushing headlong to the meeting's altar and shouting until she was hoarse. Blacks and whites at camp meetings also shared a common tendency to personalize religious experiences. Preachers of both races spoke not of abstract evil, but of a devil who actively interfered in human lives. Similarly, sinners experienced their spiritual struggles in concrete terms. Amanda Smith believed the moon and stars rebuked her willfullness and resolved her religious doubts in a debate with Satan himself. (Document 3.) Not only her mind and soul, but the real world participated in the drama of her conversion.

Secondly, many Southern men seem to have resented, rather than encouraged, religiosity in their wives. Perhaps because their slave culture made them sensitive to any loss of authority, many Southern husbands regarded the clergy as competitors for their wives' allegiance. (Document 4.) They were equally afraid that religion might relax their authority over their slaves. The biblical admonition that there was neither slave nor bond, male nor female, in the Lord threatened white Southern males on two fronts.

In sensing religion's threat to their power, Southern men accurately grasped religion's revolutionary role in women's lives, for religion did in fact help free females from male dominance. It convinced slave women such as Sojourner Truth that a divine and "dear friend" loved and would protect her. (Document 5.) It also gave women a new set of values often at odds with their husbands' or owners' values and embued them with a self-confidence and sense of righteousness that enabled them to stand up to human authority. Above all, religion gave women a field in which they could exercise their talents: occasionally as wandering seers, such as Sojourner Truth; more often as evangelists within their homes and communities.

WOMEN AS REVIVAL PROMOTERS

Women's evangelical work was a natural result of their conversions. New converts—male or female—characteristically felt a strong desire to share their experience with others and spread the "good news" of the Lord. This impulse, which was especially strong in Northern religious life during the nineteenth century, provided evangelicalism with thousands of determined proselytizers. Evangelical theology further encouraged religious activism by maintaining that the church member's daily life attested to the reality (or fraudulence) of her conversion; indifference to God's cause suggested that one had not been saved after all. To further assure that church members would take their evangelical duties seriously, clergy explicitly demanded that laity work for revivals. Although they differed on what evangelical activities laity should perform, ministers of all persuasions agreed that the state of religion was the laity's responsibility as well as the clergy's, and women's obligation as well as men's.

The evangelical role ministers found most acceptable for women was, not surprisingly, that of mother. (Document 6.) If women's proselytizing activities are understood in their broadest sense, one must include the pious mother as one of the major evangelical forces of the nineteenth century. Countless converts recalled that their "angel mother" had taught them their first prayers, shed tears over their sins, and prayed daily for their salvation. Religious magazines and anthologies of "revival incidents" contained these examples of women's redeeming love. They suggest that women acted as ministers within their homes. Children formed their congregations, and husbands, in keeping with the nineteenth century's utilitarian approach to religion, paid the church rent but did not attend services.

Devout women attempted to convert adults outside their homes as well as children within. (Document 7.) Despite an illness which kept her in bed from the age of seventeen, Hannah Hobbie (born 1806) of Dutchess County, New York, feverishly worked to foster the piety of her neighbors. The zeal with which she "spen[t] what little strength she had in doing good and glorifying God" elicited her pastor's praise. So, too, did the efforts of another Presbyterian, Jane Coombs Greenleaf (1764–1851), a Massachusetts matron who not only prayed for sinners, but wrote them pointed letters. The discretion with which Greenleaf attempted to convert others forestalled criticism, but her letter to T. C., Esq., suggests the air of command that many women assumed in matters of religion. Such imperiousness would ultimately make men anxious over women's expanding religious activities. The evangelical work among slaves, which Southern women such as Mrs. Ann Page engaged in, similarly invited male retaliation.

Individual efforts of women like Hobbie, Greenleaf, and Page produced periodic conversions, but they rarely precipitated wide-scale repentance. Far more effective in converting sinners was the prayer meeting. The prayer meeting was the most common forum for women's group evangelical efforts. If revival accounts are to be believed, prayer meetings often fostered community-wide revivals. During the nineteenth century, most Northern towns seem to have had a group of pious females who periodically met for prayer. In times of religious prosperity, the prayer meeting functioned like a Bible study group. In periods of spiritual laxity, however, it became a spearhead for moral reform.

Conscious that as church members they were within the covenant of grace and confident that God answered the prayers of His people, devout women responded to apathy with concerted weekly prayers for a revival. Their prayers helped precipitate revivals in that expectations of success made the prayer meeting members especially sensitive to others' spiritual state. Whenever they observed religious awakening in someone, they made sure she did not lose her interest and counseled her on the necessity of repentance. Apparently, members of prayer meetings also pointed out prospective converts to the minister so he, too, could help them. Such systematic efforts not only prevented individuals from lapsing into religious indifference, but also created a communal awareness of the need for reform. This, in turn, made others susceptible to demands for repentance.

As the number of inquiring sinners multiplied, the prayer meeting gained new functions. In the first place, it counseled the newly repentant for whose reform its members had prayed. It explained the steps of salvation to them, overcame their religious doubts, and soothed them during moments of despair. The minister and his elders also performed these functions, but the prayer meeting, which met nightly during revivals and which was organized by neighborhood, was more accessible and offered guidance in a more intimate setting.

Once a revival was under way, the prayer meeting served a sociological as well as religious function. Prayer meetings were usually sexually segregated. The female prayer meeting's leaders were often spinsters or married women who were older than the young single women who formed the majority of repentant sinners. As the leaders of the meeting guided these young women through the steps of conversion, they also guided them into the way of life which nineteenth century culture expected from married women. This way of life separated the single female from the frivolous youth culture that had previously dominated her life and replaced it with a circle of sober religious friends whose lives centered on home and church. In short, the prayer meeting provided crucial support for young women coming of age.

Ministers were grateful for women's evangelical efforts and in fact often depended on them to foster revivals. (Document 8.) Even the most conservative ministers did not deny that female prayer meetings were useful, even necessary, instruments of moral reform. But as pleased as they were with the prayer meeting's results, some clergy worried that women's evangelical commitment might remove them from their divinely appointed sphere.

The question of what exactly women could do to promote revivals became a matter of debate beginning in the 1820s and 1830s. Within the Presbyterian Church, one group of ministers (who would become the Old Side when the Church split in 1837–1838) believed that women might pray for revivals, engage in benevolent work, and proselytize as mothers and Sunday school teachers. However, these ministers also maintained that such efforts could be successful only if women were meek and did not leave their sphere or put themselves in a position superior to men. In particular, they insisted that women could not pray before sexually mixed groups. (Document 9.) Such logic suggests that these clergy prized revivals, but that they prized male authority more.

Opposing the Old Side view was Charles Grandison Finney (1792–1875), who emerged from New York's "Burned-Over District" to become the nineteenth century's leading evangelist. Like Old Side Presbyterians, he emphasized the importance of lay revival efforts. Unlike them, however, he often depicted the laity as wiser and more pious than clergy. (Document 10.) He also differentiated himself from the Old Side in allowing women to lead prayers in "mixed" meetings. Finney combined his liberal views on female evangelism with an Arminian theology and belief in perfectionism, which further alienated him from the Old Side, and in 1836 he left the Presbyterian Church to pursue an independent evangelical career.

It is significant that Finney, who allowed women greater leeway in evangelical activities than most Presbyterians, believed in the possibility of perfect sanctification: that Christians, through God's grace, might free themselves from sin. His rejection of Calvinist determinism and emphasis on the power of the Spirit recalled Quaker religious concepts. Such principles had led Quaker women to disregard society's sexual determinism and to gain equal authority with men in testifying to the Spirit within. Nineteenth century perfectionists never allowed women as much freedom as the Friends had, but their theology seems to have encouraged women to expand their religious role. By the 1850s, perfectionist women within the Methodist denomination had begun to act as public evangelists. A prominent leader of that decade's "Holiness Movement" was Phoebe Palmer (1807–1874), who conducted revivals in the eastern United States and Canada and, later, in Great Britain.

Although perfectionist denominations such as the Methodist permitted women to preach publicly, they were reluctant to recognize officially female clerical ability. Palmer may have broken sexual barriers by conducting revivals, but she always worked side by side with her husband, and the Methodist Episcopal Church never ordained her. It was not until after the Civil War that a licensed female evangelist with a popular following emerged.

In 1869, Margaret Newton Van Cott (1830–1914) became the first woman licensed to preach in the Methodist Episcopal Church in the United States. (Document 11.) Raised an Episcopalian in a wealthy New York family, she converted to Methodism when her husband became ill and a daughter died. An enterprising and forcible woman, Van Cott supported her family by running a wholesale drug company. As her devotion grew, she transferred her considerable energies from business to religion. Like other pious women, Van Cott attended prayer meetings. Unlike most, however, she dared to speak before an all-male meeting. Again, like other women, Van Cott distributed tracts to New York's destitute, but unlike them, she exhorted the poor in groups up to 150. Her evangelical fervor gradually overcame her self-doubts and enabled her to accept individual preaching invitations and finally to apply for and receive an Exhorter's License in 1868 and a Local Preacher's License the following year. Until her retirement in 1902, Van Cott preached throughout the nation.

The female revivalist was the logical result of women's nineteenth century evangelical activities, but few besides Van Cott dared to assume such a public role. The vast majority of women confined their revival efforts to their homes and immediate communities. Prevented from publicly proslytizing men, devout women sought converts mainly among their own sex. Ironically, this assured that more women than men would become church members. For every male minister or elder who attempted to convert males, there were dozens of women who brought their sisters into the fold. Cultural expectations and the circumstances of female life may have made women more susceptible to the evangelical message, but the fact that women were compelled to recruit converts largely among other females assured that evangelical religion would remain women's domain throughout the nineteenth century.

In their evangelical work women occasionally attained fame and often gained a new forum for their talents. They also won a sense of solidarity with other women. The "Cult of True Womanhood" had separated women into their own sphere, but their evangelical faith provided a common understanding of life that united women with bonds far stronger than gender alone could furnish. It made them sisters in the Spirit as well as in the flesh. At the same time that their religiosity united women, it enhanced their world. The dominance of women in evangelical religion transformed their sphere into an *ecclesia in ecclesiolae,* a church within a church, and endowed it with a spiritual significance which the male realm entirely lacked.

In this manner, piety both bound women together and uplifted them. As such, it had important implications for the development of feminism. In that piety made women's lives more bearable and provided them with a sense of importance within their assigned sphere, it lessened discontent and helped integrate them into American culture. But to the degree that feminine piety embued women with a sense of moral superiority and righteousness and bred discontent with a system that limited their evangelical work, it encouraged feminism. Until the popular basis of nineteenth century feminism has been studied in detail, it would be difficult to say how piety affected women's views of their station. What remains clear is that the periodic awakenings of the nineteenth century revived not only religion but a spirit of sisterhood and high purpose among women.

Black preacher Amanda Berry Smith was one of the most powerful evangelists and effective missionaries of the nineteenth century. James Thoburn, Methodist Episcopal bishop, testified that he learned more of actual value to him as a preacher from Amanda Smith than from any other person. [From Donald W. and Deane K. Dayton, *Discovering an Evangelical Heritage* (New York: Harper & Row, 1976), p. 107.]

Evangelist Margaret ("Maggie") Newton Van Cott became, in 1869, the first woman to be granted a local preacher's license in the Methodist Episcopal Church. In 1880, as women increasingly began to seek ordination in the denomination, the license was revoked. [Courtesy Frederick Norwood, Garrett-Evangelical Theological Seminary.]

The baptism of a woman on a farm in Kansas illustrates the religious commitment of women and men as early settlements grew in the West. Many such women went on to become effective evangelists themselves. [From Vergilius Ferm, *Pictorial History of Protestantism* (New York: Philosophical Library, 1957), p. 349.]

Abolitionist, reformer, and women's rights advocate, Sojourner Truth was one of the most famous black women of the nineteenth century. Her social commitments were based on a deep religious faith. [From the Sophia Smith Collection, Women's History Archive, Smith College, Northampton, Mass.]

Documents: Women and Revivalism

WOMEN AS REVIVAL MEMBERS

Document 1: The Ideology of Feminine Piety

A Scottish-born Presbyterian who became a popular London preacher during the 1760s and 1770s, the Reverend James Fordyce (1720–1796) was interested in women's place on earth as well as in the hereafter. He wrote several works on feminine character, of which his 1765 Sermons to Young Women *was the most popular. Repeatedly published in the colonies during the revolutionary era, it taught Americans that religion was both necessary and natural in "the true woman."*[10]

That your sex are, in a particular degree, susceptible of all the tender affections, will, I presume, be allowed by most. Their propensity to those, with which the passion of love is more immediately complicated, has been charged upon them by many as matter of reproach. What to me appears in general to do them honour is the warmth of their attachments, and their aptitude to be affected with whatever has a tendency to touch the heart. But I have always thought that the spirit of devotion depends on sentiment, rather than ratiocination; on the feelings of gratitude and wonder, joy and sorrow, triumph and contribution, hope and fear, rather than on theological disquisition however profound, or pious speculation however exalted. . . .

Nothing can be more plain, than that Providence has placed you most commonly in circumstances peculiarly advantageous for the exercises of devotion, and for the preservation of that virtue, without which every profession of godliness must be regarded as an impudent pretence. The situation of men lays them open to a variety of temptations, that lay out of your road. The bustle of life, in which they are generally engaged, leaves them often but little leisure for holy offices. Their passions are daily subject to be heated by the ferment of business; and how hard is it for them to avoid being importuned to excess, while sometimes a present interest, frequently a pressing appetite, and yet more frequently the fear of ridicule, stimulates them to comply! How very hard for a young man to withstand

> "The world's dread laugh,
> "Which scarce the firm philosopher can scorn!"

In the case of our sex, do we not often see ranked on the side of licentiousness that reputation which ought to attend on sobriety alone? Is not the last openly laughed at by those to whose opinion giddy young men will pay most respect, their own companions? Is not its contrary cried up as a mark of spirit? And if, in their unrestrained conversation amongst a diversity of humours, they meet with affronts, are they not constantly told, that the maxims of honour require them to take revenge? Is not all this extremely unfavourable to the religious life, of which so great a part consists in purity and prayer, in regularity and coolness, in self-command and mild affections? But from such snares your sex are happily exempted. . . .

Corrupt as the world is, it certainly does expect from young women a strict decorum; nor, as we have seen before, does it easily forgive them the least deviation. Add that, while you remain without families of your own, few of you are necessarily so engaged, as not to have a large portion of time with daily opportunities for recollection, if you be inclined to improve them. I go farther and subjoin, that your improving them by a piety the most regular and avowed, if withal unaffected and liberal, will be no sort of objection to the men, but much the reverse.

A bigoted woman every man of sense will carefully shun, as a most disagreeable, and even dangerous companion. But the secret reverence, which that majestic form Religion imprints on the hearts of all, is such, that even they who will not submit to its dictates themselves, do yet wish it to be regarded by those with whom they are connected in the nearest relation. The veriest infidel of them all, I am apt to believe, would be sorry to find his sister, daughter, or wife, under no restraint from religious principle. Thus it is, that even the greatest libertines are forced to pay, at the same instant, a kind of implicit respect to the two main objects of their profligate satire, Piety and Women; while they consider these as formed for each other, and tacitly acknowledge that the first is the only effectual means of insuring the good behaviour of the last. Let them talk as long, and as contemptuously as they will, about that easy credulity, and those superstitious terrors, which they pretend to be the foundation of your religion; something within will always give them the lie, so long as they perceive that your religion renders you more steadily virtuous, and more truly lovely. . . .

That your souls are immortal is probable from reason, and certain from revelation. But the arguments from either I hold it unnecessary to propose here. To attempt the conviction of female infidels falls not within my present design. Indeed I fear it were a hopeless undertaking. The preposterous vanity, together with the open or secret profligacy, by which they have been warped into scepticism, would in all likelihood baffle any endeavours of mine. If they be not however so far gone in that unhappy system, as to be resolved against all sober inquiry, I would earnestly recommend to their perusal a few of the many excellent writings, which this age and country have produced in favour of religion both natural and revealed. At the same time I would just remind them, that the daring and disputatious spirit of unbelief is utterly repugnant to female softness, and to that sweet docility which, in their sex, is so peculiarly pleasing to ours; not to mention, that from an infidel partner a man can have no prospect of consolation in those hours of distress, when the hopes of futurity can alone administer relief.—To you, my christian hearers, I was going to observe, that the stedfast and serious belief of immortality, as pointed out in your frame, and brought to light by the gospel, will excite such a mighty concern to secure its grand interests, such a high sense of your internal dignity, such a predominant ambition of being acceptable in his sight, who can make you happy or wretched forever, as must necessarily lessen in your esteem every external and perishing advantage.

Document 2: The Conversion within the Revival

An obscure small-town girl from New Jersey, Anna Maria Smith (1811–?), described her 1827–1828 conversion with a breathlessness, drama, and lack of terminal punctuation that suggests how over-whelming the experience was for her. Like many of the Second Awakening's subjects, Smith was only sixteen or seventeen when she converted and joined the Freehold Presbyterian Church.[11]

Upper Freehold, May 1827. A special meeting of several days was during this month, held at the church in which the Rev. Mr. Perkins-Halsey and Norton assisted the Pastor the Rev. William Woodhull. At these meetings I felt the influences of the Holy Spirit saying unto me, "Sinner prepare to meet thy God," I for a time made a few feeble efforts to seek the Savior and the salvation of my soul, I prayed but trusting to my prayers and my good resolutions I tryed to feel that they were sufficient, but alas I soon found that the word of God "that his Spirit will not always strive with man" was verified in me, for I succeeded too well in stifling conviction, Tho I said it not with my lips "Go thy way for this time when I have a more convenient season I will call for thee," yet practically I did, for Thou on God knowst what a hardened sinner I became, I neglected what I knew to be duty. I held in derision thy people, and what was I not but the chief of sinners, and if Thou hadst dealt in Justice without mercy, I would now be where the offers of salvation are never made, and where hope never cometh. But glory be to God in the highest for his good will towards me, that I am still spared and as I humbly trust have been washed in the blood of Jesus, and renewed and sanctified by the Holy Spirit of God, I continued for many months in a very unhappy state of mind, and in the month of September I left home on a visit to Trenton and other places which was almost the ruin of my soul. In yielding to the solicitations and temptations of young companions, I drove the Holy Spirit from me, I ceased to pray and became hardened in sin, I reasoned with myself that I was yet too young to give up the pleasures of the world and attend the gloomy concerns of religion, Such was my state of mind when I returned home in December, God was there in the midst of his people reviving their hearts and convincing sinners of their sins, and very many were seriously impressed, meetings were held almost every evening at which Mr. Norton mostly officiated, and as it was under his preaching I had been impressed I felt a dread and fear of attending them, for I now felt a perfect disgust for him, But as the rest of the family were going on Christmas eve I concluded to go with them, Tho no one had known of my former convictions I was fearful that my friends would suspect me, I therefore endeavored more and more to harden my heart and with a thoughtless careless manner entered the sanctuary of God and there truly did I understand what my end would be if I still continued to reject the offers of his mercy, It seemed as if every word of that discourse was for me alone, I left that house of God a deeply convicted sinner, never will I forget that walk home, the agony of concealing my feelings from my friends when in the anguish of my heart I could have cryed "What must I do to be saved."

Jan the 1st 1828. This evening I again went to Church. Mr. Woodhull preached; his text was these words "Redeeming the time." The discourse was deeply affecting to me, I thought perhaps I might redeem my many mispent and misimproved hours, I prayed for God to forgive my sins, I felt as if every moment I was in danger of my being consigned to an everlasting Hell and that each moment I was spared was a surprise. There was no comfort for my poor sinsick soul, for I have since found I sought not in Christ. There was anxious meetings held but I was ashamed to go for I did not wish my parents or friends to know that I was under conviction, I continued in this state of mind a most unhappy being for six weeks, afraid to let my feelings be known, spending sleepless nights and anxious days, When one evening my Father and sister Rebecca were about starting to church I concluded to go with them, Mr. Woodhull's remarks were upon the danger of stifling conviction, and of delaying to seek the salvation of the soul, and in the conclusion of his remarks earnestly invited all defering until some future time the concerns of their souls but at some other time intended to repent, If a dagger had then pierced my heart I do not think I could have felt it more forcibly. It almost seemed to me as if all Hell was let loose for my destruction and all Heaven for my conversion, I thought it strange how Mr Woodhull knew the feelings of my heart so well but I felt as if the invitation was intended for me. Tho the struggle was great God assisted me to tell my parent and sister I intended to remain, Several others also stayed, Mr W conversed with each of us, he said he was most surprised to see me there as he was not at all aware of my being in such a state of mind, but oh what a relief to my feelings to thus give way to the feelings so long concealed to one who could point me to the Lamb of God who taketh away the sins of the world. He prayed with and for us, that we might all of us be converted to thee and thy service oh God, When I returned home my family seemed such surprised and endeavoured to ridicule me out of the notion as they said, which somewhat disheartened me from trying my peace with God, I now felt a strong desire to attend the meetings and felt a love for Gods people and that they would do me good, and not evil as I once thought, but my mother was not willing that I should go without some of the rest of the family went with me, I one evening expressed a strong desire to go to which she was unwilling, After the regular services which were very affecting to me there was one of inquire, my Father was willing I should stay if Mr W would accompany me home, to which he kindly consented, At that meeting and in that walk home he urged me freely to make known my feelings to him and wished me to renounce all self dependance and to seek reconciliation with that God against whom I felt I had sinned and who was justly offended with me through his Son the great propiation which he had provided and through whom alone salvation could come, He reminded me of Jacob to like him wrestle in prayer and poor helpless sinful heavy ladened sinner as I felt myself to be, to still cry "I will not let thee go except Thou bless me," When we separated he entreated me to no longer postpone but at once give myself to Christ and yield my self a willing captive, . . . I sometimes thought I would cease to seek his favour, and then I again would try to gain his favour by some good act of my own, by my prayers, tears and repentance, I thought I looked to Christ but it was through my own merits, and yet I felt that I had no merit within me, and that there was no hope or mercy for me, and God would not hear me, I continued to attend the religious meetings, and to visit my pastor for instruction, but still could not feel that there was mercy for me, March the Sacrament of the Lords Supper was administered, a great many then joined themselves with the people of the Lord, I also felt a great desire to do so, but knew that I had no evidence of an interest in Christ and the devil and my own wicked heart almost urged me to despair, whilst the flattering charms and pleasures of the world were placed in bright array before me to allure me from the pleasant fruits of religion and I began to feel that God was a hard master that he would not hear, and that he had given me up to a hard and reprobate heart, But I resolved to make one more effort, another agonising struggle, a complete renunciation, and oh then light shone around my path I now felt that it was not God who would not accept me, but that I would not accept Christ on his terms, I endeavoured to examine myself, and prayed that God would assist me, which he graciously did, I now found that I had been trying to put my sins from me, before I came to him, but I now flew to him a guilty heavy ladened sinner, and ever blessed be his holy name he took my load of guilt upon himself, washed me in his blood, clothed me with his robe of righteousness, and put a new song in my mouth even that of redeeming love. On the 21st of June 1828 I went before the session of the Church as a candidate for admission but how great the effort, Tho not openly opposed by my friends, yet I was in no way encouraged by them, young in years, with but little experience and of a naturally timid and shrinking disposition with every inducement to turn to the world, with not one pious relative to cheer me on my way, what was it but thy grace oh God that supported me . . . , But God raised me up a faithful friend in my beloved pastor, To him I had confided both my temporal and spiritual sorrows, and when in much weakness and many misgivings I appeared amongst Gods people to give some account of his dealings with my soul he my pastor was as it were my mouthpiece, and recommended me as a fit person to be named as one of Christs followers, . . . oh that he may never be deceived in me, but grant me grace oh my Father in heaven to always adorn the profession which I have now made, And as I have stood in the presence of men, angels, and Thee, and have been baptised in the name of the Father, the Son, and the Holy Ghost, so may the presence of the sacred Three ever abide upon me. Some time before I joined the church I became a member of the female prayer meeting where I spent many delightful hours, I also had become a teacher in the Sabbath school. I had also become acquainted with that dear friend M. C. L. tho afflicted more than words can express, yet always exhibiting a cheerful patient christian spirit, oh how much has her example done for me at this great turning point of my life, and perhaps has been effectual in the salvation of my soul, Truly the promise of God that those who seek him early shall find him has been verified in me, and I know that if I am thine none can [illegible] me out of thy hand. . . .

Document 3: The Conversion within the Camp Meeting

In her 1893 autobiography, Amanda Berry Smith (1837–1915) described the conversion she experienced as a young wife of nineteen.

Her piety helped Smith endure two unhappy marriages and hard labor as a washerwoman. After Smith experienced "sanctification" in 1868, she devoted herself entirely to evangelicalism. During the last third of the nineteenth century, she preached at "holiness" camp meetings in the United States and Britain and evangelized the people of Africa and India. Although she was never ordained, Smith gained an international following unusual for both her sex and her race.

In this excerpt from her autobiography, Amanda Smith describes her own conversion through a struggle with Satan and God.[12]

In 1855 I was very ill. Everything was done for me that could be done. My father lived in Wrightsville, Pa., and was very anxious about my soul. But I did not feel a bit concerned.

I wanted to be let alone. How I wished that no one would speak to me. One day my father said to me, "Amanda, my child, you know the doctors say you must die; they can do no more for you, and now my child you must pray."

O, I did not want to pray, I was so tired I wanted to sleep. The doctors said they must keep me aroused. In the afternoon of the next day after the doctor had given me up, I fell asleep about two o'clock, or I seemed to go into a kind of trance or vision and I saw on the foot of my bed a most beautiful angel. It stood on one foot, with wings spread, looking me in the face and motioning me with the hand; it said "Go back," three times, "Go back. Go back, Go back."

Then, it seemed, I went to a great Camp Meeting and there seemed to be thousands of people, and I was to preach and the platform I had to stand on was up high above the people. It seemed it was erected between two trees, but near the tops. How I got on it I don't know, but I was on this platform with a large Bible opened and I was preaching from these words:—"And I if I be lifted up will draw all men unto me." O, how I preached, and the people were slain right and left. I suppose I was in this vision about two hours. When I came out of it I was decidedly better. When the doctor called in and looked at me he was astonished, but so glad. In a few days I was able to sit up, and in about a week or ten days to walk about. Then I made up my mind to pray and lead a Christian life. I thought God had spared me for a purpose, so I meant to be converted, but in my own way quietly. I thought if I was really sincere it would be all right.

I cannot remember the time from my earliest childhood that I did not want to be a Christian, and would often pray alone. Sometimes I would kneel in the fence corner when I went for the cows to bring them home. Sometimes upstairs, or wherever I could be alone. I had planned just about how I was going to be converted. I had a strong will and was full of pride. When I said I would not do anything, I was proud of my word, and people would say, "Well, you know if Amanda says she won't do anything, you might as well try to move the everlasting hills." And that inflated me and I thought, "O, how nice to have a reputation like that." I would stick to it; I would not give in; my pride held me. I went on in this course till 1856.

In a watch meeting one night at the Baptist Church in Columbia, Pennsylvania, a revival started. I lived with Mrs. Morris, not far away, and I could hear the singing, but I did not mean to go forward to the altar to pray. I didn't believe in making a great noise. I said, "If you are sincere the Lord will bless you anywhere, and I don't mean to ever go forward to the altar; that I will never do." So I prayed and struggled day after day, week after week, trying to find light and peace, but I constantly came up against my will. God showed me I was a dreadful sinner, but still I wanted to have my own way about it. I said, "I am not so bad as Bob Loney, Meil Snievely, and a lot of others. I am not like them, I have always lived in first-class families and have always kept company with first-class servant girls, and I don't need to go there and pray like those people do." All this went on in my mind.

At last one night they were singing so beautifully in this Church, I felt drawn to go in, and went and sat away back by the door and they were inviting persons forward for prayers. O, so many of them were going, the altar was filled in a little while, and though I went in with no intention of going myself, as I sat there all at once,—I can't tell how,—I don't know how.—I never did know how, but when I found myself I was down the aisle and half way up to the altar. All at once it came to me. "There, now, you have always said you would never go forward to an altar, and there you are going."

I thought I would turn around and go back, but as I went to turn facing all the congregation, it was so far to go back, so I rushed forward to the altar, threw myself down and began to pray with all my might: "O, Lord, have mercy on me! O, Lord, have mercy on me! O, Lord, save me," I shouted at the top of my voice, till I was hoarse. Finally I quieted down. There came a stillness over me so quiet. I didn't understand it. The meeting closed. I went home.

If I had known how to exercise faith, I would have found peace that night, but they did not instruct us intelligently, so I was left in the dark. A few days after this I took a service place about a mile and a half from Columbia, with a Quaker family named Robert Mifflins. This was in January. I prayed incessantly, night and day, for light and peace.

After I had got out to Mr. Mifflins', I began to plan for my spring suit; I meant to be converted, though I had not given up at all, but I began to save my money up now. There were some pretty styles, and I liked them. A white straw bonnet, with very pretty, broad pink tie-strings; pink or white muslin dress, tucked to the waist; black silk mantilla; and light gaitar boots, with black tips; I had it all picked out in my mind, my nice spring and summer suit. I can see the little box now where I had put my money, saving up for this special purpose. Then I would pray: O, how I prayed, fasted and prayed, read my Bible and prayed, prayed to the moon, prayed to the sun, prayed to the stars. I was so ignorant. O, I wonder how God ever did save me, anyhow. The Devil told me I was such a sinner God would not convert me. Then I would kneel down to pray at night, he would say, "You had better give it up; God won't hear you, you are such a sinner."

Then I thought if I could only think of somebody that had not sinned, and my idea of great sin was disobedience, and I thought if I could only think of somebody that had always been obedient. I never thought about Jesus in that sense, and yet I was looking to Him for pardon and salvation.

All at once it came to me, "Why, the sun has always obeyed God, and kept its place in the heavens, and the moon and stars have always obeyed God, and kept their place in the heavens, the wind has always obeyed God, they all have obeyed."

When I set my people down to tea in the house I would slip out and get under the trees in the yard and look up to the moon and stars and pray, "O Moon and Stars, you never sinned like me, you have always obeyed God, and kept your place in the heavens, tell Jesus I am a good sinner." One day while I was praying I got desperate, and here came my spring suit up constantly before me, so I told the Lord if he would take away the burden that was on my heart that I would never get one of those things. I wouldn't get the bonnet. I wouldn't get the shoes. O, I wanted relief from the burden and then all at once there came a quiet peace in my heart, and that suit never came before me again: but still there was darkness in my soul. On Tuesday, the 17th day of March, 1856, I was sitting in the kitchen by my ironing table, thinking it all over. The Devil seemed to say to me (I know now it was he), "You have prayed to be converted."

I said, "Yes."

"You have been sincere."

"Yes."

"You have been in earnest."

"Yes."

"You have read your Bible, and you have fasted, and you really want to be converted."

"Yes, Lord. Thou knowest it; Thou knowest my heart, I really want to be converted."

Then Satan said, "Well, if God were going to convert you He would have done it long ago; He does His work quick, and with all your sincerity God has not converted you."

"Yes, that is so."

"You might as well give it up, then" said he, "it is no use, He won't hear you."

"Well, I guess I will just give it up. I suppose I will be damned and I might as well submit to my fate." Just then a voice whispered to me clearly, and said, "Pray once more." And in an instant I said, "I will." Then another voice seemed like a person speaking to me, and it said, "Don't you do it."

"Yes, I will."

And when I said, "Yes, I will," it seemed to me the emphasis was on the "will," and I felt it from the crown of my head clear through me, "I WILL," and I got on my feet and said, "I will pray once more, and if there is any such thing as salvation, I am determined to have it this afternoon or die."

I got up, put the kettle on, set the table and went into the cellar and got on my knees to pray and die, for I thought I had made a vow to God and that He would certainly kill me, and I didn't care, I was so miserable, and I was just at the verge of desperation. I had put everything on the table but the bread and butter, and I said, "If any one calls me I won't get up, and if the bread and butter is all that is to go on the table, Miss Sue [the daughter] can finish the supper, and that will save them calling for me, and when they come down cellar after it they will find me dead!"

I set the tea pot on the table, put the tea cady down by it, so that everything would be ready, and I was going to die; and O, Hallelujah, what a dying that was! I went down into the cellar and got on my knees, as I had done so many times before, and I began my prayer. "O Lord, have mercy on my soul, I don't know how else to pray." A voice said to me, "That is just what you said before."

"O, Lord, if Thou wilt only convert my soul and make me truly sensible of it, for I want to know surely that I am converted. I will serve Thee the longest day I live."

"Yes," the Devil says, "you said that before and God has not done it, and you might as well stop."

O, what a conflict. How the darkness seemed to gather around me, and in my desperation I looked up and said, "O, Lord, I have come down here to die, and I must have salvation this afternoon or death. If you send me to hell I will go, but convert my soul." Then I looked up and said, "O, Lord, if thou wilt only please to help me if ever I backslide don't ever let me see thy face in peace." And I waited, and I did not hear the old suggestion that had been following me, "That is just what you said before," so I said it again. "O, Lord, if Thou wilt only please to convert my soul and make me truly sensible of it, if I backslide don't ever let me see Thy face in peace."

I prayed the third time, using these same words. Then somehow I seemed to get to the end of everything. I did not know what else to say or do. Then in my desperation I looked up and said, "O, Lord, if Thou wilt help me I will believe Thee," and in the act of telling God I would, I did. O, the peace and joy that flooded my soul! The burden rolled away; I felt it when it left me, and a flood of light and joy swept through my soul such as I had never known before. I said, "Why, Lord, I do believe this is just what I have been asking for," and down came another flood of light and peace. And I said again, "Why, Lord, I do believe this is what I have asked Thee for." Then I sprang to my feet, all around was light, I was new. I looked at my hands, they looked new. I took hold of myself and said, "Why, I am new, I am new all over." I clapped my hands; I ran up out of the cellar, I walked up and down the kitchen floor. Praise the Lord! There seemed to be a halo of light all over me; the change was so real and so thorough that I have often said that if I had been as black as ink or as green as grass or as white as snow, I would not have been frightened. I went into the dining room, we had a large mirror that went from the floor to the ceiling, and I went and looked in it to see if anything had transpired in my color, because there was something wonderful had taken place inside of me, and it really seemed to me it was outside too, and as I looked in the glass I cried out, "Hallelujah, I have got religion; glory to God. I have got religion!" I was wild with delight and joy; it seemed to me as if I would split! I went out into the kitchen and I thought what will I do, I have got to wait till Sunday before I can tell anybody. This was on Tuesday; Sunday was my day in town, so I began to count the days, Tuesday, Wednesday, Thursday, Friday, Saturday, Sunday. O, it seemed to me the days were weeks long. My! can I possibly stand it till Sunday? I must tell somebody, and as I passed by the ironing table it seemed as if it had a halo of light all around it, and I ran up to the table and smote it with my hand and shouted, "Glory to God, I have got religion!"

Document 4: Southern Male Opposition to Female Piety

Converted at age sixteen in a camp meeting, Peter Cartwright (1785–1872) became the most powerful Methodist evangelist on the nineteenth century Southern and Illinois frontiers. His Autobiography *(1857) provides invaluable accounts of the forces at work within the Southern revival. In this description of an 1814 Tennessee camp meeting, he suggests that the revival was, in effect, a duel for woman's soul.*[13]

There was another incident which occurred at this meeting that I will relate. Not very distant from Hopkinsville, near which town I lived, there was a very interesting, fashionable, wealthy family, who were raised with all the diabolical hatred that a rigidly-enforced predestinarian education could impart against the Methodists. It had pleased God, at a camp-meeting near them, that I superintended, to arrest the wife and two of the daughters of the gentleman who was the head of this family, and they were powerfully converted, and joined the Methodist church, and, as is common, they felt greatly attached to me as the instrument, in the hands of God, of their salvation. This enraged the husband and father of these interesting females very much. He not only threatened to whip me, but to kill me. He said I must be a very bad man, for all the women in the country were falling in love with me; and that I moved on their passions and took them into the Church with bad intentions. His eldest daughter, a fine, beautiful, intelligent young lady, wanted to attend the above-mentioned camp-meeting, and bespoke a seat in my carriage, in company with others going to the same meeting. At first her father swore she should not go; but on second thought he consented, but told his wife and daughter that he would go along, and that he would watch me closely, and that he had no doubt, before he would return, he would catch me at my devilment, and be able to show the world that I was a bad man, and put a stop to the women all running mad after this bad preacher. His daughter made ready, and we all started. We had about twenty-eight miles to go to reach the encampment. His daughter thought it her duty to tell me the designs of her father, and said she hoped I would be on my guard, for she verily thought that her father was so enraged that if he could not get something to lay to my charge to ruin my character as a preacher, he would kill me from pure malice. I told her, of course, I was wide awake, and duly sober, and I had not the least fear but what God would give me her father as a rescued captive from the devil before the camp-meeting closed. Said I, "You must pray hard, and the work will be done." I said to her, "It is not the old big devil that is in your father; it must be a little weakly, sickly devil that has taken possession of him, and I do not think that it will be a hard job to cast him out." "Now," said I, "if God takes hold of your father and shakes him over hell a little while, and he smells brimstone right strong, if there was a ship-load of these little sickly devils in him, they would be driven out just as easy as a tornado would drive the regiments of mosquitoes from around and about those stagnant ponds in the country. Cheer up, sister; I believe God will give me your father before we return." Seeing me so bold and confident, she wept, and raised the shout in anticipation of so desirable an event. When we got to the camp-ground, I had the company and their horses all taken care of, and then said to this man, "We have a large preachers' tent well provided with good beds; come, you must go with me and lodge in the preachers' tent." He seemed taken by surprise, and hesitated, but I took him right into the tent. "Now, sir," said I, "make yourself at home, for I hope to see you soundly converted before this camp-meeting comes to a close." I saw his countenance fall, and perhaps this was the starting point of his deep and pungent convictions. The trumpet sounded for preaching; I mounted the stand and preached; this man came and heard me. I saw clearly from his looks that he was convicted, and had a hard struggle in his mind. He said to me, after the meeting was over, that my taking him into the preachers' tent and treating him so kindly was the worst whipping he ever got; he could not sleep, he said. Sometimes he thought he was a poor mean devil to treat me as he had done; and surely I must be a Christian or I never could treat him so kindly after he had said so many hard and bitter things about me. As the meeting progressed, his convictions increased till he could neither eat nor sleep.

On Sunday night, when such a tremendous power fell on the congregation, and my gang of rowdies fell by dozens on the right and left, my special persecutor fell suddenly as if a rifle ball had been shot through his heart. He lay powerless, and seemed cramped all over, till next morning; and about sunrise he began to come to. With a smile on his countenance, he then sprang up, and bounded all over the camp ground, with swelling shouts of glory and victory, that almost seemed to shake the encampment. This was a glorious time for his daughter; she came leaping and skipping to me, and shouted out that those little mean and sickly devils were cast out of her father. He joined the Church, went home, and for days the family did little else but sing, pray, and shout the high praises of God.

Document 5: The Religious Experience of the Female Slave

Born a slave in New York state, Sojourner Truth (1797–1883), known as Isabella until 1843, was the most famous black female religious figure in antebellum America. After she gained her freedom in 1827, she wandered the country in response to mystical voices and preached that God was loving and kind. Her Narrative of Sojourner Truth, *which the abolitionist Olive Gilbert wrote for her in 1850, provides one of the few accounts of a black woman's religious experience. Sojourner Truth was in her twenties at the time she underwent this conversion.*[14]

She talked to God as familiarly as if he had been a creature like herself; and a thousand times more so, than if she had been in the presence of some earthly potentate. She demanded, with little expenditure of reverence or fear, a supply of all her more pressing wants, and at times her demands approached very near to commands. She felt as if God was under obligation to her, much more than she was to him. He seemed to her benighted vision in some manner bound to do her bidding. . . .

She at first commenced promising God, that if he would help her out of all her difficulties, she would pay him by being very good; and this goodness she intended as a remuneration to God. She could think of no benefit that was to accrue to herself or her fellow-creatures, from her leading a life of purity and generous self-sacrifice for the good of others; as far as any but God was concerned, she saw nothing in it but heart-trying penance, sustained by the sternest exertion; and this she soon found much more easily promised than performed.

Days wore away—new trials came—God's aid was invoked, and the same promises repeated; and every successive night found her part of the contract unfulfilled. She now began to excuse herself, by telling God she could not be good in her present circumstances; but if he would give her a new place, and a good master and mistress, she could and would be good; and she expressly stipulated, that she would be good *one* day to show God how good she would be *all* of the time, when he should surround her with the right influences, and she should be delivered from the temptations that then so sorely beset her. But, alas! when night came, and she became conscious that she had yielded to all her temptations, and entirely failed of keeping her word with God, having prayed and promised one hour, and fallen into the sins of anger and profanity the next, the mortifying reflection weighed on her mind, and blunted her enjoyment. Still, she did not lay it deeply to heart, but continued to repeat her demands for aid, and her promises of pay, with full purpose of heart, at each particular time, that *that* day she would not fail to keep her plighted word. . . .

[Isabella was sold to a new and kind master, and in his service she ceased prayer. But one day just prior to a religious holiday,] she says that God revealed himself to her, with all the suddenness of a flash of lightning, showing her, "in the twinkling of an eye, that he was *all over*"—that he pervaded the universe—"and that there was no place where God was not." She became instantly conscious of her great sin in forgetting her almighty Friend and "ever-present help in time of trouble." All her unfulfilled promises arose before her, like a vexed sea whose waves run mountains high; and her soul, which seemed but one mass of lies, shrunk back aghast from the "awful look" of Him whom she had formerly talked to, as if he had been a being like herself; and she would now fain have hid herself in the bowels of the earth, to have escaped his dread presence. But she plainly saw there was no place, not even in hell, where he was not: and where could she flee? Another such "a look," as she expressed it, and she felt that she must be extinguished forever, even as one, with the breath of his mouth, "blows out a lamp," so that no spark remains.

A dire dread of annihilation now seized her, and she waited to see if, by "another look," she was to be stricken from existence,—swallowed up, even as the fire licketh up the oil with which it comes in contact.

When at last the second look came not, and her attention was once more called to outward things, she . . . [said] aloud, "Oh, God, I did not know you were so big," walked into the house, and made an effort to resume her work. But the workings of the inward man were too absorbing to admit of much attention to her avocations. She desired to talk to God, but her vileness utterly forbade it, and she was not able to prefer a petition. "What!" said she, "shall I lie again to God? I have told him nothing but lies; and shall I speak again, and tell another lie to God?" She could not; and now she began to wish for someone to speak to God for her. Then a space seemed opening between her and God, and she felt that if some one, who was worthy in the sight of heaven, would but plead *for* her in their own name, and not let God know it came from *her*, who was so unworthy, God might grant it. At length a friend appeared to stand between herself and an insulted Deity; and she felt as sensibly refreshed as when, on a hot day, an umbrella had been interposed between her scorching head and a burning sun. But who was this friend? became the next inquiry. Was it Deencia, who had so often befriended her? She looked at her with her new power of sight—and, lo! she, too, seemed all "bruises and putrifying stores," like herself. No, it was some one very different from Deencia.

"Who *are* you?" she exclaimed, as the vision brightened into a form distinct, beaming with the beauty of holiness, and radiant with love. She then said, audibly addressing the mysterious visitant—"I *know* you, and I *don't* know you." Meaning, "You seem perfectly familiar; I feel that you not only love me, but that you always *have* loved me—yet I know you not—I cannot call you by name." When she said, "I know you," the subject of the vision remained distinct and quiet. When she said, "I don't know you," it moved restlessly about, like agitated waters. So while she repeated without intermission, "I know you, I know you," that the vision might remain—"Who are you?" was the cry of her heart, and her whole soul was in one deep prayer that this heavenly personage might be revealed to her, and remain with her. At length, after bending both soul and body with the intensity of this desire, till breath and strength seemed failing, and she could maintain her position no longer, an answer came to her, saying distinctly, "It is Jesus." "Yes," she responded, "it is *Jesus.*"

Previous to these exercises of mind, she heard Jesus mentioned in reading or speaking, but had received from what she heard no impression that he was any other than an eminent man, like a Washington or a Lafayette. Now he appeared to her delighted mental vision as so mild, so good, and so every way lovely, and he loved her so much! And, how strange that he had always loved her, and she had never known it! And how great a blessing he conferred, in that he should stand between her and God! And God was no longer a terror and a dread to her.

She stopped not to argue the point, even in her own mind, whether he had reconciled her to God, or God to herself, (though she thinks the former now,) being but too happy that God was no longer to her as a consuming fire, and Jesus was "altogether lovely." Her heart was now full of joy and gladness, as it had been of terror, and at one time of despair. In the light of her great happiness, the world was clad in new beauty, the very air sparkled as with diamonds, and was redolent of heaven. She contemplated the unapproachable barriers that existed between them, and the union existing between herself and Jesus,—Jesus, the transcendently lovely as well as great and powerful; for so he appeared to her, though he seemed but human; and she watched for his bodily appearance, feeling that she should know him, if she saw him; and when he came, she should go and dwell with him, as with a dear friend.

WOMEN AS REVIVAL PROMOTERS

Document 6: The Mother as Evangelist

This example of a mother's redeeming love, taken from a popular mid-nineteenth century revival anthology, was one of literally thousands published in Victorian America. Women must have read such accounts with a sense of gratification, for they promised ultimate, if delayed, vindication.[15]

"MY MOTHER'S PRAYERS HAUNT ME."—A mother with several children was left a widow. Feeling her responsibility as a parent, she gave diligence to train her household for Christ. That her instructions might be blessed and her children converted, she was unceasing in her supplications at the throne of mercy. She would arise at midnight, and in the chamber where her little ones were sleeping, would kneel and pray for them with wrestling importunity.

Her eldest son becoming restless under religious restraints, abandoned his mother and the home of his childhood. He bent his steps to a seaport, and enlisted as a sailor. He was absent several years, made a number of voyages, and under the influence of wicked companions became profligate.

At length he was induced to visit the place of his nativity. His mother, who had heard nothing of him from the time of his departure, was dead, and the residue of her family scattered. Of her death the sailor felt an interest to learn some particulars, and whether any members of the family were still living, or remained in the vicinity of his birth. But how was he to obtain the desired information! "A man's heart deviseth his way, but the Lord directeth his steps." It was a time of religious revival in the congregation where his mother had been accustomed to worship. He was told of a prayer-meeting in the neighborhood; and knowing that his devout parent used to attend such meetings, he directed his course thither, thinking that he might there meet some of her old acquaintances.

When the sailor arrived at the place of worship, he found the meeting in progress. He entered and took a seat in an obscure corner, intending, at the close of service, to ask for the information he was seeking. The assembly was one of great stillness and solemnity, such as a genuine revival of religion usually produces. The mariner would not have been dismayed at the thunder of the storm upon the heaving ocean, but he could not brave the silent power of the prayer-meeting and religious conference. He could hear nothing, save the voice of one and another relating what God had done for their souls, or the suppressed sign and stifled sob, which arose from different parts of the congregation. The "still, small voice" of the Holy Spirit, who had conducted him thither, was speaking to his conscience. Unable to quench the fire within, or longer conceal his anguish, he exclaimed vehemently, *"My mother's prayers haunt me like a ghost!"*

Those who well remembered the praying mother, and had a slight recollection of the wayward boy, now became deeply interested in the distressed man. Such counsel was imparted as the circumstances and state of his feelings seemed to demand; but he writhed with keen conviction for several weeks. At length he found peace in hopeful reconciliation to God and faith in the Lord Jesus Christ; and in due time became an exemplary and useful member of the same church with which his mother had been connected.

Document 7: Individual Efforts to Foster Piety

Hannah Hobbie and Jane Coombs Greenleaf tried to foster revivals by accosting or writing to neighbors and relatives and demanding that they repent. Mrs. Ann Randolph Page (1781–1838) of Virginia inculcated piety in a different group: her slaves. Here she records her anxieties over her slaves' souls. After her husband died in 1826, Mrs. Page freed her slaves and sent them back to Africa.

Rev. Robert Armstrong describes Hannah Hobbie's evangelical activities:[16]

It is painful to witness the apathy of multitudes who profess to be the followers of Christ, and their habitual neglect of *effort to save sinners*—to see them idle in the Lord's vineyard, even in the possession of firm health, and apparently contented, while hardly evincing a desire to spend and be spent in the Lord's service. The *aged* can look back without alarm upon a long series of years in which they have made few if any efforts for the salvation of a single soul. The *young,* in all the vigor of youthful enterprise, are laying plans to consume their years and spend their strength in the pursuit of worldly interests, and not in labors and sacrifices for the salvation of men. Such was not the piety of Hannah Hobbie.

She was anxious *to do* something for the salvation of souls—to spend what little strength she had in *doing good* and glorifying God. Few would have done anything situated as she was—nothing would have been attempted. Sickness is often considered a plea for giving up every thing like active effort; but her views of obligation were such that she could not rest while any strength and opportunity remained to promote the Savior's cause. Her obedience to his commands was *cheerful,* and therefore universal and persevering; as she loved God's work, she panted continually after more extensive usefulness. Having done what she had purposed, she devised other plans of doing good, that she might still pursue her Master's work.

Think of her practice of conversing with the impenitent friends who visited her on the subject of their salvation—of the *letters written* from her sick bed, all breathing an ardent desire to be useful, and some of them expressly designed as a personal effort for the salvation of a soul. Think of a suffering and feeble young female exerting successfully her influence to form those of her own sex around her into a *society for assisting the Missionary and the Tract cause;* endeavoring also to assemble around her sick bed her sisters in Christ; in a stated *concert of prayer,* and resolving to take part in the necessary exercises of the meeting; and then think of such an one, almost wasted away by years of excruciating pain, using her influence with her friends to collect the wandering children of her destitute neighborhood into a Sabbath school; and when she found those efforts fruitless, girding up her own loins to the work, and gathering them *every Sabbath into her sick chamber,* that she might herself instruct them in eternal things. Think of all this, ye that are blest with health, and opportunity, and means to do good, and yet neglecting them; and is there no reason to fear that she will in judgment rise up and condemn you?

The following letter was written by Jane Coombs Greenleaf to T. C., Esq., of Newburyport.[17]

Presuming on your goodness to forgive this intrusion, I take my pen to address a few lines to you, sir, upon the interesting subject of real religion.

I venerated your father; and I do not give up the pleasing hope, which I have entertained for many years, that you, his beloved son, may become truly pious, and preach the everlasting gospel to perishing sinners. . . .

When I hear that Mr. C. attends this and that lecture in the week, I begin to think that your dear father's prayers will be answered, and that you are to be called into the sheepfold of Christ. What a shining Christian you may yet make! Let me entreat you to engage on the Lord's side with all your heart; read the Bible, and pray; attend the most lively means of grace; ask for the teachings of the Holy Spirit; forsake every sin, and soon you may find "the pearl of great price." . . . But, perhaps, Mr. C. thinks that to pass through this mighty change of heart, of which I have been writing, is not essential to salvation. Let us, however, look into the Word of truth, and see how it is represented there. It is called "being born again,"—"made a new creature,"—"passing from death unto life,"—"being born of the spirit." If your father were now on earth, I believe he would explode this new divinity, which is termed liberality of sentiment. I sat under his ministry for several years, and expect to give an account hereafter of the improvement I made of his faithful preaching. He used often to close his sermons in this way: "I have set life and death before you; choose you this day whom you will serve."

For many years I have had a great desire for your real conversion, and I could not resist the impulse I have felt to take this method of addressing you on this great subject. When I think of the worth of one immortal soul, I am willing to lay aside all ceremony, and to be called a fanatic, if I may be the humble instrument of awakening any to seek for "the pearl of great price." Separate from our future happiness, "virtue carries its own reward with it." To "fear God and keep his commandments is the whole duty of man." The true penitent is the only happy man.

I know that the spirit of God only can convince us of the importance of eternal realities; but we are free agents, and are commanded to seek for wisdom "as for silver, and search for it as for hid treasure." Our Saviour says, "Ask, and you shall receive; seek, and ye shall find"; but our misery is that we will not leave this vain, dying world, for joys that will last for ever.

Your friend,

J. G.

The following excerpts were taken from the private writings (1825) of Mrs. Ann Page Randolph:[18]

[1825] Regard in mercy, O God! the whole sad scene which thou hast caused me in mercy for so many years to mourn over, and bring before thee by night on my often sleepless bed—sleepless from pressing thoughts for some remedy for evils which continue because, alas! they are not considered evils. Thy Sabbaths are profaned; thy word is not made known to the throngs who inhabit the smoky huts, and till our fields. Their souls are so dear to thee as ours, who have the priceless treasure of thy word committed to us. Wilt thou not then visit for these things? Will not thy long-suffering at last come to an end? Shall thy Sabbaths and thy word be deposited in our hands for the use of souls, and we wrap ourselves up in selfishness and forget that thou hast said that for all these things thou wilt bring us into judgment? Forbid it, Lord. Awake us—arouse us—strike an alarm from the vast ocean of eternity which rolls so near! Give us to believe the awful threatenings against those who slight thy Sabbaths and neglect to labor for souls committed to their charge, who let ignorance reign, and suffer thy people to be destroyed for lack of knowledge. Open our eyes to the gross and almost heathenish darkness which surrounds us. Take away our selfishness, and give us to care more for the bodies as well as the souls of our slaves, knowing that we must give an account of our stewardship.

[1823] Added to my own especial needs, I have to lay before Thee this night, the case of one who professes to belong to thy fold, and dear to me for thy sake, my servant according to the flesh, but my sister in thy love. She lacks knowledge to adorn her profession, and I have often to reprove her for conduct which would be wrong in such as make no profession. This she takes not alright. Give her for Christ's

sake a clearer light, that she may know how to walk, so as to bring
honor to thy name, which she professes. I have ardently desired to
try every means to bring her right, yet let me not give up in despair.
Of myself, I never could have borne what I have with her, but faith
and patience must be tried. To keep closer to thee, and feel thy
wisdom working for me, is my only support. Correct what is wrong,
both in her soul and mine, as thou seest what is wanting in both.

Document 8: The Female Prayer Meeting

*Perhaps the most common female revival effort was the prayer
meeting. By the 1820s, its evangelical efforts were so accepted that a
Presbyterian magazine could suggest that God showers down His
grace in direct proportion to women's prayers.*[19]

(Furnished by a Clergyman)

Soon after I was constituted the pastor of one of the Congregational churches in Connecticut, it was ascertained, that some fifteen or
twenty females of this church were usually solicitous for the salvation
of sinners. They conversed much respecting the long continued and
distressing declension, which had obtained among them, and their
christian friends with whom they were associated. Their tears and
prayers were mingled together before God, and they silently, yet
critically, watched the signs of the times. It was not long before, at a
lecture in a part of the parish remote from the centre, there were
found three persons evidently under the special operations of the
Holy Spirit. One of this number, to the great joy of these sisters in
Christ, soon gave evidence of a change of heart. A second lecture,
without much delay, was preached in the same neighborhood; at
which meeting eleven persons were found, who were deeply affected
in view of their spiritual state. At the close of the service an opportunity was improved for personal conversation with each of them, and
not many days were suffered to pass before they were seen and
conversed with the second time. A part of them were now supposed
to be under pungent convictions of sin. Their pastor was then necessarily absent from town a few days.—On his return, his first business
was to visit these anxious sinners; but alas, he found them not in a state
of anxiety like that in which he left them. All, without exception, were
far less solicitous respecting the salvation of their souls; and the serious impressions of no small proportion of them were erased, and they
were unwilling to make religion a subject of conversation. It was so
ordered, that on the same day in which this mournful fact was ascertained, the little band of pious females, of whom mention has been
made, were assembled together. Their minister, without communicating to them a knowledge of this fact, asked them individually,
what had been their religious feelings and conduct for a few days

previous. There was, substantially, but one answer given to the interrogation. Each person was constrained to confess, that she had not, during that period, had so lively an interest at the throne of grace—she had been involved more deeply in the cares of the world—and had thought less of the condition of impenitent sinners. It was then stated to them, that the persons, who were a short time before viewed as being convicted of sin, were now in an unpromising state, having lost, in a great degree, their serious impressions.—This statement called forth, as we trust, tears of repentance. A resolution was unanimously adopted, to devote a certain portion of time to special fasting and prayer. The convictions of the eleven persons, to whom allusion has been made, were renewed—their hopeful conversions succeeded, one after another; and all of them, together with *fifty-six* other persons, were in a few months added to the church.

Document 9: The Conservative View of Women's Evangelical Activities

Ashbel Green (1762–1848), influential Presbyterian minister, used a Philadelphia magazine, The Christian Advocate, *as a forum for his conservative theological and social views. Green was president of the College of New Jersey (1812–1822) and also president of Princeton Seminary's board of directors (1812–1848). In the following sermon, he was attempting to draw the line between proper and improper female religious activities.[20]*

> *Mark 14:8—First part.*
> *"She hath done what she could—."*

These words are found in the narrative of a very interesting incident in the life of our blessed Redeemer. Six days before the Jewish Passover at which he entered on his last sufferings, a supper, or festival entertainment, was made for him at Bethany; . . . Martha and Mary, were both present. With her characteristic activity, Martha served at the supper-table; and Mary, with her wonted reverential love to her Lord and Redeemer, and animated no doubt with the liveliest gratitude for the interposition of his almighty power, in calling her beloved brother from the tomb, gave him, on this occasion, a signal expression of sense of obligation, and of the high estimation in which she wished that others should hold him. . . . His recumbent attitude, then always in use at the supper table, was peculiarly favourable to her design. Approaching him in this reclining posture, she broke the box of liquid Nard, and poured it, first on his head, and afterwards on his body and his feet. And then, while the house was filled with the odour of the ointment, this holy devoted woman kneeled at the feet of Jesus, and wiped them with the flowing tresses of her hair.

Christian sisters, are you tempted to envy your sister Mary?—To envy the opportunity she had to express, in a most striking and affecting manner, her humble, ardent attachment, to your common and adored Redeemer? Envy not—but imitate her. Opportunities still occur, to express love and gratitude to your unseen Saviour, by acts as acceptable to him as that of Mary was; and which he will, ere long, acknowledge and reward, before the assembled universe. . . .

We propose, therefore, in the sequel of this discourse, *to endeavour to ascertain and state, what Christian women may do; and what they may not do; in manifesting their love to Christ, and their desire to do him honour.*

It may be proper just to remark, in a preliminary way, that genuine love to Christ, and a rational desire to do him honour, will always manifest themselves in earnest endeavours to render the Redeemer precious in the estimation of others.—In using all proper means to propagate the knowledge of his glorious person; of his excellent doctrines; of his great salvation; of the obligations which sinners owe him; and of the absolute necessity of their embracing for themselves his offered mercy, as the only sure ground of their hope for eternity. . . .

In prosecuting our purpose, as already stated, we may find it advantageous to consider—

I. The negative part of our subject; namely, what Christian women may not do, in manifesting their love to their Saviour, and their desire to do him honour.

It is plainly intimated in the text, that Mary's efforts to honour her Redeemer, were limited. When it is said, "she hath done what she could," the implication is obvious, that she would have done more, if more had been in her power—if propriety would have permitted, or if means and opportunity had not been wanting. By what circumstances and consideration, then, were her efforts limited? *In the first place,* I answer—by the bounds prescribed to her by her sex itself. Happy is that woman who always finds that she *cannot* do, what it is improper for her to do *as a woman;* whose whole mind and feelings are so set against whatever misbecomes her, that she experiences a fortunate incapacity to attempt it. The Saviour, to whom Christian women are to manifest their attachment, is their Creator and Lord. He framed them with that shrinking delicacy of temperament and feeling, which is one of their best distinctions, which renders them amiable, and which, while it unfits them for command, and subjects them, in a degree, to the rougher sex, gives them, at the same time, an appropriate and very powerful influence. It was therefore not to be expected, that he who formed them with this natural and retiring modesty, and under a qualified subjection to man, would ever require, or even permit them, to do anything in violation of his own order; and least of all that he would permit this, in his own immediate service. Hence I apprehend it is, that we find in the New Testament, such texts as the following—1 Timothy 2:11–14: "Let the woman learn in silence with all subjection. But I suffer not a woman to teach, nor to usurp authority over the man, but to be in silence. For Adam was first formed, then Eve. For Adam was not deceived, but the woman being deceived was in the transgression." ...

The same apostle, who, under the unerring guidance of Divine inspiration, delivered these plain and positive injunctions, has also said—1 Corinthians 11:5: "Every woman that prayeth, or prophesieth, with her head uncovered, dishonoureth her head; for that is even all one as if she were shaven." Here, unquestionably, is a direction how women ought to appear and act, when speaking in a publick Christian assembly; for the connexion of the passage shows clearly, that it is of such an assembly that the apostle is here treating. This latter direction, therefore, has the appearance of militating pointedly with the texts before recited; and as we know that inspired truth can never contradict, or be inconsistent with itself, it becomes a serious question—how is this apparent inconsistency to be cleared up? We answer, that in our apprehension it can be done in one way only; but in that way, easily and perfectly. Let it be carefully observed then, that during the period of miraculous endowments, under the Gospel dispensation, as well as under that of Moses, the gift of supernatural inspiration was sometimes conferred on women, as well as on men. We are told expressly, that Philip the Evangelist "had four daughters, virgins, that did prophesy." Now, in the last quoted passage, the apostle is plainly speaking of women under supernatural inspiration; but in the other passages, of women under no such inspiration. It appears, therefore, that by a miraculous gift, the great Head and lawgiver of the church, took the case of the women on whom he bestowed that gift out of the general rule; and authorized them to utter, even in publick assemblies, what his own Spirit dictated at the time. But on all other and ordinary occasions—to which our first quotations refer—they are absolutely required not to speak, but to keep silence in the churches. It is also worthy of special remark, that even when divinely authorized to speak, they were still commanded to be covered; as indicative of a delicate reserve, and as recognising a state of subjection. But as we assuredly believe, that miraculous inspiration has long since ceased in the Christian church, no such excepted cases as those we have mentioned, can any longer occur. The general rule, therefore, laid down by the Spirit of Christ, speaking by the mouth of St. Paul, is now in force, without an exception. Women are, in no case, to be publick preachers and teachers, in assemblies promiscuously composed of the two sexes. ...

Let us now consider, more directly,

II. What Christian women may properly do, as a manifestation of their love to their Saviour, or for the promotion or extension of his religion. . . .

First, that Christian women should be very sensible that the religion of their Saviour is greatly adorned, and sometimes directly promoted, by an exemplary discharge of all the customary duties of life. Perhaps it belongs to women to prove the truth of this observation, more frequently and strikingly than can be done by men. . . . It should, therefore, never be forgotten, that Christian women ought practically to demonstrate, that the influence of their religion has rendered them better wives, better mothers, better daughters, better sisters, better neighbours, and better friends, than they would otherwise be; and more active, punctual, conscientious, and persevering, in the discharge of all the ordinary duties of life. . . .

Secondly, it is one of the peculiar and most important duties of Christian women, to instruct and pray with children, and to endeavour to form their tender minds to piety, intelligence, and virtue. Here is a wide fertile field of their appropriate labours, in the service and for the honour of their Redeemer. The earliest years of children are usually and necessarily past, almost wholly, under female care; and it is much earlier than is commonly supposed, that their minds and moral feelings take a cast, which is often as lasting as life. Of what inconceivable importance is it then, that this first moulding of the mind and heart should be favourably made; and that mothers should know and remember that if *so* made, it must commonly be made by them. They have the capacity of mingling, as it were, their own souls with the souls of their children—of breathing into them, with a maternal tenderness and sympathy for which there can be no substitute, those sentiments of filial reverence for their Creator and Redeemer, and of veneration for all that is holy and lovely in the religion of the Gospel, which, under the Divine blessing, may become, and do often in fact become, the germs of early and vital godliness. . . .

Nor does maternal influence, in favour of piety and virture, terminate with the infant, or early years of children. A mother's influence is of the utmost consequence—very often it is greater than any other influence—through the whole of youth, and even to a more advanced age. The young man, or young woman, on whom the counsels, prayers, and tears of a pious mother have lost their commanding effect, has indeed reached the threshold of hopeless perdition. . . .

5. Christian women may manifest their love to their Saviour, to his cause, and to communion with himself, by associations for prayer among themselves; and by keeping up the worship of God in their households, in the absence of a male head of the family. . . . The supposition is, that in female prayer meetings, women *only* meet with women. In the devotional exercises carried on in such circumstances, there is surely no ground for the charge of arrogant assumption, or of any trespass on female decorum. Why then should any object to

this sacred communion of sisterhood, in which devout women mingle their prayers and their praises—their prayers for each other, for their husbands, for their children, and for the church of God? Verily, we believe that these female offerings come up as sweet incense, before the throne of a prayer-hearing God; and that often, in the most signal manner, he returns to the offerers answers of peace. . . .

7. Bible Societies, Tract Societies, Education Societies, Jews Societies, Charity Schools, Orphan Asylums, Widows' Asylums, and all institutions of a similar character to these, present to Christian women objects and opportunities for manifesting their love to their Saviour and his cause, which they may seize and improve, with the greatest freedom and advantage. And truly they have, in our day, seized and improved them, with an activity, and to an extent, which are worthy of the highest praise. In several instances, within the knowledge of the speaker, the energy, perseverance, and success of Christian women, in cultivating these fields of pious usefulness, have reproved the more sluggish efforts of men. It was reserved for the age in which we live, and it is among the indications, as we hope, of a better age approaching, that female agency should be called on, to take part in almost every plan and effort for extending the Gospel, or for abating the sufferings, or meliorating the condition of mankind. . . .

Go on, Christian sisters. "Be not weary in well doing, for in due time you shall reap, if you faint not." Often think of the number of immortal souls, that are everyday and every hour passing into eternity, from the multitudinous population of India—vicious, polluted throughout, and totally ignorant of that Saviour, whose blood alone "cleanseth from all sin." Often think on your special obligations to "God who hath called you unto his kingdom and glory." Often think on the distinguishing and merciful allotment of his providence, in giving you birth and education, in a Christian, instead of a heathen or Mahomedan land. And while you perceive, as you cannot fail to perceive, that women have a peculiar interest in the propagation of revealed truth—since the influence of that alone has ever raised them to their proper rank in society, and sustained them in it—feel that you are under peculiar obligations to extend the knowledge of that truth, by all means in your power; to extend it for the benefit of all, but especially for the benefit, both temporal and eternal, of your own sex. . . .

Men and brethren, who hear me on this occasion. Be reminded that there is a divine injunction laid on us, in relation to the subject, which has now been discussed. The apostle Paul, speaking as he was moved by the Holy Ghost, has said—"Help those women that laboured with me in the Gospel." Yes, it is the sacred duty of us all, to help these female gospel labourers; to help them with our countenance and encouragement; with our prayers and our purses; with every aid and every facility which we can afford them, in their benevolent exertions. For whom do they labour? Not more for themselves than for us. Nay, in many of these pious labours, they are directly helping us; they are taking part of that burden on themselves, which used to be borne by us alone.—They are doing for us, generously and nobly, a part of our special business. And shall there be a creature in the form of a man, so much without the spirit of a man, as to hinder, and not help them, while thus employed—to mock them with laughter or ridicule, or even to treat them with a cold and discouraging neglect? Such a being, I trust there is not in this assembly. . . .

Document 10: Charles Grandison Finney on Female Evangelicalism

During the 1830s, Charles Grandison Finney delivered a series of sermons in New York City on how to create a revival. Published as his Lectures on Revivals *in 1835, they show his utilitarian approach to the revival. They also inadvertently suggest his dependence on women in evangelicalism; most of his examples of successful lay revival efforts feature women rather than men, and many of those women were more strongly evangelical than their ministers.*[21]

A revival may be expected when Christians have a spirit of prayer for a revival. That is, when they pray as if their hearts were set upon a revival. Sometimes Christians are not engaged in prayer for a revival, not even when they are warm in prayer. Their minds are upon something else; they are praying for something else—the salvation of the heathen and the like—and not for a revival among themselves. But when they feel the want of a revival, they pray for it; they feel for their own families and neighborhoods, and pray for them as if they could not be denied. What constitutes a spirit of prayer? Is it many prayers and warm words? No. Prayer is the state of the heart. The spirit of prayer is a state of continual desire and anxiety of mind for the salvation of sinners. It is something that weighs them down. It is the same, so far as the philosophy of the mind is concerned as when a man is anxious for some worldly interest. A Christian who has this spirit of prayer feels anxious for souls. It is the subject of his thoughts all the time, and makes him look and act as if he had a load on his mind. He thinks of it be day, and dreams of it be night. This is properly praying without ceasing. . . .

When this feeling exists in a church, unless the Spirit is grieved away by sin, there will infallibly be a revival of Christians generally, and it will involve the conversion of sinners to God. This anxiety and distress increases till the revival commences. A clergyman in W——n told me of a revival among his people, which commenced with a zealous and devoted woman in the church. She became anxious about sinners, and went to praying for them; she prayed and her distress increased; and she finally came to her minister, and talked with him, and asked him to appoint an anxious meeting, for she felt that one was needed. The minister put her off, for he felt nothing of it. The next week she came again, and besought him to appoint an anxious meeting; she knew there would be somebody to come, for she felt as if God was going to pour out his Spirit. He put her off again. And finally she said to him, "If you don't appoint an anxious meeting I shall die, for there is certainly going to be a revival." The next Sabbath he appointed a meeting, and said that if there were any who wished to converse with him about the salvation of their souls, he would meet them on such an evening. He did not know of one, but when he went to the place, to his astonishment, he found a large number of anxious inquirers. Now don't you think that woman knew there was going to be a revival? Call it what you please, a new revelation or an old revelation, or any thing else. I say it was the Spirit of God that taught that praying woman there was going to be a revival. "The secret of the Lord" was with her, and she knew it. She knew God had been in her heart, and filled it so full that she could contain no longer.

If you have the Spirit of God, you must expect to feel great distress in view of the church and the world. . . .

You will be often grieved with the state of the ministry. Some years since I met a woman belonging to one of the churches in this city. I inquired of her the state of religion here. She seemed unwilling to say much about it, made some general remarks, and then choked, and her eyes filled, and she said, "O, our minister's mind seems to be very dark." Spiritual Christians often feel like this, and often weep over it. I have seen much of it, and often found Christians who wept and groaned in secret, to see the darkness on the minds of ministers in regard to religion, their earthliness and fear of man; but they dared not speak of it, lest they should be denounced and threatened, and perhaps turned out of the church. I do not say these things censoriously, to reproach my brethren, but because they are true. And ministers ought to know, that nothing is more common than for spiritual Christians to feel burdened and distressed at the state of the ministry. I would not wake up any wrong feelings towards ministers, but it is time it should be known, that Christians do often get spiritual views of things, and their souls are kindled up, and then they find that their minister does not enter into their feelings, that he is far below the standard of what he ought to be, and in spirituality far below some of the members of his church. This is one of the most prominent, and deeply to be deplored evils of the present day.

Document 11: The Evolution of the Female Revivalist

Margaret ("Maggie") Van Cott was rebuffed the first time she spoke in a men's prayer meeting, but in time friends recognized her gifts and invited her to preach. These excerpts from a contemporary's reminiscences show how she gained in confidence and emerged as an authoritative and effective evangelist by 1868.[22]

One cold, snowy day [in the early 1860s in New York City], being obliged to take a large package of pills to the Broad-street firm, and settle some accounts, she passed through Fulton-street. So terrible was the storm, that she saw no other lady on the street, when, presently, her eye caught the sign of the noonday prayer-meeting. Looking at her watch she knew she had time to drop in, get a blessing from heaven, and reach her desired place of business. About forty gentlemen were present, and she the only lady. The prayers were glorious, the testimony grand, and her heart began to feel the glow of Jesus' love. Five minutes before one o'clock she arose, and occupied three minutes testifying of the power of Christ to save. She was sweetly blest. The meeting closed, and as they descended the stairs, she was met by one, who, after considerable clearing of his throat, and a polite bow, said, "Ah, madam, ah—we—do not—ahem"—

Quick as thought the truth flashed through her mind that she was a woman, and had dared to speak of her precious Savior in the presence of men. She caught his words, and continued them, "You do not permit ladies to speak in your meetings."

"I won't say permit," was the reply, "but it is strictly a men's meeting; and there are plenty of places elsewhere where women can speak."

"I am aware of it, sir, thank God; but I thought I felt the Spirit of the Lord, and I am taught that 'where the Spirit of the Lord is there is liberty.' Please excuse me, sir; I will never intrude again."

"O, no intrusion, madam; come again."

"Thank you; I will when I can go nowhere else."

As she passed on, choked with deep emotion, a gentleman stepped to her side, and said,

"Don't weep, lady; I know what you have passed through; but they have dealt gently with you. I have known them to tell ladies of great refinement and talent to stop and sit down, when the room has been full of people, but as true as you live, I feel that that is just what the Fulton-street meeting wants, to make it a power greater than it ever has been."

[In February, 1868, Mrs. Van Cott went to visit some friends in Greene County, New York.]

In the morning the family gathered in the cozy sitting-room for prayers. The aged father in Israel conducted the devotions. He was one of those great, good-hearted men, whose Christian deportment and sound judgment impressed all with whom he associated—tall and heavy, with full chest, high forehead, and white hair, he was one of the noble of earth. A slight stroke of palsy had disturbed his nerves, and his whole frame trembled, despite his strong will and best endeavors to steady his hand. They sat in quiet meditation for a moment after devotions, when Rev. John Battersby arose, took the family Bible, crossed the room, and handed it to Mrs. Van Cott, saying,

"Child, I want you to take this book, look out a subject, and preach for us at the school-house to-night."

Completely overcome with surprise, she turned pale, hesitated, and finally said, "Sir, I can not preach."

"Why, Charley"—his son at the Leonard-street mission—"writes us that you preach three or four times each week, and it is a pity you can not preach for us once."

"Father Battersby, I never attempted to preach; I do not understand the first rule. I do the best I can to talk for Jesus, and praise his name—he saves precious souls—but as to leading a meeting here, I can not do it; but if you will go on with your meeting, I will do my part."

"No, you must preach."

"Excuse my rudeness; but I will not."

"Why not?"

"Because I am not willing to show myself so foolish. You tell me there are four local preachers within a mile of this place, and they know much more of the Bible than I. The people on the Five Points are very illiterate, and I do not mind speaking to them, but I can not here."

Placing the Bible in her lap, he continued, "The people expect it, and you must."

"If the people expect it, it is your fault"; and she began to weep.

"Don't feel bad; we never have more than ten or twelve persons out, and Charley says you sometimes speak to a hundred and fifty at your meeting. Come, cheer up, God will help you."

Left alone with the thought "you must preach," strange memories ran through her mind. The word "preach," as applied to her efforts, was always harsh, and undesirable; and then some thoughtless persons were ever putting "Rev." on her letters, a thing she could never sanction; and then she remembered a certain dream of some months agone. Of dreams she cared but little, but this one was peculiar. It ran thus:

In her accustomed place at church she heard a voice saying, "You must preach."

"You are mistaken; I do not know how to preach," she replied to the unseen messenger.

"It makes no difference; you must preach."

"I am a lady; it is the work of the gentlemen to preach."

"Come," the voice continued, "the church is crowded, and the people expect it."

As she obeyed, and ascended the pulpit, the thought arose, "I'll do the very best I can to tell the people of the love of Jesus."

The house was indeed crowded, but she saw no one in particular, save a dear old gentleman sitting near the altar. After services she asked one of the brethren, "Can you tell me who that gentleman is, with his silver hair dressed in a cue?"

"That is Rev. John Wesley, the founder of Methodism."

A shudder passed over her frame, and she asked again, "Have I been speaking before one so talented as Mr. Wesley?"

At this moment he stepped forward, took her trembling hand, saying, "Do not be alarmed, my child; you will speak before greater than I."

The whole dream had such a vividness, and so many things in harmony with the duties then before her, that to hesitate longer might be sin. True, Wesley was dead, dreams were nothing; but an aged veteran was before her, and others would be there of sound mental and theological culture.

And then, again, previous to her leaving the city, a lady friend, to whom she had intrusted her class-meeting, asked, "Was you ever called to preach?"

To which she answered, "No, never."

"Was you called for a class-leader?"

"No."

"What was you called for, then?"

"I do not know, unless it was to live for God, and make my way to heaven; and I find this about as much as I can do. Take good care of my children and, God willing, I will be at home next week."

But to return: Evening came, and at "early candle-light" the family started for the school house, which they found crowded with people. She was conducted to the desk, but it was so small and near the wall there was no room for a chair, or a place for her to sit down, and for people of her size it would be exceedingly difficult even to kneel down, and so she was obliged to conduct the meeting standing all the time.

The Word was opened, and the story of the cross told to the believing and the erring.

At the close a score or more pressed around, calling, "Please, sister, have meeting to-morrow night."

She was somewhat embarrassed, but after a moment in prayer, saying, "Here am I, Lord," she consented, and the news flew all over the neighborhood.

Next evening the school-house could not hold the people, who had come from all directions. Some tarried outside as long as they could endure the cold. The meeting was good, and after the curiosity was over, some felt the need of clean hearts and pardon in Jesus. As the place could not hold the people, she was asked, "Will you conduct services in the Hervey-street Baptist Church, about a mile from here, if it can be obtained?"

To this she consented. Then another delegation wanted to know if she would "preach there on Sunday night."

"I have no objections to talking for Jesus at that hour," was the reply.

"Will you also hold meeting on Monday evening?"

"No; I must return to New York on Monday."

Sunday evening a grand sleigh-load drove up to the Baptist Church, which had been locked for more than a year where already an audience had assembled. As soon as she arrived at the table in front of the stand she found that the two candles on the sides of the wall, and the one over the pulpit, did not give sufficient light for reading the hymn. Asking the gentleman who acted as janitor to get another light, he replied, "Why don't you go into the pulpit?"

To this she objected; and, waiting a moment, he continued, "I can't get a lamp very well; go in the pulpit, everybody does."

No sooner had her feet touched that spot than she felt overpowered by the step taken. In the silent prayer that followed, the burden of her prayer was, "If this step is right, O God, give me to see souls seeking thee this very night."

This burden had not been before her mind on the evenings previous, but now the great question of standing in the pulpit and proclaiming salvation to all, nearly overwhelmed her. She remained longer kneeling than usual, but arose with a sweet consciousness of the presence of Christ. When speaking she soon forgot the pulpit, left it, and in the strong exhortation for sinners to "flee from the wrath to come," she found herself part way down the aisle. Eight persons came forward for prayers, and knelt at the "anxious seat," weeping in deep anguish of spirit.

Sabbath day a storm raged till three o'clock, but the family had a good day at the parsonage, reading sermons. In the evening the clouds scattered, and it became clear, and very cold. The church was so full of people that many feared for their safety. The house trembled under its great burden, but no sill nor timber gave way during all of the meetings.

When the opportunity was offered, the "anxious seat" was again filled, this time with middle-aged and old people. Some found peace in Jesus, while others were yet in sorrow and deep penitence. Near the time of closing she bade the congregation and friends farewell, expecting to return home in the morning.

Father Battersby arose, laid his trembling hand on her shoulder, shaking her whole frame, and pointing toward the mourners, asked,

"Do you dare to go away, and leave that work?"

"That is not my work; it is God's work," she replied.

"Yes; but He sent you here to do it."

"But, sir, you told me that six ministers were in the house to-night; you can conduct the meetings. I must go home; you know I have left my business and my child."

"Yes; but these immortal souls?"

"I understand; but I don't see how I can possibly remain."

At last she consented to stay until Wednesday; but when the work of that evening was closing, fifteen souls were yet at the altar of prayer, many of them for the first time; most all of them over thirty, and two or three between sixty and seventy years of age. And now the people, and especially the young converts, urged so strongly, that she consented to remain for a time indefinite.

Six weeks passed, and God gave her seventy-five souls, as seals to the work, and the step she had taken had received the Divine approval.

[Mrs. Van Cott soon became a skillful revivalist.]

One evening the sick pastor sent word for Mrs. Van Cott to come home earlier, and take more rest, as he knew the severe work was telling unfavorably on her health. Her average hours for sleep were scarcely more than four; and the advice from the man of God was good. But the young converts held midnight meetings; their companions were seeking the Lord, and their songs and prayers could be heard till nearly morning.

"Please, sister, do go and sit in the room, and we will lead the meeting," were words she could not hear unheeded. In front of the church, across the street, at a private house, these meetings were held long after the exercises in the church had closed. Entering the capacious parlor, she found about sixty persons gathered, and soon others came, till the room was completely filled. She had scarcely been seated when an old man, tottering with age, came in, and in a moment she insisted upon his taking her comfortable chair. The devotions started immediately, and penitents were weeping in different parts of the room. One was standing by the door, his face bathed in tears, and near by him another, for whom his mother had long been praying. To the one standing by the door she said, "Do you desire to seek Jesus?"

With a distressing wail, he answered, "Yes ma'am."

"Come with me, then, where we all can kneel around and pray for you."

To the audience she said, "Here is one who desires salvation; let us all look to God for him."

The company bowed, and prayed fervently. The penitent wept, pleaded, groaned, and uttered the most dismal howls, until they were almost unbearable. He tossed about, to and fro, like a wild man, keeping up his terrible noise, fully twenty minutes.

Something must be done for him, was the present conviction of her mind, for if he was in earnest his agony was fearful; if he was not sincere, it was time some words of instruction were given, that the melting power of the Holy Spirit might touch him. A moment of silent prayer, and with strong faith she said, "Now, Lord, receive this captive of sin and Satan."

Suddenly he sprang to his feet, crying in a loud voice, "Seek, O seek God at once! Don't put it off; you will perish! Do come! Glory be to God, he has saved me! I'll tell it while I live, and shout it when I die! I am saved; yes, sing it, shout it! I'm glad salvation's free!"

It was now past midnight, and Mrs. Van Cott thought it best to close the meeting; but before doing so, she asked, "Is there not another soul that would have me pray for the blessing of God to come upon it?"

Just before her a young lady screamed out, "What shall I do to be saved?"

"Seek Jesus," answered the new-born soul; "O, yes, seek him; he will be found of you!"

She fell into Mrs. Van Cott's arms, and continued her screams, intermingled with sighs of deep anguish. The exhaustion of overwork brought on dizziness and fainting, and Mrs. Van Cott needed assistance for a few moments. The dear young lady was converted in less than half an hour, and joy and gladness filled the believers' hearts. The meeting closed about one o'clock, and the still, cold, frosty air echoed the praises of God as the happy throng scattered to their several homes.

Women in Utopian
Movements

ROSEMARY RADFORD RUETHER*

The second quarter of the nineteenth century saw a great flow-
ering of utopian movements in America. Some of these groups were heirs
of Reformation radicalism, such as the German communities of the Rappite Harmonists, the Zoarite Separatists, and the Amana Inspirationists.
The Shakers were an English Quaker sect that came to America at the
time of the American Revolution. Several of the other sects considered
in this chapter were born on American soil. The Oneida Perfectionists,
led by John Humphrey Noyes, was a revolt against New England Calvin-
ism. The transcendentalist communities of Brook Farm and Fruitlands,
and Christian Socialist Hopedale, expressed utopian impulses in New
England Unitarianism and Universalism. The Sanctificationists of Belton, Texas, had their roots in Methodist perfectionism. The Church of
Latter Day Saints was born in the revival atmosphere of Western New
York and developed communal structures as they moved west.

Secular utopian communities, mostly with European or English roots,
also brought their experiments to America in the second quarter of the
nineteenth century. Among the most prominent were the Owenites in
New Harmony, Indiana, the Phalansterians inspired by French utopian
Charles Fourier, and the Icarians, led by Etienne Cabet. The interracial
community of Nashoba, envisioned by radical feminist Frances Wright
to free American slaves, was supported by the Owenites.[1]

The secular socialists were anticlerical, but there was much exchange
between them and religious utopians. Members visited each other and
moved from one community to another. Most utopian socialists con-

*ROSEMARY RADFORD RUETHER is Georgia Harkness Professor of Applied Theology
at Garrett-Evangelical Theological Seminary in Evanston, Illinois. She has taught at Howard University School of Religion, Harvard Divinity School, and Yale Divinity School. She
is author of numerous books and articles on women in religion, among them *New Woman/
New Earth* (Seabury Press, 1974).

sidered the idea of presenting their movements as the new Christianity. Cabet, for example, wrote a book called *The True Christianity* (1846) in which he argued that Jesus was a revolutionary journalist who taught communism in veiled language to hide his intentions from hostile sacerdotal power.[2]

All these movements shared some version of the belief in the perfectibility of humanity. They were millenarians, transcendentalists, or spiritualists. They saw themselves as the avante-garde of a new redeemed age of humanity, anticipating and leading the transformation of the world toward a new level of spiritual perfection. The two noncommunal groups considered in this chapter, the Seventh Day Adventists and the Christian Scientists, shared these millenarian or spiritualist perspectives with the utopians.

In this chapter, I will discuss and document four aspects of utopian views: (1) the androgynous God and the new humanity, (2) the marriage question, (3) patterns of female leadership, and (4) utopianism and feminism.

THE ANDROGYNOUS GOD AND THE NEW HUMANITY

Many of the utopians believed that God was dual or androgynous. These ideas went back to ancient gnosticism. In the seventeenth and eighteenth centuries they had been revived in various forms by mystical philosophers, such as Jacob Boehme and Emmanuel Swedenborg. For example, Boehme believed that the original Adam was androgynous. Only with the Fall was there a separation into distinct sexes. From this comes sin, death, and the need for carnal union and physical reproduction. The redeemed Adam will be restored to androgynous form. Sex and reproduction will disappear.[3] The German pietist movements, such as the Rappites and Zoarites, were influenced by Boehme. (Document 1.)

Swedenborg believed that spiritual reality was divided into male and female principles, representing the complementarity of truth and goodness. Even the angels are divided into male and female spirits. The union of these two principles is the pivot of spiritual development.[4] The transcendentalist and spiritualist movements in America were heavily indebted to Swedenborg. (Document 2.)

Shaker doctrine stressed the parallelism of male and female on all levels, in God, creation, and redemption. The male-female dualism of humanity images God as both Father and Mother. Likewise redemption must be carried out by both a male and a female Messiah. (Document 3.)

For most utopians, androgyny is linked with celibacy. The separation of the sexes and the fall into carnal union is regarded as the beginning of sin. Spiritual androgyny is restored by a transcendence of sexuality. An exception to this view is the perspective of the Mormons, who also believed that there is a "Mother in Heaven" alongside God the Father.

But they imaged this as a heavenly marriage, the divine prototype of the patriarchal marriage of Mormon families.[5]

Not all androgynous concepts promote equality for women. The male traditions of androgyny, represented by Boehme, are androcentric. The separation of the female from the male is regarded as the fall from wholeness. Females as separate beings are seen as the source of sin and death.

Only in female-founded communities, particularly Shakerism and Christian Science, is the promotion of the female divine figure used to promote the equality of women. The Shakers, founded by Ann Lee, also believed that redemption meant transcendence of sexuality. But they saw maleness and femaleness as parallel principles that must always have equal representation in order to reflect the image of God. Just as the Messiah must be both male and female, so the Shaker community must be divided into male and female orders. Every leadership position must have a dual office, male and female.[6]

Mary Baker Eddy, foundress of Christian Science, regarded the Feminine as the principle of spiritual perfection. She identified maleness with carnality and materialism. The appearance of Christian Science as the spiritual Christianity she saw as completing the old revelation on a higher level of spiritual perfection. She was fond of identifying herself as the new Virgin Mary, or with "woman clothed with the sun" of the book of Revelation, who brings forth the new and spiritual messianic child, Divine Science. Christian Science, governed not by the Masculine Principle of material force, but by the Feminine Principle of spirit and love, will usher in a spiritualized humanity. (Document 4.)

THE MARRIAGE QUESTION

Marriage, sexuality, and procreation were hotly debated issues in the utopian movement. The private nuclear family was a dissonant factor in communal experiments. Most communities sought to modify the private family in one way or another. The favored solution was celibacy, either as a condition of membership, as in the Shakers, or as in the direction of spiritual growth, as in the Rappites, Zoarites, Inspirationists, Belton Sanctificationists, Mountain Cove Spiritualists, and the New York Christian Scientists under Augusta Stetson. Even the transcendentalist community of Fruitlands tried celibacy for a period of time under Charles Lane and broke up when Bronson Alcott finally decided to reject it in favor of his family.[7] Celibacy also corresponded to the millenarian or perfectionist concepts of redeemed humanity held by many utopians.

Contrary to what is often believed, celibacy did not cause groups like the Shakers to die out. The celibate communities generally lasted longer than those who accepted, unmodified, the nuclear family.[8] Celibacy abolished competing interests of private families within a community and allowed all to submerge their interests in the total group. Although the Shakers began to die out in the twentieth century because of failure to recruit new members, generally the conversion of adults is a better way to perpetuate an intentional community than natural progeny. Many successful experiments, such as the Oneida Perfectionists and the Belton Sanctificationists, lasted through the lifetimes of the original members, but died out because the next generation failed to be converted into the community.

Celibacy had an ambivalent effect on the status of women. In a patriarchal context, it throws suspicion on women as responsible for sexual temptation. But in the female-founded communities, such as the Shakers, the Christian Scientists, and the Belton Sanctificationists, it presented a liberating choice for women. Celibacy allowed women to throw off dependency on men for an autonomous identity.

Besides celibacy, there were other attempts to modify the marriage bond. The most notorious was the experiment in "complex marriage" among the Oneida Perfectionists. This group believed in a realized eschatology in which the commandment "all love another" was taken literally. All members were regarded as married to each other. All might have sexual access to each other (only on a heterosexual basis, apparently). But this access was regulated so that each liason was exchanged with the consent of the governing structure of the community. Jealousy was prevented by a strict ban on special attachments between either couples or parents and children. The Oneida Perfectionists also believed in birth control, eugenics, and women's equal right to sexual pleasure. The procreative should be separated from the amative function so that no woman would bear an unwanted child. (Document. 5.)

Mormon polygyny represented a quite different marriage experiment. Originally the privilege of the leadership, Mormon polygyny was strictly patriarchal. It was also hostile to birth control. Women should have as many children as possible in order to cloth the souls in heaven with bodies.[9] (Document 6.)

Some of the socialist communities advocated free love. Fanny Wright and Robert Dale Owen were notorious in the 1830s for linking free love with the experiments at New Harmony and the interracial community of Nashoba. Josiah Warren's anarchist colony of Modern Times in Long Island (1851–1857) rejected all community regulation of marriage. (Document 7.) But the socialists were basically interested in free choice and women's right to divorce, not promiscuity. The few cases where a sexually exploitative relation developed between the leader and the members of a community happened in the fringe authoritarian religious communities (such as Cyrus Spragg's New Jerusalem, Illinois) and not in the socialist movements.[10]

Some groups tried to retain the private monogamous marriage within the community. In the case of the short-lived Christian socialist experi-

ment of Hopedale, Massachusetts, monogamy was not only preserved,
but idealized. Each couple was encouraged to grow into higher levels of
fidelity and mutuality.[11] Adin Ballou did defend birth control as women's
right to choose maternity. But divorce was only allowed on proof of
adultery and couples could not remarry. (Document. 8.) Generally speaking, if utopians modified the marriage bond, it was not in order to allow
chaos to reign, but rather to regulate the union in a new way more
compatible with communal work, property, and identity.

PATTERNS OF FEMALE LEADERSHIP

Female founders and leaders abounded in radical sects. But these
women exhibited very different styles and values. Fanny Wright (1795–
1852) was a militant feminist, abolitionist, and socialist. Although she was
associated with New Harmony and founded her own colony in Nashoba,
her utopianism was more ideological than practical. She had neither the
time nor the ability to settle down to regular residence in these communities. Basically she was an individualist lecturer and radical journalist.[12]
(Document 9.)

Two woman who played important roles in sectarian movements were
Barbara Heinemann (1795–1883) of the Amana Inspirationists and Ellen
Harmon White (1827–1915) of the Seventh Day Adventists. Both were
valued for their special gifts as ecstatic visionaries. The Amana Inspirationists were an illuminist sect that believed it should be governed by
personal vehicles of the Spirit. Barbara Heinemann, along with Christian
Metz, was regarded as a vehicle of the Spirit (*Werkzeuge*) in America.
From 1867 through 1883, she was the sole head of a thriving colony of
sixteen thousands. Her utterances were collected and preserved as oracles of God. She dictated the sacramental, moral, and spiritual life of the
community.[13] But political and economic government was in the hands
of males. Heinemann's role was special to herself and did not affect the
status of other women. (Document 10.)

Ellen White also was regarded as a prophetess of the Seventh Day
Adventist Church from 1845 to 1915. Her repeated visions, received in
trances throughout her life, were regarded as authoritative guides to
interpreting the Scriptures for the movement. (Document 11.) Her many
other concerns, such as health, diet, temperance, educational reform,
antislavery, and even women's dress, shaped the Adventist Church for
seventy years. She also encouraged missionary activity and spent ten
years as a missionary educator in Australia.[14] But her role came from her
visionary gifts. The regular leadership of the community has been maintained in male hands. If her example had any continuing effects, it has
been primarily in the special importance of Adventist women in the
missionary field.

The special role of Mary Baker Eddy as foundress of Christian

Science was unique to her also. During her lifetime, her control over the movement she founded was absolute. (Document 12.) She brooked no competition from other leaders. Her career was marked by a series of destructive power struggles between herself and men or women whom she perceived as threatening her singular domination. One of the most notable of these struggles took place between Mrs. Eddy and her most talented female disciple, Augusta Stetson, and resulted in Stetson's expulsion from communion with the Mother Church.[15] (Document 13.) Christian Science reflected the Victorian doctrine of the Feminine, as well as woman's special role in sickness and health. Women have tended to predominate as healing practitioners. But Mrs. Eddy generally preferred to lodge the governance under herself in the hands of docile male followers.

The only female-led religion that developed a consistent system of equal empowerment of women was the Shakers. The Shaker theory of dual orders of male and female in creation and salvation ensured that Mother Ann Lee's position would be inherited by a line of elderesses of the female order of the community. Lucy Wright (1780–1821),[16] first successor of Ann Lee, and Anna White (1831–1910), Shaker historian, peace worker, and active feminist, were among the notable Shaker elderesses.

While sectarians sometimes offered exceptional roles for women, this did not always result in ongoing female leadership. Continuing female leadership of a group was more likely if the founder was a woman. But even then it was not assured unless there was a definite theory of female empowerment in the ideology and structure of the community. Female leaders of utopian and sectarian movements did not differ from the general leadership style of such movements, which tended to center on charismatic, authoritarian figures.

UTOPIANISM AND FEMINISM

The secular socialist movements were generally explicit advocates of women's rights. Frances Wright was America's first feminist socialist in the 1820s. The Owenites of England and the French Fourierites and Icarians advocated equal rights for women. The Fourierites developed a special theory about the connection of feminism and utopianism. They believed in ascending levels of civilization, each one advancing the status of women until full equality was reached in the stage of Harmony.[17] They thought that communal households would transform the prospects of women entrapped in the private family. (Document 14.)

The German pietist groups were generally more patriarchal, although some gave more rights to women than the traditional society. Rappites and Zoarites gave women the vote.[18] The last leader of the

Rappite community of Economy, Pennsylvania, was a woman, Suzie Duss. Shakers were the most politically equalitarian. Not only did they give equal power to women in their community, but some, like Elderess Anna White, were active in women's peace and suffrage association.

Mrs. Eddy was not active in suffrage organizations, but she continually defended women's political and educational rights.[19] She also exalted the Feminine Principle as superior to the coarse, materialist Masculine Principle and believed that her movement embodied this superior Feminine Principle to uplift and perfect humanity.

Utopians appear least innovative in the economic roles assigned to women. Generally women did the traditional women's work of house-cleaning, cooking, child-raising, and gardening. Most groups maintained a strict sexual division of labor. In the Shaker communities, women's work was indoors; men's work outdoors. The Oneida Perfectionists were the only ones who consciously tried to modify this sexual role division. Women were encouraged to do outdoor work, to drive the team of horses, and to work in the machine shop. Men were assigned to the communal nursery to participate in raising the children. The bloomer outfit and short hair of Oneida women expressed their belief that women should use their bodies in a healthy and vigorous way, contrary to the Victorian concept of repressive femininity. (Document 15.)

But even when considering those communities where women did traditional women's work, it is important to remember that theirs was the division of labor of the preindustrial village, not that of average middle-class Americans of that period. From the point of view of most women in industrializing America, utopian women appeared economically self-sufficient and possessed of a great variety of productive skills. These were the skills of a self-contained agricultural and handicraft economy that were being lost to both men and women in nineteenth century America. Shaker women pioneered in the invention of household labor-saving devices and were the first in America to sell packaged flower and vegetable seeds.[20]

The communalization of housework and child-raising transformed women's work in community. Many utopians believed that abolishing the private household would overcome women's economic dependency. In communal societies, women as well as men would be equal participants and shareholders. Occasionally utopian women experimented with forming separate women's work collectives to ensure their economic independence. A group of women at Brook Farm tried for a while to pool their "fancy work" in a collective. (Document 16.)

The most impressive example of a community built around a women's work collective was the Sanctificationists of Belton, Texas. Under the leadership of Martha McWhirter, these Methodist matrons emancipated themselves from their husbands by pooling their butter and egg money in a common fund. Eventually they were able to build separate houses and even buy a hotel, which they used to support their independence as a women's cooperative. (Document 17.)

CONCLUSION

The utopian movements of nineteenth century America were janus-faced phenomena. On the one hand, they represented a protest of the preindustrial, agrarian, handicraft economy against the alienation of the new industrial world. Industrialization deprived the worker of owner-ship of the means of production by taking the spinning wheel from the woman and the cobbler's bench from the man. Utopians sought to restore the old self-sufficiency in idealized form.

Industrialization also transformed women's work. Women were los-ing the agricultural and handicraft skills of their foremothers. They were being forced into the low wages and exploitative conditions of the facto-ries or relegated to the repressed dependency of the middle-class household. This revolution in women's roles, affecting both proper-tied and poor women in different ways, explains why the agitation for women's rights arose in this period.

The utopians restored the old self-sufficient communal village. But this protest against industrial alienation also stimulated radical specula-tion and experimentation. Communalization would create a new econ-omy, a new family, even a new type of humanity. They imagined that their experiments would be the harbingers of a new redeemed society, millennial or communist (which, in this period, meant communalist).

Utopians failed to achieve the hoped-for impact on the larger society. Many communities arose and fell in a few years or decades. The religious groups had better discipline and generally lasted longer than the secular, socialist ones. Nevertheless, they were laboratories for new ideas and practices. They provided free space, in a relatively unsettled land, to play with alternative religious visions, alternative sexual life-styles, alternative economic and political relations. The vindication of the female side of humanity, was, in one way or another, on the agenda of most of them.

Women of the Oneida Perfectionist Community adopted short hairstyles to enhance their greater freedom. [From Pierrepont Noyes, *My Father's House: An Oneida Boyhood* (New York: Farrar and Rinehart, 1937), p. 79.]

Sister Phoebe Lane was a member of the Mount Lebanon Shaker Community in New York. The Shakers not only advocated equality of the sexes but equality of the races. [From *The Shaker Image* (Boston: New York Graphics Society, 1974), photo no. 203. Used by permission of Shaker Community, Inc., Hancock, Massachusetts.]

Augusta Stetson, disciple of Mary Baker Eddy, was for a time her rival for the leadership of Christian Science. Stetson founded the prominent First Church of Christ Scientist in New York City. When she was excommunicated by Eddy from the mother church in 1909, Stetson went on to found her own Christian Science Movement. [From Augusta Stetson, *Reminiscences, Sermons, and Correspondence* (New York: Putnam's Sons, 1913), p. 4.]

Mary Baker Eddy, founder and leader of Christian Science until her death in 1910, continued to command absolute loyalty from her followers even from her retirement in Pleasant View, Concord, New Hampshire. This photo shows her addressing ten thousand Christian Scientists from the balcony of her home in June, 1908. [From Virgilius Ferm, *Pictorial History of Protestantism* (New York: Philosophical Library, 1957), p. 315.]

Oneida women, shown here at work in the business office and bakery, adopted a short skirt and bloomer outfit. [From Frank Leslie, *Illustrated Newspaper,* April 2, 1870.]

Ellen G. White's prophetic utterances guided the Seventh Day Adventist Church for sixty years. She is shown here in 1899, at seventy-two years old, just before her return from missionary work in Australia. [From Ellen G. White, *Prophet of Destiny* (New Canaan, Conn.: Keats Publishers, 1972.]

Anna White, Eldress of the Shaker Community of Mount Lebanon, New York, was a leading historian and a theoretician of the Shaker community and also a prominent leader in the international Peace Movement. [From *The Shaker Image* (Boston: New York Graphics Society, 1974), photo no. 134. Used by permission of Shaker Community, Inc., Hancock, Massachusetts.]

Documents: Women in Utopian Movements

THE ANDROGYNOUS GOD AND THE NEW HUMANITY

Document 1: The Rappite Harmonists

The Rappites were a German pietist sect that immigrated to the
United States in 1804 and formed several successive communities in
Indiana and Pennsylvania. They took from Jacob Boehme a mystical
doctrine of the original androgynous Adam. Adam, created in God's
image, was originally a bisexual being. Like God he could create life
from himself without a separate female partner. In his original form,
Adam lacked "bestial sex organs." Trustee of the Harmonist Society,
R. L. Baker summarized Rappite anthropology in these words, which
he delivered on January 19, 1857:[21]

The first influence practised on man by the serpent's head (or by
the evil spirit) was to inflame his imagination in favor of an external
helpmate, when he discovered the animals before him to be male and
female. Genesis 2:10–20. Just at this juncture the first fall of man took
place, by which Adam violated his own inward Sanctuary and his own
female function by means of which he could have been (as Genesis
1:28 has it) fruitful and multiply without an external helpmate, after
the order of a Hermaphrodite then, and after the order now, see
Luke 20:34–36.

According to the Rappites, the new order of humanity was being
constituted by transcendence of sexuality and a restoration of the
original hermaphodite humanity. By abstaining from sex, the members of the Harmony society were preparing for the Second Coming
of Christ and the advent of the new humanity of the Kingdom of God.

However, their celibate piety took the form of a fervent devotion
to the Divine Sophia, whom they saw as the feminine virginal spirit
of God. An example of their sophiological piety is seen in the following extracts from the "Hymns to Sophia."

> O, Sophia, when thy loving hands
>   carefully have guided my path
> Through the thorny rose-bush,
> Let my shadow soar;
> You, the Harmonists' goddess, play
>   now your golden strings;
> Bind with loving golden chains
>   those who follow you to the designated goal.

> Tell me, where do I find one like you,
>   Sophia, whom all revere,
> Whom shall I entreat to show
>   me, you, you angel?
> You must be a goddess of
>   radiant beauty
> Who receives all who see her.

Sophia, from your glances rapture flows into my
      heart
When a friendly love delights my soul;
O the pure instincts your charm arouses in me;
This flame feeds the blessed heavenly love.

You surmise in silence all wild passion,
And uncover what is hidden within us;
For my endeavors rob me of all rest;
Beloved, would you desert me if I am unwise?

Beloved, let me experience the gentleness and faith
      if we were united,
With your sweet caress many an anxious hour would
      flee,
My wounds would be healed,
Pure fire would be drawn to love.

Let no Delilah sneak into
      my heart, and rob me of my strength!
Let me be constant and true,
Let nothing ever weaken me
      through its false brilliance.

O, heal what was wounded,
      cut what is unclean!
Give me, noble Virgin, a virgin-heart;
Give me a hero's spirit for my sufferings;
Let brightly burn in me the light
      of truth.

Sophia, I cannot let go,
      my heart burns with sweet fire;
My heart desires to hold you, and
      wants to let go all the mire
Until my spirit rests with you;
Nothing but you I want to love,
My heart is refreshed with increasing fiery-zest;
Call me yours, then I am free.

Document 2: The Spiritualist Brotherhood of the New Life

*The Brotherhood of the New Life was a spiritualist sect dominated
by the paternalistic authority of their leader, ex-Universalist minister
Thomas Lake Harris. They believed in an androgynous God and the
gradual cessation of sexual relations as humanity became spiritualized. The following letter from Harris to W. A. Hinds, written on
August 22, 1877, from Fountain Cove, Santa Rosa, California, illustrates these views:*[23]

This is a kingdom that does not come with observation: ... It
grows simply by its power of organic diffusion and assimilation. We

believe it to be a germ of the Kingdom of Heaven, dropped from upper space and implanted in the bosom of the earthly humanity:—in fine, the seed of a new order; the initial point for a loftier and sweeter evolution of man.

Two only of our Families, so far as I am aware, have fallen under the eye of correspondents of the press; that in the town of Portland, Chautauqua Co., N.Y., and this, my private residence, in California. These are practically one. In both of them the social order may perhaps be termed patriarchal, there being no community of possessions. I may quote from the old dramatist, and say: "A poor house, sir but mine own." I hope I shall not trespass on the modest privacy of my guests and kinsmen, if I add that, under no stress of compulsion, but in the evolution of character, they have become, in the natural sense, celibate as I am: some entering from a state of monogamic marriage, but others virginal from the first.

Of the other Families in the Society, I may say that they are in different stages of advancement, from a starting-point of accepted altruism; that they begin from germs of individual households, with no break in the continuity of relations; the new growth forming in the old wood of the tree; the internal first changing, and then, by evolution, "that which is without" becoming "as that which is within." . . . Gradually the family partnerships have ceased, without a struggle, and all have entered into this order.

In serving me these tender hearts believe that they are also serving God, working for a kingdom of universal righteousness. They do not think that I possess any thing, except as representatively; nor that I rule in them, except as aiding to lift and direct them into a larger freedom, wisdom and purity. I consider the Family at Salem-on-Erie and that at Fountain Grove as one: the germ of a solar family in the midst of a planetary family system.

I find no difficulty in the solution of the painful and perplexing problem of the sexes. Monogamists who enter into union with me rise, by changes of life, into a desire for the death of natural sexuality. Those whose lives have been less strict first, perhaps, may pass through the monogamic relation, though not always; but the end is the same. Others, who have lived singly, holding the fierce passion in restraint, find themselves gliding out of the passional tempest into a bodily state of serenity and repose. Still I do not believe that sexlessness characterizes man in his higher and final evolution.

Among my people, as they enter into the peculiar evolution that constitutes the new life, two things decrease: the propagation of the species and physical death. In the large patriarchal Family that I have described but one death has occurred since its formation in 1861, and this under circumstances and with results which demonstrated to us that the dear and honored subject of the visitation was simply taken from his more visible place to serve as an intermediate for higher services. One young pair in our borders have had three children, I am sorry to say; but with this exception the births in seventeen years have been but two, and of these the younger is almost a man. We think that generation must cease till the sons and daughters of God are prepared for the higher generation, by evolution into structural, bisexual completeness, above the plane of sin, of disease, or of natural mortality. . . . I may add here that our views are not the result of mere scriptural study, nor based on textual interpretations, and that we have no especial sympathy that unites us to one school of religionists more than to another. If we find one vein of knowledge, or possibly correct surmise, in Swedenborg, we find other veins in Spinoza, or Boehme, or Comte. Using the term in its metaphysical sense, we aim not to be partialists but universalists of inquiry and knowledge . . . but we further conclude that the Creative Logos, "God manifested in the flesh," is not male merely, or female merely, but the two-in-one, in whose individual and social likeness, in whose spiritual and physical likeness, we seek to be re-born, is the pivot of our faith and the directive force of our life. The ages wait for the manifestation of the sons of God. Thus we are adventists, not in a sectarian sense, but in the sense of a divine involution, and thence of a new degree in human evolution.

Document 3: Shakerism

The following extracts from Shaker elderess and historian Anna White illustrate the views of the United Society of Christ's Second Appearing (Shakers) on the bisexual God, the Female Messiah, and the spiritual development of humanity.[24]

The revisers of the "Millennial Church" assert that as "the light of Divine Truth is progressive in the Church, and as the preparatory work of salvation and redemption increases on earth,—so the solemn and important truths of the Gospel will continue from time to time to be more clearly manifested to mankind.

Among the revelations to Ann Lee and imparted through her life and teachings, were ideas new to the Christian world. Contrasting these ideas with the formulas of belief cherished and insisted upon by Christians of her day and for one hundred years later, the claim of a special gift of spiritual enlightenment is not extravagant; comparing them with the thought of the Churches of day; it will be apparent that the masses of Christian thinkers are slowly climbing up to the standard set more than a century ago by Ann Lee. Among these great truths are:

God is Dual

Shakers believe in One God—not three male beings in one, but Father and Mother. And here the Bible reader turns at once to Genesis 1:26. "And God said"—in the beginning of creative work, whether by fiat or evolution matters not—"let us make man in our image, after our likeness." Did three masculine beings appear, in contradistinction to every form of life heretofore known? Nay! Verse 27 says: "So God created man in His own image, in the image of God created He him, male and female created He them."

The ancient language of Scripture distinguishes God when power or truth are emphasized as masculine; when love or wisdom is the important attribute, the masculine name has the feminine complement. O Theos agapa estin, God is Love (feminine). The term Adam is well known to mean humanity, male and female. How can it "image" a Being utterly unlike itself? Simple and beautiful becomes the relation between God and the man when the true meaning is accepted. Hence comes

Equality of Sex

Woman appears in her rightful place, at once the equal of man in creation and office at the hand of God. Ann Lee's followers, 1900 years after Jesus uttered the words, "Neither do I condemn thee, go and sin no more;" and sent Mary to tell the Good News of a risen Lord and living Savior, along of all humanity, have taught the doctrines that have placed woman side by side with man, his equal in power, in office, in influence and in judgment. To Ann Lee may woman look for the first touch that struck off her chains and gave her absolute right to her own person. To Ann Lee may all reformers among women look as the one who taught and through her followers teachers still perfect freedom, equality and opportunity to woman. The daughters of Ann Lee, alone among women, rejoice in true freedom, not alone from the bondage of man's domination, but freedom also from the curse of that desire "to her husband" by which, through the ages, he has ruled over her.

God the Father-Mother

Fatherhood and motherhood exist in the complete human being. One is correlative of the other. The apostle said: "The invisible things of Him are clearly seen, being understood by the things that He has made, even His eternal power and Godhead." And as all life in the "things that He has made" originates, as scientists tell us after most careful experiments, not from spontaneous generation, but always from seed or germinal principle, from a father and mother, so in the highest form of earth life, humanity, in the spiritual realm are souls born of God, the Absolute, Self-existent, infinite Perfection of Being,

Father and Mother. The very name God, Almighty, in its original Hebrew form, El Shaddai, reveals the infinite quality. El, God, its first meaning, Strength: Shaddi, the plural whose singular, Shad, signifies a Breast and is feminine.

In the beautiful and lofty strains of that magnificent psalm found in the eighth chapter of Proverbs, "Doth not Wisdom Cry," etc., Wisdom is feminine, and all through the wondrous passage the Mother in Deity utters her voice. In the forty-fifth Psalm, the Queen is pictured standing at the right hand of the King. . . . The spiritual children of Ann Lee, who forsook all fathers of church and creed and covenant, of old relationships of blood, old ties and bonds of idea, custom and conformity, and through supreme toil and anguish came to the heritage of spiritual motherhood, render easy of fulfilment the promise,—"I will make thy name to be remembered in all generations; therefore shall thy people praise thee for ever and ever." We may look up through Nature to God. Our natural father and mother, with their united strength and wisdom, truth and love are types of that Perfect Parentage our Father and Mother which are in Heaven.

Document 4: Christian Science

Mary Baker Eddy's religious creation was embodied primarily in her book Science and Health, With Key to the Scriptures, *which she continually developed in successive editions. In this volume, she comments on the Scriptures by means of a spiritualist allegory. At many points, her view of the Feminine as the higher and more spiritual principle is evident, as in these extracts from her comments on Genesis 1:27 and Revelations 12:1.*[25]

Genesis 1:27. So God created man in His image; in the image of God created He him; male and female created He them.

To emphasize this momentous thought, it is repeated—that God made man in His own image, to reflect the divine Spirit. It follows that man is a generic term. Masculine, feminine, and neuter genders are human concepts. In one of the ancient languages the word for man is used also as the synonym of mind. This definition has been weakened by anthropomorphism, or a *humanization* of Deity. The word anthropomorphic, in such a phrase as *"an anthropomorphic god,"* is derived from two Greek words, signifying *man* and *form,* and may be defined as a mortally mental attempt to reduce Deity to corporeality. The Life-giving quality of Mind is Spirit, not matter. The ideal man corresponds to creation, to Intelligence, and Truth. The ideal woman corresponds to Life and Love. We have not as much authority, in Divine Science, for considering God masculine, as we have for considering Him feminine, for Love imparts the highest idea of Deity.

Revelation 12:1. And there appeared a great wonder in Heaven—

a woman clothed with the sun, and the moon under her feet, and upon her head a crown of twelve stars.

Heaven represents harmony, and Divine Science interprets the Principle of heavenly harmony. The great miracle, to human sense, is divine love.

The Revelator beheld the spiritual idea from the mount of vision. Purity was the symbol of Life and Love. He saw also the spiritual ideal, as a woman clothed in light, a bride coming down from Heaven, wedded to the Lamb of Love. To him, the Bride and the Lamb represented the correlation of divine Principle and spiritual idea, bring harmony to earth.

John saw the human and divine coincidence, as shown in the man Jesus, as divinity embracing humanity, in Life and its demonstration, —reducing to human perception and understanding the Life which is God. In divine revelation, material and corporeal self-hood disappear, and the spiritual ideal is understood.

The woman in the Apocalypse is the vignette, which illustrates as man the spiritual idea of God,—and God and man as the divine Principle and divine idea. The Revelator symbolizes Spirit by the sun. The idea is clad with the radiance of spiritual Truth, and matter is put under its feet. The light portrayed is really neither solar nor lunar, but spiritual Life, which is "the light of men."

John the Baptist prophesied the coming of the immaculate Jesus, and he saw in those days the spiritual idea as the Messiah, who would baptize with the Holy Ghost,—Divine Science. As Elias represents the Fatherhood of God, through Jesus, so the Revelator completes this figure with woman, as the spiritual idea or type of God's Motherhood. The moon is under her feet. This idea reveals the universe as secondary and tributary to Spirit, from which it borrows its reflected Substance, Life, and Intelligence.

The spiritual idea is crowned with twelve stars. The twelve tribes of Israel, with all mortals,—separated, by belief, from man's divine origin and the true idea,—shall through much tribulation yield to the activities of the divine Principle of man, in the harmony of Science. These are the stars in the crown of rejoicing. They are the lamps in the spiritual heavens of this age, which show the workings of the spiritual idea by healing the sick and the sinful, and by manifesting the light which shines "unto the perfect day," as the night of materialism wanes.

THE MARRIAGE QUESTION

Document 5: The Oneida Perfectionists

In this extract from John Hymphrey Noyes' pamphlet on Male Continence, *Noyes describes how his discovery of this "natural" meth-*

od of birth control through the male's withholding of emission in coitus originated in his concern about his wife's repeated pregnancies. Noyes sees a direct connection between birth control, eugenics, a woman's rights to sexual pleasure and voluntary motherhood, and a new, more mutual relation of the sexes. His theories on these issues became the basis of the Oneida experiments in "complex" or communal marriage.[26]

I was married in 1838, and lived in the usual routine of matrimony till 1846. It was during this period of eight years that I studied the subject of sexual intercourse in connection with my matrimonial experience, and discovered the principle of Male Continence. And the discovery was occasioned and even forced upon me by very sorrowful experience. In the course of six years my wife went through the agonies of five births. Four of them were premature. Only one child lived. This experience was what directed my studies and kept me studying. After our last disappointment, I pledged my word to my wife that I would never again expose her to such fruitless suffering. I made up my mind to live apart from her, rather than break this promise. This was the situation in the summer of 1844. At that time I conceived the idea that the sexual organs have a social function which is distinct from the propagative function; and that these functions may be separated practically. I experimented on this idea, and found that the self-control which it requires is not difficult; also that my enjoyment was increased; also that my wife's experience was very satisfactory, as it had never been before; also that we had escaped the horrors and the fear of involuntary propagation. . . . In the course of the next two years I studied all the essential details and bearings of the discovery. In 1846 we commenced Community life at Putney, Vt. . . .

The amative and propagative functions of the sexual organs are distinct from each other, and may be separated practically. They are confounded in the world, both in the theories of physiologists and in universal practice. The amative function is regarded merely as a bait to the propagative, and is merged in it. The sexual organs are called "organs of reproduction," or "organs of generation," but not organs of love or organs of union. But if amativeness is the first and noblest of the social affections, and if the propagative part of the sexual relation was originally secondary, and became paramount by the subversion of order in the fall [as had previously been shown], we are bound to raise the amative office of the sexual organs into a distinct and paramount function.

Our theory, separating the amative from the propagative, not only relieves us of involuntary and undesirable procreation, but opens the way for *scientific* propagation. We are not opposed, after the Shaker fashion, or even after Owen's fashion, to the increase of population.

We believe that the order to "multiply" attached to the race in its original integrity, and that propagation, rightly conducted and kept within such limits as life can fairly afford, is a blessing second only to sexual love. But we are opposed to involuntary procreation. A very large proportion of all children born under the present system are begotten contrary to the wishes of both parents, and lie nine months in their mother's womb under their mother's curse or a feeling little better than a curse. Such children cannot be well organized. We are opposed to *excessive,* and of course oppressive procreation, which is almost universal. We are opposed to random procreation, which is unavoidable in the marriage system. But we are in favor of intelligent, well-ordered procreation.

The physiologists say that the race cannot be raised from ruin till propagation is made a matter of science; but they point out no way of making it so. Propagation is controlled and reduced to a science in the case of valuable domestic brutes; but marriage and fashion forbid any such system among human beings. We believe the time will come when involuntary and random propagation will cease, and when scientific combination will be applied to human generation as freely and successfully as it is to that of other animals. The way will be open for this when amativeness can have its proper gratification without drawing after it procreation, as a necessary sequence. And at all events, we believe that good sense and benevolence will *very soon* sanction and enforce the rule that women shall bear children only when they choose. They have the principal burdens of breeding to bear, and they rather than men should have their choice of time and circumstances, at least till science takes charge of the business.

The separation of the amative from the propagative, places amative sexual intercourse on the same footing with other ordinary forms of social interchange. So long as the amative and propagative are confounded, sexual intercourse carries with it physical consequences which necessarily take it out of the category of mere social acts; . . . it is not to be wondered at that women, to a considerable extent, look upon ordinary sexual intercourse with more dread than pleasure, regarding it as a stab at their life, rather than a joyful act of fellowship. But separate the amative from the propagative—let the act of fellowship stand by itself—and sexual intercourse becomes a purely social affair, the same in kind with other modes of kindly communion, differing only by its superior intensity and beauty. Thus the most popular, if not the most serious objection, to communistic love is removed. The difficulty so often urged, of knowing to whom children belong in complex-marriage, will have no place in a Community trained to keep the amative distinct from the propagative. . . . In a society trained to these principles, as propagation will become a science, so amative intercourse will have place among the "fine arts." Indeed, it will take rank above music, painting, sculpture, etc.; for it combines the charms and benefits of them all. There is as much room for cultivation of taste and skill in this department as in any.

The practice which we propose will give new speed to the advance of civilization and refinement. The self-control, retention of life, and ascent out of sensualism, which must result from making freedom of love a bounty on the chastening of physical indulgence, will raise the race to new vigor and beauty, moral and physical. And the refining effects of sexual love (which are recognized more or less in the world) will be increased a thousand-fold, when sexual intercourse becomes an honored method of innocent and useful communion, and each is married to all.

Document 6: Mormonism

When Joseph Smith first began to take additional wives, he encountered stiff opposition from his wife Emma Smith. In order to win her obedience to this new ordinance of polygyny, Joseph Smith received a special revelation from God describing its scriptural basis and commanding her assent.[27]

Revelation on the Eternity of the Marriage Covenant, including Plurality of Wives. Given through Joseph, the Seer, in Nauvoo, Hancock County, Illinois, July 12th, 1843.

1. Verily, thus saith the Lord unto you, my servant Joseph, that inasmuch as you have inquired of my hand, to know and understand wherein I, the Lord, justified my servants Abraham, Isaac and Jacob; as also Moses, David and Solomon, my servants, as touching the principle and doctrine of their having many wives and concubines: . . .

34. God commanded Abraham, and Sarah gave Hagar to Abraham to wife. And why did she do it? Because this was the law, and from Hagar sprang many people. This, therefore, was fulfilling, among other things, the promises.

35. Was Abraham, therefore, under condemnation? Verily, I say unto you, Nay; for I, the Lord, commanded it. . . .

37. Abraham received concubines, and they bear him children, and it was accounted unto him for righteousness, because they were given unto him, and he abode in my law, as Isaac also, and Jacob did none other things than that which they were commanded; and because they did none other things than that which they were commanded, they have entered into their exaltation, according to the promises, and sit upon thrones, and are not angels, but are Gods.

38. David also received many wives and concubines, as also Solomon and Moses my servants; as also many others of my servants, from the beginning of creation until this time; and in nothing did they sin, save in those things which they received not of me.

39. David's wives and concubines were given unto him, of me, by

the hand of Nathan, my servant, and others of the prophets who had
the keys of this power; and in none of these things did he sin against
me, save in the case of Uriah, and his wife; and, therefore he hath
fallen from his exaltation, and received his portion; and he shall not
inherit them out of the world; for I gave them unto another, saith the
Lord.

40. I am the Lord thy God, and I gave unto thee, my servant
Joseph, an appointment, and restore all things; ask what ye will, and
it shall be given unto you according to my word: ...

51. Verily, I say unto you, a commandment I give unto mine
handmaid, Emma Smith, your wife, whom I have given unto you, that
she stay herself, and partake not of that which I commanded you to
offer unto her; for I did it, saith the Lord, to prove you all, as I did
Abraham; and that I might require an offering at your hand, by
covenant and sacrifice;

52. And let mine handmaid, Emma Smith, receive all those that
have been given unto my servant Joseph, and who are virtuous and
pure before me; and those who are not pure, and have said they were
pure, shall be destroyed, I saith the Lord God;

53. For I am the Lord thy God, and ye shall obey my voice; and
I give unto my servant Joseph, that he shall be made ruler over many
things, for he hath been faithful over a few things, and from hence-
forth I will strengthen him.

54. And I command mine handmaid, Emma Smith, to abide and
cleave unto my servant Joseph, and to none else. But if she will not
abide this commandment, then shall my servant Joseph do all things
for her, even as he hath said; and I will bless him and multiply him,
and give unto him an hundredfold in this world, of fathers and
mothers, brothers and sisters, houses and lands, wives and children,
and crowns of eternal lives in the eternal worlds.

56. And again, verily I say, let mine handmaid forgive my servant
Joseph his trespasses; and then shall she be forgiven her trespasses,
wherein she has trespassed against me; and I, the Lord thy God, will
bless her, and multiply her, and make her heart to rejoice. ...

Document 7: Individualism at Modern Times

*In response to outraged reports of general promiscuity in their
community, some of the solid citizens at Josiah Warren's individualist
colony of Modern Times published a pamphlet explaining their principles. They declared that most families lived conventional sexual
lives. If some of their members had more irregular habits, it was not
condoned out of a general advocacy of free love, but rather because
it was believed that sexual relations are a private matter and should
not be subject to legal constraints or community crusades.*[28]

But the most bitter criticisms made upon our Modern Times
movement and its Equitable Commerce theory, have been based upon

their supposed hostility to the Family Institution. The immorality of the periodical press at the present day, is exhibited to us here in a striking light by the falsehoods repeatedly uttered about us in this respect. . . .

We do not, indeed, by any means regard our Movement as really capable of effecting so vast a change as is very evidently needed. Some of the advocates of Equitable Commerce may have so regarded it, but we do not. We have, on the contrary, settled ourselves here rather with a view to our own amendment; to the better conduct of our own lives, and the better bringing up of our children. The universal rapine and treachery which characterize the ordinary conduct of business, were sufficiently hateful to us to make us forego all the chances of material advantage we might have enjoyed elsewhere, in hopes of finding ourselves surrounded here by persons ready to conduct their mutual dealings upon more honorable principles.

At the same time we instinctively felt that the attempt to make men moral by legislation, was necessarily destined to be a failure. Whether in regard to sexual intercourse or sobriety, or any other purely moral obligation, the civil government will, certainly, always fail in really regulating human conduct. Our ideas were at first unsettled as to the true solution of the difficult moral questions then beginning to agitate the public mind; but we were quite confident that political assemblies were totally incompetent to their solution. That which was grossly immoral in New York state could not be perfectly virtuous in Ohio; yet the same thing was legal in one place, illegal in the other. We hoped that by free discussion, and equally free experimentation under our principle of Individual Sovereignty, a true solution might be found. And if finally we have had to look elsewhere for such a solution, its acceptance, at least, has been facilitated by that which has actually transpired at Modern Times. . . .

The only real difference between Modern Times and any other village, in this respect, is, first that there is more social intercourse than is usual among a population of equal numbers, secondly, that that social intercourse is much more polite on the one hand, and much more genial on the other, thirdly, that there is a total absence of the obscenity that commonly intermingles with the conversation of the male portion of a village population (or a city one either) when it happens to be freed from the restraints imposed by the presence of the better sex, fourthly, that there is very much less, and with a continual decrease, of the scandal and backbiting that usually prevail elsewhere in exclusively feminine intercourse, and finally that conscientious differences of opinion on all matters whatever, including therefore questions relating to marriage, and the family, are actually respected here, that toleration and recognition of the "Right of private Judgment" which is elsewhere only professed being here fully, sincerely and manfully practised.

It is quite true that there are persons, highly respectable and virtuous persons too, among our neighbors, who have exercised their sovereignty in protesting practically as well as theoretically against the interference of the civil government in matters of domestic morality, persons who have married themselves, and divorced themselves, and even remarried without asking leave of either priest or magistrate. We confess we do not think this course either right or wise, but we know how to respect conscientiousness when it differs from us ever so widely. . . . The persecution of our "Free Love" neighbors would but make martyrs of them, and add new enthusiasm to the followers of their faith.

Certainly we in no wise share such a faith. We frankly confess however to having for a long time formerly believed marriage an institution destined finally to pass away, and a social condition more or less resembling that announced by Charles Fourier as destined to take its place. Persecution always deepened this faith of ours so long as we held it; and instead of disposing us to abandon it made it so much the harder for a truer and nobler doctrine to take its place. We have great respect for the democracy—when we see it ranged, as it ever is in conditions of real social order, under the guidance of wise and worthy Leaders and Teachers, true Priests; but we have no respect at all for a disorderly multitude pretending to regulate by mere power of numbers whether represented by a Dogberry lawfully elected or an impromptu Judge Lynch, matters that belong not to the domain of force but to that of wisdom.

But the important fact to be noted here is, that while equitable Commerce or Modern Times was neither of them heard of till four or five years ago, the troubles affecting the shattered families whose dispersed members come to take refuge among us (and whom we are immoral enough to treat with kindness), must have sprung from influences of far more distant date. What had we to do with that which was passing among people who had never heard one word about us or our principles either? The plain truth is, that "Free Love," like most of the other modern "isms"—like all the varied forms of Socialism—like Modern Times itself, with its Equitable Commerce theory in all its ramifications is merely an indication of a profound and immense movement, an under current, and therefore, to most observers unseen, but still continously going on throughout all modern society; a movement essentially constituting a transition from an old social condition long in decay, and of which only the ruins now remain, to a new social condition, all the fundamental elements of which have been spontaneously preparing for centuries, but which have now to be systematically co-ordinated into a ONE WHOLE as harmonious in all its parts as contemporary society is discordant and chaotic.

Document 8: The Hopedale Community

The Christian Socialists of Hopedale, Massachusetts, rejected all sexual experimentation in favor of strict monogamous marriage. The members pledged "never to violate the dictates of chastity by adultery, polygamy, concubinage, fornication, self-pollution, lasciviousness, amative abuse, impure language or cherished lust." Group counseling sessions, called Perceptive and Parentive Circles, were arranged to deal with marriage and family conflicts in the community. When a couple espousing free love arose in their midst, the Hopedale community, under Adin Ballou's leadership, was quick to reject them. The offending couple moved to the anarchist community of Modern Times on Long Island, which was more receptive to their views.[29]

A Free Love Episode. As we at Hopedale, wherever we were known, had a reputation for hospitality to new ideas and a friendliness towards everything calculated to benefit our fellowmen, we were frequently confronted with theories and doctrines, good, bad, and indifferent, claiming, through their apostles, consideration and acceptance on the ground that they were helps to human progress or panaceas for the maladies of mankind. Some of these were thoroughly false in principle and mischievous in tendency and effect. It was impossible to prevent the introduction of these pernicious theories and doctrines without our borders and the discussion of them among our people. It was no part of our policy to attempt to do this; but it was a part of our policy to prevent them from doing any of us harm; it was a part of our policy to be continually watchful concerning them, lest they get a foothold among us, captivating the unwary and causing injury to personal character and the social well-being.

Among these reprehensible speculations was that, which, under a plea for the broadest and largest liberty, contemplated the removal of all conventional restraints pertaining to the relation of the sexes to each other, and especially in the matter of marriage, and granting to each and every one the privilege of forming connubial alliances and dissolving them at will, as inclination, pleasure, convenience, or whatever else, might dictate, under the general name of Free Love. But notwithstanding our vigilance, and an utter contravention of our solemn declaration concerning chastity and of our well-known adherence to the principle of monogamic marriage, there arose in our midst during the year 1853, a case of marital infidelity and illicit intercourse that caused great unpleasantness, perplexity, and scandal, and that required, at length, Community intervention.

The story is simply this: One of our male members, the head of a family, became enamoured of a woman, also a member who had for sometime resided in his household, and proportionally estranged from his faithful and worthy wife. Suspicions of something wrong

arose among outsiders, causing considerable talk of a scurrilous nature, though nothing was absolutely known or could be proved to that
effect. At length the unhappiness of the wife was revealed, and the
cause of it, upon investigation, made public. The matter then very
properly received attention from the Council, who summoned the
delinquents before them for examination and discipline. Upon being
questioned and confronted with proof of misconduct, they acknowledged culpability, professed regret, and penitence, and promised
amendment. But these professions proved insincere, or at least, tran-
sient, and the parties were again called to account. They then did not
deny or attempt to conceal their criminality, but rather justified it on
the ground that it was consonant with the principles of the new
philosophy touching personal liberty, sexual relations, and the conju-
gal bond, which they had embraced—in a word, they openly and
unhesitatingly avowed themselves to be Free Lovers, from conviction
and in practice also. Having taken that position they could not do
otherwise than withdraw from Community membership and leave the
locality where both their theory and their action were held in almost
universal derision and abhorrence. They went from us to the settlement of kindred *Individual Sovereigns* on Long Island already adverted to—"Modern Times," where they undoubtedly found congenial
companionship, and unbridled liberty to carry their doctrines out to
the farthest possible limit, with no one to question or reproach them,
or say them nay. For, as one who had been unwittingly induced to take
up his residence among that "peculiar people" for a time, and who
knew them well—a man of ability and character, well qualified to
judge and to judge wisely—said: "There is a lurking combination
among the leaders to do away entirely with the name and essence of
marriage and to introduce instead an open and respectful sanction of
promiscuous cohabitation. They not only cut the bonds of legality and
set at nought the proprieties of custom, but they also scout the idea
of constancy in love, and ridicule the sensitiveness of one who refuses
to barter connubialities. Wife with them is synonymous with slave and
monogamy is denounced as a *vicious monopoly of affection.*"

This case of marital infidelity and contempt of the marriage covenant occurring in our very midst and at a time when the most lax,
corrupting, and dangerous sentiments concerning the general subject
to which they relate were bruited abroad and extolled throughout the
general community under the specious and captivating guise of *Liberty* and *Reform,* led us at Hopedale to declare our views and make our
position known to the world beyond all doubt or peradventure. This
we effected in a series of resolutions covering the whole ground
involved in the divinely appointed distinction of sex, so far as it applies
to the human race, which was passed in Community meeting held July
10, 1853. The series culminated in the last one which records most

unequivocally and emphatically our conviction concerning the pernicious assumption adverted to, as follows:

"*Resolved,'* (10) That, with our views of Christian Chastity, we
contemplate as utterly abhorrent the various 'Free Love' theories and
practices insidiously propagated among susceptible minds under pretext of higher religious perfection, moral exaltation, social refinement,   individual   sovereignty,   physiological   research   and
philosophical progress; and we feel bound to bear our uncompromis-
ing testimony against all persons, communities, books and publications which inculcate such specious and subtle licentiousness."

PATTERNS OF FEMALE LEADERSHIP

Document 9: Frances Wright's Plan for Nashoba

*Frances Wright was America's first radical feminist, abolitionist,
and socialist. In the 1820s, she developed a plan for emancipating
black slaves through the principles of cooperativism. She believed that
slavery debased the Negro by servile labor. It was unjust simply to free
them without helping them to overcome this conditioning. The cooperative colony would emancipate the Negro by allowing them to pay
off their own bondage in a work cooperative. In the process, the slave
would recover the habits of free and self-directed labor. The plan was
advertised and promoted through the Owenite journal,* New Harmony Gazette. *Robert Dale Owen, Robert Owen's son, was Frances
Wright's close friend and supporter in this as well as other projects.
The plan soon floundered, however, because of lack of practical
leadership. Frances Wright ended the enterprise by personally conveying the emancipated slaves to Haiti.*[30]

*A Plan for the Gradual Abolition of Slavery in the United States,
Without Danger of Loss to the Citizens of the South*

It appears superflous, in proposing a plan for the general abolition of slavery in the United States, to observe upon the immensity
of the evil, and the gloomy prospect of dangers it presents to the
American people—disunion, bloodshed, servile wars of extermina-
tion, horrible in their nature and consequences, and disgraceful in the
eyes of the civilized world.

It is conceived that any plan of emancipation, to be effectual, must
consult at once the pecuniary interests and prevailing opinions of the
southern planters, and bend itself to the existing laws of the southern
states. . . . The following plan is believed to embrace all these objects
and is presented to some southern and northern philanthropists, in
the hope that, if meeting with their approbation, it will also meet with
their support. It was originally suggested by the consideration of the
German society, lately conducted by Mr. Rapp, at Harmony, Indiana

and (since the purchase of that property by Mr. Owen,) at Economy, Pennsylvania. . . . The great advantages of united, over individual labor, have been evinced by the practice of several religious communities—Moravians, Shaking Quakers, and Harmonites. . . . In directing the attention to the advantages of a co-operative system of labor, as practised in the above-named societies, it is necessary at the same time, to compare those advantages with the disadvantages of existing slave labor.

It is conceived to be an admitted truth, that slave labor, considered in itself, independent of the nature of the produce it is employed in raising, is profitless. In Maryland and Virginia, and in other states and districts, where slave labor is brought in direct competition with the free labor of the north, agriculture yields indifferent profit. . . .

This effect, whenever and by whatever produced, will tend towards the adoption of some other mode of labor, even in that section of the Union, where reform may at present appear the least practicable. It is thought, however, that if a more humane and profitable system should be brought to bear in any one state, the example must gradually extend through all.

To render these advantages more immediately apparent, and to bring the first experiment within the reach of a small capital, it is proposed:

To purchase two sections of congress lands, within the good southwestern cotton line—say in some tract bordering on Tennessee, either in Alabama, or Mississippi, unless within Tennessee itself, or elsewhere, some suitable and advantageous purchase of improved property, should present itself.

To place on this land from fifty to one hundred negroes, (the greater the number the more will the advantages of a system of united labor be apparent,) and to introduce a system of cooperative labor, conducted, as far as shall be advisable in the given case, on the plan of the German and other communities above mentioned, holding out, as the great stimulus to exertion, the prospect of liberty, together with the liberty and education of the children.

To open a school of industry which, on the Lancasterian plan shall carry order and cooperation from the school-room into the field, the children working, under the direction of their monitors, with such intermission as shall keep their minds cheerful, and their bodies vigorous. . . . It appears unnecessary to enlarge on the probable effect, which a mild but steady system of order and economy, together with the improved condition and future destinies of the children, and an induced personal and family interest in the thriving of the establishment, will produce on the dispositions and exertions of the parents. The better to insure those effects, the parents will be gradually brought to understand, in weekly evening meetings, the object of the establishment, and taught orally (in simple language) the necessity of industry, first for the procuring of liberty, and afterwards the value of industry when liberty shall be procured. . . . The term of five years has been chosen as an average term, in which a good laborer will return his first purchase money with interest. On sugar, rice and some cotton lands, the term is now esteemed much shorter, from one to three. . . .

It is hoped, that, after one successful experiment, a similar establishment will be placed in each state; and that when the advantages of the system shall be ascertained, many planters will lease out their property, to be worked in the same way, receiving an interest equal or superior to that returned at present, while the extra profits may be devoted to the general system.

The experiment farm, which it is proposed to establish by subscription, will as it is hoped, among other advantages, offer an asylum and school of industry for the slaves of benevolent masters, anxious to manumit their people, but apprehensive of throwing them unprepared into the world. . . .

This plan, proposed in a spirit of equal good will to master and slave, is intended to consult the interests of both. To prepare the latter for liberty, before it is granted, and in no case to grant liberty, but in accordance with the laws of the state, by removal out of the state.—To remove, by gradual and gentle means, a system fraught with danger, as well as crime.

Document 10: Barbara Heineman (Landmann) as Werkzeuge of the Amana Inspirationists

As Werkzeuge, *Barbara Heineman Landmann was regarded by the German pietist sect of Amana Inspirationists as an incarnate vehicle of the Holy Spirit. In 1874, Charles Nordhoff, a student of American communalism, visited Amana and gave the following, rather gloomy view of their generally repressive manners toward women in contrast to the spiritual authority held by their female leader. Celibacy was encouraged as a higher spiritual state at Amana, although it was not always successfully enforced.*[31]

The women and young girls wear dingy colored stuffs, mostly of the society's own make, cut in the plainest style, and often short gowns, in the German peasant way. All, even to the very small girls, wear their hair in a kind of black cowl or cap, which covers only the back of the head, and is tied under the chin by a black ribbon. Also all, young as well as old, wear a small dark-colored shawl or handkerchief over the shoulders, and pinned very plainly across the breast. This peculiar uniform adroitly conceals the marks of sex, and gives a singularly monotonous appearance to the women.

The sex, I believe, is not highly esteemed by these people, who think it dangerous to the Christian's peace of mind. One of their most esteemed writers advises men to "fly from intercourse with women, as a very highly dangerous magnet and magical fire." Their women work hard and dress soberly; all ornaments are forbidden. To wear the hair loose is prohibited. Great care is used to keep the sexes apart. In their evening and other meetings, women not only sit apart from men, but they leave the room before the men break ranks. Boys are allowed to play only with boys, and girls with girls. There are no places or occasions for evening amusements, where the sexes might meet. On Sunday afternoons the boys are permitted to walk in the fields; and so are the girls, but these must go in another direction. "Perhaps they meet in the course of the walk," said a member to me, "but it is not allowed." At meals and in their labors they are also separated. With all this care to hide the charms of the young women, to make them, as far as dress can do so, look old and ugly, and to keep the young men away from them, love, courtship, and marriage go on at Amana as elsewhere in the world. The young man "falls in love," and finds ways to make his passion known to its object; he no doubt enjoys all the delights of courtship, intensified by the difficulties which his prudent brethren put in his way; and he marries the object of his affect, in spite of her black hood and her sad-colored little shawl, whenever he has reached the age of twenty-four. . . .

In every village four or five of the older and more experienced elders meet each morning to advise together on business. This council acts, as I understand, upon reports of those younger elders who are foremen and have charge of different affairs. These in turn meet for a few minutes every evening, and arrange for the next day's work.

Women are never members of these councils, nor do they hold, as far as I could discover, any temporal or spiritual authority, with the single exception of their present spiritual head, who is a woman of eighty years. . . .

They regard the utterances, while in the trance state, of their spiritual head as given from God; and believe—as is asserted in the Catechism—that evils and wrongs in the congregation will be thus revealed by the influence, or, as they say, the inspiration or breath of God; that in important affairs they will thus receive the divine direction; and that it is their duty to obey the commands thus delivered to them.

There were "inspired instruments" before Christian Metz. Indeed, the present "instrument," Barbara Landmann, was accepted before him, but by reason of her marriage fell from grace for a while. . . .

The words of "inspiration" are usually delivered in the public meetings, and at funerals and other solemn occasions. They have always been carefully written down by persons specially appointed to that office; . . .

The "inspired" words are not always addressed to the general congregation, but often to individual members; and their feelings are not spared. Thus in one case Barbara Landmann, being "inspired," turned upon a sister with the words, "But you wretched creature, follow the true counsel of obedience"; and to another: "And you, contrary spirit, how much pain do you give to our hearts. You will fall into everlasting pain, torture, and unrest if you do not break your will and repent, so that you may be accepted and forgiven by those you have offended, and who have done so much for you."

The warnings, prophecies, reproofs, and admonitions, thus delivered by the "inspired instrument," are all, as I have said, carefully written down, and in convenient time printed in yearly volumes, entitled "Year-Books of the True Inspiration Congregations: Witnesses of the Spirit of God, which happened and were spoken in the Meetings of the Society, through the Instruments, Brother Christian Metz and Sister B. Landmann," with the year in which they were delivered. . . .

The celebration of the Lord's Supper is their greatest religious event. It is held only when the "inspired instrument" directs it, which may not happen once in two years; and it is thought so solemn and important an occasion that a full account of it is sometimes printed in a book. . . .

The present inspired instrument being very aged, I asked whether another was ready to take her place. They said No, no one had yet appeared; but they had no doubt God would call some one to the necessary office. They were willing to trust him, and gave themselves no trouble about it.

Document 11: Ellen Harmon White, Seventh Day Adventist Prophetess

In the 1840s, the Millerite movement predicted the Second Coming of Christ in 1843. The Harmon family were among the many swept into this expectation. When the Day of the Lord failed to materialize, many Millerites drifted back to their old churches. Shortly after the Great Disappointment, Ellen Harmon, soon to be married to Adventist preacher James White, began to have ecstatic visions. Through these visions she reinterpreted the Adventist expectations. Adventists regard her prophetic gifts as falling in the line of inspired prophets. In this extract from her early writings, Ellen White describes the importance of this visionary guidance during the early development of Adventism and recounts a particular vision that she had at Howland House in Topsham, Maine, on April 3, 1847, where the continued validity of the Sabbath observance was revealed to her.[32]

In 1842, I constantly attended the second advent meetings in Portland, Maine, and fully believed that the Lord was coming. I was hungering and thirsting for full salvation, an entire conformity to the will of God. . . . I had never prayed vocally in meeting, and drew back from the duty, fearing that if I should attempt to pray I would be confounded. Every time I went before the Lord in secret prayer this unfulfilled duty presented itself, until I ceased to pray, and settled down in a melancholy state, and finally in deep despair. . . .

There was to be a prayer meeting that evening, which I attended, and when others knelt to pray, I bowed with them trembling, and after two or three had prayed, I opened my mouth in prayer before I was aware of it, and the promises of God looked to me like so many precious pearls that were to be received by only asking for them. As I prayed, the burden and agony of soul that I had so long felt left me, and the blessing of God came upon me like the gentle dew. I gave glory to God for what I felt, but I longed for more. I could not be satisfied till I was filled with the fullness of God. Inexpressible love for Jesus filled my soul. Wave after wave of glory rolled over me, until my body grew still. Everything was shut out from me but Jesus and glory, and I knew nothing of what was passing around me.

I remained in this state of body and mind a long time, and when I realized what was around me, everything seemed changed. Everything looked glorious and new, as if smiling and praising God. I was then willing to confess Jesus everywhere.

From this time, up to December, 1844, my joys, trials, and disappointments were like those of my dear Advent friends around me. At this time I visited one of our Advent sisters, and in the morning we bowed around the family altar. It was not an exciting occasion, and there were but five of us present, all women. While I was praying, the power of God came upon me as I had never felt it before. I was wrapped in a vision of God's glory, and seemed to be rising higher and higher from the earth, and was shown something of the travels of the Advent people to the Holy City.

Subsequent Visions

The Lord gave me the following view in 1847, while the brethren were assembled on the Sabbath, at Topsham, Maine.

We felt an unusual spirit of prayer. And as we prayed the Holy Ghost fell upon us. We were very happy. Soon I was lost to earthly things and was wrapped in a vision of God's glory. I saw an angel flying swiftly to me. He quickly carried me from the earth to the Holy City. In the city I saw a temple, which I entered. I passed through a door before I came to the first veil. This veil was raised, and I passed into the holy place. Here I saw the alter of incense, the candlestick with seven lamps, and the table on which was the shewbread. After viewing the glory of the holy, Jesus raised the second veil and I passed into the holy of holies.

In the holiest I saw an ark; on the top and sides of it was purest gold. One each end of the ark was a lovely cherub, with its wings spread out over it. Their faces were turned toward each other, and they looked downward. Between the angels was a golden censer. Above the ark, where the angels stood, was an exceeding bright glory, that appeared like a throne where God dwelt. Jesus stood by the ark, and as the saints' prayers came up to Him, the incense in the censer would smoke, and He would offer up their prayers with the smoke of the incense to His Father. In the Ark was the golden pot of manna, Aaron's rod that budded, and the tables of stone which folded together like a book. Jesus opened them, and I saw the Ten Commandments written on them with the finger of God. On one table were four, and on the other six. But the fourth, the Sabbath commandment, shone above them all; for the Sabbath was set apart to be kept in honor of God's holy name. The holy Sabbath looked glorious—a halo of glory was all around it. I saw that the Sabbath commandment was not nailed to the cross. If it was, the other nine commandments were; and we are at liberty to break them all, as well as to break the fourth. I saw that God had not changed the Sabbath, for He never changes.

Document 12: Mary Baker Eddy, Pastor Emeritus of the Mother Church

None of the other women discussed in this volume held such final authority in the religious institutions they led as did the foundress of Christian Science, Mary Baker Eddy. In the Manual of the Mother Church, *she developed a handbook of church bylaws that mediated her personal authority and direction. In her Christmas letter of 1903, she told the directors: "If I am not personally with you, the Word of God and my instructions in the By-Laws have led you hither and will guide you safely on. . . . The change of Mrs. Eddy's title from Mother to Leader was made in response to attacks by Mark Twain and other publicists who inferred that Mrs. Eddy regarded herself as a female divinity.*[33]

Article XXII
Relation of Members to Pastor Emeritus

The Title of Mother Changed. Section I. In the year eighteen hundred and ninety-five, loyal Christian Scientists had given to the author of their textbook, the Founder of Christian Science, the individual, endearing term of Mother. At first Mrs. Eddy objected to being called thus, but afterward consented on the ground that this appellative in the Church meant nothing more than a tender term such as sister or

brother. In the year nineteen hundred and three and after, owing to
the public misunderstanding of this name, it is the duty of Christian
Scientists to drop the word *mother* and to substitute Leader, already
used in our periodicals.

Working Against the Cause. Sect. 2. If a member of this Church shall,
mentally or otherwise, persist in working against the interests of another member, or the interests of our Pastor Emeritus and the accomplishment of what she understands is advantageous to this Church
and to the cause of Christian Science, or shall influence others thus
to act, upon her complaint or the complaint of a member for her or
for himself, it shall be the duty of the Board of Directors immediately
to call a meeting, and drop forever the name of the member guilty
of this offense from the roll of Church membership.

No Unchristian Conduct. Sect. 3. If a member of this Church were
to treat the author of our textbook disrespectfully and cruelly, upon
her complaint that member should be excommunicated. If a member,
without her having requested the information, shall trouble her on
subjects unnecessarily and without her consent, it shall be considered
an offense.

Not to Learn Hypnotism. Sect. 4. Members of this Church shall not
learn hypnotism on penalty of being excommunicated from this
Church. No member shall enter a complaint of mental malpractice for
a sinister purpose. If the author of *Science and Health* shall bear witness
to the offense of mental malpractice, it shall be considered a sufficient
evidence thereof.

Reading and Attesting Letters. Sect. 5. When a letter or a message
from the Pastor Emeritus is brought before a meeting of this Church,
or she is referred to as authority for business, it shall be the duty of
the Church to inquire if all of the letter has been read, and to require
all of it to be read; also to have any authority supposed to come from
her satisfactorily attested.

Unauthorized Reports. Sect. 6. Members of this church shall not
report on authority an order from Mrs. Eddy that she has not sent,
either to the Boards or to the executive bodies of this Church. The
Pastor Emeritus is not to be consulted on cases of discipline, on the
cases of candidates for admission to this Church, or on the cases of
those on trial for dismissal from the Church.

Interpreting Communications. Sect. 7. If at a meeting of this Church
a doubt or disagreement shall arise among the members as to the
signification of the communications of the Pastor Emeritus to them,
before action is taken it shall be the duty of the Clerk to report to her
the vexed question and to await her explanation thereof.

Unauthorized Legal Action. Sect. 8. A member of this Church shall
not employ an attorney, nor take legal action on a case not provided
for in its By-Laws—if said case relates to the person or to the property

of Mary Baker G. Eddy—without having personally conferred with her on said subject.

No Adulterating Christian Science. Sect. 9. A member of this Church shall not publish profuse quotations from Mary Baker G. Eddy's copyrighted works without her permission, and shall not plagiarize her writings. This By-Law not only calls more serious attention to the commandment of the Decalogue, but tends to prevent Christian Science from being *adulterated.*

Opportunity for Serving the Leader. Sect. 10. At the written request of our Pastor Emeritus, Mrs. Eddy, the Board of Directors shall immediately notify a member of this Church to go within ten days to her and to remain if needed twelve months consecutively, and it shall be the duty of this member to comply therewith. A member, who leaves her in less time without her consent, or who is discharged, is liable, on Mrs. Eddy's complaint, to have his or her name dropped from the Church.

The aforesaid members who remain with her three years consecutively shall be paid semi-annually at the rate of twelve hundred dollars yearly in addition to rent and board. Those members, whom she teaches the course in Divinity, stay with her three years, and receive the degree D.S.D. of the Massachusetts Metaphysical College.

Publications Unjust. Sect. II. If a member of The Mother Church publishes, or causes to be published, an article that is false or unjust, hence injurious, to Christian Science or to its Leader, and if, upon complaint by another member, the Board of Directors finds that the offense has been committed, the offender shall be suspended for not less than three years from his or her office in this Church and from Church membership.

Document 13: Augusta Stetson, the Faithful Disciple

Mary Baker Eddy's most brilliant disciple in Christian Science healing was Augusta Stetson. Mrs. Stetson pushed many of the ideas hinted at in Mrs. Eddy's writings to their logical extreme. She believed that the Christian Scientist would gradually overcome sin, sickness, and death, and, with it, the need for procreation. She also believed Mrs. Eddy herself to be the incarnation of the female Divine Principle. Her ecstatic loyalty to her teacher is expressed in her many letters to Mrs. Eddy. By 1900, Mrs. Stetson had become a powerful leader of a large following in New York City. She was widely regarded as Mrs. Eddy's logical successor. But in 1909, Mrs. Eddy moved suddenly to press charges of false teachings and "malicious animal magnetism" against Mrs. Stetson and to expel her from communion with the Mother Church.

In the following letter written in July of 1895 to Mrs. Eddy, Mrs. Stetson gives us a glimpse of her attachment to her leader. A second

*letter, written in July of 1909 and presented here, protests her con-
tinued devotion to her leader, despite the notice of Mrs. Eddy's actions against her. Even after her excommunication, Mrs. Stetson
continued to regard Mrs. Eddy as divine and to interpret even her
own expulsion as a pedagogical measure from her all-wise Teacher.*[34]

The Dream

Winter Hill, Mass., July 10, 1895.

My precious Leader and Teacher:—

I received these two letters some days ago, which I enclose to you.
Deception and falsity have at least been uncovered in this student.
One night I felt that I could not endure another hour of such mental
agony. At this point I laid my head upon my pillow and went to sleep
with this prayer: "Father-Mother God, I can do no more for this
student. Thou knowest that I have tried to be faithful and true according to my understanding. I leave all with Thee. I turn from this dream
forever. Do with me as Thou wilt, only let Spirit be manifest in me as
I kiss the rod and carry the cross." Then I dreamed this:

That you had sent for me. I was shown into a large square room
with one window, and one door which opened on a lawn. In the room
was a very large bed. You approached me, and smiling, whispered,
"Rest, dear, rest." You then glided to the bed and lay down on the
edge. I followed and laid myself on the other side. As I lay there I
thought it was night and I said to myself, how quiet she is! Oh, how
sweet and peaceful to be with her; I wonder what she wants me to do!
I must not sleep; when she awakes she will tell me. Then it seemed
to be morning.

You quietly arose and went to a dressing-table and began to arrange your hair. I said, "Oh! Mother dear, may I dress it?" You
immediately sat down and whispered, "Yes, dear." I carefully arranged it, feeling so happy that I was permitted to do it. I exclaimed,
"Oh, your hair is so lovely, dear mother!" Then you arose and went
to the door. Turning to me again whispered, "Come." I said, "I must
dress my hair," and I quickly pinned it up and went after you. You
were away beyond, tripping like a fairy over a beautiful green plateau
which seemed to extend as far as I could see, with nothing to obstruct
the view. I said to myself, "Oh, I must hurry; she is so light and walks
so fast, and I am so slow and heavy, I must run faster." And I
increased my efforts, calling on God to help me to follow, when you
turned and smiled and waited for me.

As I reached you, you put your arm around my waist and I put
mine around yours, and like two school girls we walked on together,
so happy, but not a word was spoken. When you reached what seemed
to be the edge of this plateau, there was a steep descent, and you
continued right on down it till, when at its foot, I found we were on

a wide, smooth, sandy beach. You walked right into the water and I said, "How delicious the water is to my feet!" You still went on, farther in where the water was quite deep, and I said, "Oh! it is cold, is it not, Mother?" You said nothing, but kept on walking into deeper water until I said, "It is cold, but I am not afraid when God and Mother are with me." Then I seemed to lose the sense of a river bed, and the thought that I was not touching bottom with my feet gave me a little shudder, but I said: "I will follow where you lead." Instantly I felt a solid substance under my feet. I said, "This seems like a large rock." I saw we were in the middle of an immense lake—quiet, and clear as crystal—and we slipped on the rock for a moment, still with our arms around each other. Then we turned towards the shore, walked on the water, and ascended the hill, over the same green plateau, and entered the same room we had left. You had not spoken a word. The room was filled with people waiting for you, and many were outside. Some one brought in a tray with food, but you turned away to talk to the people, and I also refused to eat. I then said, "I wonder what she wants me to do. I must not interrupt her, she is feeding the truth to so many people. I will go to God and He will tell me." Then I awoke. The sun had risen; it was early morning and all was quiet in my room. I said, "God will tell me what I am to do"; for strength and peace and joy assured me that I had been walking with an angel. I then arose, and took up my Bible.

My eyes rested on the sixth verse of the sixth chapter of Isaiah, which I read to the close of the chapter. Since then I have been seeing wondrous things out of God's law. I have no fear which Love will not cast out. I have always, when recalling that dream, felt the impression of that rock under my feet as sensibly as when in my night vision.

7 West 96th Street, New York City
July 24, 1909

Reverend Mary Baker Eddy,
    Chestnut Hill, Brookline, Mass.

My precious Leader:—

Your dear letter of to-day is before me. I thank you for your continued watch-care during this perilous passage (through material sense to Soul) from the will of the flesh, or human energy, which embodies itself in physical personality, to the will of God, or divine energy, which dissolves finite personality together with all the phenomena of the carnal mind, and reveals Spirit, God, as the only creator, and man as His image and likeness, the compound idea or divine personality, the reflection of the infinite Person. . . .

I have always tried to teach my students to differentiate between finite and infinite personality, between the physical personality, which is the image of the beast or so-called mortal mind, specifically named animal magnetism, and the divine personality, which is the image of God—the spiritual idea or Christ. By failing to discern this difference some of my students in the past have lost "the way." . . .

The sensuous world refused, and continues to refuse, to follow and obey the impersonal Christ which Jesus and you, my beloved Leader, have declared. . . .

I have always taught my students to love and reverence you as the one whom God has appointed to voice His word to this age.

My students know that I am endeavoring to obey your teaching and demonstrate Christ, and for this reason they, in turn, have confidence in me as a teacher and demonstrator of Christian Science. For twenty-five years, "the enemy of good" has been using every subtle suggestion to separate me from the Christ which you represent, and are demonstrating, but it has signally and utterly failed. If my students have shown more zeal than wisdom in expressing their love for their Leader, and for their teacher, I will try still further to warn them of the danger of deifying physical personality. I believe, however, that they are clear on the fact that "none is good, save one, that is, God," and His idea.

As you continue to demonstrate the "infinite calculus defining the line, plane, space, and fourth dimension of Spirit" (*Miscellaneous Writings,* p. 22), may wisdom enable me to maintain through you, God's idea, the consciousness of my unity with Him. This I believe I have always done in the letter, and in an ever increasing degree in the spirit. I have taught my students to look straight at and through the brazen serpent of *false* personality, and to behold the immortal idea, man, where the mortal seems to be. Malicious animal magnetism still persists in its efforts, by its indiscriminate denunciation of personality in general, to slay the spiritual idea, Christian Science, to which you have given birth. I understand your teachings held him in the bonds of personal sense. The wise see you to-day as the Messiah, or the Anointed of God to this age, fulfilling the law of Love. They do not deify your human personality, but will not lose sight of your spiritual individuality, or God with us. Although all of my students have been taught this, doubtless some have not assimilated it.

In your letter to me, which was published in the *Sentinel* of July 17th, you thanked me for acknowledging you as my Leader. I have always delighted to revere, follow, and obey you as my Leader, to whom I pay loving, loyal allegiance. I am abiding by the divine rules laid down in your writings, and am following your Christly example so far as Love reflected in love illumines the way. This sincere endeavor to possess the Mind of Christ must bring its blessing. Your comforting assurance that I am "aware that animal magnetism is the opposite of divine Science" (*Christian Science Journal,* vol. xxvii., p. 313) gives me renewed courage to wield the two-edged sword of Truth and Love with intent to decapitate this opponent, the beast and false prophet; for the lie, lust, and hypocrisy, which contend against innocence and truth—the Lamb of Love, shall not continue to engender and develop, for God worketh with us.

Precious Leader, I am watching and praying that "the enemy of good" cannot "separate" me from you, my Leader and Teacher. "For I am persuaded, that neither death, nor life, nor angels, nor principalities, nor powers, nor things present, nor things to come, nor height, nor depth, nor any other creature, shall be able to separate us (me) from the love of God, which is in Christ Jesus our Lord"—and Mary Baker Eddy, my beloved Leader, "and best earthly friend."

Your loving child,
Augusta

UTOPIANISM AND THE EMANCIPATION OF WOMEN

Document 14: The Fourierite Plan of Female Emancipation

Several leading American communalists, including George Ripley of transcendentalist Brook Farm and Albert Brisbane, author of The Social Destiny of Man *(1840), cooperated to produce the* Phalanx, *a journal designed to promote Fourierite principles in America and to report on the news of developing Phalanxes. In the August 10, 1844, issue of the journal, they published a translation of a French article that described the cooperative household as the key to women's emancipation.*[35]

Condition of Women in Harmony
Translated from the French of Madame Gatti De Gamond

Since social questions have been generally mooted, the condition of women is that which is most obscured by prejudices. Their emancipation is essential to real progress; but the word alone alarms and irritates one-sided minds, who couple liberty with immorality, or turn a serious subject into ridicule. In irresponsible disunity no liberty can be allowed to women, it is true, without exposing them to danger and depravity; but in associative unity, the case is very different. The corporation everywhere protects the individual from vice.

Fourier expresses the greatest solicitude for the condition of women; in them he sees at once the class the most oppressed, and the most powerful instruments of social regeneration. His system of attractive industry enables them to act in groups, securing independence by their industry, and raising them from degradation liberates them from their misery.

No class is so interested as that of the women in the realization of his system. It solves all the difficulties of their position, and assures them the full emancipation which they need. What is this emancipation? This is a word which has been so much abused, that it requires some explanation.

By the emancipation of women do we only wish to express modification, amelioration, progress? Who can deny that the condition of woman is susceptible of improvement as well as all human institutions?

Woman in the savage state, whose destiny is often so sad that when she brings into the world a child of the weaker sex, will destroy her new-born babe, that it may be spared a painful existence, must she not desire to advance a step in social progress? It is from this excess of degradation and misery that woman, in passing through the various social phases from complete barbarism to the present state of civilization, has always been released from servitude, and raised to a degree of dignity. Since, then, her condition has been already modified, what may she not desire, what may she not hope for?

The most immediate cause of woman's misery is poverty. If she asks for emancipation, she does but ask, as the first condition toward her melioration, a reform in the social economy, effectual in removing distress, affording to all some education, the bare necessaries of life, and the right to labor.

It is not only the wives of the people, but women of all classes, whose evils result from the present social state. The great majority possess but a moderate portion, insufficient for their support; those who have a competency are in danger of losing it from mismanagement. They have not, like men, opportunities for earning an independence, and they are everywhere surrounded by dangers and difficulties. Marriage and the cares of a family are their destination; the law, the customs, education, permit woman only to form her social position by marriage. Unmarried, she is solitary, dependent, and subject to perpetual humiliations.

Fourier's system gives independence, and opens a career to woman; it reconciles her household cares, and the duties of maternity, with intellectual development and art and general employments. It does even more—it gives her a high place in general estimation, a dignified and pure position, favorable to her own improvement and society's regeneration. . . .

We must then understand, by moral emancipation for woman, an independent position, conducive to the free exercise of her affections and her talents, without the necessity of making engagements contrary to her inclinations.

The subject of woman, her state of miserable and precarious dependence, is the first cause of her moral degradation. . . .

It must be understood, that all progress in the condition of woman depends upon a social renovation, which, securing her independence, permits her to act with honesty and sincerity in all the relationships of life. . . . Let the social state be changed, so that woman can think and act freely, then will she revive all that is good and true in morals and in manners—then will she prove herself to be, what God designed her, the dispenser of peace, harmony, and happiness in all societies. . . .

The system of education, which fashions woman, is quite different to that which fashions men. With these, it is all matter of fact, scepticism, dogmatism; with woman it is innocence, modesty, ingenuousness, golden dreams—Love around her deceiving, flattering, bewildering. From her childhood, all speak to her of Love—conversations, books, theatres, society, beneath the deceiving mask of gallantry, her own illusions, unknown emotions, involuntary sighs and tears.

Soon all these early illusions give way to reality—soon does woman herself conform to the customs of the age, and calculation, as a sum in arithmetic, is consulted in her destiny. Already has Love undergone its first transformation in her soul; Love now means marriage. Love in marriage is woman's second dream. . . . But one step more into actual realities, and the world, with all its contradictions, is opened before her. . . .

Civilization, or the system of separate households, offers no remedy for the ills of woman, offers no escape from sorrowful and painful subjection, to the daughters of people. It is in vain, that legislation, morals, and education combine to reform the manners, to stem the tide of corruption, to regenerate woman, to strengthen family relationships: all must fail, as society is now constituted. Remove the cause of corruption, then you efface misery; establish unitary education, then you give a free development to the faculties, and assure independence by labor. . . . But perhaps it may be said, that in the present state, every industrious, artistic, and scientific path is opened to woman, and that a great number earn their own livelihood; but nevertheless, the difficulties of a profession for a woman are very great: first, by education, which seldom prepares her for it; secondly, by the obstructions which surround all social undertakings. Besides, how can women, absorbed in household details, the fatigues and the cares of maternity, occupy themselves with regular labor? It is in this sense that the independence of woman cannot be reconciled with separate households, and that even the right to labor cannot be granted her. What can become of an unhappy woman, when her husband is either a gambler, drunkard, dissipated, or extravagant? What can become of her if she has children and no fortune? Even when the laws permit divorce, is she in circumstances to profit by it—must she not endure all, suffer all, for the sake of her children? In the present social state, no remedy can be found for the ills and oppression of woman.

Fourier's system insensibly introducing, without struggle, without injury to any interest, a society in society, resolves all the difficulties in the position of woman. Without changing the legislation or proclaiming new rights, he stops at once all the sources of corruption, reforms education and manners by the effects that naturally flow from his system in which Unitary Education and the independence of women are ensured by the rights of labor; independence rendered possible by Associated Households, Attractive Industry and Wealth increasing rapidly. Women are no longer the mere slaves of solitary household duty; they are organized in corporations of industrial, artistic and religious unity and have a morally collective, a truly social existence in addition to their individual position in the private family. The daughter or the wife at home, in private domesticity, is known to the collective body of the Plalanx as a useful member of society connected with some corporations of importance with regard to art or industry, religion or instruction. She is an artist, or an educator, is adept in floriculture or in needlework, a useful member of society, in fact, as well as wife and daughter in the private family and when society is organized on unitary principles, the wife and daughter will have time for all her duties, social and domestic.

Document 15: New Roles for Women at Oneida

For over thirty years, the Reports of the Oneida community and their journal, the Circular, *discussed, among other things, advances in the status of women in their movement. The following extracts give some glimpses into their feminist concerns.*[36]

First Annual Report of the Oneida Association
January 1, 1849
'SHORT DRESSES

In connection with this new fashion of making rooms, it will be appropriate to allude to one or two other novelties which the Association has fallen into by free-thinking. Early in the summer, in consequence of some speculations on the subject of women's dress . . . some of the leading women in the Association took the liberty to dress themselves in short gowns or frocks, with pantaloons (the fashion of dress common among children), and the advantage of the change soon became so manifest that others followed the example, till frocks and pantaloons became the prevailing fashion in the Association. The women say they are far more free and comfortable in this dress than in long gowns; the men think that it improves their looks; and some insist that it is entirely more modest than the common dress.

CHANGE IN HAIR-DRESSING

Another new fashion broke out among the women in the following manner. The ordinary practice of leaving the hair to grow indefinitely, and laboring upon it by the hour daily, merely for the sake of winding it up into a ball and sticking it on the top or back of the head, had become burdensome and distasteful to several of the women. Indeed there was a general feeling in the Association that any fashion which requires women to devote considerable time to hair-dressing is a degradation and a nuisance. The idea of wearing the hair short and leaving it to fall around the neck, as young girls often do, occurred frequently but Paul's theory of the natural propriety of long hair for women (1 Corinthians 11) seemed to stand in the way. At length a careful examination of this theory was instituted and the discovery was made that Paul's language expressly points out the object for which women should wear long hair and that object is not ornament but "for covering." In this light it was immediately manifest that the long hair of women as it is usually wórn, coiled and combed upward to the top of the head, instead of answering Paul's object of covering actually exposes the back part of the head more than the short hair of men. It then occurred also that Phrenology, in pointing to the back of the head and neck as the seat of amativeness, has given a rational basis to Paul's theory of the propriety of women's making their hair a covering. It was evident moreover that the hair is not needed as a covering where the person is covered by the dress. These considerations seemed to establish satisfactorily the natural and scriptural propriety of women's wearing their hair in the simple mode of little girls, "down in the neck." Accordingly some of the bolder women cut off their hair and started the fashion, which soon prevailed throughout the Association, and was generally acknowledged to be an improvement of appearance as well as a saving of labor.

CIRCULAR, April 26, 1855

Some conversation this evening on woman's education, and the new course she has entered upon here. It was resolved that our women ought not to let a day pass without engaging in some manly work. A lesson in manly work every day would do more for their education than ever so much playing on the piano, or sewing and sweeping. We calculated that every woman in the Association could give as many as two hours a day to outdoor manly industry, and a proposal to this effect was well received. The profit of health, spirit, and value of character, it is expected, will show six months hence. A thorough experiment for converting farm work and gardening from drudgery into sport will be tried here this summer. The social harmonies and the virtue of frequent alternatives, change of groups, etc., will be brought to bear. If there is any power in youth and beauty in feminine attractiveness, it is not going to draw towards the house and laziness, but towards useful industry and productiveness on the domain.

CIRCULAR, February 15, 1855

If women wish to get rid of effeminacy, they must be willing to wear thicker shoes and fabrics of coarser texture than they have been accustomed to. Why should not woman be as independent of the weather and outdoor elements as man? Is there any reason in her original constitution for the inequality which exists? The speaker referred to the present extreme cold and the temptation there is in such a time to curl up, shrug the shoulders, and hover over the register and around the stove; and remarked that so long as we act on the defensive merely, and retreat before the cold, it will crowd us. We must put the weather on defensive—take the initiative of war. Instead of seeking protection by outside appliances, we should arouse the center, and let courage conquer both fear and cold together. This was the value of our Brooklyn practice of a daily plunge into the salt brine of the harbor, which some of us enjoyed quite regularly until we left the city in December.

CIRCULAR, April 25, 1864

What's the excitement now? What's this buzz in our bee-hive? What are the women talking about that makes them look so important? Well, they have been promoted in business. They have received a sort of agency—an Express agency. The Community necessarily have a great deal of business at the Depot, and it is of two kinds; one involves heavy freight and important transactions, and the other consists of light errands. The women are to "run" a horse and carriage for light errands; for the mail for instance. The Board of Expenses has appropriated a horse and carriage this spring for the women's exclusive use. But it is deemed almost an effeminacy by Community women to ride for no object but to ride, and if this business had not been given them we doubt whether the previous gift of the horse and carriage would have been worth much. As it is, a sense of usefulness will make excursions attractive. And if this thing grows, perhaps we shall have the credit by and by of extending "woman's sphere."

CIRCULAR, May 22, 1865

To the Community:

I can truly say that I am proud of our women, young and old. I see that in will and principle, and to a good extent in practice and feeling, they have conquered the fashions of the world in themselves, and are substantially free from bondage to the spirit of dress and ornament, and special love. The long discord I had with them about these things has passed away. They have, in many respects, had to bear the brunt of the battle for Communism. The reproach of the short dress and our social theory has fallen on them more than on the men. And when I look back and remember the terrible scenes that some of them went through at Putney; and the shame that others endured and despised here when they were brought before magistrate; and the steady, long-continued, unflinching obedience to discipline which all have shown in our fifteen years warfare with the fashions and passions of the world inside from without, I wish to praise and thank them. They have proved themselves good soldiers; and they will have their reward. Already it is evident that the short dress, which our women invented and have bravely won the right to wear, is coming to acceptance and honor in the world. And so it will be with every social improvement that they have suffered shame for. Their time of honor is coming. God bless them!

JOHN H. NOYES.

CIRCULAR, March 6, 1866
Wallingford

One subject of interest in our evening meetings lately has been the education of women. In our future University it is determined to make the education of women a prominent object. Girls shall have all the advantages of boys. They shall be encouraged to study everything that boys do. We have made a beginning in having our girls learn to swim. They have been admitted to a field there which has belonged to men alone, and it appears that they excel in swimming. They shall be admitted to all the sciences, to the whole course of education considered useful to men. We maintain the ground that if the women are thoroughly educated, the education of men will take care of itself. The subject of systematic reading has engaged attention. The appetite for good strong standard works should be cultivated among the women. There are certain books which may be called the tap-roots of learning to which the literature of the day is but as the leaves on the outmost branches of the tree. That a taste for solid reading has already somewhat developed among our women and girls, appeared in the fact that there were classes reading Malthus and Burges's translation of Plato, with great relish. G. W. N., having himself a new attraction for Greek history and literature, is giving us the benefit of his research in lectures and reading on the subject.

CIRCULAR, January 5, 1874

We have what we call a family machine shop, instituted partly with a view to admit the women. It is in the parlor of the old Willow Place house. This room contains five lathes. Mr. Inslee, whose skill and experience have had very much to do with the manufacturing success of the O. C., presides over this shop and has afforded the women not only the benefit of his instruction but the most hearty encouragement.

They began with turning chuck screws of various sizes. Then they were set to cutting the threads of these screws, a nice operation, particularly in the case of the smaller ones; but Mr. I. reports that they have succeeded in cutting the finest screws in first-rate style. He appreciates the women in the shop not only for their work, but for the influence of their inalienable tidiness and order, not to say anything about the attractions of their personal presence, to which he is the last man in the world to be insensible. On the whole he thinks women can do many kinds of light work on the lathe just as well as the sex who have heretofore monopolized its use. Admitted to the machine shop, perhaps the next census will record women inventors.

Document 16: A Women's Work Collective at Brook Farm

From 1844 to 1854, Marianne Dwight was a member of the transcendentalist Brook Farm community, including the period when they reorganized as a Fourierite Phalanx. Her many letters to her friends and relatives are a vivid source of information on daily life at Brook Farm. On August 20, 1844, Miss Dwight wrote to her best friend, Anna Parsons, describing plans to form a women's work collective.[37]

And now I must interest you in our fancy group, for which and from which I hope great things—nothing less than the elevation of woman to independence, and an acknowledged equality with man. Many thoughts on this subject have been struggling in my mind ever since I came to Brook Farm, and now, I think I see how it will all be accomplished. Women must become producers of marketable articles; women must make money and earn their support independently of man. So we, with a little borrowed capital (say twenty-five or thirty dollars; by we, I mean a large part of the women here), have purchased materials, and made up in one week about forty-five dollars worth of elegant and tasteful caps, capes, collars, undersleeves, etc., etc.,—which we sent in to Hutchinson and Holmes, who have agreed to take all we can make. If they find a ready sale, we shall be greatly encouraged,—and be able to go on extending our business, as far as our time and numbers will allow. Of course, if we succeed (and we are determined we will), it will be very desirable for other ladies to come here on purpose to take a part in our fancy work; then our domestic work which now presses too heavily, will get more divided, and we shall each have less house-work and more fancy work. By and by, when funds accumulate (!) we may start other branches of business, so that all our proceeds must be applied to the elevation of woman forever. Take a spiritual view of the matter. Raise woman to be the equal of man, and what intellectual developments may we not expect? How the whole aspect of society will be changed! And this is the great work, is it not, that Association in its present early stage has to do? Do, as you love and honor your sex, bear our fancy group in mind, and bring or send us patterns and designs of every sort of thing you see or can conceive of that will be useful to us.

Document 17: Auto-Emancipation in Belton, Texas

The Belton Sanctificationists are the most striking example of a women's work collective formed exclusively by women to create the financial base for autonomy. George Garrison, Texas historian, spent two weeks in the summer of 1892 with the community and published, in the Charities Review, *what is still the most authoritative account of its rise and development.*[38]

The original leader of the Sanctificationists, and their present head, is Mrs. Martha McWhirter, whose maiden name was White. She was born in Jackson county, Tennessee, in 1827. At sixteen she joined the Methodist church, and continued a most zealous member up to 1870. After this time, though remaining nominally a member some years longer, she gradually drew away from it. In 1845 she married George M. McWhirter, of Wilson county, Tennessee, and in 1855 they moved to Bell county, Texas. Mr. McWhirter died in 1887. They had twelve children. Five of these, two unmarried sons and three married daughters, are yet living. One of the daughters and one of the sons are members of the community. . . .

Mrs. McWhirter's account of the original cause of the whole matter ascribes it to an extraordinary religious experience of hers. In 1866 she lost, at short intervals, two children and a brother. She regarded this as a chastisement from God, and resolved that she would try to lead a better life. While she was in this state of mind, a protracted meeting was held in Belton. She was much exercised on behalf of her unconverted children, but all her anxiety appeared to be in vain. At the end of the week during which the meeting lasted, as she walked home in the evening, a voice within her asked if she did not believe what she had seen in the meeting that week to be the work of the devil. All that night she struggled and prayed against the suggestion; but on the morning after, while she was in her kitchen and busy about breakfast, she experienced a kind of pentecostal baptism, through which it became clear to her that the voice of the night before was from God. Thenceforth she professed sanctification, and taught the doctrine in a way that led her to antagonize strongly the views of her successive pastors, but not to break openly with the church. Her convictions were most effectively set forth in a ladies' weekly prayer-meeting which was held from house to house in the town for some years succeeding her "sanctification." This finally merged into a meeting of her followers alone. . . .

From this time Mrs. McWhirter and her followers were more and more out of harmony with the churches. They developed and dwelt upon their peculiar views in regard to sanctification, and declined to be any longer subject to pastoral control or advice. . . .

But now a more serious trouble had begun to manifest itself. What this was may be gathered from a petition for divorce which was based upon it. . . .

The following extract from the petition will suffice:

"Plaintiff further charges 'that this band teach and enforce the doctrine that it is sinful for a wife who is a member to live with a husband who does not believe the doctrine; that such a husband is a serpent in the house, and the wife should separate and depart from him.'

"He alleges that in 1879 his wife joined this band at the solicitation of her mother, and during his temporary absence permitted the band to hold its meetings in his house, and encouraged them to instill into the minds of his children their accursed doctrines.

"That influenced by her mother, who taught her it was a sin to live with him, defendant withdrew herself from plaintiff's bed and board in January, 1879," etc. . . .

The communistic practices of the Sanctificationists had a definite beginning near the end of 1879. Previous to this time Mrs. McWhirter had refused to accept money from her husband for household expenses, and had managed to provide it herself by selling milk and butter from four or five cows which she kept. This refusal seems to have originated in the circumstance that he threatened to withhold what she required unless she would account for him for its use. Others of the Sisters followed her example. At the time which has been mentioned they had a meeting upon one occasion and discussed the propriety of living in common, dwelling mainly upon the question as to whether their faith required it. While the discussion was in progress one of the Sisters, who had been supporting herself by teaching school, and had saved, in this way, twenty dollars, took the money and laid it down in the presence of all, saying that there was what she had. This money was the beginning of a common fund. Mrs. McWhirter was treasurer, and the fund grew by the addition, at irregular intervals, of such amounts as the Sisters had been respectively able to lay by. It was paid in mostly at the meetings held each week, and averaged at first perhaps fifteen dollars weekly. The money was saved in various ways, among them being the sale of milk and butter and of rag carpets, for the weaving of which they bought a loom out of the common fund and contributed material and labor. . . .

Pretty soon a use was found for this fund. One of the Sisters had lost her home as well as her husband by a divorce, and she had to be provided for. A room was rented for her from Mr. McWhirter, and the rent was paid from the fund. After a time he gave his wife the rent that should be collected subsequently, and she declined to collect it, thereby causing this drain to cease.

During all this time any one of the Sisters who had anything about her house she could spare would give it to any other one that stood in need of it.

In August, 1882, some of the Sisters overheard the complaint of a lady living in the town that she could get no one to wash for her family. They sent to her for the clothes, and washed them at Mr. McWhirter's house. The story went abroad, and they were soon asked to do work of the same nature for others. They consented, and the business grew until, without any soliciting on their part, they were unable to meet the demand for their services. At length it became the source of quite a considerable income to them. The washing was done in the old-fashioned way, without the help of any machinery. It passed from house to house among the Sisters until it came to one of them whose husband had most decided objections to its being done upon his place; so when they had gathered there, at an appointed time, for that purpose, he drove them away with sticks and stones. In doing this he struck his wife and unintentionally no doubt, cut a quite severe gash in her head. That evening the Sisters gathered at the house again, where those of them most prominent in the affair were arrested on the charge of assault. They were tried, and four were fined twenty dollars and costs each, making the total about one-hundred dollars. This was paid out of the common fund.

The Sister at whose home the trouble occurred went back there no more after the trial, but lived with one or another of the rest until the next spring, when it was thought best to provide her with a house. Accordingly a lot belonging to Mr. McWhirter was selected for its location, the material was purchased out of the common fund, and the work was done by the Sisters themselves, with the help of the young sons of two of them, and with about two days' assistance from a regular house-builder. The building was nearly completed before Mr. McWhirter knew of it. As soon as he learned what was going on, he expostulated earnestly with his wife, but did not interfere with the occupation of the house by the Sister for whom it was intended. Mrs. McWhirter claimed that as she had brought a large portion of the McWhirter estate into the family herself, she was exercising a moral, if not a legal, right in taking possession of a part of it. . . .

The building of the house which has been mentioned, exhausted the common fund, but it soon began to grow again. The Sisters showed themselves ready to undergo any hardship that might be necessary in order to secure a living. To the other means used for obtaining an income they added that of selling wood. Two of them had each a horse, and a wagon and harness were purchased. Then, buying wood at twenty-five cents per cord as it stood in the forest, they cut and hauled it themselves, and sold it at three dollars per cord. This is the more remarkable from the fact that several of them had been reared in easy, and some in almost affluent, circumstances. The one whose husband had stopped their laundry work on his place, had charge of the wood hauling, and worked at it like the rest. He was a man of means, and while she was in the enjoyment of his wealth she had all the servants she needed at her own bidding, instead of acting the part of a servant herself.

From the summer of 1883 the Sisters began to make money fast. Just after that time the receipts from the sale of milk and butter were sometimes five or six dollars per day, from that of wood eight or ten dollars per day, and from the laundry work as much as two hundred dollars per month. . . .

Within a year and a half from the time the first house was erected by the Sisters, three others were built for rent, in order to invest the surplus money on hand. They were located upon lots belonging to Mr. McWhirter, and, as in the first case, he protested, but suffered the houses to be rented and the rent to be collected by his wife. In November, 1883, the man that had refused to let the laundry work be done at his house died, and his wife at once took possession of the homestead. From this time it was partly occupied by herself, and partly rented as a boarding-house, for which it was favorably located. When it was first rented, twenty-five dollars per month was paid for it; but more rooms were needed for the boarders, and when these were built the rent was raised to fifty dollars per month. May 10, 1886, the Sisters took charge of the place themselves and opened a hotel. . . .

The community now owns property worth at cash value fifty thousand dollars, nearly all of which has been purchased with the surplus of the common fund. . . .

The net income of the community is about eight hundred dollars per month. Most of this is from the hotel, a considerably smaller portion being from the rents of store houses and dwellings. The laundry, as it is now managed, brings in no money, but simply reduces the general expense account.

The management of the hotel, together with that of the farm, of which only a part is rented, is very systematic. Usually two of the women and four of the children are kept at the farm, which is about two miles from the hotel. During the winter the weaving of rag-carpets is carried on at the former. . . .

There is a change all round, including the farm, every month, and the cooks are now changed every two weeks. The average day's work is only about four hours, and, when that is done, each is free to amuse herself as she chooses. . . .

The Sisters spend their leisure in various ways, such as reading, practising on the piano, painting, etc. They read especially such works as those of Tolstoi and Bellamy. Among the periodicals which they take, or receive with considerable regularity from one source or another, are the Forum, the North American Review, the Arena, Frank Leslie's illustrated Weekly, the Woman's Journal published in Boston, a dental magazine published in New York, and the principal daily papers of Texas. They take also the Flaming Sword, published by Cyrus Teed, of Chicago, but they do not subscribe to its doctrines.

No uniform is worn by the Sanctificationists, nor have they ever adopted one, though it has been their custom to dress plainly. There seems to be a tendency among them now to allow themselves a little more latitude in this respect. Formerly they wore sun-bonnets without exception, but now they wear hats a great deal.

While the Sisters do not visit, and while they are usually to be found only where their work is, they have not despised to travel and see something of the world. In the summer of 1880, the whole band visited New York, making quite an excursion of it. They went in three divisions, each of which was gone about six weeks. Most of the time was spent in New York City, and in order to make the trip more pleasant and less expensive they rented a house on Madison Avenue near Central Park, and made it their home while they were there. They went by various routes, including that by ocean steamer from Galveston, and exchanged tickets to return, so that each came back a different way from that she followed going. The total expense was about three thousand dollars. It is their intention to see in a similar manner the World's Fair at Chicago.

It is the desire of the Sisters to make their community as complete within itself and as independent of the world as practicable. To this end they keep up a school for the smaller children, which is taught by one of themselves. It is kept up most of the time, but has not been very regular in its hours since the hotel was occupied. Only the younger members of the community are taught, and the instruction is not very extensive including only the elementary branches up to geography, grammar and arithmetic. The community has also its own dentist, in the person of one of the Sisters. She has learned the art mostly from books, with some instruction from dental surgeons who practice in Belton and the neighboring town of Temple. She does all the work for the band, extracting teeth, filling them, and putting in new sets whenever necessary. An office has been properly equipped for her, and she has done a considerable amount of work for the boarders at the hotel and the people of the town. . . .

As to the present faith of the Sanctificationists, it is worth while perhaps to say but little. They claim to be "living the Bible," but, of course, the life is according to their own interpretation of the book. They do not hesitate to work on Sunday when it is either necessary or convenient. They no longer have formal worship of any kind. In this, they have changed greatly from what they were at first. They then had regular and frequent devotional exercises. At present the nearest approach to such exercises is to be found in their discussion among themselves of their religious experience, which they try to interpret so that it will serve to guide them. They frequently obtain this guidance from dreams; but Mrs. McWhirter claims that they get their greatest help from a delicate sense which belongs to the entire community rather than to any individual member, and which enables them to detect any mistake they have made or false step they have taken, by causing an unpleasant reaction to be felt by the whole body.

There seems to be at work in this community no disorganizing force due to disatisfaction arising from equality of service. No one appears to toil unwillingly, or to think that the others do less than their respective shares.

The whole matter is summed up by Mrs. McWhirter in the statement that it is the work of God, under whose protection the Sisters live, and by whom a way will always be opened for them. The people of Belton sum it up by saying that Mrs. McWhirter is the centre and the soul of the organization, that its prolonged existence and success are due to her really extraordinary powers and to her strange influence over her followers, and that when she is gone there will be the end of it.

The Leadership of Nuns in Immigrant Catholicism

MARY EWENS O.P.*

Roman Catholic nuns or "sisters," as they are popularly called, exerted an important influence on the Catholic Church in America in the nineteenth century. Catholicism in that period faced the challenge of preserving and fostering its faith among millions of immigrant members, and of establishing her credibility in an alien and often hostile society. If adequate means could be found to measure the relative importance of personal influences, it might well be shown that sisters' efforts were far more effective than those of bishops or priests in the Church's attempts to meet these challenges. It was they who established schools in cities and remote settlements to instruct the young in the tenets of their faith, who succored the needy, who brought the consolations of religion to soldiers in military hospitals, who changed public attitudes toward the Church from hostility to respect. Their numbers grew from under forty to more than forty thousand during the nineteenth century. (Document 1.) They outnumbered male church workers in the last half of the century in almost every diocese for which we have records, and there were almost four times as many nuns as priests by the century's close.[1]

Sisters performed many charitable works, but their chief preoccupation was with teaching. They staffed several kinds of schools: elementary ones, academies, free and pay schools, night schools, industrial, parochial, private, and public ones. There were 3,811 parochial schools by 1900, most of them run by sisters, and 663 girls' academies (but only 102 Catholic academies for boys). Sisters taught their students, mostly girls, the rudiments of their religion, prepared them to receive the sacraments, and gave them a solid grounding in Christian living and a sense of responsibility for the maintenance of a Christian atmosphere in the

---

*MARY EWENS, O.P., is Professor of American Studies at Rosary College in River Forest, Illinois. She received her Ph.D. from the University of Minnesota, writing on the adaptation of Catholic women's religious orders to the United States. Her study has been published by the University of Notre Dame Press.

homes they would one day run and for the religious instruction of their children.

Schools like those established in the Indiana woods by Mother Theodore Guerin and Mother Angela Gillespie were found in many remote frontier outposts and were attended by Protestants as well as Catholics because of their reputation for learning and piety. Many young women brought up to believe the anti-Catholic propaganda of the times learned in these schools to respect and even love the sisters and later helped to change the attitudes of their Protestant families and friends towards the Catholic Church. Sisters' schools won friends for the Catholic Church wherever they were established, and were a potent force in lessening the virulence of anti-Catholic sentiment.

Nowhere was the Church's charity towards others more readily apparent than in the nursing done by sisters in private homes, almshouses, and hospitals. The scanty statistics available to us indicate that sisters administered at least 265 hospitals in America during the century.[2] They also did heroic work during the cholera and yellow fever epidemics that ravaged the country periodically and in every American war of the nineteenth century.

It was particularly through their nursing in military hospitals of both the North and the South during the Civil War that sisters brought about a dramatic change in public attitudes towards Catholicism. In the military hospitals in which they nursed, thousands of men who had never before come into contact with sisters or Catholics had a chance to observe them firsthand. Accounts of sisters' military nursing are full of testimony to the changed attitude towards things Catholic that resulted from this work. Reports of their work in both the Civil and the Spanish-American wars make it clear that they had an important spiritual ministry. They prepared men to receive the sacraments, helped them to face death, encouraged lapsed Catholics to return to the Church, and instructed patients in the beliefs of the Catholic faith. They did not interfere with the beliefs of non-Catholics, but responded to requests for information and often did the actual baptizing when a soldier so desired it.

The priest came, often from a nearby town, to say mass and administer the sacraments to those who had been prepared for them by the sisters. When we consider that there were only eighty-four official Catholic chaplains in the Civil War, but 640 sister-nurses serving in the military hospitals, we get a clearer picture of just who it was who represented the Catholic Church to the soldiers and hospital personnel in that war. Nor was the situation any different in the Spanish-American War, in which were thirteen Catholic chaplains but 282 sister-nurses. Surgeons, doctors, officers, and patients were all impressed by the devotion of the sisters to the sick, their willingness to nurse patients with deadly contagious diseases whom no one else would approach, their honesty and genuine virtue in the most trying circumstances, their concern for others rather than themselves.

In addition to their major works of teaching and nursing, sisters ran day-care centers, infant and maternity homes, homes for the aged, mental institutions, settlement houses, residences for working women, and homes for delinquent girls and unwed mothers. In the convents there was ample scope for the talents of any woman, and the opportunity for travel and adventure as well. (Document 8.) Large numbers of young women were attracted to this life. Indeed, there were complaints in some places that the convents were removing too many of the marriageable girls from the countryside.

Many nuns responded to a call to leave their families, friends, and homelands to spread the Gospel message on foreign shores. They came to America as foreign missionaries. Ninety-one of the 119 communities of sisters established in America in the nineteenth century had European or Canadian origins. The letters and journals of these women who came to America as immigrants are full of the lively details of their travels: the long Atlantic journey by sailing ship (on which they encountered pirates, gales, seasickness, sand bars, and thirst); the problem with luggage, dishonest porters, and customs officials; the journey across America by canal boat, ferry, stagecoach, open wagon, and railroad; the travel up the Mississippi by steamboat, overland to the Southwest, around South America to San Francisco. Their observant comments on all that they saw—buildings, manners and customs, climate, geography, foods, and especially people—are full of wit. (Document 2.) Immigrant sisters sympathized with their own countrymen in America. German sisters complained about the predominance of Irish bishops, and French ones disdained the Americans as cold, calculating boors.

A European class consciousness was not only a part of their world view; it was also built into the structure of their religious life. Many communities had two classes of members, choir sisters (who possessed some degree of education and chanted the Divine Office, the official prayer of the Church) and lay sisters (who had less education, were often from the lower classes, and performed the manual labor). Often there was a distinction in color or detail in the habits worn by the two groups. Americans found this lack of equality shocking, and European sisters were highly suspicious of American democracy.

As the targets for the attacks of two groups of bigots, sisters encountered a great deal of hostility and persecution in nineteenth century America.[3] Their foreign language, customs, and methods roused the ire of nativists, and their religion and manner of life were denounced by the anti-Catholic forces in American society. Often the membership of the two groups overlapped. Several events of the first half of the century roused the anti-Catholic feeling that had always been latent in American Protestantism, among these events the storm of resentment that greeted the passage of the Catholic Emancipation Act in Britain in 1829 and a meeting of all American Catholic bishops that was held in Baltimore in the same year. In the hostility towards Catholicism that swept the country in waves in the 1820s, 1850s, and 1890s, sisters were prime targets for abuse because their distinctive costume and their retired lives set them apart. Indeed, sisters soon learned that it was dangerous to wear their religious garb on the streets as they went about their work of mercy. Many adopted contemporary dress.

In the 1830s and 1850s, the country was flooded with pamphlets, books, and newspapers that purported to reveal what "really" happened behind convent walls. The tales of secret tunnels, rape, seduction, infanticide, prison cells, and absurd penances that appeared in print were reinforced by the sermons of ministers who enlarged upon the "Catholic threat." Prominence was given to lectures delivered by ex-nuns and ex-priests. The revelations of "escaped nuns" attracted large audiences. The most famous of them all, the prototype of those who came after her, was Maria Monk, a girl who had suffered brain damage in childhood. After her escape from a Montreal asylum for wayward girls, she came to New York with tales of her alleged experiences in a convent. Ministers were not slow to turn her stories to profitable use. Reverend J. J. Slocum, with the advice of Reverend George Bourne and Theodore Dwight, undertook the task of writing her story for publication, calling the book that appeared in 1836 *Awful Disclosures of the Hotel Dieu Nunnery of Montreal.* This book and its sequels roused a storm of controversy, with charges and countercharges, delegations to the Montreal convent, and so forth. Miss Monk's public appearances helped to sell the book. Over three hundred thousand copies were sold prior to the Civil War, and it has remained in print into the 1970s.

It is no wonder that people who believed these tales insulted nuns on the streets, organized mobs to attack convent property, tried to undermine sisters' schools, and proposed convent inspection laws with the intention of freeing nuns from their prisons. As anti-Catholic sentiment grew, attacks on sisters and convents became more serious. Bigots focused attention on the convent as a symbol of the evils of Catholicism. Mount St. Benedict, the flourishing Ursuline academy in Charlestown, Massachusetts, was destroyed by a mob in 1834. (Document 6.) This incident was denounced by sensible people everywhere, but it established a precedent for attacks on convents that was followed later in Baltimore, Frederick, St. Louis, Galveston, and elsewhere. In the mid-1850s, when the activist Know-Nothing Party enjoyed success in state and national elections, bills aimed at the inspection of convents were introduced in the legislatures of several states. Sisters in Roxbury, Massachusetts, and elsewhere suffered the indignity of being visited unexpectedly by a dozen or more unruly men. It was only after large numbers of Americans actually saw sisters in action, nursing in the Civil War, that the attitude toward Catholicism began to change. (Document 7.)

Many communities of sisters who were denounced as foreigners, minions of the pope, prisoners, etc. may have unwittingly provoked some of this abuse themselves by the European customs that were a part of their lives. As they came to understand the American milieu and the needs of the American Church, they saw that adaptations had to be made, if religious life were to be lived successfully in their adopted country. The Church's canon law regulations, which formed the framework for the constitutions that governed communities of nuns, dated back to the thirteenth century. They reflected the medieval view of women as child-ish, emotional, "misbegotten males" who were incapable of controlling their own lives. These rules were formulated in an age when young women were sometimes consigned by their families to convents against their will and had to be carefully supervised lest they seek to escape or indulge in behavior not suitable for a nun.

Such regulations, intended to preserve the virtue of cloistered nuns who devoted themselves to prayer and penance and never stepped out-side their convent walls, were unsuitable in nineteenth century America. Here sisters served others through active works of charity. The American culture stressed the freedom of every individual. But the constitution of each religious order reflected the culture of the time and place in which it had been written. A serious problem for communities with European roots (and for American sisterhoods that imitated European ones) was the question of whether their constitutions could be adapted to American ways and still retain what was essential for an authentic religious life. European superiors often insisted on exact adherence to the constitu-tions as the *sine qua non* of eternal salvation.

Sisters who saw the needs of the American Church, and heard their bishops' pleas for adaptation and flexibility, pondered the best solution to their dilemma. Often it was found in a complete break with the Euro-pean motherhouse. As the century progressed, Rome established the practice of giving its approval to new constitutions. This freed the sisters, to a certain extent, from the jurisdiction of the local bishop. Many superi-ors spent long years in their attempts to achieve this independent status for their communities.[4]

The careful study of constitutions was essential because they were a religious community's bill of rights, which clearly stated privileges and obligations on all sides. Constitutions could not be changed by the action of a single individual, even a bishop, so they were a protection against the occasional bishop who sought to interfere in a community's internal affairs. In the few instances in which bishops tried to overstep the limits of their authority, as in the dispute between Bishop Hailandiere and the Sisters of Providence, sisters were within their rights in refusing to trans-gress their constitutions. (Document 4.)

Instances of such high-handedness on the part of bishops were not common in the nineteenth century, though they loomed large in the communities in which they occurred. The instances in which bishops worked to the detriment of a community are far outweighed by those in which they were helpful. Usually a bishop who invited a community to his diocese was delighted to have such capable workers and gave them every support and encouragement. Though the bishop was responsible for all church activities in his diocese, he usually left the sisters to run their own internal affairs. Often he appointed an ecclesiastical superior as his delegate in matters that concerned the community. In practice, the ecclesiastical superior usually became a close friend, advisor, spiritual director, and defender of the community, especially of its leaders. The histories of most communities recount the names of many priests and bishops whose advice and help have been invaluable to them.

In the disputes which did sometimes arise between religious communities and bishops in this period, the disagreement was often over a difference of opinion regarding policy rather than male-female polarities. Disputes were usually negotiated or arbitrated. The sisters were equals, not subordinates, in the discussions. Perhaps the primary cause for disagreement was the question of the adaptation of European customs to the needs of the American Church. American bishops who were concerned with satisfying the needs of large numbers of immigrants became irritated with sisterhoods whose rules forbade contact with male students and orphans, choir work, employment at schools at a distance from the convent, or adaptation to American teaching practices.

Constitutions which had been adequate for a community under the jurisdiction of the bishop of a European diocese were not sufficient when that group established convents all over America. Sometimes the lines of demarcation between the authority of the bishop, the ecclesiastical superiors, and the sisters' superiors were not clearly drawn. Bishops especially resented the control of personnel in schools, hospitals, orphanages, and similar settings by motherhouse superiors. It was precisely because they were independent that such superiors were resented. Indeed, they often had more church workers under their jurisdiction than did the bishop in whose diocese they lived. It was natural that many bishops should come to prefer diocesan communities that would be responsible to them rather than to some bishop or sister superior in another diocese.

There was often no clear-cut right or wrong answer in disagreements over policy, and there were sisters and male clerics on either side. Thus when the administrators and ecclesiastical superior of the Sisters of Charity of Emmitsburg decided to seek affiliation with the French Daughters of Charity, they thought they were doing what was best for their community. Their sisters in New York and Cincinnati, however, in conjunction with their bishops, deplored the move as a betrayal of the ideals of their foundress, Elizabeth Seton, and seceded from the parent group. This alternative of forming a new community when there were ideological differences was fairly common. Sometimes it was basically a clash of personalities that led one group to back a particular leader and form a separate community. Sometimes priests or bishops stepped in when they sincerely felt that it was important for a community's well-being that changes be made.

Bishops and priests came to have a healthy respect for the power of sisters, and with good reason. The sisters were important influences in the Catholic community and ran most of the Church's charitable institutions. In disagreements sisters fought for their rights and usually won. Then too, they could and did vote with their feet, or threatened to, when the occasion warranted it. There was always another bishop, just over diocesan borders, who needed the services the sisters provided. Communities like that of the Sisters of the Holy Cross and the Dominicans, which included both male and female branches, often went through various stages in their relationship with male members of the group, as one or the other seemed to be in control. There were benefits and disadvantages on both sides, so no generalizations can be made. Thus we see the Dominican sisters seeking affiliation with the male branch of the order and Holy Cross priests. (Document 5.)

An interesting aspect of the relationship of nineteenth century American nuns with men is the number of friendships that flourished between sisters and priests. The long distances from home and lack of communication must have encouraged support and friendship among sympathetic souls. Thus we see, for example, Mother Philippine Duchesne confiding to Fathers Barat and Varin in France, Mother Pia Backes counting on Father May, Mother Guerin turning to Bishop Bouvier for advice, Sister St. Francis Xavier unburdening her soul to Father (later Bishop) Augustine Martin, and Mother Theresa Gerhardinger writing long intimate letters to Father Siegert.[5] (Document 3.) In many ways, these relationships are impressive as models of mutual respect between equals.

In many aspects of their lives, nuns in nineteenth century America enjoyed opportunities open to few other women of their time: involvement in meaningful work, access to administrative positions, freedom from the responsibilities of marriage and motherhood, opportunities to live in sisterhood, and egalitarian friendships. Perhaps it was this freedom from the restrictive roles usually ascribed to women that enabled them to exert such a powerful influence on the American Church. Though barred from the priesthood, they exercised a sacramental and educational ministry that was essential for Catholicism's continued existence. They administered its charitable institutions, conducted its religious instruction, prepared its members for the sacraments, were exemplars of its holiness, and won a grudging acceptance and even respect for Catholicism from other Americans. We can only speculate on what the fate of the Church would have been, had they not been willing to labor so valiantly for its survival.

Sister Blandina Segale's pioneering work in the American Southwest is recorded in her letters to her sister Justina during the last decades of the nineteenth century. [From Sister Blandina Segale, *At the End of the Santa Fe Trail* (Milwaukee: Bruce, 1948). Used by permission of Crowell, Collier and Macmillan.]

Mother Elizabeth Bayley Seton was the first American saint and foundress (in 1809) of the Sisters of Charity, the first American women's religious order. [Courtesy the Archivist, St. Joseph's Central House, Emmitsburg, Maryland.]

Catholic nuns won acceptance into American life in no small measure because of their devoted nursing during the Civil War. This photo shows the staff and nurses outside the Satterlee Military Hospital near Gettysburg, Pennsylvania, during the war. [Courtesy the Archivist, St. Joseph's Central House, Emmitsburg, Maryland.]

These four members of the America Congregation, an Indian sisterhood, nursed during the Spanish-American War at Camp Onward,
Savannah, Georgia. They are shown with their chaplain, the Reverend Francis Craft. The four sisters are, left to right, Sister Josephine
Two Bears, Sister Ella Clarke, Sister Bridget Pleets, and Sister Anthony Bordeaux. Sister Bordeaux died in Cuba and was given a military
funeral. Sister Bridget Pleets treasured to the end of her life the
apron on which dying soldiers had written their names and addresses
so that she could write to their relatives. [Courtesy the Milford (Pennsylvania) Historical Society.]

Photographs from an article by Lida Rose McCabe entitled "The Everyday Life
of a Sister of Charity" (below and on the following pages) show the sisters not only
performing the corporal works of mercy but also teaching immigrant women
work skills. [From *Cosmopolitan* magazine 23 (1897), pp. 289–96. Photo courtesy
the Newberry Library, Chicago, Illinois.]

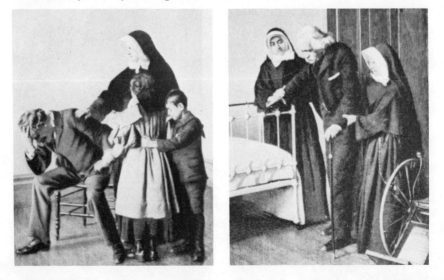

Documents: The Leadership of Nuns in Immigrant Catholicism

Document 1: The First Indigenous American Women's Order

Mother Elizabeth Bayley Seton was a widow with five children when she founded the Sisters of Charity in 1809. In this letter approving the community's constitution, Archbishop John Carroll, the first American Catholic bishop, touched on several important themes. He wanted the sisters to control their own internal affairs, to be free from ties with male communities (the Sulpicians, in this case), and to have a way of life adapted to American conditions.[6]

Baltimore Sept. 11th. 1811

To Elizabeth Seton

Hond. & dear Madam. Shall I confess that I am deeply humbled at being called on to give a final sanction to a rule of conduct & plan of religious government, by which it is intended to promote and preserve amongst many beloved spouses of Jesus Christ, a spirit of solid & sublime religious perfection? ... it affords me great pleasure to learn that all the material points on which a difference of opinion was thought to exist have been given up by Messrs de Sulpice in their last deliberations. If they had not, I do not think that I should have approved the Constitutions, as modified in the copy thereof which has been before me. Mr. Dubois has not exhibited the rules of detail & particular duties of the Sisters, but they being matters of which yourselves & your Rev. Superior will be the best judges, I commit you & them with the utmost confidence to the guidance of the Divine Spirit. I am exceedingly anxious that every allowance shall be made not only to the sisters generally, but to each one in particular, which can serve to give quiet to their conscience, provided that this be done without endangering the harmony of the Community & therefore it must become a matter of regulation. I am rejoiced likewise to know that the idea of any other connexion than that of charity, is abandoned between the daughters of St. Joseph's & the society of St. Sulpice; I mean that their interests, administration & government are not to be the same, or at least under the same control. This removes many inconveniences for you & for Messrs of St. Sulpice. No one of the body but your immediate Superior residing near you will have any share in the government or concerns of the Sisters, except (on very rare & uncommon occasions) the Superior of the Seminary of Balte, but not his society. This however is to be understood so as not to exclude the essential superintendance & control of Archbp over every Community in his Diocese. Your own particularly situation required special consideration on account of your dear children. It seemed to me that only general principles for your & your family's case should be now established, grounded on justice & gratitude & that any special considerations should be deferred to the period when the circumstances may require them. At present too many persons would be consulted

& amongst them some who are incompetent to judge; and even they who are most competent might find their most equitable provisions rendered useless by the changes produced in a few years. Mr. Dubois has been very explicit in communicating, I believe, whatever it was proper for me to know; on my side it has been my endeavor when I read the Constitution to consult in the first place the individual happiness of your dear Sisters & consequently your own; 2ndly, to render their plan of life useful to religion & the public; 3dly, to confine the administration of your own affairs & the internal & domestic government as much as possible to your own institutions once adopted & within your own walls. Your Superior or Confessor need be informed or consulted in matters where the Mother & her Council need his advice. I shall congratulate you & your beloved Sisters, when the Constitution is adopted. It will be like freeing you from a state in which it was difficult to walk straight, as you had no certain way in which to proceed. In the mean time assure yourself & them of my utmost solicitude for your advancement in the service & favor of God, of my reliance on your prayers; of your prosperity in the important duty of education which will & must long be your principal, & will always be your partial employment. A century at least will pass before the exigencies & habits of this Country will require & hardly admit of the charitable exercises towards the sick sufficient to employ any number of the [illegible] sisters out of our largest cities; and therefore they must consider the business of education as a laborious, charitable & permanent object of their religious duty. Mention me in terms of singular affection to your dear, sons & daughters. . . . The Baltimore girls in your school form a special object of my affection, though I cannot name half of them. Your account of Miss Wiseman has added much to my high estimation of her. Julianna & Maria White, Mary Anne Jenkins, Ann Cox & Ann Nelson occur this moment to my memory, yet I omit some equally dear to me. Mr. Harper thinks of sending up his daughter. I have not seen her since her return home. Adieu. Mr. Js Barry still in Washn. as is our ever honored friend. I am with esteem & respect Honord & dr. Madam Yr. sevt in Xt.

> J. Abp. of Balt
> C SJCH

Document 2: Travel and Settlement

Mother Theodore Guerin led a small band of Sisters of Providence from their motherhouse near Lemans, France, to the woods of Indiana in 1840 to establish the American foundation of her community. Her travel journal and letter to Canon Lottin, rector of the Cathedral in Lemans, gives us a vivid impression of how the strange American society looked to an aristocratic Frenchwoman.[7]

It would be difficult to describe what passed in my soul when I felt the vessel beginning to move and I realized that I was no longer in France. It seemed as if my soul were being torn from my body. Finally we left the harbor. Fort Francis First was the last object we beheld. It too disappeared, for we were already on the ocean.

We watched the sails being unfurled one after the other; we saw them swelled by the wind, hurrying us away from our beloved France. I shall not undertake to describe what was going on aboard the ship. Sad, and leaning against the cordage, I was contemplating the shore of my country, which was flying away with inconceivable rapidity and becoming smaller and smaller at every moment. All was commotion and noise on deck, but, absorbed in painful reflections, we neither saw nor heard anything. We again offered up to Heaven the sacrifice of all that we loved, and we thought of those who were weeping for us.

O my dear friends! O my Country! How much it costs to give you up! And you, my sister, the only one left of my family, I did not see before my departure but you were not forgotten, nor will you ever be, nor will he who has been such a father to me [Monsieur de la Bertaudiere, benefactor at Soulaines].

While I was thus preoccupied, my poor companions were weeping also; nearly all had bid adieu to a tender father or beloved mother. How their hearts were bleeding at that time! . . .

At New York

"At last, we have arrived," we said to one another, "the perils of the sea are passed!" We threw ourselves on our knees, and with hearts full of gratitude we offered our thanks to God for all the benefits He had bestowed upon us. We prayed to Him also for our future; we could not but feel some anxiety about it. The ship ceased to move. What joy for the Americans! They were going to see again those that were dear to them. They were expected. The telegraph, in announcing the arrival of the *Cincinnati*, had caused many a heart to throb; but not one was anxious about us, not one was throbbing for us. "Behold," we said, "houses, but not our dear Providence home. Behold people, but not our Sisters. We shall not meet with friendly faces, with devoted hearts, in this foreign land. Here we shall be looked upon with contempt, perhaps with hatred; at most, we shall meet only pity."

While these painful reflections were oppressing our hearts, the Custom House officers came to visit the ship. They were very friendly but no one was so kind as the good doctor of whom I have already written, and who came now bringing refreshments to us. In our circumstances his kindness did more good to our hearts than to our stomachs. I am happy to give you the name of this gentleman—Doctor Sidney A. Doane. Later he told the people it would bring a blessing to any one who would render us the least service. Do pray for him, for he is a Protestant. Without him, what would have become of us in New York? It was he who informed the Bishop of our arrival, because the deputy of Monseigneur de la Hailandiere the Bishop of Vincennes had not yet arrived in the city. It was he who spoke to us the first consoling words we heard in the New World, so new to us. "Soon," he said, "you will be surrounded by numerous friends who will be happy to see you. The Bishop of New York will be much pleased to make your acquaintance. You will find in his Vicar General, Father Varela, a real father. He is a Spanish priest who speaks French, and an excellent man whose life is spent in doing good."

Doctor Doane presented us with some beautiful peaches which he himself had gathered, and the other good things he had brought. His words, and his manner of acting—a stranger, a non-Catholic, and an American—surprised us so much that we were almost mute. I could stammer out only a few words of thanks....

I wrote you also about the Church, St. Peter's, Barclay Street, of its elegance, of its being as light as if it had been made of crystal, of the dazzling whiteness of its walls, of the pews which were of solid mahogany, of its galleries with four rows of seats placed in tiers, which give it the appearance of a theatre. The speaker seemed to be talented, though we really understood nothing of his sermon. His audience listened attentively. The Mass and Vespers were sung to music which, however, did not particularly please me. I had a great deal more devotion in our poor barn at Soulaines, notwithstanding the lack of harmony there. The church was filled with men, there were at least as many men as women, and all comported themselves perfectly well. We did not see one woman who did not have on a bonnet. Here the shepherdess wear bonnets and even the milkmaids while milking their cows. The milk is carried around in quite a stylish conveyance drawn by two horses at such a rate that one might think it were the president's carriage rolling along. The men who distribute the milk from door to door are dressed up as if for a wedding. It is impossible to have any idea of the extravagance of the Americans without having witnessed it.

The houses have an elegant appearance, especially those in the country. The city of New York is beautiful, but of a beauty severe and sombre—quite depressing. The houses are mostly red brick, extremely high. The streets are over thirty feet wide, with fine brick sidewalks, above which are suspended awnings to shade the numerous stores. At certain distances there are crossings paved with a stone that looks very much like our slate stone. The Americans never cross a street but at these places, which are at right angles. The other streets are badly paved. There are here, as at Paris, many fine carriages, especially a new style which is unusually elegant.

There are separate sections in the city for different kinds of business; for example: for the sailors, for the soldiers, for the whole-sale merchants, etc., etc. In the latter, and in the navy quarter, no women are to be seen; not from fear of being insulted, however, for women are much respected here, more so than in Europe. To be wanting in respect towards them would be a shameful thing, and would brand the guilty one with an indelible mark. We saw no public buildings other than the City Hall and the Post Office which, however, offered nothing remarkable. The Catholic churches are small and badly built, even the cathedral.

In Philadelphia

During our stay in the city the good Bishop gave us constant marks of friendliness. He came frequently to see us and received us always with admirable benevolence. As soon as our arrival was known in the city, a crowd of French people came to visit us. Our costume was admired by all. And indeed ours is much superior to that of our good Sisters, who are dressed in black serge and wore a little lustring cap not worth two sous. They have also a sort of bonnet made of paste-board covering with lustring; and, truly, holy poverty loses nothing here. . . .

Baltimore

Frederick is rather small and built on a level. A carriage sent by the Sisters was waiting to take us to their house, as they also had been notified of our coming by the Bishop of Philadelphia. We were gra-ciously received by Mother Rose, former Superior General of the Sisters of Charity. This good ex-Mother is a model religious, filled with the virtues of her state, especially humility and charity. All the Community regret her, but she is delighted to be relieved of the burden of the superiorship. She told us all about the beginning of her institute, which had very trying times. These good Americans had, in fact, to undergo inconceivable privations; but Heaven blessed their sacrifices, for they have now a Community that does great good. It is destined especially for the instruction of the poor and chiefly of orphans: however they have a fine Academy. They teach the various sciences scarcely known in our French schools, but they excel in music, which is an indispensable thing in this country, even for the poor. No piano, no pupils! Such is the spirit of this country—Music and Steam! At Frederick, of the five Sisters three teach piano and guitar. These Sisters have an excellent religious spirit; tender piety, great charity, regularity,—in fine, all the virtues of the true Religious. I am happy to render them this testimony.

At last we had arrived at Vincennes! Vincennes!! The conveyance stopped. We were taken to the Sisters of Charity, who live near the episcopal residence, and who had been requested by the Bishop to take care of us until his return. After partaking of some food and putting on again our religious dress, we begged to be taken to the cathedral. Ciel! What a Cathedral! Our barn at Soulaines is better ornamented and more neatly kept. I could not resist this last shock and wept bitterly, which relieved me somewhat. I could not possibly examine this poor church on that day—the following day I did so with more calm. . . .

The Journey's End

I cannot tell you what passed within me during the next half hour. I do not know myself, but I was so deeply moved that I could not utter a word. We continued to advance into the thick woods till suddenly Father Buteux stopped the carriage and said, "Come down, Sisters, we have arrived." What was our astonishment to find ourselves still in the midst of the forest, no village, not even a house in sight. Our guide having given orders to the driver, led us down into a ravine, whence we beheld through the trees on the other side a frame house with a stable and some sheds. "There," he said, "is the house where the postulants have a room, and where you will lodge until your house is ready." . . .

The day after our arrival we went to look at our new house, now building. Like the castles of the knights of old, it is so deeply hidden in the woods that you cannot see it until you come up to it. Do not conclude, however, that it is built on the model of Father Buteux's. No, indeed. It is a pretty two-story brick house, fifty feet wide by twenty-six feet deep. There are five large openings in front. The first stone was laid August seventeenth and it is already roofed. Today they began plastering, but there are yet neither doors nor windows; all is being done, little by little. As to our garden and yard, we have all the woods. And the wilderness is our only cloister, for our house is like an oak tree planted therein.

Here is the list of our movables: twelve folding beds, an old bureau, a small cupboard or buffet—bois blanc—for the dishes and bread, a dozen wooden chairs and a table for the kitchen. Our dining-room table belongs to the farmer. As to the kitchen it is only a stove placed outside. We have pots, pans, etc., also a soup tureen, two dozen plates, two dozen spoons and forks, and one dozen knives. Besides these we have the trunks and boxes in which we brought our belongings from France. Some unbleached muslin was bought for sheets. This, then, is what we have for the foundation of a house, which the Bishop foresees will one day be a flourishing institution. No doubt; but we shall have to suffer much. Many things are wanting us, yet we dare not complain. Shall we not be, and are we not already, in our own little nook? Besides, did we not come here to suffer—we who were so well provided for in France?

Early Experiences

I am not sure whether I told you of the insupportable pride of the
Americans. However, I shall give you a little incident which happened
yesterday, and which came very near putting me in the bad graces of
everybody. Well, yesterday we had our washing done, the first of this
kind, probably, ever done here. I shall not relate all the trouble we
had to organize things, to get a tub, etc. I leave that for you to imagine.
But I shall tell you that we had employed a young woman, an orphan,
wretchedly poor and miserably clad, to help us wash. I attempted to
show her what to do. At first she refused to take any direction, but,
by coaxing, I secured the favor of showing her.

When dinner time came, there was my washerwoman sitting down
at the table with us. I was so indiscreet as to say it would be better for
her not to take dinner with the Community. I wish you could have
seen the change in the countenances of our American postulants! I
had to compromise by telling the girl she might eat with the reader
at the second table. The mere name of "servant" makes them revolt,
and they throw down whatever they have in their hands and start off
at once. You cannot hire either a man or a girl for more than a month
at a time.

It is astonishing that this remote solitude has been chosen for a
novitiate and especially for an academy. All appearances are against
it. I have given my opinion frankly to the Bishop, to Father Buteux,
and, in fine, to all who have any interest in the success of our work.
All have given reasons that are not entirely satisfactory; yet I dare not
disregard them. The spirit of this country is so different from ours
that one ought to be acquainted with it before condemning those who
know more about it than we do; so I await the issue before passing
judgment in a positive manner. If we cannot do any good here, you
know our agreement, we will return to our own country.

Dear France? Though far away, it is nevertheless who, like a good
mother, sends help to this poor diocese.

*Mother Guerin's account is continued in a letter on May 25, 1841
to Canon Lottin.*

We have at present ten postulants, exclusive of those we have
dismissed and some others who have offered themselves but whom
we cannot accept on account of our poverty. In this country no dowry
is given to girls even at marriage. They come with a silk dress, a fine
hat, and a tiny trunk. . . . The education of our candidates corresponds with their poor exterior. In religion they are ignorant of the
first essentials, and I am now beginning to teach them a little catechism, often with an interpreter. They ask me questions as learned
as that of St. Paul the Simple, who asked of his father Anthony

whether our Lord lived before the Prophets. They tell me that the Son
of God is a thousand years younger than the Eternal Father, and the
Holy Spirit still younger. I should never finish if I gave you details of
the absurdities which they retail. Can it be otherwise when these poor
children have seen a priest only once or twice a year? And is it not
surprising that God inspires in persons who know Him so little the
desire of consecrating their lives to His service, and submitting themselves to strangers, this latter a virtue which costs so much to the pride
of Americans, who long only for liberty and independence? There is
great fervor among those good children. Uncertain though we may
be of the success of our boarding school, such is not the case with our
Novitiate. If we had thirty Sisters all formed and ready to go on
mission, they could all be placed within a year and would accomplish
an infinite amount of good in their poor Indiana, which has needs so
great, so pressing, and so acutely realized. The Protestants are as
eager as the Catholics in asking for Sisters, although motivated by
self-interest and business, which are the two great wheels by which all
America goes forward. God who knows how to draw good from evil
will doubtless cause these inclinations to tend to His Glory.

In truth, how much good there is to do here, and how great and
sublime the mission confided to us! But one must be a saint to fulfill
it, and I own to you, Father, that I understand better each day how
far I am from the perfection of my state and from the qualities
necessary for the important duty which is mine. . . .

This thought makes me tremble, and I have written to our venerated Mother begging her to send us someone who has indeed the
spirit of God and especially profound humility, great piety, and an
earnest spirit of sacrifice. With these, one could perform miracles
here. . . . I conjure you, Father, in the name of Jesus, in the name of
the countless souls which we could win here, to induce our good
Mother to send us the two Sisters for whom I am asking with so much
earnestness, one to replace, or at least to assist me, a musician for our
boarding school, and Irma to teach drawing. With this help I have
assured her that we shall succeed, and without it, we shall fail. Only
after studying the circumstances with the most scrupulous care do I
repeat this. You have been our father and our friend. Be our advocate
now, and if you accept, our suit is won.

The Bishop of Vincennes seems to take the keenest interest in our
establishment and has given me during my illness very great proofs
of devotedness. His exterior, however, is of icy coldness, and our
chaplain, who is the same northern temperature, asked me lately to
write to our Mother that he was an ill-conditioned bear. They are,
nevertheless, men of a sanctity terrifying for my cowardice. If my
illness seems to last too long, Monseigneur will probably send me back
to France. In that case, I shall go to my little room in the Rue des

Portes, to my dear friends, but in that as in all else, my desire is to wish for nothing. . . .

If Sisters come to us, it is essential for them to write to the Bishop of New York before leaving the ship. He will send for them and have them accompanied to Mme. Parmentier's house where the tenderest attentions will be showered upon them, and their persons and their belongings will be in perfect safety. I recommend these dear Sisters especially to you. They will not need a passport except perhaps to go to Havre, and in that case a single one will suffice. I am awaiting a long letter from you, and what joy shall I have in receiving it! Have you my address? Terre Haute, Indiana, is sufficient.

Document 3: Letters to a Priest-counsellor: The Trials of School-teaching in America

Mother Theresa Gerhardinger, foundress of the School Sisters of Notre Dame, came from her motherhouse in Munich to open dozens of convents in America and other countries in her lifetime. She traveled with a pioneer band of sisters to America in 1847 and remained several months to study conditions there. During this period she wrote long letters to Father Mathias Siegert, the ecclesiastical superior of her congregation in Munich, with whom she shared her fears and hopes and appealed for counsel. Her letters are full of shrewd observations on American manners.[8]

J.M!

Baltimore, December 22, 1847

To Reverend Mathias Siegert

Dear Reverend Father

We have sent you more than twelve letters, and still have no news from you since July 17. This is doubly painful for us, since we are concerned about you, and we miss your advice in our trouble. . . .

We can write in all sincerity that we are concerned day and night about you, and all we have left behind, and in general about the young and sorely tried work of God. Let us hope our presentiments are unfounded. We would gladly bear your pain if we could. . . .

Difficult as it is for us to do, we are forced to beg to be supplied with money, until this work of God has developed sufficiently to allow us to pay it back. In our earlier letters we asked you, Reverend Father, to procure for us, through the mediation of the Most Reverend Archbishop and the Reverend court chaplain Mueller, a check for 18,000–20,000 florins, because our motherhouse, whose financial burdens and capabilities we so well know, is not in a position to help.

We are to pay to the Reverend Redemptorists at least 60,000 dollars (15,000 florins) soon, since it is very necessary to pay them promptly. They themselves are burdened with many debts. There are also alterations to be made, and many necessary articles to be bought during the coming spring. We have not yet sufficient income to procure the necessities of life. Perhaps it will be several years before this is possible.

We can count on nothing now but the small tuition, not even enough to hire the secular personnel we need; we must depend on candidates. The money brought with us from the loved motherhouse in Munich will soon be completely spent. Since we do not consider it prudent to make known our poverty, we trust entirely in the almighty and merciful God, and ask help from you. It is with a heavy heart that we do this, because we have heard from immigrants that scarcity of goods and even famine is prevalent in our beloved Fatherland. If this should be the case, there is no hope of our receiving money from Germany. . . .

Of course, the hardships and dangers of the journey, and the unhealthy climate here can be not endured without injury except by a few. There is an abundance of the best of food here, but the prices are exorbitant, so that a religious community like ours will experience difficulties if the community does not possess investments, or a large farm which can be worked by our own members. The Benedictine Fathers and the Christian Brothers from Alsace intend to do this at St. Mary's. We could never undertake it profitably; in fact it would be impossible here as well as there.

The Carmelite sisters here, who do not own a farm and are not provided with capital, experience great difficulties. They are obliged to teach school for their livelihood. The same is true of the colored sisters, who can not improve their situation. In fact, they were in danger of dispersing, but some priests helped them by increasing the number of school children, and entrusting more children of the poor to them for education. This is the harsh fate of religious societies that are not provided with capital which bears a large annual interest; 6% is the lowest interest rate.

Convents which are not in want of the necessary means of support are able to live according to their Rule with no disturbance or hindrance. Should circumstances force you and our entire Congregation to come here, Reverend Father, the Lord has already provided accommodations, as I have said. We trust we will have sufficient work in a few years with the children in cities close by: Pittsburgh, Philadelphia, New York and Buffalo. Of course, until these places become available, the sisters would have to live on their means; therefore, it would be advisable to save every penny and article of clothing and bring it along. How delighted we would be to see you, and all our sisters here with us!

It is impossible to learn to know America from the writings and oral accounts of others; one must live here and experience it. Things are different from the ideas prevalent in Europe. One can not possibly write about it.

Much consideration must be given to the dispensations from Holy Rule which will become necessary for America, and which must be obtained from Rome. Here again, I cannot write about it. We are concerned about this, and are very anxious about it. It requires much prayer. We beg you and our dear companion sisters to remain faithful in prayer, faith, hope and love for Jesus, Mary, and the dear children. . . .

In our earlier letters we asked our order for three or four house sisters. Now that we have been in Baltimore for three months, we know that in this case, too, things have developed entirely differently from what we originally planned. In case not every one comes, send us only teachers. I would like to remind you that these should be healthy, strong, robust and courageous; each must be capable of filling the post of superior, and must be a competent teacher in the elementary school and the Industrial Arts department. The requirements for German are not as rigid here as in Munich. Great prudence is needed to manage the children and their parents successfully, and only a keen insight and strong will can meet and conquer the various difficulties that arise in the school room and outside it. Without these qualities it is not apparently possible to hold one's own in a German-American school. Neither are mannish, rough sisters acceptable. They would be a torment to themselves, to the children, to their parents and the priests, and they could accomplish nothing, bringing shame and disgrace upon the order.

We cannot use sisters and young ladies who desire only to live a quiet, retired conventual life, those who cannot be employed in school; unless they bring with them considerable funds which bear a yearly interest of at least 200 dollars. This is considered the lowest amount annually needed for the support and needs of an individual. Several young ladies have already applied for domestic service; this will save us traveling expenses for sisters from Bavaria. Besides, these people are accustomed to the climate and are familiar with the habits and customs. They know the temperment of the people, and speak English. Therefore, for the present we have no need of sisters to do cooking, gardening, painting, gilding, shoemaking and cobbling, bookbinding or secretarial work. Neither do we require a hired man or extern, for we could not support them and we can hire people here for these services. Crescentia Schrupp, if she changes for the better, could cook in German style for us, since she would be aided by a sister in charge of the kitchen. A lady whom we brought from St. Mary's is gardener, and does this for a small compensation. She also tends animals, and does other work around the house. Such a lay person is of more use to us in this country than a house sister would be, because she can also deal with people, which the sisters could not do. The method of painting and gilding employed here is quite different from the one used at home, because of the different materials used.

Should necessity arise, Crescentia Schrupp, who has learned something of these two trades from painter Petzer, could take care of them in the manner in which they are done here. Sister Magdalene is able to attend to the shoes we wear in the house. Leather shoes will have to be provided by a shoemaker in any case. Under the present circumstances there is no need for book binding, since the Redemptorists have all the needed school books on hand, and intend to have our grammar printed. Perhaps the sister proposed for the bookbindery could be of use here, since we shall need copybooks for the private school. However, we hesitate somewhat, because of Sister Emmerana's health, work habits, self-conceit, and hearty appetite. A dollar a day would scarcely suffice to support her. She could be employed with delicate craftwork in pasting and basket weaving, and thereby earn her livelihood. Perhaps she can still learn something along these lines. Small wax figures of the Infant Jesus might also find a market here.

French is not needed, as English is the national language. Probably all our teaching sisters should learn it. The schools are half German, half English. For this reason it would have been good if our motherhouse might have been established in an entirely German Catholic city, as St. Mary's is. Perhaps in five or six years this may become possible. We are deeply concerned about these half English-speaking, half-German schools, since we are afraid that the English language, English customs, and English attitudes might also enter our convent. May God preserve us from this!

We have accepted three school candidates, 20 years old. With God's help we will succeed with them. An eleven-year-old pupil joined them, but we shall have to see what God's plans are in her regard. This coming Sunday four more young ladies are coming. All of them, however, are without financial means; only our eleven-year-old boarder pays.

It is advisable for the sisters who come to reduce the amount of luggage as much as possible. We recommend they not take more than they are able to carry and watch it personally. . . .

Difficult tasks are awaiting these dear children, even if they come invested with the habit. It is possible that one or other will experience what happened to our novice Colette when she was sent to Pfaffenhofen. We wish those sisters who make profession might be entirely prepared or even better, that they make profession before coming, so that they would need only renew their vows here. We want to avoid dealing with the Archbishop until we can present our Rule to him as approved by Bishop Reisach. Without a letter from our Archbishop in Munich there is no thought of approaching the Ordinary here. It would be good if the letter were brief, and would explain that until now we have lived according to the Rule of Notre Dame, have been received and made profession in it, and that we beg for permission to continue thus until the required dispensations in the Rule have been obtained from Rome, and that the Archbishop of Munich will inform him as soon as they have been granted. . . .

About four weeks ago our church and little convent were threatened with burning, and we were closely guarded for a week. The Lord will be our protector. We wonder, too, how many trials have befallen you and the Congregation during our absence. We suspect sickness and death, and our worries about all of you are increased by your silence. Perhaps our houses cannot help each other any more. . . .

Here are some experiences we have had in our three schools which might prove helpful in sending personnel. Schools will not become large, for there are too many of them, and attendance is voluntary, which is bad. Children attend one school today, another tomorrow, just as they please. If they are corrected they do not come back; learning they often consider recreation. All they want to do is eat cookies, taffy and molasses candy, a cheap sweet. This causes us much trouble. If we forbid it they threaten not to come to school any more. At the slightest punishment the parents say, "In this country one may not treat children so severely; they, too, must be given freedom." They do not listen to any one, and even strike their parents if they do not give in to them. They laugh and jeer at priests. They ask boldly, "Can I go down stairs? I want to go home now." They will not write one letter of the alphabet at home. "I go to school for that," is their answer. Homework cannot be introduced here; the parents do not want it either. Therefore, everything must be studied with them in school. They do not manifest the slightest eagerness to learn German. English, however, they want to learn to read and write. They hate German. All one hears is English. If they want to insult each other they say, "You German!"

They comprehend little or nothing if one tries to convey ideas to them, because they do not know enough German to understand what we mean. They will never learn spelling, for they neither speak German correctly, or do they understand it. Because of the English they inevitably write ch for g and other similar errors. It is difficult to give them grades or keep school records; today one or other leaves, and four to six weeks absence is not uncommon. They show little or no interest in needlework. What is most to their liking is jumping, running, dancing, tagging, singing and fighting. They are like wild animals, and try out all their naughtiness in school.

Children sit in the school benches with legs crossed, backs leaning and arms folded like men at the theater in our country. They even speak to priests in this position, and the latter must put up with it in order not to displease the parents. It is difficult to make them come to holy Mass on Sundays and holy days. As soon as it becomes a bit warm they use fans, want a drink constantly, and do not want to study. If it is cold, only a few come to school; these do not take off their wraps, but write with their mittens on. This is how pampered and spoiled even German children are in America. If they do not know something they answer boldly, "Teacher did not know it either when she was little."

They mumble all kinds of abusive language in English. One of the reasons the children do not want to study is the fact that their minds are filled with concern for boys. They write little notes to each other, exchange gifts, etc. They consider this all right, and parents laugh about it if told. In the lavatories they behave indecently, do not close the door, talk, laugh and sing while there. This is common in America, even with adults. Clothing, too, is immodest. All wear pants; the girls' dresses are low-cut and short, only to the knee. The smallest girls appear like women and acrobats. Naturally they do not want to hear about prayer. Teaching school is difficult and we implore the dear Lord fervently for his grace. . . .

When we tell parents they ought punish their children for their own good they say in the children's presence, "I can not punish my own flesh and blood." A mother who came to call for her child whom we had detained for disobedience said, "It is already twelve o'clock; come, Mary, and eat something." She wept because the child had not had anything to eat for so long. A father said, "My child is handsome and talks sensibly; I can not strike him; it would hurt me too much."

Stealing is a daily occurrence in school. Some one even took the pen from my desk. Another child stole an earring from a classmate which I found on her. Like confirmed thieves they know how to hide what they have taken. One hears horrible things about their parents from the children. "My father, the scoundrel, was shot. I am glad." Or, "I wish my mother were hanged, and my father forced to go begging," said a girl, angry because she did not get her will.

At St. James school we will employ only two persons, one sister and a candidate, who will teach in English. It is not possible for the sisters to live there, and we shall continue to drive to school. The missions here can hardly develop as the branch houses in Bavaria did.

Dear Reverend Father, pardon my poor writing and many mistakes; it is late at night, and I am sleepy. Time does not permit me to read over this letter. A thousand greetings to all the sisters, boarders, and school children. . . .

Write to us. We can not describe the depth of our loneliness and the desires of our hearts. If God had not borne with us, what would have become of us, and what will become of us? If I could only speak with you, Father, for an hour, and with the most Reverend Archbishop as well. . . .

I feel urged to take care of everything which needs to be completed; to put all things in order, but my hands are tied without both of you. This fact would make my death doubly difficult.

I feel less capable of being a superior here than in Europe, and I must take steps to resign: otherwise I shall spoil everything. Sisters Caroline and Seraphina have a calling for America; their views are opposite mine, and I am sure the Lord will assist them when they are in a position of authority.

I must tear myself away from writing, but again beg you to write us. I can not adequately express my anxiety for the order and for you.

Document 4: Struggles with Bishops

The constitutions of religious orders were designed to set forth clearly the rights and obligations of sisters, ecclesiastical superiors, and bishops to each other. In spite of this, nuns sometimes had to struggle against the efforts of bishops to usurp undue power over them. Mother Guerin and the Sisters of Providence in Indiana were placed in this position when Bishop de la Hailandiere of Vincennes repeatedly interfered in their internal affairs, reassigning sisters to different convents, closing and opening missions without consulting them, intercepting their mail, refusing them the sacraments, and forcing them to accept candidates they regarded as unsuitable. Finally, after exercising much patience, Mother Guerin gave the bishop an ultimatum, threatening to move the sisters to the diocese of Detroit. This forced Bishop de la Hailandiere to accede to their conditions rather than lose the services of the sisters.[9]

Letter Circular

St. Mary-of-the-Woods, March 8, 1846

Very dear Sisters,

It is a joy to me to be able myself to tell you that, thanks to your fervent prayers, Our Lord still permits me to live and to suffer with you. We will thank Him together, and to prove our gratitude we will repeat to Him from the depth of our hearts that we will belong to Him more perfectly than ever. And this we will more particularly prove to Him by the tender charity that unites us; for it is by this that we shall preserve the spirit of God amongst us, and that we can rely on His assistance—assistance of which we have no greater need than ever before; as, my dear daughters, the moment has come when we must leave the distressing state in which we have been for so long a time.

During the first days of my illness we received a letter from the Bishop whom you know about [the Bishop of Detroit]. He offered, together with his fatherly protection, to approve our Rules and Constitutions for his diocese, and he entreated our Father [Corbe] to come with us to continue to be our Superior. But this is all he can do for us at the present time.

I also received on the 27th of January, a letter of ten pages from the Bishop of Vincennes. It is full of accusations and reproaches which are personal, three-fourths of which are palpably untrue. I am obliged to communicate this to you, for in a little corner your names are written; as is also that of Father Corbe, who read only two pages of it and then threw it aside with the greatest indignation.

Notwithstanding, we think here that before taking the final step it would be more according to the spirit of God to renew again our petitions to His Lordship, the Bishop of Vincennes, without mention of the past. In view of this we are sending you the letter that we are addressing to him, in order that you may sign it, if, as we do not doubt, you share our opinion in the matter. . . .

Your devoted
Sister St. Theodore
Sup'r Gen'l

You know, my dear Sisters, you are not obliged to sign the letter I am sending, if it is contrary to your views. You also know that in signing it you engage yourselves to remain in the diocese of Vincennes, if the Bishop grants us what we ask, and of leaving soon if he does not grant it. Reflect well and act according to your lights and intentions. Write to me as soon as you will have taken your determination. You understand that this letter is for you alone.

Always yours in our Lord,
Sr. St. T.

To the Right Reverend Cel. de la Hailandiere, Bishop of Vincennes

Saint Mary-of-the-Woods, March 8, 1846

My Lord:

It has not been possible to reply sooner to your letter of January 25; even today we can speak of only one item of that letter. We are confronting circumstances too grave to be deterred by personal considerations.

You say that we are mistaken in thinking that your refusal to reply to our letter of the month of August is equivalent to a refusal to those things we asked of you. If such is the case, we take the liberty to renew, once more, those same requests.

The first is, as you know, that you give in writing, with your signature and under your episcopal seal, permission to dwell in your diocese according to the Rules and Constitutions which we brought from France, in order that we may have the assurance of being allowed to follow them as perfectly as is possible for a body not yet organized. The second is that you give us the deed of the property of Saint Mary's so that we may begin to build. Your Lordship knows that we have never asked aught but these things in order to establish ourselves in Indiana as a Congregation subject to you. Many times you have said, and even written, that you intended to grant us these things, but that we had put obstacles. These obstacles are now all removed—all the Sisters of Providence can now hold property legally; therefore, we dare hope that you will not delay to give us this last proof of your good will, which, in putting an end to a state so painful for all, will open to our view a brighter future and afford us the occasion to prove to you by our gratitude and submission how it has pained us to be, in a way, compelled to afflict your heart.

However, faithful to the spirit of candor which we have always followed, we must say that, after all that has occurred since our first request, your silence, or any reply which would not be the Acts we ask for, could not but be regarded by us, this time, as a formal refusal; in which case we would consider ourselves obliged to take a definitive resolution, and that with very little delay.

The fate of our Congregation is yet in your hands. We shall pray with even greater fervor than in the past that God may inspire you to act in the manner that will procure Him more glory and unite us more closely to Him. In these sentiments we remain, with the most profound respect, my Lord.

Of Your Lordship
>>>The very humble and obedient servants,

SISTER ST. VINCENT	SISTER MARY JOSEPH
SISTER ST. FRANCIS XAVIER	SISTER MARY CECILIA
SISTER MARY LIGUORI	SISTER ST. THEODORE

Document 5: Securing the Freedom of the Order to Work in America

In the European Dominican tradition, nuns of the "second order" were strictly cloistered, while "third order" nuns were allowed to live a more active life in the world. Many orders sought direct approval of their constitution from the Vatican, because in becoming a papal or exempt congregation, they were independent of the control of the local bishop. In this letter Mother Hyacintha, administrator of the Dominican community in Racine, Wisconsin, explains to Mother Pia, superior of the Dominican community in San Jose, California, the reasons for seeking third order status and Vatican approval.[10]

Racine, December 31, 1889

Dear good Reverend Mother Pia:
>>>Your inquiry regarding affiliation necessitates a long explanation.

Our Convent became affiliated with the Dominican Order as early as 1877 as a convent of the Third Order through J. Sanvita, at that time master general. More than this cannot be claimed by the Sisters of our Order who are engaged in the schools, especially if they have charge of institutions and orphanages. The Second Order cannot dispense with the strict canonical enclosure. This enclosure forbids under penalty of excommunication travel under any pretext whatsoever. All visits, moreover, from externs are forbidden; and only a limited number of members may be received. Under these circumstances what would we be able to do and how could we obtain our livelihood? For a long time we were confused about the conditions and, like many other Dominican Communities in this country, considered ourselves Sisters of the Second Order. Our confessor, who for many years was professor of Canon Law, called our attention to this mistaken view of ours, and pointed out that we were not members of the Second Order and could not hope ever to be such, because we would never be able to observe strict enclosure. He told us, moreover, that if we desired to be members of the Dominican Order, we would have to be affiliated with the Order; that is, that our Convent must be recognized as Dominican by the Master General. . . .

His answer clearly indicated that we could only become Dominicans by becoming affiliated with the Third Order and that bishops and priests did not have the power of admitting members into the Third Order unless they were especially empowered to do so. We had no choice but to follow the advice of our Confessor and to accept the offer made by the master general. Since then we have the assurance of really belonging to the Order and of really being Dominicans. We have a quiet conscience and are happy. Don't hesitate to follow our example. Remember that the privileges and the spiritual advantages of the Third Order are scarcely less than those of the Second Order. Besides as members of the Third Order we have the privilege of following our good judgment in the circumstances that arise. Simple affiliation in the Third Order does not satisfy us, however. We strive after higher things. We want the approval of our Congregation by Rome. If a Congregation is not recognized by Rome, it is simply an episcopal association and depends in every respect upon the bishop of the diocese, who has full charge of the Sisters, and who can act at will in their regard. It is, moreover, of greatest importance to have a Rule designed for our special circumstances and approved by the Holy See. Our Father Confessor went to Rome last year in the interests of the convent. . . . The strict fast and abstinence of the Order was declared incompatible with the duties of Sisters engaged in teaching. Our Reverend Confessor is engaged at present in writing a Rule for our Community in accordance with directions he received in Rome.

It will consist for the most part of the ordinary regulations, but it will be arranged to conform with the Third Order requirements. It will, therefore, contain little that is new to us, and, on the whole, will require only what we have been observing up to the present. . . . The Reverend Confessor hopes to complete the task within a few months. It will then be printed and sent to Rome for approval. It will probably be several years before the approbation is given, as Rome is very deliberate in matters of this kind. . . .

The matter is so important for all of us. No doubt I have surprised you by the contents of this letter, but I hope that I have convinced you of the necessity of affiliating with Rome, for we can get help from no one else—neither bishop nor priest. If we do our part, God will supply what is missing.

With heartfelt greetings,
Mother Mary Hyacintha, O.S.D.

Document 6: Conflicts with American Protestant Bigotry

When Catholic sisters first began to be seen in America in the first half of the nineteenth century, they were greeted with hostility and suspicion. Rumors of evil practices and women held by force in convents were circulated, and Protestant ministers argued against Catholicism from their pulpits, directing their attacks particularly against nuns. Nuns were frequently insulted or pelted in the streets. Occasionally riots broke out, and mobs pillaged and burned the convents.

One of the most famous of such cases was the burning of the Ursuline convent in Charlestown, Massachusetts, on August 11, 1834. This incident was inspired by misinformation circulated by Rebecca Reed, who had been dismissed from Mount St. Benedict as unsuited to religious life after a six-month novitiate. (She later wrote the first of the anticonvent books, Six Months in a Convent, *published in 1835.) A second nun, Elizabeth Harrison, had left briefly because of a breakdown caused by overwork, but then had petitioned to reenter. It was falsely rumored that she was being held by force. The mob looted the buildings and desecrated the chapel, even digging up the bodies of the sisters in the cemetery, before burning the convent and academy. In the following account from the transcript of the trial, Sister Mary Edmund St. George, the Ursuline superior, describes the scene followed by two other nuns, including Miss Harrison.*[11]

From the Boston Transcript—Trial of the Convent Rioters.

The trial of the convent rioters commenced yesterday, at East Cambridge. . . .

The district attorney, after opening the case, called as the first witness Mary Ann Ursula Moffat, otherwise called Mary Edmond St. George, the Lady Superior of the Ursuline Community. . . . She gave the following testimony, as reported by the Atlas:

I am the superior of the Ursuline Community in this state. I had the entire jurisdiction of the institution at Charlestown. Have held my present rank ten years. There was a school in our establishment, of which I was director. On the Thursday preceding the day on which the outrage was committed, I was told that the convent would be pulled down, and on the Saturday following several papers were sent to the institution concerning the "mysterious lady." On Sunday one of the selectmen of Charlestown called upon, and told me the convent would be destroyed if the "mysterious lady" could not be seen. By the "mysterious lady" I understood him to mean Miss Harrison.

On Monday the selectmen, five in number, came and were shown over the whole establishment. They remained three hours, and searched the building from the cellar to the highest apartment, looking in every box—even the paint boxes; also into all the drawers and closets. Two of the sisters went with me; one of these was the "mysterious lady," Miss Harrison. I do not know whether the out-buildings were examined. The selectmen went away at about six in the afternoon, and at a little after nine, I heard a great noise on the Medford Road, and distinguished the words—"Down with the convent!" I sent to tell the community that I thought we were in danger.

There were fifty pupils, from the age of six to eighteen years, and ten sisters in the establishment at this time. Two of the latter were novices. One of the sisters has died since. . . . After I had alarmed the inmates of our house, I went into a room on the second story, opened the window, and asked the people outside what they wanted. I told them they were disturbing the peaceful slumbers of the pupils, some of whom were the children of their most respectable fellow citizens. They then asked to see "the nun that had run away," and I sent up to fetch her, but found her lying insensible in the arms of four of the sisters. She had fainted with fright. I returned to the window and told the people that this was the case. She was incapable of showing herself to them that night, but if they would come the next day, they should receive every satisfaction.

I also told the mob that the selectmen had examined our institution and were satisfied; but if they [the mob] were not satisfied, they might come on the following day and investigate for themselves; I said the report of the selectmen would appear in the Morning Post. They replied, that all I said was false; that they had one of the selectmen with them, and that he had opened the gate for them. They asked if we were prepared to meet them. I did not wish them to know that our male domestics had left us. The mob shortly after this went away, saying they would not return til Thursday, when they would pull down the convent.

Before they went, they had fired a gun from under a willow tree near the house. I told them at the time they were making a noise, shouting and screaming, that my sister was ill of a consumption, and that the state of alarm they had thrown her into would cause her death. They replied, "So much the better." My sister is since dead. When they were gone, I thought there was no longer any cause for apprehension, and told the pupils and sisters to retire to their dormitories. They had no sooner done so, than the men returned and began to break the fence to make a bonfire.

At this time Mr. Runey, the selectman, came up with another person and told me he did not think he could quell the mob, but if I and the pupils would throw ourselves on his protection, he would do the best he could for us. I told Mr. Runey, if he wished to show himself friendly to us, to go and tell the people to desist from breaking the fences. He said he would go and do all in his power to prevent them. About five or six minutes after this I heard renewed shouts of "Down with the convent," and I then told the pupils and sisters it would be best for them to get to the summer-house, but before the former had time to leave their dormitories, the mob commenced breaking the doors and windows.

I went to each of the dormitories afterwards to see if all the pupils had escaped. I called at every door and found that they were all gone. I then went down to my own room, in which was a drawer containing valuables, but when I opened the door I saw the mob had already entered. I turned to go away, and saw twenty or thirty men in the same passage with me; they were about ten or twenty feet from me. I then went to the summer-house, where I found about forty of the pupils, some in their fright having climbed over the fence and gone to Mr. Cutter's; I sent the remainder after them, and went myself to Mr. Adam's whither all the pupils were eventually brought.

I never recovered any of the property of the institution, excepting a few articles of very small value. . . .

Mary Ann Barber, otherwise Sister Benedict Joseph, was next called. This lady is very beautiful. She gave her testimony with great clearness and self-possession, and her manner and language were those of a highly educated and accomplished female: I have been more than eight years in the Ursuline Community. I was in the convent on the night of the 11th Aug. Was awakened from sleep by the superior, who told me to dress quickly and arouse the community. I did so, and went afterwards to a window, from which I saw the mob, and heard them using abusive language towards the superior. They called her "a figure head, and said she was made of brass." The remainder of the witness's testimony was similar to that of the lady who preceded her, and which had been already before our readers. She identified a work-box and cross, as forming part of the property taken from the convent.

Miss Elizabeth Harrison (otherwise Mary St. John, the individual who left the convent) examined: I have been a member of the Ursuline Community for thirteen years. I was a teacher of music in the establishment. I did not leave the convent in consequence of any difficulty with the Lady Superior. The cause of my leaving was mental derangement. Had any one told me I should have done what I did, I should have thought it impossible. Everything was done in the institution to contribute to my happiness and that of the other inmates. I had never before felt any desire to leave the convent. I gave 14 lessons per day, and of 35, 40, and 45 minutes each. The witness further stated that her recollection of what took place after she left the community was very indistinct; she was bereft of reason.

Mr. Farley was proceeding to put other questions, when she suddenly covered her face with her handkerchief and burst into tears. Mr. F. under these circumstances, and considering what had been said respecting the witness's state of health, expressed his willingness to refrain from further interrogations. Miss Harrison was then suffered to retire from the court, which she did under the escort of the Russian consul.

In a somewhat more humorous style, Sister St. Francis Xavier of Saint Mary-of-the-Woods, Indiana, writes back to her family in France of the anti-Catholic hostility and superstitions of the Americans as well as of newfound friends.[12]

This good news [of the conversion of a hardened sinner] will console you a little for the burning of the house of the Sisters of Charity at Fredericktown. The incendiaries, before enkindling the fire, disabled the fire engines so that the progress of the fire could not be arrested. The house was burned to the ground. We may, perhaps, have to endure a similar misfortune. A few days ago we received an anonymous letter warning us to be on our guard. For two or three nights our workmen have watched, armed with guns. Some men were found hiding in our fields, but God permitted one of our neighbors to see them. We trust that the Blessed Virgin, who has always been a mother to us, will continue to protect our poor community.

I have already told you that our mission at Madison is greatly exposed to the persecutions of the enemies of Catholicity. Not long since, our Sisters wrote that the Presbyterian minister assembled his congregation in the church, and then, transported by the *Spirit,* disclosed all the infamies perpetrated by priests and nuns since the beginning of the Church! He ended his harangue by hurling anathemas against the parents who sent their children to Catholic schools, and he predicted that they would not escape the divine vengeance. "When we go to Mass," wrote one of our Sisters at this time, "the little rogues of boys, seeing us with our pupils, run after us, screaming,"

'Sheep, sheep, sheep!' They also pelt us with snowballs (but that does not hurt us), and sometimes even with eggs and stones."

The persecutions that our Sisters have been suffering at Madison are somewhat abated. Their most formidable adversary, however [Mr. Curtis], called together three hundred ministers last month, in order to devise in council some means of doing away with the *nuns*. But God laughs at the designs of men. Their ridiculous assembly inspired only contempt, and since that time the people are more favorably disposed toward our holy religion.

There is here an apostate monk from Italy, who goes from city to city giving lectures on the progress and danger of Catholicity. He was lately at Cincinnati, and I read a portion of his sixth discourse from which I quote: "When the demon wished to introduce evil into the world he made use of woman to corrupt man; now, to introduce Catholicism in America, he makes use of the nuns, true Eves, with their sweet and engaging manners, their knowledge, and their attractions. The Jesuits are dangerous, but the nuns are their agents, and are still more to be feared. Guard against sending your children to their schools, and even against placing among them servants trained by the Sisters, for they will instill their bad principles into the hearts of your children. The evil is greater than you think; and I know better than you that Catholicism is daily increasing," etc.

We do indeed remove the prejudices of our pupils. The parents have to choose between the inferiority of the other schools and what they call the *superstition* of ours; but, as many prefer having their children well instructed, they send them to us. Our boarding school is the best in Indiana, and would be considered very good even in France. We have about eighty pupils and several others are expected. I have never met young girls better taught than our first pupils. Mr. Pinatel, an old naval officer, was astonished at their knowledge of mathematics and astronomy. As these subjects and drawing were the ones to which he had principally devoted himself, this part of the examination pleased him best. The children especially excel, however, in Christian doctrine and in sacred and ecclesiastical history. They were highly commended, and with good reason, for the skill they show with the needle, particularly in plain sewing.

Every kind of absurdity and calumny finds acceptance with some of the people here. They were even so foolish as to believe that our chaplain had horns. One mischievous little woman, now a Catholic, told the villagers that if each of them would give her twenty-five cents, she would beg Father Corbe to take off his hat and let them see the horns. Not seeing them on his head the people wanted to look in his hat, supposing he had left them there.

A solicitous friend wrote as follows to an old lady who had her daughter in our school at Terre Haute: "Dear Madam: Although I have not the honor of your acquaintance, the interest I take in your daughter prompts me to tell you that, if you leave her with the nuns, she will be lost. Twenty years from now she will remember the detestable principles she has imbibed there; and if she does not become a Catholic, she will at least defend the Sisters all her life and on all occasions."

The good lady replied that she was old enough to judge for herself and wise enough to know how to bring up her own children; that not only would she leave her daughter with the good Sisters, but that she herself, when her dear husband should be no more, would offer herself to the Sisters, not to teach in the boarding school, but to serve them in their houses, an office she would consider an honor. We have the strangest imaginable applications for admission. Some, like this lady, still have their dear husbands, and are not even baptized; others ask to be received for a year only, in the absence of their husbands; others would like to be Sisters, but have not yet decided to become Catholics, and so on.

Document 7: The Sisters as Nurses: Turning the Tide of Bigotry

At a time when nursing was still considered a daring profession for a woman, Catholic nuns offered their services to all in the most dangerous circumstances, such as the yellow fever epidemics in the 1850s in Charleston, North Carolina. In the following account, a Sister of Mercy of Charleston describes their work in that city during the epidemics.[13]

The first yellow fever I remember was the terrible epidemic of 1852. There was a new hospital just built, called the "Roper Hospital." The Rev. Dr. Lynch, then in charge, Bishop Reynolds being absent and requested not to return (on account of the danger), opened it as a relief hospital. Here the Sisters worked day and night with Dr. Lynch and Dr. Corcoran. . . . Numbers of valuable lives were saved, and many who had neglected their religion for years were prepared for happy deaths; whilst others at the sight of their danger made their peace with God. . . .

When Bishop Reynolds arrived, he found his flock almost decimated, and a large number of orphans to be provided for. The Sisters had been obliged to contract a considerable debt, which the city of Charleston generously assumed as its own and paid.

In 1854, 1856, and, I think, 1858, the city received visits from the same dread disease. During these years the Sisters had no hospital, but went about from street to street, through lanes and alleys, wherever the sick might be found, carrying baskets filled with the necessaries of life and medicine, as these were needed. They worked heroically, all through the periods of disease, and all classes of citizens recognized the debt of gratitude due to these noble women. Some, such as Sister Mary Joseph, and Sister Mary Peter, fresh from Ireland and full of vigor in body and soul, were as little alive to human respect as they were to danger, and I remember on one occasion during the wet season, it was quite laughable to see them wade through the mire, with large boots, their habits and cloaks tied up, and lugging along their baskets, which seemed twice as large as themselves, that they might bring relief to the sick in the poor quarter of the town. When the troubles were over, our Sisters quickly returned to their school-rooms and seemed to have forgotten, what no one had seen them could ever could ever forget, that they had but a short time before been active amid the dark scenes of death from yellow fever haunting an entire community. It was not strange then that the people of Charleston should have been greatly attached to these nuns, and honored the little black bonnet. In truth the ladies of South Carolina called to a religious life think no dress so respectable as that of the Sisters of Mercy. In later years, whenever the epidemic broke out, the Sisters were supplied with vehicles in order that they might carry out their mission to the sick with greater facility and despatch. At times no one was seen in the streets but the doctors, the priests, and the Sisters on their rounds, and no sound was heard but the rumble of carts that were carrying off the dead. Coffins were often heaped one upon the other. About this time a society was formed among the first Protestant gentlemen of the district for the relief of the yellow fever sufferers, called the "Howard Society." The members worked heartily with the Sisters in their way, and frequently alms were distributed from the society through the Sisters. Natives of the region or those who were acclimated were not subject to the fever, except the children. Hence it was possible to hire good nurses; but they required to be well paid and well looked after. The Sisters managed to bring many of these nurses under their direction, and whilst the Howard Society usually paid for the lay service, the influence of the Sisters could not be paid for nor equalled by any hired service. Indeed the nuns so impressed the people by their efficiency and unselfish charity that they were not infrequently called to the sick before priest or doctor would be consulted. Finally, an hour had to be fixed after which people could not call the Sisters out of the convent. The d ʼor or gate was then to be locked, and no further calls to be answered. This was a great relief, as our poor Sisters were almost exhausted.

Although Catholics were a small percentage of the American population at that time, one-fifth of the nurses during the Civil War were Catholic nuns. Ninety-one Sisters of Charity, under the direction of Sister Gonzaga Grace, nursed at Satterlee Military Hospital near Gettysberg. In this account by Sister Gonzaga, the affection and esteem of the soldiers for the sisters is described.[14]

Cases of small-pox had occurred in the hospital from time to time, but the patients were removed as soon as possible to the Small-pox Hospital, which was several miles from the city. The poor fellows were more distressed on account of their being sent away from the Sisters to be nursed than they were on account of the disease. It was heart-rending when the ambulance came to hear the poor fellows begging to be left, even if they had to be entirely alone, provided the Sisters would be near them to have the Sacraments administered in the hour of danger. We offered our services several times to attend these poor sick, but were told that the Government had sent them away to avoid contagion. At last, however, the Surgeon in Charge obtained permission to keep the small-pox patients in the camp some distance from the Hospital. The tents were made very comfortable, with good large stoves to heat them, and "flys" (double covers) over the tops. The next thing was to have the Sisters in readiness, in case their services were required. Every one was generous enough to offer herself for the duty, but it was thought more prudent to accept one who had had the disease. As soon as the soldiers learned that a Sister had been assigned to the camp, they said: "Well, if I get the small-pox now, I don't care, because one of our Sisters will take care of me." From November, 1864, until May, 1865, we had upward of ninety cases—of whom nine or ten died. Two had the Black Small-pox. They were baptized before they died. We had, I may say, entire charge of the poor sufferers, as the physician who attended them seldom paid them a visit, but allowed us to do anything we thought proper for them. The patients were very little marked, and much benefited by drinking freely of tea made from Saracenia Purpura, or Pitcher Plant. When the weather permitted, I visited those poor fellows almost every day. Like little children, at these times they expected some little treat of oranges, cakes, jellies, apples and such things, which we always had for them. They often said it was the Sisters who cured them and not the doctors, for they believed they were afraid of the disease. Our small-pox patients appeared to think that the Sisters were not like other human beings, or they would not attend such loathsome contagious diseases, which every one else shunned. One day I was advising an application to a man's face for poison—he would not see one of the doctors, because, he said, the doctor did him no good—and I told him this remedy had cured a Sister who was poisoned. The man looked at me in perfect astonishment. "A Sister!" he exclaimed. I answered "Yes." "Why!" said he, "I didn't know the Sisters ever got anything like that." I told him "To be sure they did. They are liable to take disease as well as any one else." "To be sure *not!*" he said. "For the boys often say they must be different from other people, for they do for us what no other person would do. They are not afraid of fevers, small-pox or anything else." The physicians acknowledged that they would have lost many more patients had it not been for the Sisters' watchful care.

In Ward R, there was a patient named John Smith. He was a month in the ward, and suffered very much. Morally speaking, he was a good man, and very patient and respectful. He had never been baptized, and did not know that it was necessary to salvation. As Sister saw that he was ignorant on that point, she explained it to him. He dreaded death, and could not think it was so near. He was conscious until the last. During the last three days of his life he seemed to be in deep thought. Sister said but little of death to him; she saw it was in vain. An hour before his death, she was passing near his bed, when he called her, and said in a tone of despair, "Oh, Sister, I am going to die!" Sister asked him if he was sorry for not having been baptized? He answered, "Oh, yes!" Sister told him it was not yet too late. He appeared overjoyed at hearing this, and she asked who he wished should baptize him? He answered, "A Catholic priest." Sister replied: "There is no Catholic priest here, and there is no time to send for one, but in a case like yours, the Catholic Church permits anyone to administer Baptism." He said at once: "Sister, baptize me. I want to be a child of God." He repeated some prayers after Sister in a very fervent manner. She asked him: "If you recover, do you intend to be a faithful Catholic?" He replied: "Oh, yes." He recited the Hail Mary with her, and in five minutes after he was baptized, he died in great peace.

In the same ward, another patient, an Indian named James Graham, who had been brought up where God was not known, was altogether ignorant of Him and His goodness. Sister told him of his danger, and of the little hope there was of his recovery, and of the necessity there was of preparing for a happy death. As well as he knew how, the poor man tried most fervently to prepare himself. He appeared never to have had any care, and the little we showed him won him so much that he thought nothing was right except what Sister did. He asked to be baptized in the Church that Sister thought was the right one and in no other. She gave him some instructions and left him a few days to consider them. He wore a medal of the Blessed Virgin, and would kiss it, and say: "My sweet Mother, I will soon see you in heaven!" A Protestant minister came to see him, and Sister asked him if this was the one he would choose to have baptize him. He asked: "Is this the one you would bring?" She told him "No," and he said: "Well, bring the right one." The priest had not yet arrived and he was sinking rapidly, so Sister baptized him as he earnestly desired, praying at the same time that God would have mercy on his soul. He died about two hours after, in peace.

From our taking charge of the Hospital, June the 9th, 1862, until we left it on August 3rd, 1865, ninety-one Sisters had been on duty there. The war being over in April, 1865, the Government only desired our services after that until the convalescents could obtain their discharge. The physicians, however, requested us to remain until all the sick were removed to the Soldiers' Home, or returned to their own homes. I am happy to be able to state that during our whole sojourn at Satterlee Hospital, there never was an unpleasant word between the physicians or officers and the Sisters. The eve of our departure, the Executive Officer said to me: "Sister, allow me to ask you a question. Has there ever been any misunderstanding or dissatisfaction between the officers and the Sisters since you came to this Hospital?" I answered: "None at all." "Well," he said, "I will tell you why I asked. The other evening we were at a party. The conversation turned on the Sisters in the Hospitals, and I said there had never been a falling-out between us at Satterlee—that we were all on the same good terms as on the first day we met. Some of the City Hospital doctors said they did not believe that forty women could live together without disputing, much less that they could be among such a number of men without it."

The number of Baptisms we have on record is fifty-seven. The number of communicants could not be ascertained, as some approached the Holy Table every Sunday. . . .

Document 8: Nuns on the Frontier: Sister Blandina's Adventures in the Southwest

Sister Blandina Segale, a Cincinnati Sister of Charity, was a remarkable woman who traveled alone to Colorado in 1878 at the age of twenty-two and spent eighteen years working in Colorado and New Mexico. During this period she put up a school and a hospital without prior resources, ended the lynch law in New Mexico, tamed Billy the Kid, built the tallest building in the territory, and proved herself more than the equal of the forces of greed and violence that surrounded her. She described these adventures in a personal journal written to her sister Justina, also a sister of Charity.[15]

Ending the Lynch Law in Trinidad, Colorado

One of my oldest pupils came to ask to have his sister excused from school. He looked so deathly pale that I inquired, "What has happened?" He answered, "Haven't you heard?"

"Nothing that should make you look as you do."

"Sister, dad shot a man! He's in jail. A mob has gathered and placed men about forty feet apart from the jail to Mr. McCaferty's room. The instant he breathes his last, the signal of his death will be given, and the mob will go to the jail and drag dad out and hang him."

"Have you thought of anything that might save him?" I asked.

"Nothing, Sister; nothing can be done."

"Is there no hope that the wounded man may recover?"

"No hope whatever; the gun was loaded with tin shot."

"John, go to the jail and ask your father if he will take a chance at not being hanged by a mob."

"What do you propose doing, Sister?"

"First to visit the wounded man and ask if he will receive your father and forgive him, with the understanding that the full force of the law be carried out."

"Sister, the mob would tear him to pieces before he was ten feet from the jail."

"I believe he will not be touched if I accompany him," I said.

"I'm afraid he will not have the courage to do as you propose."

"That is the only thing I can see that will save him from the mob law. Ask your father to decide. This is Friday. I'll visit the sick man after school this afternoon. Let me know if he will consent to go with me to the sick man's room."

Immediately after school, with a companion, I went to see the wounded man. Sister Fidelis had preceded me. She was writing a letter to his mother bidding her good-bye until they would meet where the Judge was just, and their tears would be dried forever.

I looked at the young man, a fine specimen of honesty and manliness. My heart ached for the mother who expected frequent word from her son, then to receive such news! To be shot unjustly, to die in a strange land, among strangers, so young!

As soon as Sister Fidelis and companion took leave of the sick man, the subject of the present visit was broached. The young man was consistent. He said, "I forgive him, as I hope to be forgiven, but I want the law to take its course."

Fully agreeing with him, he was asked: "Will you tell Mr. _____ this if he comes to beg your pardon?"

"Yes, Sister," he answered.

Friday evening the prisoner's son came to say his father was very much afraid to attempt to walk to Mr. McCaferty's room, but if Sister would walk with him, he would take the chance of having the court pronounce sentence on him.

Early Saturday morning we presented ourselves to the Sheriff in his office.

"Good morning, Sister!" was the Sheriff's pleasant greeting.

"Good morning, Mr. Sheriff. Needless to ask if you know what is taking place in our two principal streets."

"You mean the men ready to lynch the prisoner who so unjustly shot the young Irishman?"

"Yes. What are you going to do to prevent the lynching?"

"Do! What has any sheriff here ever been able to do to prevent a mob from carrying out its intent?"

"Be the first sheriff to make the attempt!"

"How, Sister?" Standing to his full height—he must be six feet four—he reminded me of a person with plenty of reserve strength, and on the qui vive to use a portion of it.

"The prisoner was asked if he would be willing to walk between the sheriff and Sister to the victim's sick bed and ask his pardon." The sheriff interrupted:—"Sister, have you ever seen the working of a mob?"

"A few, Mr. Sheriff."

"And would you take the chance of having the prisoner snatched from between us and hanged to the nearest cottonwood?"

"In my opinion, there is nothing to fear." He straightened himself and looked at me, shrugged his shoulders and said, "If you are not afraid, neither am I."

We—the sheriff, my companion and myself—started to walk to the jail. All along the main street and leading to the jail were men at about a distance of a rod apart. These were the men who were to signal Mr. McCaferty's death by three taps of our school bell, in order that the mob might proceed to the jail, take the prisoner and hang him. Our group arrived at the jail, where we encountered the greatest discouragement. The prisoner saw us coming. When we got near enough to speak to him, he was trembling like an aspen. We saw his courage had failed him. We paused while we assured him he was safe in going with us.

He hesitated, then said: "I'll go with you." All along the road we kept silence, and no one spoke to us. When we got within a block of the sick man's room, we saw a crowd of men outside his door. It was at this juncture that my fears for the prisoner began. Intent upon saving our protégé from mob law, we hastened to the sick man's door. The crowd made way. Intense fear took possession of me. "Will the prisoner be jerked away when he attempts to enter his victim's room?"

The Sheriff and I remained at the foot of the few steps which led into the room. Meanwhile, I quietly said to the prisoner: "Go in," which he did, myself and companion following. The sheriff remained outside. The door was left wide open that those standing outside might hear the conversation taking place within.

The culprit stood before his victim with bowed head. Fearing a prolonged silence, I addressed the prisoner: "Have you nothing to say?"

He looked at the man in bed and said: "My boy, I did not know what I was doing. Forgive me."

The sick man removed the blanket which covered his tin-shot leg, revealing a sight to unnerve the stoutest heart. The whole leg was mortified and swollen out of proportion, showing where the poisonous tin had lodged and the mortification creeping toward the heart.

"See what you have done!" said the wounded man.

"I'm sorry, my boy, forgive me."

"I forgive you, as I hope to be forgiven, but the law must take its course."

I added, "Yes, the law must take its course—not mob law." Those outside the door with craned necks distinctly heard the conversation.

We returned to the jail where the prisoner was to remain until the Circuit Court convened.

Encounters with Billy the Kid

My scattered notes on "Billy the Kid's Gang" are condensed, and some day you will be thrilled by their perusal.

The Trinidad Enterprise—the only paper published here—in its last issue gave an exciting description of how a member of "Bill's Gang" painted red the town of Cimarron by mounting his stallion and holding two six-shooters aloft while shouting his commands, which everyone obeyed, not knowing when the trigger on either weapon would be lowered. This event has been the town talk, excluding every other subject, for the past week.

Yesterday one of the Vigilant Committee came to where I was on our grounds—acting as umpire for a future ball game—and said: "Sister, please come to the front yard. I want you to see one of 'Billy's gang,' the one who caused such fright in Cimarron week before last." My informant passed the news to the Nine and their admirers, so that it became my duty to go with the pupils, not knowing what might take place.

When we reached the front yard, the object of our curiosity was still many rods from us. The air here is very rarefied, and we all are eagle-eyed in this atmosphere. We stood in our front yard, everyone trying to look indifferent, while Billy's accomplice headed toward us.

He was mounted on a spirited stallion of unusually large proportions, and was dressed as the *Toreadores* (Bull-Fighters) dress in old Mexico. The figure passed from our sight. I tried to forget it, but it was not to be. Our Vigilant Club, at all times, is on the alert to be of service. William Adamson, a member of the Club, came excitedly, to say—"We have work on hand!"

"What kind of work?" I asked.

"You remember the man who frightened the people in Cimarron, and who passed our schoolhouse some weeks ago?"

"Yes, William."

"Well, he and Happy Jack, his partner, got into a quarrel, and each got the drop on the other. They kept eyeing and following each other for three days, eating at the same table, weapon in right hand, conveying food to their mouth with left hand.

"The tragedy took place when they were eating dinner. Each thought the other off guard, both fired simultaneously. Happy Jack was shot through the breast. He was put in a dugout 3 × 6 ft.

Schneider received a bullet in his thigh, and has been brought into Trinidad, thrown into an unused adobe hut, and left there to die. He has a very poor chance of living."

"Well, William, we shall do all we can for him. Where did this all take place?"

"At Dick Wootton's tollgate—the dividing line between Colorado and New Mexico."

At the noon hour we carried nourishing food, water, castile soup and linens to the sick and neglected man. After placing on a table what we had brought, my two companions, William Adamson and Laura Menger, withdrew. I walked towards the bed and, looking at the sick man, I exclaimed, "I see that nothing but a bullet through your brain will finish you!"

I saw a quivering smile pass over his face, and his tiger eyes gleamed. My words seemed heartless. I had gone to make up for the inhuman treatment given by others, and instead, I had added to the inhumanity by my words.

After a few days of retrospection, I concluded it was not I who had spoken, but Fear, so psychologists say.

At our first visit I offered to dress the wound, but to my great relief the desperado said, "I am glad to get the nourishment and the where-with to dress my wound, but I shall attend to it myself." Then he said: "What shall I call you?"

"Sister," I answered.

"Well, Sister, I am very glad you came to see me. Will you come again?"

"Yes, two and three times a day. Good-bye."

We continued these visits for about two months, then one day the sick man asked: "Sister, why is it you never speak to me about your religion or anything else?"

I looked and smiled.

He continued: "I want to tell you something. I allude to the first day you came. Had you spoken to me of repentance, honesty, morals, or anything pertaining to religion, I would have ordered you out. 'I see that nothing but a bullet through your brain will finish you.' Sister, you have no idea what strength and courage those words put into me. I said to myself, 'No shamming here, but the right stuff.' "

Dear Sister Justina, imagine what a load was lifted, to know for a certainty I had not added pain to the downtrodden culprit.

Another month passed by and the patient was visibly losing strength. I managed to get his mother's address. She lives in California.

After a week we resumed our visits. At the noon call our patient was quite hilarious. I surmised something unusual had taken place. He lost no time in telling me that Billy and the "gang" are to be here,

Saturday at 2 P.M., and I am going to tell you why they are coming.

"Do you know the four physicians who live here in Trinidad?"

"I know three of them," I answered.

"Well, the 'gang' is going to scalp the four of them" (and his tiger eyes gleamed with satisfaction) "because not one of them would ex-tract the bullet from my thigh."

Can you imagine, Sister Justina, the feeling that came over me? One of the gentlemen is our Convent physician!

I looked at the sick man for a few seconds, then said: "Do you believe that with this knowledge I'm going to keep still?"

"What are you going to do about it?"

"Meet your gang at 2 P.M. next Saturday."

He laughed as heartily as a sick man could laugh and said, "Why, Sister, Billy and the gang will be pleased to meet you. I've told them about you."

I cannot give you any idea of the anxiety of the days previous to the coming ordeal of meeting the gang.

Saturday, 2 P.M., came, and I went to meet Billy and his gang. When I got to the patient's room, the men were around his bed. The introduction was given. I can only remember, "Billy, our Captain, and Chism."

The leader, Billy, his steel-blue eyes, peach complexion, is young, one would take him to be seventeen—innocent-looking, save for the corners of his eyes, which tell a set purpose, good or bad. Mr. Chism, of course this is not his real name—has a most bashful appearance. I judge he has sisters. The others, all fine looking young men. My glance took this description in while "Billy" was saying: "We are all glad to see you, Sister, and I want to say, it would give me pleasure to be able to do you any favor."

I answered, "Yes, there is a favor you can grant me." He reached his hand toward me with the words: "The favor is granted."

I took the hand, saying: "I understand you have come to scalp our Trinidad physicians, which act I ask you to cancel." Billy looked down at the sick man who remarked: "She is game."

What he meant by that I am yet at a loss to understand. Billy then said: "I granted the favor before I knew what it was, and it stands. Not only that, Sister, but at any time my pals and I can serve you, you will find us ready."

I thanked him and left the room.

Building the Tallest Building in New Mexico

April, 1878

The question of building is assuming large proportions. I smile, knowing the financial condition of the convent treasury. . . .

Sister Augustine called me to her office and very suavely broached the subject of building. In part she said, "Most Rev. Archbishop Lamy thinks one great need in the Territory is a Trade School for girls. Now, Sister, will you undertake to build it?"

"How much money have we with which to begin building?"

"Nothing, Sister. Do as you did in Trinidad. I was told you had not a cent when you started to build your adobe schoolhouse, and you finished it without debts."

"Ah! Sister, that was only an insignificant matter compared to what a Trade School should be."

"Well, Sister, keep the size of the building within the boundary of your judgment."

"And the money within the same boundary?"

She smiled and continued, "Use your originality as you did elsewhere, and with God's blessing you will get through."

I immediately thought of the young artist, Mr. Projectus Mouly, son of Antoine, whose feelings made him shrink from meeting his friends.

Mr. Mouly has come to the Convent. I saw at once he was strangely touched that I should send for him. I told him my plans for building an Industrial School. The plans are out of all proportions to any building here, and far away from the imagination of the present population of Santa Fe.

I must confess, I have a strong repugnance to building; not on account of the hardships the work will entail, but because some things are not clear to me. At an interview with His Grace, he said: "One great need of the territory is a Trade School. Go at it with my full blessing." Here is the interview with the Rector of the Cathedral, Rev. Augustine Truchard. He thinks the object of the training school is most laudable and greatly needed.

"How much money have you to begin with, Sister?"

"Not a cent, Father."

"And you want to build a three-story house in a country where there is not a planingmill, not a brickyard, nor a quarry of your own, nor limekilns, and, worst of all, not a cent on hand!" Yet you want to begin to dig the foundation Monday morning. Do you know what some of us will say of you?"

"I can surmise, but if you will do what I ask of you I'm not afraid to begin work Monday morning."

"Let me hear, Sister, what you wish me to do."

"Simply to announce at the next Sunday Masses that the Sisters of Charity wish to build a house where girls in need can be trained in industries by which they can make a livelihood. Please say that our present wish is that a number of peons be paid by those disposed to do so, and sent to our front grounds to work on Monday and continue daily until the foundations are laid, each man to bring pick and shovel."

"Well, Sister, I will make the announcement, but I do not believe the men will come."

Monday, June 3, 1878

Seven o'clock. Twelve men with picks and shovels came to work. I registered the names and became timekeeper.

June 17, 1878

Two weeks ago we started work on the foundations for an Industrial School. Part of the land excavated makes a natural foundation, so we are ready for masonry work.

I had another interview with the Rector of the Cathedral. When he saw me he said: "Now, Sister, what do you want?" The answer was, "Wagons, mules, drivers."

"And how do you propose getting them?"

"If you please, in the same way we got men, picks, and shovels."

"Well, Sister, I shall announce your second plea at all the Masses tomorrow."

Meanwhile, a quarry had been opened and the men who were not needed to work on foundations were quarrying stone. After the second announcement in the church so many men and wagons were sent to us that they were in one another's way. A Mr. Antonio Ortiz y Salazar, who has taken an active interest in our plan of building without money, said to me:

"Sister, when you dismiss these men and wagons, I shall send you a regular team on one condition that when the mules need shoeing and the wagon needs repairs you send them to Mr. Paul's blacksmith shop and charge to me."

"Thank you, Sir!" I said gratefully. You will note, Sister Justina, that by this arrangement we will have a steady team to depend on.

We have given a contract to a native who will employ his own men to cut the trees and handsaw the lumber to the dimensions required. The nearest place trees are available for lumber is twenty-three miles from Santa Fe.

We have started our own brickyard, 250,000 bricks will be burnt at the first firing. We have eight gentlemen pledged to send workingmen to wait on the bricklayers.

The intersecting interior walls are to be of adobe laid in mortar. This will make the school cool in summer, and warm in winter. The work is to settle for months before the bricks and adobe walls are interlocked.

We have neither gas nor water-works here, but we are going to install pipes for both commodities in case we ever "wake up." This place is not a "Sleepy Hollow" only "Sunshine Asleep."

July 26, 1878

The bricks are all piled ready to use.

I sold the span of horses and wagon for $200, paid the owner of the horses $150, and gave $40 to the poor family who had no use for the wagon, and thereby gained $10. This will help pay for lime.

We have made no financial appeal to the people of Santa Fe, yet they have shown themselves most liberal. Seldom do I go to the plaza to order supplies, but I return with much more money than I started out with. God provides when one does his best.

I must tell you, dear Sister Justina, that the erection of this building has brought out many ludicrous opinions. Some asked; "How can a building sixty feet high, and a cupola on top of that, stand? The first big wind will blow it down." Others said that if the inside adobes were not laid with mud, the first rainy weather would melt the building. These critics thought the roof would be mud-covered.

We started our own brickyard, opened our own quarry, had our lime burnt to order, and had our lumber hand-sawed by our natives. After this had been done, a sawmill was started at Glorieta and planing-mill was opened in Las Vegas. There was a sawmill sixty miles this side of Trinidad, but having to rely on teams to haul the lumber, it was better economy to do as we did. Can you picture what work this entailed?

February 12, 1880

Here is the latest criticism on the Industrial School Building. Some ladies who are not troubled for want of money took this view: "If those Sisters who had no cash to build succeeded in putting up the finest building in the Territory, why cannot we, who have money, build our own homes?" It would take pages to note all that has been said about the structure.

The Jewish Woman's Encounter with American Culture

ANN BRAUDE*

The transformation of the religious role of women has been among the most far-reaching results of the Jewish tradition's encounter with American culture. Thousands of years of tradition were radically reshaped on American soil. It is within the context of this encounter that we can best understand the story of Jewish women in nineteenth century America.[1]

The first Jewish settlers arrived on the North American continent in 1654 when the Portugese recaptured eastern Brazil and expelled the Jews and Dutch who were living there. Twenty-three Jews landed at the Dutch port of New Amsterdam. Before the end of the seventeenth century, the Jews of New York had gained the right of public worship and established the Portugese-speaking Congregation Shearith Israel (the Remnant of Israel). Jews continued to migrate to America in small numbers throughout the seventeenth and eighteenth centuries. The rate of intermarriage was high, and the pressure to convert was great.

As late as 1820 there were probably no more than three thousand Jews in the United States, about half of them Sephardic (Spanish and Portugese) and half Ashkenazic (western and eastern European). Although small in number, the Sephardim retained a degree of influence as the elite of American Jewry. They were soon outnumbered by the two or three hundred thousand Jews among the five million Germans who came to the United States between 1820 and 1880. These German Jews and their children were the dominant force in the emergence of American Judaism in the nineteenth century. In 1881, the bloody pogroms of Russia and eastern Europe began a stream of Jews fleeing to the United States. This group amounted to three million before the gates of immi-

*ANN BRAUDE is studying for her Ph.D. in Religious Studies at Yale University. She received her M.A. degree from the Divinity School of the University of Chicago and her B.A. from Vassar College. She is specializing in the religious history of American women in her Ph.D. program.

gration were closed in 1923. The arrival of these Jews, and the wave of anti-Semitism in eastern Europe that precipitated it, had a profound impact on the existing American Jewish community, but not until the twentieth century was the practice of Judaism in America once again transformed by this new majority.[2]

In the United States, Jews from distant countries and disparate cultures came into contact for the first time. In order to understand the role of women in the religious synthesis that resulted from the encounter of these diverse groups with each other and with American civilization, we must first look briefly at the cultural background which each group brought to America.

During the several centuries preceding their arrival in the United States, European Jews lived in isolation from the Christian cultures of their host countries. In cities they lived in restricted areas called *ghettos*. In the country they lived in small villages called *shtetlach*. Barred from civil rights in the larger society, Jews had legal authority over their own affairs inside their own communities. In the autonomous Jewish culture that developed inside the ghetto and the shtetl, piety was seen as the first priority of communal life. Piety was achieved by fulfillment of religious obligations. Women were exempt from most male obligations because they were responsible for the physical needs of the family. However, many obligations could be fulfilled only with the cooperation of women, so women were enjoined to do many things to help men fulfill their religious obligations. Procreation was a duty for men, so women were to marry and bear children as soon as they were able. A man was not to look at a woman in a synagogue because he might be aroused to desires that would distract him from his prayers; therefore the women had to sit in a curtained balcony of the synagogue where they could not be seen. A man could not touch a menstruating woman, so a woman had to avoid her husband during menstruation and visit the mikvah, the ritual bath, to purify herself following menstruation before her husband could resume sexual relations with her. Women provided all of the physical elements that allowed men to conform with Jewish religious practice. They provided clean clothes and a special meal for the Sabbath, kept the household in conformity with dietary laws, and made ready all the ritual objects necessary for special observances. In the synagogue, women were permitted only where they would not distract men and were prohibited from playing an active role in the worship service or the organization of the synagogue. They could not be counted in a minyan, the quoram of ten required for public prayer, and did not receive extensive education because they were exempted from the male requirement to study the Torah. Tradition taught that piety in this life led to heaven in the next. But a woman could get to heaven only through her husband's godliness, so she could never place anything before her constant striving to aid him in the fulfillment of his religious obligations.[3]

It should not be concluded from this brief description that European Judaism held a uniquely negative view of women. Many women excelled in spite of cultural restrictions. The paper by Ray Frank on "Woman in the Synagogue" describes the many exceptional Jewish women who were renowned for their learning and their piety.[4] Women outside the ghetto walls had as few opportunities as their Jewish sisters and fewer legal protections. During a period when Christian women were being burned as witches, injunctions to bathe and shave one's head cannot be seen as extraordinarily oppressive. Rabbinic literature codified negative attitudes toward women into specific limitations on women's role.

As in many cultures where women are excluded from male religious activities, many Jewish rituals were performed exclusively by women. These practices may almost be seen as a parallel religion with its own set of rituals and standards of piety. Among the rituals practiced by women were attendance at the mikvah, baking challah (holiday bread), observance of kashrut (dietary laws), lighting the Sabbath candles, and Rosh Chodesh, the New Moon ceremony. Women had their own prayer books, printed in the vernacular. These contained prayers for specific events in a woman's life, including prayers for the safe delivery of a child, prayers for the safe return of a husband who was on a journey, exercises for a woman who was unhappily married, and exercises for a woman who was married to an irreligious husband. In the woman's section of the synagogue, a woman who could read the Hebrew text served as zogerkeh, leading the other women through the service.[5]

Women's religion in the shtetl has been beautifully described in Bellah Chagail's book *Burning Lights,* in which she recounts the religious events of her childhood in Russia. The parallel religion of Jewish women is especially suggested in her description of the feast of Purim, which celebrates the triumph of Queen Esther over the enemy of the Jews. The observance of Purim includes the public reading of the Book of Esther. In Chagall's description, her mother could not go to the synagogue to hear the book read because she could not take time away from her attendance on the family store and the preparations for the feast which she must have ready when the male members of the family returned from synagogue. Rather than miss the account of Queen Esther's triumph, Chagall's mother hired a reader to come to the house. The reader was greeted at the kitchen door by the cook, who then gathered the female members of the family for the reading. Little Bellah was so overwhelmed with the glory of Queen Esther that she nearly missed her role in the event where the children had to make enough noise to outshout the enemy of the Jews.[6]

The autonomy and isolation of Jewish culture began to change in western Europe with the Enlightenment of the eighteenth century. One of the impacts of the Reign of Reason in the Enlightenment was the beginning of the trend toward the relocation of religion in society.

French Jews enjoyed a brief period of citizenship under Napoleon Bona-
parte, and more limited rights and privileges were extended to Jews in
other countries in western Europe. Jews began to seek secular education.
Especially in Germany, they began to participate in the intellectual life
of modern Europe. However, the cost of emancipation quickly became
clear. The French National Assembly stated it clearly: "To the Jew as an
individual—everything; to the Jews as a nation—nothing." The national
identity of the Jews and the constant prayer that the Chosen People
would someday be returned as a nation to the promised land of Israel
were incompatible with modern citizenship.[7]

Because of these experiences in Europe, the German Jews who came
to the United States were prepared to accept the voluntary model of
religious life that was the norm in America. Though much attached to
their native identity as Germans, they were prepared to participate in a
secular national culture in the United States just as they had in Germany.
This was not true of the eastern European and Russian Jews who later
followed them. Although Jewish enlightenment thought, called *haskahla*,
eventually worked its way eastward from Germany to Russia, the continued enforced isolation and persecution of Jews in Russia left them
without reason to exchange Jewish nationalism, or Zionism, for a secular
national identity. Likewise, the Russian Jews found fewer opportunities
awaiting them in America than did their German predecessors, and so
they had little incentive to identify themselves with the values of their new
home.

Many of the German Jews brought with them a form of religious
practice that reflected the influence of enlightenment and the desire to
participate in modern culture: Reform Judaism. The Reform movement
was just beginning in Germany when the flow of immigration began, but
as it progressed it continued to send outstanding rabbis to the United
States. The goal of Reform was to preserve the essence of Judaism but
to modernize the ritual and practice of Judaism according to the principles of reason.

In Europe, women with secular educations found social and intellectual opportunities in gentile circles which were not available to them in
the traditional Jewish community. The apostasy and conversion of several well-known and admired German Jewish women at the beginning of
the nineteenth century alerted male leaders of the Reform movement
that liberally educated women would gravitate toward the greater freedom and status offered by Christianity if Judaism could not offer the
same advantages. The Reform Synod of 1846 made women the religious
equals of the male laity.[8]

The German Jews who brought the Reform movement to the United
States were anxious to be accepted in their new country. In America, they
had citizenship and freedom to follow their own religion. Although they
brought little with them to America, they were able to take advantage of

the economic opportunities offered by the growing cities and westward expansion, and many rose to affluence within one or two generations. Many of these Jews saw America as the new Zion, the promised land for Jews. To them, archaic attitudes toward women were an embarrassment. Isaac Meyer Wise, the leader of Reform Judaism in the United States, advocated all the changes in women's role made by the German reformers, and then some. Besides counting women in the minyan, allowing them to sit in the main body of the synagogue, and giving them equal access to religious education, Wise instituted a double-ring ceremony with reciprocal vows to replace the traditional Jewish wedding in which the woman was silent and passive. He also advocated women's suffrage and the ordination of women, but neither of these reforms was enacted during his lifetime.[9]

Although most frequently articulated by reformers, Americanization was the aim of many nineteenth century Jews who did not identify themselves as reformers. The great internal debate of American Judaism in the nineteenth century was what amount of American practice could be adopted before religious practice ceased to be Jewish. Reform and Americanization were two converging trends that encouraged a new role for women.

Even before Reform ideas began to arrive from Germany, the United States showed itself to be fertile ground for innovation in Jewish practice. As early as 1825, in the large Jewish community of Charleston, South Carolina, a small group broke away from a Sephardic congregation to start the Reformed Society of Israelites. This group openly admitted its desire to conform with American Protestant religious practice. Calling their rabbi a minister, the members of this group stated that they did not follow rabbinic teachings, but "only the laws of Moses, and those only as far as they can be adapted to the institutions of the Society in which they live and enjoy the blessings of liberty." By 1840 the group was large enough to take over the congregation from which it had originally departed.[10]

Although ostensibly orthodox, other early American Jews showed signs of adapting to American religious practice. The letters of Rebecca Gratz are among the most vivid and intimate accounts of American Jewish life before the beginning of the German immigration. She and her gentile sisters-in-law read the Bible and other religious books together and discussed them in their letters. The ease and frankness of their religious discussions show a remarkable lack of friction between their faiths. The Jewish Sunday school that Gratz founded preceded other Jewish religious schools which met on Saturday. Her description of the dedication ceremony of the new synagogue of the Mikveh Israel Congregation in Philadelphia in 1826 suggests that Jews accepted certain American practices without question until more recent arrivals from Europe reasserted traditional practices. The mixed choir that sang at the ceremony attracted contemporary comment only for the sweetness of its song, while the acceptability of mixed choirs in the synagogue was much debated during the following decades because of the traditional view that a woman's voice caused sexual arousal in men.[11] (Document 1.)

The Americanization of Judaism required radical changes in the role of women. The formative period of Judaism in America coincided with a period in American Protestantism which has been called the "feminization of American religion." Women were believed to possess a natural piety that made them especially suited to spiritual affairs. Barred from other public activities, many women took leading roles in churches and religious organizations. The religious forms and practices which were the model for Americanization were substantially concerned with what society considered to be the feminine sphere.[12]

All of the changes made by Reform Judaism encouraged and enhanced women's increased participation in the synagogue. (Document 2.) Many of the changes later identified with Reform were more universally accepted by American congregations in the nineteenth century. (Document 3.)

The introduction of the vernacular and of instrumental and choral music into the worship service encouraged women's participation even where they were not counted in the minyan of called to the Torah. After her congregation installed an organ in 1841, Penina Moïse, a Sunday school superintendant, gained international recognition for her English language hymns. At the same time, the Reform movement and the lack of facilities discouraged the traditional religious activities of Jewish women: attending the mikveh, keeping kashrut, and keeping the Sabbath in the home. With some significant exceptions, the shapers of Reform Judaism found that male religious practices were rational and essential, while female religious practices were temporal and superstitious. This often placed women in the position of the defenders of orthodoxy, as they wished to continue their own rituals which were rejected by Reform. Women had complete control over whether their families continued to observe the dietary laws. In the United States, this "kitchen religion" sometimes outlasted male religious observance. The first synagogue in Chicago, Kehilath Anshe Mayriv, is said to have been founded because a pious woman, Dilah Cohn, refused to eat meat that was not kosher. Her sons despaired of seeing their mother subsist on vegetables and so organized the Chicago Jews into a congregation which could support a shohet (kosher butcher) to slaughter meat according to Jewish law.[13]

Women who accepted Reform rechanneled their religious lives into the previously male realm of the synagogue. They were included in confirmation classes and Sunday schools. Early reports in the *Occident*, the first periodical concerned with the current events of the American Jewish community, indicate that women often made up the majority of both students and teachers in these classes.[14]

The changing role of the rabbi reflected the changing sexual composition of the congregation. The traditional European rabbi had been a legal authority in matters of Jewish law and ritual. His main obligation had been to study the Torah, an activity limited to men. American rabbis, like their Christian counterparts, were expected to present a weekly sermon in the vernacular which pertained to both sexes. Besides leading services, American rabbis were expected to advise women's organizations in their charitable activities and take leadership in the social life of the community. In a sense, their duties shifted from the exclusively masculine sphere of the book to the increasingly feminine sphere of the synagogue.

The expanding role of women in the synagogue was not limited to the Reform movement. American women who were committed to the practices of the old country often saw themselves as the guardians of orthodoxy in the synagogue rather than the kitchen, just as their Christian contemporaries acted as guardians of Christian piety. In response to the radical reforms adopted by Congregation Beth Elohim in Charleston, a group of women started a coeducational religious school. The *Occident* reported:

> This sacred and laudable undertaking emanates from the mothers and daughters of Israel who are opposed to the innovations lately established in this congregation, and whose zeal and energies will be actively employed in impressing upon the tender minds of their pupils the *orthodox* tenets of our religion....[15]

The school was supported and operated exclusively by women. Sixty Jewish women enrolled as members, indicating sizable opposition to reform among the Jewish female population of Charleston. The *Occident* went on to express a characteristically American view of female religiosity, which directly contradicts the traditional Jewish view of women.

> It is ever so with women, and particularly so with the daughters of Israel, who are more deeply embued with the true spirit of our religion than the "sterner sex" and are (as this society will prove) the *Guardians of the Faith* and the ministering angels of its divine precepts.[16]

The *Occident* was edited by Isaac Leeser, who became the leader of the American Jews who did not accept all of the sweeping reforms advocated by Isaac Meyer Wise. Although Leeser opposed some of the suggested reforms relating to women, the contents of the *Occident* reveal a strong recognition of the importance of the role of women in American Judaism. Besides reporting the activities of women's benevolent societies, sewing circles, and Sunday schools, the *Occident* frequently printed poetry, fiction, and religious writing by and about women. Female scriptural characters were a popular subject in many of the nineteenth century Jewish periodicals. Rose Emma Salaman, Martha Allen, and Rebekah

Hyneman were among the women published in the *Occident* whose works were later collected into books.[17]

The American Jewish reading public was also exposed to the much-acclaimed work of English women writers. Grace Aguilar, who wrote both about Judaism and about women, was among the most popular Jewish writers of the nineteenth century. After her death, Grace Aguilar libraries and societies were founded to promote Jewish knowledge and literature. The *Occident's* review of Aguilar's *Women of Israel* made special note of her assertion that the soullessness of women was not a true Jewish belief, but must have been grafted on from the beliefs of the countries where Jews dwelled. George Eliot was also widely praised by American Jews for her novel *Daniel Deronda,* in which she advocated the creation of a Jewish national homeland in Palestine. Emma Lazarus wrote that Eliot had done more than any other writer "toward elevating and enobling the spirit of Jewish nationality." Lazarus' writing also received tremendous popular acclaim even though contemporary Jewish leaders opposed her suggestions for a Jewish homeland.[18] (Document 4.)

In 1881, Russian Jews fleeing from anti-Semitic violence began to swell the ghettos and sweatshops of America's industrial cities. For the German Jews, these new arrivals were a ready supply of cheap labor for the garment industry, but a threat to their carefully nurtured identity as patriotic Jewish Americans. Little of the modern world had reached the isolated shtetlach of Russia and eastern Europe. To the German Jews, the Russians represented everything they had fought against since arriving in the United States: foreignness, backwardness, and superstition. To the Russian Jews, the Germans represented the most heinous forms of apostasy. They ate food that was not kosher; they failed to keep the Sabbath; they worshipped like Christians. While the Germans started a campaign to Americanize the Russians, the Russians fought an uphill battle to keep their own ways against the harsh economic realities of the American ghetto. (Document 5.)

The German Jews' separation of religious practice and social practice allowed women to form organizations that identified themselves as Jewish and aimed at the promotion of Judaism, but followed models established by their Protestant sisters. The Russian immigrants who eventually formed the majority of American Jews did not initially adopt this separation between the social and religious realms. For women who aspired to goals that were prohibited by the traditional values of the shtetl, Judaism often seemed inextricable from the roles they were trying to escape. The United States offered new rights and opportunities to women only if they were able to fight their way out of the ghetto. After a short youth in sweatshops helping to support her family, a Jewish girl was expected to marry young and immediately start keeping house and bearing children, in fulfillment of her husband's obligation of procreation. Autobiographies of immigrant women who refused this role tell bitter stories of estrangement from beloved parents who could not accept their daughters' American ways and of alienation from the only community where they felt at home.[19] (Document 6.)

Although many women were forced to reject Judaism to pursue goals that took them outside the home, they often retained an identification with Judaism which was not related to religious practice. During the nineteenth century, Christian principles were voiced on both sides of nearly every struggle for reform. When Christian truth was held up as a roadblock to reform, religion appeared to be the enemy. Yet when Christian principles were voiced in favor of reform, it was only a short ideological step to the inclusion of the propagation of Christianity as part of the reform package. Jewish reformers responded to this dilemma by working against religious affiliation of any kind for their projects. Especially instructive of this conflict is the long battle between Jewish human rights advocate Ernestine Rose and Reverend Antoinette Brown Blackwell over whether the women's rights movement should adopt resolutions stating the biblical basis of their position. Rose succeeded in preventing the adoption of a religious platform as long as she lived, although her victory was not reflected in the activities of the other leaders of the movement.[20]

The tendency to support secular rather than Jewish institutions can also be seen in education. Rather than attempt to establish an independent school system, Jews fought to reduce the Protestant bias of public education. Likewise, Annie Nathan Meyer founded Barnard College to provide equal educational opportunities for all women, not just for Jews.[21]

The Congress of Jewish Women, which took place as part of the World Congress of Religions at the Columbian Exhibition at Chicago in 1893, was the highest moment of the century for American Jewish women. Crowds packed the halls to hear papers about Jewish women presented by such well-known figures as Henrietta Szold, Josephine Lazarus (Emma's sister, also a successful writer), and Ray Frank. (Document 7.) Although the congress was composed mainly of German Jewish women, it resulted in a permanent organization, the National Council of Jewish Women, for which the needs of Russian Jewish women were a primary concern for several decades. The United States Government eventually sought the assistance of the council in handling the problems of immigrant women on Ellis Island.[22]

In the opening address of the Jewish Women's congress, Hannah G. Solomon said: "Living as we do in this renegade city, belonging to radical synagogues, thoroughly in sympathy with all endeavours to break down barriers, we are loyal to our history and to the traditions of our families." (Document 8.) For Solomon and the thousands of women who joined the National Council of Jewish Women and other organizations like it, loyalty to Judaism took the form of a willingness to adapt their faith to a modern society. Twentieth century Jews often criticize the trends toward Reform and Americanization of which the council was an expression. However, women of the more recent immigration have followed the council's example by assuming a central role in the life of the synagogue and the Jewish community. The vital participation of women of all degrees of orthodoxy has been an essential, creative, and sustaining tone throughout the history of American Judaism.[23]

Emma Lazarus, Jewish poet and author whose
"New Colossus" was selected to be inscribed on the
base of the Statue of Liberty, wrote particularly
about the plight of Jewish refugees from Europe.
[Courtesy the American Jewish Archives, Cincinnati, Ohio.]

Hannah G. Solomon was the organizer of the Congress of Jewish Women at the World Parliament of
Religions of the Columbian Exhibition in 1890, the
beginning of what came to be the National Council
of Jewish Women. [Courtesy the American Jewish
Archives, Cincinnati, Ohio.]

Rebecca Gratz, Jewish philanthropist concerned with women and children, founded and was the superintendent of the first Hebrew Sunday School. [From a portrait by Edward Greene Malbone, original owned by Kathleen Moor, Montreal. Courtesy the American Jewish Archives, Cincinnati, Ohio.]

Rose Kohler, the daughter and granddaughter of prominent rabbis, was an early advocate of the equality of women with men in Reform Judaism. She was a painter, sculptor, and the author of *Art as Related to Judaism*. [Courtesy the American Jewish Archives, Cincinnati, Ohio.]

Rosa Sonneschein, founder of the *American Jewess*, the first English language publication for Jewish women in the United States, was an early supporter of Zionism and criticized the Americanization of Jewish women. [Courtesy the American Jewish Archives, Cincinnati, Ohio.]

Documents: The Jewish Woman's Encounter with American Culture

THE JEWISH WOMAN IN THE EARLY
NINETEENTH CENTURY

Document 1: Rebecca Gratz

Rebecca Gratz (1781–1869) was born into a well-established Jewish family in Philadelphia. Her extensive philanthropic activities included the Female Association for the Relief of Women and Children in Reduced Circumstances, the Philadelphia Orphan Society, the Female Hebrew Benevolent Society, the Jewish Foster Home, the Fuel Society, and the Sewing Society. In 1838 she founded the Hebrew Sunday School, the first Jewish Sunday school. She served as superintendent of the school for thirty-two years.[24]

These excerpts, from the Letters of Rebecca Gratz, *were written to her brother Benjamin and his Christian wife, Maria.*[25]

To Benjamin Gratz

[This letter describes the dedication of the new synagogue of the Mikveh Israel congregation of which the Gratz family were prominent members.]

Feb'y 27, 1825

I am surprised you have no account of the consecration except from the newspaper as it was a subject engaging universal attention. . . .

I have never witnessed a more impressive or solemn ceremony or one more calculated to elevate the mind to religious exercises—the school [synagogue] is one of the most beautiful specimens of ancient architecture in the city, and finished in the Stricklands best manner—the decorations are neat yet rich and tasteful—and the service commencing just before the Sabbath was performed by lamplight—Mr. Keys was assisted in the service by the Hazan [cantor] from New York, Mr. Peixotto, a venerable learned & pious man who gave great effect to the solemnity—the doors being opened by our brother Simon and the Blessing pronounced at the entrance—the processions entered with the two Reverends in their robes followed by nine copies of the Sacred Rolls—they advanced slowly to the Tabah [reading desk] while a choir of five voices chanted the appointed psalms most delightfully when the new Hazan had been inducted into his office and took his place at the desk. Mr. P. in slow and solemn manner preceded the Sephers [scrolls of the law] in their circuit round the area of the building between the desk and the ark—whilst such strains of sacred songs were chanted as might truly be said to have inspiration in them—between each circuit, the prayers appointed (as you will see in the book our brother sent you) to be performed by the Hazan and the congregation were said and among the most affecting parts of the service—Mr. Keys in a fine full voice and the responses by Mr. Peixotto in a voice tremulous from agitation and deep feeling. I have no hope of conveying by description any idea of this ceremony—you must have seen the whole spectacle—the beautiful ark thrown wide open to receive the sacred deposit, with its rich crimson curtains fringed with gold—the perpetual lamp suspended in front with its little constant light like a watchman at this post—and with the humble yet dignified figure of the venerable Mr. P. as he conducted the procession in its seven circuits and then deposited the laws—after which Mr. Keys recited with an effect amounting almost to eloquence that impressive prayer of King Solomon (1 Kings 8) the whole audience was most profoundly attentive and tho' few were so happy as to understand the language—those who did—say they have never heard the Hebrew so well delivered as by Mr. Keys—the bishop expressed his opinion—and all who were there acknowledge there has never been such church music performed in Phila—you will wonder where "these sweet singers in Israel" were collected from—the leader, teacher and principal performer is Jacob Seixas and his female first voice his sister Miriam, they were fortunately on a visit to their sister Mrs. Phillips and induced a class to practice for some weeks—Miriam and Becky Moses [nieces of Rebecca Gratz] contributed very considerably and all in the congregation who Mr. S. found teachable assisted— he is now resident here and we hope by his assistance to keep up a very respectable class of singers in the synagogue. The service continues to be finely performed and the congregation behave with the utmost decorum and propriety during the service. I scarcely know how to answer your questions concerning Mr. Keys—I do not believe he is a learned man—nor indeed a very sensible one—but he is a good Hebrew scholar—an excellent Teacher, and a good man, he is moreover very popular with the congregation and reads the prayers in a manner as to make his hearers feel that he understands and is inspired with their solemnity—perhaps his usefulness is not lessened by his diffidence—he is modest and unassuming, which suits the proud, the ignorant & presumptuous—these require most reformation and he is so respectable on the Tabah that he gives general satisfaction— Mr. P. is such a man as you describe, he was a merchant before the death of Mr. Seixas but has since his clerical appointment studied and become as learned as he is intelligent—Mr. K. had had a congregation which only required him to perform his school duties—now that he is among more intelligent people he too will feel the necessity of study—he has a wife and three clever children and when he gets over his West Indian indolence he will show what he can become—one very important talent he certainly possesses—he is a good Hebrew teacher —yesterday one of his pupils read a barmitzvah portion very handsomely altho' he had only a few weeks instruction. Our brothers have all become very attentive to school matters—Hyman is Gaboy [War-den] and they rarely omit attending worship. We all go Friday evening as well as on Saturday morning—the gallery [women's area] is as well filled as the other portion of the house—I think continually of you My dear Brother when I enter that temple and I pray that I may again see you worshipping within its walls—I know your faith is unchangeable and will endure even tho' you are alone in a land of strangers. May God be merciful to us all and keep us stedfast to our duties. I love your dear Maria, and admire the forbearance which leaves unmolested the religious opinions she knows are sacred in your estimation. May you both continue to worship according to the dictates of your conscience and your orisons be equally acceptable at the throne of Grace. . . .

To Maria Gist Gratz

[probably April, 1832]

.   .   .   .   .

That which you call the misfortune of single ladies, My dear Sister, is in my case converted into a blessing—for by sharing the troubles I gain admittance into the affections of my friends—and what should I do with the heart nature had given me if all its warm pulsations were to beat against closed bosoms? . . .

I had my philosophy a little tried the other day by some good Christians, and as I dare not complain about it to anybody else (for I hate to set the subject in its true light at home)—I must make you my confidante—You know I promised our friend Mrs. Furness to apply for a little girl out of the Asylum for her—well there is a good little girl I have kept my eye on and she is ready for a place—and my application is rejected because it is for a Unitarian—but "Ladies," said I, "there are many children under my special direction—you all know my creed—suppose I should want one to bring up in my family?" "You may have one," said a church woman—"because the Jews do not think it a duty to convert"—but said a presbyterian "I should not consent to her being put under the influence of a Unitarian"—and so my dear after putting the question to vote—I could get nothing— and when the meeting broke up, had a mischievous pleasure in telling one of the most blue of the board that I construed their silence into consent—for only one lady voted in the affirmative—and they were all ashamed to vote no—but I do not mean to let Mrs. F. know how she is proscribed, because notwithstanding my own position, I am ashamed of such an illiberal spirit—I got into a long discussion on the subject of religion, with a lady after the meeting and though we have been more than twenty years acquainted—I expect she will look shy on me for the rest of our lives—what a pity that the best and holiest gift of God to his most favoured creatures, should be perverted into a subject of strife—and that to seek to know and love the most High should not be the end and aim of all—without a jealous or persecuting feeling towards each other. . . .

Feb 23rd 1840

. . . we are now preparing for a second examination of our Sunday school and I am gratified at the evident improvement of a large class of children in religious knowledge, more particularly as I find it influencing their conduct, and manners, and gaining consideration in the minds of their parents—it will be a consolation for much lost time—if this late attempt to improve the degenerate portion of a once great people shall lead to some good—and induce wiser and better Jews to take the work in hand. I have just received a manuscript translation of a work of Mendlesohn on Jerusalem [discussion of separation of Church and state] from which I expect great pleasure & labour too—for it is difficult to read & more difficult to understand, perhaps I might be better able to answer your questions, when I have perused it. You give me credit for more lore than I can boast.

. . . God Bless you my dear Sister believe me with true affection always yours RG

NEW ROLES FOR THE JEWESS: REFORM JUDAISM AND AMERICANIZATION

Document 2: Rose Kohler

Rose Kohler (1873–1947) was a painter and sculptor who concentrated on Jewish themes. In 1922 she wrote a monograph entitled Art as Related to Judaism. *Her father, Kaufman Kohler, and her mother's father, David Einhorn, were among the most prominent rabbis of the more radical wing of the Reform movement in American Judaism. She was the national chairman of the National Council of Jewish Women's Committee on Religious Schools.*

The following paper was read by Miss Kohler before the New York branch of the National Council of Jewish Women on February 10, 1895. She contends that concrete changes which bring females into positions of equality with males must be made in Reform Judaism. Only then can the Jewess "kindle anew that holy light of faith in God which her mothers kindled before her."[26]

Recently we have had occasion to read the membership list of 102 Jewish congregations, coming from every section of this country, and representing every shade of our ancestral belief. They contained of radical reformers, conservative and ultra orthodox Jews, altogether more than 20,000 names. The lists varied in size and importance, each containing different names. But in one respect they were all alike. No matter where the list came from, no matter how the name sounded,

it was prefaced by the simple *Mr.* Not even the most radical congregation on record put before its members' names *Mr. and Mrs.*____

The fact stares us plainly in the face that in Jewish congregations
married women are still debarred from membership. This ought not
to be. Our girls receive the same religious instructions as our boys,
most of our congregations are governed by laws equally well understood by women and men; and morally and materially supported by
both. Would it therefore not be befitting the spirit of our time, to
record as members of a Jewish congregation Mr. and Mrs. So-and-So?
A great deal could be said on this subject, but we prefer deeds to
words. Which will be the first congregation to combine justice with
dignity? Which will be the first to record our names?

As we saw the boys and girls standing together before the the holy
shrine, and heard their united confession of faith, and noticed how
with equal convictions representatives of both sexes took upon themselves the same obligations, and how the same religious duties were
assigned to the girls as well as to the boys, we ask ourselves: Why, now,
this utter equality, when afterwards their obligations become so different, when the one group grows into the law-giving and the other
only into the law-abiding party? A woman in Israel is as yet not
admitted to congregational meetings, and consequently deprived of
the full rights of membership. Even if a widow owns a pew, and pays
her taxes, she is not allowed to vote. Taxation without representation!
Is there any reason given in our Jewish law and history to justify such
illiberal proceedings? We know of none, and therefore we think a
woman should either be exempt from assessments, or be entitled to
all the privileges a member enjoys in a congregation.

The Reform Jewess ought to feel very grateful that there is no
longer a distinction made between her rank as a child of God and that
of man. That quaint benediction, which the orthodox Jew recites
every morning, thanking God that he was not made a woman, Reform
has put aside, with the women's gallery in the synagogue, as a mere
relic of Orientalism. The Reform Jewess does not *resignedly* thank her
Maker for her lesser importance. At her father's or husband's side she
reads her prayers in the House of God. And why should she not? Nay,
I say more, why should she not enjoy the same right of becoming a
member of the Temple she attends on the Sabbath morn; a member
of the Sabbath-school Board, that often sadly needs her practical
wisdom and active interest. Why is the Jewish woman behind her
Christian sister therein? There is no reason why she should not have
the same opportunities for activity and power in regard to matters
pertaining to religion, that she has in her charitable work. Has not
woman's, Jewish woman's, charity amply justified the freedom of
action she enjoys in that field? The world resounds in praise of all that
Jewish charities have accomplished, are accomplishing. Is the time not
now ripe for the Jewess to labor to re-awaken the spirit of religion?

Let her bestir herself—as she is now doing—so that no matter how much of skepticism and unbelief surrounds her, she can kindle anew that holy light of faith in God which her mothers kindled before her. Association with the world surely cannot have made her entirely lose sight of the mission she is to perform.

Document 3: Rosa Sonneschein

Rosa Sonneschein (born 1847; date of death unknown) founded, published, and edited the American Jewess *magazine in response to the great enthusiasm generated by the Congress of Jewish Women.* American Jewess, *"devoted to social, religious and literary subjects," was the first Jewish women's publication printed in English in the United States. Sonneschein was an early adherent of Theodor Herzl, the founder of modern Zionism. In 1897, at his invitation, she attended the first Zionist Congress in Basle as the representative of the* American Jewess. *Little is known about Sonneschein's life.[27]*

In the following article published in her journal, Rosa Sonneschein considers the opportunities and dangers which Americanization presents to the Jewish religion and to women of her faith.[28]

Thirty years ago the title "American Jewess" would have been a misnomer. Except in a very few isolated cases the mass of Jewesses living in America at that period were by thought, habit, education and inclination still clinging to the customs of the land of their birth. . . .

By force of circumstances the Western Jewess adapted herself, her household and her mode of living much quicker to the ways of the American people than did her Eastern sisters; just as Reform Judaism, although originating in the East, made more rapid strides in the West.

The Influence of Reform

It was then that the reform movement invaded America and religious reformation unfolded its banner. The instillation of individual inquiry began, and each Rabbi became his own and his congregation's law-giver. In the destruction of belief in religious ceremonials, the dietary laws were the first to succumb; with them disappeared other religious ceremonies in the home, of which Jewish women were the sacred keepers and safeguards from time immemorial. The pulpit pointed out to the Jewess' mind as religious contradiction almost everything upon which her mother looked with reverence. But in spite of these teachings the American-born Jewess could not entirely free herself from parental religious influence, and she thus became a sort of link between her progenitor and her progeny—a link between the Ghetto Jewess and the subject of our article—the present liberty-loving American Jewess.

The Jewess of Today

The admirable combination of circumstances, and the irresistible onward march of women has placed the American Jewess on a par with American womanhood. She came out of the conflict between the past and the present untrammeled by religious ceremonies and free from superstition. No intellectual despotism crushes her independent thought. She prefers to be a part and parcel of humanity rather than a chattel of her religion. Nevertheless, she is loyal to her faith and race, and is not favorably disposed to intermarriage. But she has utterly discarded her religious mission in the home. Even the Sabbath has lost much of its sanctity, and the American Jewesses congregate in larger numbers at the matinees than at the temples. No vestige of religious sentiment prevents her from attending Sunday service in the synagogue, and no ideal conception prompts her to go there. The advanced American Jewess can see no harm in the teachings of Moses being expounded on the same day as those of Christ, and whether Mohammed or Luther has said a good thing, she prefers it spoken by a Jewish orator or from the Jewish pulpit.

Communal Activity

The American Jewess is an important element in congregational life. Proportionately speaking, her attendance at the houses of worship is small, but the spacious and luxurious temples would be almost empty without her. She furthers by word and deed the material and spiritual progress of the Synagogue, and is most remarkable for her devotion and ardent labors in the sphere of charity. This is her realm, her scepter and her crown. All her sympathies are with the poor; she excels in benevolence.

I do not mean that she sets an example for broad and noble charity of mind, for in this she is, alas! woefully deficient—far behind the times and the present generation of American women as well. The field of the Jewess is the material. She devotes herself to charity that giveth and lightens the burden of the poor and needy. She throws her whole heart and soul into this work; solicits aid, sews the garments of the poor, arranges balls and bazaars to swell the relief funds, furthers the educational institutions, and has called into existence sisterhoods which are doing an immeasurable amount of good. Annual reports by some of the sisterhoods read as if some good fairy had set to work to lighten the heavy burdens of mankind.

The American Jewess has now her City, State and National Councils, which consist of several thousand Jewesses living in different parts of the Union. Apart from organizing, she has as yet accomplished little or nothing worthy of mention. At its first general session, held in November, 1896, the National Council declared for the reinstallation of the seventh day Sabbath in its "pristine purity," but during the past year not even the first step was officially taken to bring about that result. The local sections are divided into Bible classes, and their main work is in the field of charity. The Council has done good work in bringing into prominence Jewish women who have never before been heard of, either in a literary or social capacity; and yet these women, with the adaptability which characterizes the true American, have readily adjusted themselves to their positions, and from the very start have well represented Jewish American women.

Family Life

The family life of the American Jewess has shaped itself to the general customs of the country. She enjoys to the full all the liberties granted to her Gentile sisters. In her home she may still occupy the place assigned to her by "das Hohelied" as the wise, watchful, tireless ruler of the household, but she is by no means a home-body. She is in universal evidence—in the streets, in the shops, at the restaurants and at the parks.

While she guards her daughters with a watchful eye, they are like other American girls—totally independent of her in social matters. Marriage is the foremost aim of the American Jewess, as it was of her grandmother, but in its accomplishment she is not assisted by "shadchan" or parents; and, indeed it is not uncommon for a Jewish maiden to surprise her parents with the announcement of her engagement. She may love her father and mother as did the Jewesses of bygone ages, but she lacks in reverence. Children regard parents as dear, good friends, but not as authority. This condition, creditable or not, is simply—American.

In the busy world of American womanhood she is as yet a mere cipher. Protected, as she is, by the male members of the family, she does not work unless compelled to do so. She is, however, commencing to show some signs of intellectual activity, and we hear now and then that a Jewess has become a doctor, lawyer, writer, artist or poet. American society has as yet given the Jewess but few opportunities to display her abilities as a leader, if indeed she has any. By an unwritten law she seems debarred from official functions of local, State or national import. Western cities have made a few exceptions in this regard. Perhaps the New York Rabbi is right who, in a recent article, stated that "the Jewess was never meant for a society lady, nor for a devotee of the literary and poetical arts."

To the credit of the American Jewess be it said that she loves her country intensely. Her patriotism is innate and imperishable, and for her country she would sacrifice her gold and her jewels as readily as the ancient Jewess did for her religion.

The moral and civil virtues of the Jewess founded on remote ideal laws will ever remain the same; their influence transcends by far all boundaries of clime and country. Rachel, the mother in Israel, need not weep for her American daughters. Although a new era has dawned with changed conditions, and although she takes part in the joys and sorrows of the nation and is eager to reach the new and the beautiful, she nevertheless remains Jewish in spirit, in feeling, in faith and in conviction.

PRESERVING JEWISH IDENTITY WITHIN AMERICAN CULTURE

Document 4: Emma Lazarus

Emma Lazarus (1849–1887) and her sisters were educated at home in New York City by tutors. Here she prepared her first book, Poems and Translations, *at the age of seventeen. Her first venture away from home was a visit to Concord, Massachusetts, at the invitation of Ralph Waldo Emerson, with whom she had shared poems and correspondence. A tour of the detainment camp for Jewish refugees on Ward's Island began Lazarus' passionate and active interest in the plight of Russian Jews fleeing from the pogroms, and set her on the path toward her later advocacy of the establishment of a Jewish national homeland in Palestine.*[29]

Her views on these subjects were published in the American Hebrew *magazine (November 3, 1882 to February 23, 1883) in a sixteen-part essay, "Epistle to the Hebrews." Her sonnet, "The New Colossus," was selected from among poems submitted by Henry Wadsworth Longfellow, Mark Twain, Bret Harte, and Walt Whitman to be inscribed on the base of the Statue of Liberty.*[30]

1492

Thou two-faced year, Mother of Change and Fate,
Didst weep when Spain cast forth with flaming sword,
The children of the prophets of the Lord,
Prince, priest, and people, spurned by zealot hate.
Hounded from sea to sea, from state to state,
The West refused them, and the East abhorred.
No anchorage the known world could afford,
Close-locked was every port, barred every gate
Then smiling, thou unveil'dst, O two-faced year,
A virgin world where doors of sunset part,
Saying, "Ho, all who weary, enter here!
There falls each ancient barrier that the art
Of race or creed or rank devised, to rear
Grim bulwarked hatred between heart and heart!"

The New Colossus

Not like the brazen giant of Greek fame,
With conquering limbs astride from land to land;
Here at our sea-washed, sunset gates shall stand
A mighty woman with a torch, whose flame
Is the imprisoned lightning, and her name
Mother of Exiles. From her beacon-hand
Glows world-wide welcome; her mild eyes command
The air-bridge harbor that twin cities frame
"Keep, ancient lands, your storied pomp!" cries she
With silent lips. "Give me your tired, your poor,
Your huddled masses yearning to breathe free,
The wretched refuse of your teeming shore.
Send these, the homeless, tempest-tost to me,
I lift my lap beside the golden door!"

Excerpts from "Epistle to the Hebrews"[31]

. . . For the most ardent supporter of the scheme does not urge the advisability of an emigration en masse of the whole Jewish people to any particular spot. There is not the slightest necessity for an American Jew, the free citizen of a republic, to rest his hopes upon the foundation of any other nationality whatsoever, or to decide whether he individually would or would not be in favor of residing in Palestine. All that would be claimed from him would be a patriotic and unselfish interest in the sufferings of his oppressed brethren of less fortunate countries, sufficient to make him promote by every means in his power the establishment of a secure asylum. From those emancipated countries of Europe and America, where the Jew shares all the civil and religious privileges of his compatriots, only a small band of Israelites would be required to sacrifice themselves in order to serve as leaders and counselors. . . .

The fact that the Jews of America are civilly and religiously emancipated, should be, I take it, our strongest impelling motive for working towards the emancipation of our oppressed brethren. No other Jews in the world can bring to bear upon the enterprise such absolute disinterestedness of aim, such long and intimate familiarity with the blessings and delights of liberty. We must help our less fortunate brethren, not with the condescending patronage of the prosperous, who in self-defense undertake to conceal the social sores of the community by providing a remote hiding place for the outcase and the beggar, but with the keen, human sympathy of men and women who endeavor to defend men and women against outrage and oppression, of Jews who feel the sting of every wound and insult inflicted upon their bloodkindred. For ourselves, personally, we have nothing to ask or desire; neither our national nor our domestic happiness is bound up with the existence of any other Government in the world, than that of the United States. But by virtue of our racial and religious connection with these hapless victims of anti-Jewish cruelty, we feel that it devolves upon us to exert our utmost strength towards securing for them permanent protection.

It has become evident to a large majority of Jews that such permanent protection can never be afforded while masses of our people are concentrated in certain districts of Europe amidst hostile, or at least unfriendly, nations: where their free intellectual development is checked by legislative and social disabilities, and where at any moment an outbreak of popular fanaticism or the contagion of illiberal opinions may imperil their very existence. . . .

. . . However degrading or servile might be their avocations during the secular week, the first star of the Sabbath eve restored to them their human dignity, when they met in the Synagogue or around the family board, however humble, to sing, in the midst of bondage and oppression, those Psalms which have been for all ages, the battle cry of freedom, and to cherish the memory of days when they were a nation of princes and priests. The Sabbath was distinguished from the weekday by holiday apparel, by convivial gatherings, by music and gayety; the only limit to these was the equal right of every individual to undisturbed rest from labor. Whoever pauses to consider how large a part of the pleasures of the rich depends upon the ceaseless toil of the poor will see how great a proportion of daily amusement and luxury is cut off by this humane injunction. But such a restriction in modes of enjoyment has nothing in common with the gloomy horrors of the Calvinistic Sunday, or the asceticism, the wearisome solemnity and repeated devotional exercises of the Puritans. Ours is the joyous spirit of the Roman Catholic Sabbath.

Document 5: Anzia Yezierska

"A struggle between a father of the Old World and a daughter of the New" was the subtitle which Anzia Yezierska (1885–1970) gave to her autobiographical novel, Bread Givers. *Her many realistic stories of Jewish immigrant life on New York's Lower East Side emphasize the conflict between traditional Jewish ways and the new freedoms available to women in America. A veteran of the sweatshops, she was discovered by a movie producer and skyrocketed to fame. In the luxurious surroundings of Hollywood, she found herself unable to write and soon gave up the lucrative movie business to return to New York. The following selections are from* Bread Givers.[32]

It was now time for dinner. I was throwing the rags and things from the table to the window, on the bed, over the chairs, or any place where there was room for them. So much junk we had in our house that everybody put everything on the table. It was either to eat on the floor, or for me the job of cleaning off the junk pile three times a day. The school teacher's rule, "A place for everything, and everything in its place," was no good for us, because there weren't enough places.

As the kitchen was packed with furniture, so the front room was packed with Father's books. They were on the shelf, on the table, on the window sill, and in soapboxes lined up against the wall.

When we came to America, instead of taking along feather beds, and the samovar, and the brass pots and pans, like other people, Father made us carry his books. When Mother begged only to take along her pot for gefulte fish, and the two feather beds that were handed down to her from her grandmother for her wedding presents, Father wouldn't let her.

"Woman!" Father said, laughing into her eyes. "What for will you need old feather beds? Don't you know it's always summer in America? And in the new golden country, where milk and honey flows free in the streets, you'll have new golden dishes to cook in, and not weigh yourself down with your old pots and pans. But my books, my holy books always were, and always will be, the light of the world. You'll see yet how all America will come to my feet to learn."

No one was allowed to put their things in Father's room, any more than they were allowed to use Mashah's hanger.

Of course, we all knew that if God had given Mother a son, Father would have permitted a man child to share with him his best room in the house. A boy could say prayers after his father's death—that kept the father's soul alive for ever. Always Father was throwing up to Mother that she had borne him no son to be an honour to his days and to say prayers for him when he died.

The prayers of his daughters didn't count because God didn't listen to women. Heaven and the next world were only for men. Women could get into Heaven because they were wives and daughters of men. Women had no brains for the study of God's Torah, but they could be the servants of men who studied the Torah. Only if they cooked for the men, and washed for the men, and didn't nag or curse the men out of their homes; only if they let the men study the Torah in peace, then, maybe, they could push themselves into Heaven with the men, to wait on them there.

And so, since men were the only people who counted with God, Father not only had the best room for himself, for his study and prayers, but also the best eating of the house. The fat from the soup and the top from the milk went always to him.

Mother had just put the soup pot and plates for dinner on the table, when Father came in.

At the first look on Mother's face he saw how she was boiling, ready to burst, so instead of waiting for her to begin her hollering, he started:

"Woman! when will you stop darkening the house with your worries?"

"When I'll have a man who does the worrying. Does it ever enter your head that the rent was not paid the second month? That to-day we're eating the last loaf of bread that the grocer trusted me?" Mother tried to squeeze the hard, stale loaf that nobody would buy for cash. "You're so busy working for Heaven that I have to suffer here such bitter hell."

We sat down to the table. With watering mouths and glistening eyes we watched Mother skimming off every bit of fat from the top soup into Father's big plate, leaving for us only the thin, watery part. We watched Father bite into the sour pickle which was special for him only; and waited, trembling with hunger, for our portion.

Father made his prayer, thanking God for the food. Then he said to Mother:

"What is there to worry about, as long as we have enough to keep the breath in our bodies? But the real food is God's Holy Torah." He shook her gently by the shoulder, and smiled down at her.

At Father's touch Mother's sad face turned into smiles. His kind look was like the sun shining on her.

"Shenah!" he called her by her first name to show her he was feeling good. "I'll tell you a story that will cure you of all your worldly cares."

All faces turned to Father. Eyes widened, necks stretched, ears strained not to miss a word. The meal was forgotten as he began:

"Rabbi Chanina Ben Dosa was a starving, poor man who had to live on next to nothing. Once, his wife complained: 'We're so good, so pious, you give up nights and days in the study of the Holy Torah. Then why don't God provide for you at least enough to eat.' ..." Riches you want?' said Rabbi Chanina Ben Dosa. 'All right, woman. You shall have your wish.' ... That very evening he went out into the fields to pray. Soon the heavens opened, and a Hand reached down to him and gave him a big chunk of gold. He brought it to his wife, and said: 'Go buy with this all the luxuries of the earth.' ... She was so happy, as she began planning all she would buy next day. Then she fell asleep. And in her dream, she saw herself and her husband sitting with all the saints in Heaven. Each couple had a golden table between themselves. When the Good Angel put down for them their wine, their table shook so that half of it spilled. Then she noticed that their table had a leg missing, and that is why it was so shaky. And the Good Angel explained to her that the chunk of gold that her husband had given her the night before was the missing leg of their table. As soon as she woke up, she begged her husband to pray to God to take back the gold he had given them. . . . 'I'll be happy and thankful to live in poverty, as long as I know that our reward will be complete in Heaven.'"

Mother licked up Father's every little word, like honey. Her eyes followed his shining eyes as he talked.

"*Nu, Shenah?*" He wagged his head. "Do you want gold on earth, or wine in Heaven?"

"I'm only a sinful woman," Mother breathed, gazing up at him. Her fingers stole a touch of his hand, as if he were the king of the world. "God be praised for the little we have. I'm willing to give up all my earthly needs for the wine of Heaven with you. But, Moisheh," —she nudged him by the sleeve—"God gave us children. They have a life to live yet, here, on earth. Girls have to get married. People point their fingers on me—a daughter, twenty-five years already, and not married yet. And no dowry to help her get married."

"Woman! Stay in your place!" His strong hand pushed her away from him. "You're smart enough to bargain with the fish-peddler. But I'm the head of this family. I give my daughters brains enough to marry when their time comes, without the worries of a dowry."

"*Nu*, you're the head of the family." Mother's voice rose in anger. "But what will you do if your books are thrown in the street?"

At the mention of his books, Father looked up quickly.

"What do you want me to do?"

"Take your things out from the front room to the kitchen, so I could rent your room to boarders. If we don't pay up the rent very soon, we'll all be in the street."

"I have to have a room for my books. Where will I put them?"

"I'll push my things out from under the bed. And you can pile up your books in the window to the top, because nothing but darkness comes through that window, anyway. I'll do anything, work the nails off my fingers, only to be free from the worry for rent."

.   .   .   .   .

"Women! Have your way. Take in your boarders, only to have peace in the house."

The next day, Mother and I moved Father's table and his chair with a back, and a cushion to sit on, into the kitchen.

We scrubbed the front room as for a holiday. Even the windows were washed. We pasted down the floppy wall paper, and on the worst part of the wall, where the plaster was cracked and full of holes, we hung up calendars and pictures from the Sunday newspapers.

.   .   .   .   .

"Ach!" sighed Mother, looking about the furnished room complete, "God should only send a man for Bessie, to marry herself in good luck."

"Here's your chance to get a man for her without the worry for a dowry. If God is good, he might yet send you a rich boarder—"

From the kitchen came Father's voice chanting:

"When the poor seek water, and there is none, and their tongue faileth for thirst, I, the Lord, will hear them. I, the God of Israel, will not forsake them."

. . . Silent, breathless, we peeked in through the open crack in the door. The black satin skullcap tipped on the side of his head set off his red hair and his long red beard. And his ragged satin coat from Europe made him look as if he just stepped out of the Bible. His eyes were raised to God. His two white hands on either side of the book, his whole body swaying with his song:

"And I will bring the blind by a way that they know not; I will lead them in paths that they have not known; I will make darkness light before them, and crooked things straight. These things will I do unto them and not forsake them."

Mother's face lost all earthly worries. Forgotten were beds, mattresses, boarders, and dowries. Father's holiness filled her eyes with light.

"Is there any music on earth like this?" Mother whispered to Muhmenkeh.

"Who would ever dream that in America, where everything is only business and business, in such a lost corner as Hester Street lives such a fine, such a pure, silken soul as Reb Smolinsky?"

"If he was only so fit for this world, like he is fit for Heaven, then I wouldn't have to dry out the marrow from my head worrying for the rent."

Suddenly, it grew dark before our eyes. The collector lady from the landlord! We did not hear her till she banged open the door. Her hard eyes glared at Father.

"My rent!" she cried, waving her thick diamond fingers before Father's face. But he didn't see her or hear her. He went on chanting:

"Schnorrer!" shrieked the landlady, her fat face red with rage. "My rent!"

Father blinked his eyes and stared at the woman with a far-off look. "What is it? What do you want?"

"Don't you know me? Haven't I come often enough? My rent! My rent! My rent I want!"

"Oh-h, your rent?" Father met her angry glare with an innocent smile of surprise. "Your rent? As soon as the girls get work, we'll pay you out, little by little."

"Pay me out, little by little! The cheek of those dirty immigrants! A fool I was, giving them a chance another month."

"But we haven't the money." His voice was kind and gentle, as hers was rough and loud.

"Why haven't you the money for rent?" she shouted.

"The girls have been out of work." Father's innocent look was not of this earth.

"Hear him only! The dirty do-nothing! Go to work yourself! Stop singing prayers. Then you'll have money for rent!" She took one step towards him and shut his book with such anger that it fell at her feet.

Little red threads burned out of Father's eyes. He rose slowly, but quicker than lightening flashed his hand.

A scream broke through the air. Before we had breath enough to stop him, Father slapped the landlady on one cheek, then on the other, till the blood rushed from her nose.

"You painted piece of flesh!" cried Father. "I'll teach you respect for the Holy Torah!"

Screaming, the landlady rushed out, her face dripping blood as she ran. Before we knew what or where, she came back with two policemen. In front of our dumb eyes we saw Father handcuffed, like a thief, and taken away to the station house.

Document 6: Lucy Robins Lang

Lucy Robins Lang (1887–?) was born in Kiev and immigrated to the United States with her family at a young age. As the eldest child, she was immediately set to work in a cigar factory, where she was introduced to anarchism and political activism. She devoted the rest of her life to the labor movement. This scene from her autobiography, Tomorrow Is Beautiful, *shows the sharp conflict between immigrant culture and American culture that was a common experience among Jewish women.* [33]

Romance as well as politics played a part in the life of the cigar factory. My cousin Abe, a son of Aunt Yente Chave, worked at the same table as gracious, attractive Jenny. Soon he announced that he had chosen a bride and wished to bring her to his home to receive his mother's blessing. Of course Aunt Yente Chave would not consent. She was shocked that a son of hers should even propose such indecent behavior. Summoning the clan, she expressed her indignation. To Abe she said: "You are not to have anything more to do with this Jenny. You will marry the girl that I choose, a girl with a good dowry." To the members of the clan it was inconceivable that Abe should oppose the will of the matriarch. Why, he would be banished from the family, from Chicago, from the world! And Abe could only see things as the clan saw them. Although he continued to adore Jenny, he never again spoke of her at home, and in the end he married the girl Aunt Yente Chave selected.

I had been enchanted by the romance between Abe and Jenny, and I was filled with righteous indignation against Aunt Yente Chave. I called her an old tyrant, and denounced her on every possible occasion. When she heard of this, she said that I, "big as a pea and old as a drop of dew," had better stop meddling in her affairs or she would take me in hand.

She was as good as her word. Her opportunity came just before Christmas. I passed night-school examinations with honors, and the teacher, praising me before the class, presented me with a book. Of course Father and Mother boasted of my triumph, and Aunt Yente Chave heard of it. She shook her head. My teacher was a man? A goi? She shook her head again. Obviously his intentions were dishonorable. But I was only twelve. So much the worse. She convoked a family council, and solemnly asked what should be done. Her husband, her sons and daughters, their wives and husbands, and a host of more distant relatives, all trained to obey her every word, were properly horrified. They surrounded my parents as if some unspeakable calamity had befallen them, and I almost became convinced that I really had committed some terrible sin. My mother and father had no choice but to agree; I must drop out of night school.

What was even worse, I was forbidden to go to Hull House. I had recently been asked by motherly Jane Addams to assist a girls' dancing class, and this little recognition filled me with joy. Aunt Yente Chave wanted to know what I did at Hull House, and when she heard that I was connected with a dance group, she cocked her head and put on an expression of deep significance, as she always did when she was investigating sins. "So that's it!" she said. "No good will come of her!"

Seething with rage, I ran to tell Jane Addams. After listening patiently to my story, she agreed to talk with Aunt Yente Chave. When these two met, the contrast was magnificent. They were both strong-willed women, but their backgrounds were utterly different. Behind Aunt Yente Chave were generations of men and women who had suffered every kind of hardship and persecution in order to live in the way they believed to be right. To her, the least deviation from the established code threatened the whole structure. Jane Addams, on the other hand, the product of generations of freedom and security, believed that standards of conduct could and should be based on reason.

Aunt Yente Chave, wearing a black peruke that formed bangs over her high forehead, was not in the least humble or apologetic when she confronted the founder of Hull House. Nor was Miss Addams in any way critical or condescending. She knew the strength and validity of the way of life Aunt Yente Chave represented, and she did not seek to destroy it, but she also knew that the younger generation in America had to adapt itself to new ways of living, and she was trying to aid in the adjustment.

Hardly speaking the English language, the matriarch from the Russian Pale understood the lady from Cedarville, Illinois, and made herself understood. "Traditions of the home," said Aunt Yente Chave, "and commands of the parents must be the basis of training the young."

"The young must be free to experiment," Miss Addams replied. "They must learn to understand the meaning of right and wrong. Life should be interesting and joyful for them."

"Ah," said the matriarch, "we have joy in our homes. We have our celebrations, our weddings. And we know the needs of girls. First, they need loving, watchful parents. Then early marriage and a happy home of their own. I have daughters, so I know this."

"I cannot speak from experience," Miss Addams interrupted. "I have no daughter."

"Only boys?"

"No children at all."

"God have mercy."

"I have never married."

"So you don't know nothing at all."

It was funny, and yet it was sad. Poor Aunt Yente Chave knew how easily a family could be destroyed, its members set to wandering along the highways and byways of exile, never safe from persecution, never secure. What greater opportunity could America offer her than the chance to build an abiding home for her tribe for generations to come? How could she tolerate the least weakening of her power, which was the essential instrument of the only kind of survival she could understand.

Jane Addams could not budge Aunt Yente Chave, but she convinced my parents, and I was grudgingly permitted to return to Hull House. But by now my eyes were dazzled by a brighter vision of freedom, and my feet were set on paths of which Jane Addams might not have approved.

THE WOMAN'S RESPONSIBILITY IN MAINTAINING JUDAISM

Document 7: Ray Frank Litman

Ray Frank Litman (1864–1948) was born to orthodox parents in San Francisco. Because of her great learning and her devotion to Judaism, she often acted as temporary rabbi for western Jewish communities that had no ordained rabbis. The establishment of the first congregation in several West Coast towns resulted from her preaching. She later traveled to the Hebrew Union College in Cincinnati to continue her education, and then to the Congress of Jewish Women in Chicago, where she presented the following paper on "Women in the Synagogue." A Reform rabbi in Chicago wanted to start a new congregation with Frank as its spiritual leader. As on other occasions, she refused the title of rabbi and permanent affiliation with any congregation because she felt that to accept such a title or position would limit her freedom to serve her faith.[34]

Woman in the Synagogue
September 5, 1893, 9:30 A.M.

Duality manifests itself in all things, but in nothing is this two-foldness more plainly seen than in woman's nature.

The weaker sex physically, it is the stronger spiritually, it having been said that religion were impossible without woman. And yet the freedom of the human soul has been apparently effected by man. I say apparently effected, for experience has demonstrated, and history records, that one element possessed by woman has made her the great moral, the great motive force of the world, though she be, as all great forces are, a silent force.

It may be true that sin came into the world because of the disobedience of the first woman, but woman has long since atoned for it by her loving faith, her blind trust in the Unknown. Down through the ages, traditional and historical, she has come to us the symbol of faith and freedom, of loyalty and love.

From the beginning, she sought knowledge; perceive, it does not say wisdom, but knowledge; and this was at the expense of an Eden. She lost Eden, but she gained that wisdom which has made sure of man's immortality.

... [W]hen the Lord said to Moses, "And ye shall be unto Me a nation of priests and a holy nation," the message was not to one sex; and that the Israelites did not so consider it, is proved by the number of women who were acknowledged prophets, and who exercised great influence on their time and on posterity.

The Talmud speaks of seven prophetesses: Sarah, Miriam, Deborah, Hannah, Abigail, Huldah and Esther. Ruth not being mentioned in this list, we infer that she was regarded simply as a religious teacher. Except in the Talmud, Sarah is not mentioned as possessing the inspirational power, which made the prophets of old; yet, there is that chronicled of her which gives rise to the assumption that, for a time at least, she was the greatest of them all. For in Genesis 21:12 is recorded the only instance of the Lord's especially commanding one of His favorites to listen carefully to a woman: "In all that Sarah may say unto thee, hearken unto her voice."

Evidently, the Almighty deemed a woman capable both of understanding and advising.

That Miriam, the sister of Moses, was a woman of extraordinary mind is evidenced by the words of Moses to herself and Aaron when he journeyed to the mount; and from the prominence given the word prophetess prior to recording the words of her triumphant song, it is evident that she must have been one of the leaders in Israel before the journey across the sea was made. ...

The life of Hannah inculcates more deeply a lesson which we women must learn than that of any of our sex mentioned in the Bible.

Greatest and best among women is she who is a wise mother; for the children are the Lord's, the heirs of Heaven. Blessed beyond all is she who dedicates her offspring to the Eternal. Who need wonder at the song which rose so joyously from the heart of Hannah, for she was truly an inspired prophetess, she was a wise mother!

Abigail, Huldah and Esther are the others mentioned in the Talmud. ... [T]he narratives serve to show that weak woman was regarded as capable of performing for God and country heroic deeds, deeds from which strong men might have shrunk. Her faith under the most trying circumstances was sublime; and nothing more effective is recorded of piety embracing death than the martyrdom of the Maccabean Hannah or Miriam, who unhesitatingly gave to immortality herself and her seven sons.

Among the women of early mediaeval times, Ima Shalom, Rachel and Beruria are representative. The father of Ima was president of the Sanhedrin, and a descendant of Hillel. Her husband, the most noted rabbi of his day, found in her an intellectual equal, and many were the knotty questions submitted to her judgment. Had it not been for the self-sacrificing and deeply religious nature of Rachel Sabua, history would scarcely have had an Akiba, while Beruria, wife of Rabbi Meir, who lived about 100 A.D., was of such powerful intellect that she became noted throughout the land. All that she said concerning disputed points of the Halacha received the attention of her contemporaries. Poetry and prose testify to her worth.

During the Graeco-Roman period, two queens stand out as prominently influencing religious matters. Queen Salome, who was born in Jerusalem about the year 143 B.C., was of great wisdom and remarkable energy. Filled with the spirit of the Chasidim, with ideals pure and lofty, she early resolved to aid the faith in which she believed. The times were among the fiercest recorded by Israel, and great diplomacy was necessary to avoid dissensions. But through disasters of every nature, she remained constant to her principles, and at all times level-headed. Her tact and her power to remain impassive under the most awful circumstances are almost unparalleled in history. Her sole ambition was to preserve to the people their Pharisaic worship, and this she did by the most heroic teachings.

Among proselytes, Helena, Queen of Adiabene, born 152 years B.C., is mentioned in the Talmud as having done much for Judaism. She and her son were both converted to this faith, and in turn became teachers of religion, remaining true to the Jewish nation to the end.

The position of the mediaeval woman differed from that of her ancient sister. Forced by circumstances at times to become a leader, her personality no longer merged itself in that of her husband, but ran parallel with his. ... The princes of Judah were dethroned, their lands, the possession of strangers; yet the law lived, better understood and more sacredly guarded than ever. That this was owing, in the greatest degree, to the women is shown by the numbers mentioned in the Talmud as learned mothers and teachers. The Jews were stripped of many precious things by their oppressors, ofttimes their relentless persecutors, yet the Torah held such consolations that the family-home became to the Jew the most beautiful, the most sacred thing in the world.

From the book of the memorial of the dead of the Jewish congregation at Worms, I have taken the following names, they serving to show what the women of Israel at this time did for religion. Here is an epitaph: "Eva, daughter of Isaac Leipnitz, wife of Abraham Samuel, Rabbi of Worms. Her name shall be remembered because she was profoundly learned, and because she was conversant in the Bible and all its commentaries and the Midrash. There was no woman before her so deeply learned." "Remembered, the aged Rebecca, daughter of Jeremiah Neustadt, because she regularly attended synagogue, morning and evening, devoting all her life to benevolence. She spun without charge Tzitzith for all who needed them, and gave of her own money to the synagogue." "Remembered, the pious and esteemed Miriam Sinzheim, daughter of Joseph Sinzheim of Vienna, who went regularly to the synagogue, morning and evening, praying with devotion and giving all her life to benevolence. She supported students of the Bible in various congregations, especially in ours of Worms. She built the synagogue of the great Rabbi Rashi (Solomon ben Isaac), establishing free seminaries and stipending students." Women of the nineteenth century! These are but a few names from among the many on the old grave stones, testifying to the splendid work done for the synagogue by women, at a time when obstacles made up their lives. In the early part of the eighteenth century, Krendel Steinhardt, a member of a gifted family of rabbis, obtained distinction for her knowledge of the festival prayers, the Machsor, and for cleverly interpreting the Midrash. She was known as the "Rebbezin." Sarah Oppenheimer, daughter of the chief rabbi of Prague, wrote a Meghilla, a scroll of the book of Esther, while Sprenza Kempler, blessed with beauty, knowledge and piety, could quote the Mishna from memory. Bienvineda, wife of Rabbi Mordecai, of Padua, was of such rare intelligence that she held disputations on the Talmud and the Mishna with some of the greatest scholars of her day.

The list is a long one, and each name reflects intelligence and piety. But enough has been given to disprove all doubts as to the Jewish woman's capability in religious matters, both as pupil and instructor. If to the men of these times be accorded credit for having performed their duties well, if as scholars, as expounders of the Law, they live in fame, what shall we say of the women who, under the most adverse circumstances, rose to eminence in this same field of labor?

With one or two exceptions, they were all wives and mothers, most of them wives of rabbis, and in the discharge of their duties no one thing was done at the expense of another.

Intellectually they were the compeers of their husbands; practically, they excelled them. They built synagogues, controlled colleges, and stipended students. All in all, they have in the past earned the right to the pulpit, even as nature created their sensitive beings to act as its finest interpreter.

Jewish woman had earned the right to the pulpit, though she never formally asked it of the people, but that they would not have wholly opposed it, may be inferred from a romance of Bernstein's, "Voegele, der Maggid," probably founded on facts.

Voegele was an itinerant preacher, and that she combined the lovable qualities of the woman with her chosen work is shown by the fervent words of the hero who says to her, "Your hand makes the *Bethhamedrash* light." To our times and to our country in particular, the Jewish woman is indebted for many changes in her relation to the synagogue, and this progress is mainly due to one man, whose decided stand as a liberalist, in all matters concerning woman and her work, earns our hearty thanks. I refer to our revered rabbi, Dr. Wise, of Cincinnati.

With added privileges and numberless innovations, let us see what is the religious status of the Jewish woman of to-day.

Centuries have passed; the wilderness is the pride of the world, for it is all a land of freedom, of homes; and the Jew, we find him so grateful that he has well-nigh forgotten to what he owes his salvation. He has forgotten, else how explain the empty temples, the lack of religious enthusiasm, lack of reverence of children for parents, lack of that sacred home life which has made us an honored place in history? That our women have not made of themselves Dinah Morrises and "Voegele der Maggids" we can forgive, but that we have removed so many of the ancient landmarks which our fathers established, can we forgive ourselves for that?

That we have not possessed ourselves of the wisdom of her who builded her own house can hardly be pardoned us, for what can replace the priceless love which has bound the members of the Jewish family to each other and to their God? Learning is not wisdom. Innovation is not progress, and to be identical with man is not the ideal of womanhood. Some things and privileges belong to him by nature; to these, true woman does not aspire; but every woman should aspire to make of her home a temple, of herself a high priestess, of her children disciples, then will she best occupy the pulpit, and her work run parallel with man's. She may be ordained rabbi or be the president of a congregation—she is entirely able to fill both offices —but her noblest work will be at home, her highest ideal, a home.

Where are the wise mothers of Israel to-day? As we sow, so we must reap. Costly temples with excuses for congregations will not do, friends. Better the old tent for a dwelling, the trees and skies for synagogues, and reverent, God-fearing men and women, than our present poor apology for religious worship.

That we are now in the position of backsliders is owing to us women.

Where are the Hannahs who cry as she of old, "For this lad did I pray; and the Lord hath granted me my petition which I asked of Him. Therefore also have I lent Him for my part to the Lord; all the days that have been assigned to him shall he be lent to the Lord."

Sisters, our work in and for the synagogue lies in bringing to the Temple the Samuels to fulfil the Law. As mothers in Israel I appeal to you to first make of our homes temples, to rear each child a priest by teaching him to be true to himself.

If the synagogues are then deserted, let it be because the homes are filled, then we will be a nation of priests; edifices of worship will be everywhere. What matter whether we women are ordained rabbis or not? We are capable of fulfilling the office, and the best way to prove it is to convert ourselves and our families into reverent beings. To simply be ordained priest is not enough, and the awful punishment which befell Eli is the best illustration of this. Nothing can replace the duty of the mother in the home. *Nothing can replace the reverence of children, and the children are yours to do as ye will with them.*

Mothers, ye can restore Israel's glory, can fulfil the prophecy by bringing the man-child, strong love of the Eternal, to his Maker.

Letter of Farewell and Appreciation
From Congregation Emanu-el, Victoria, B.C.

October 5, 1895

Dear Miss Frank,

We feel that we should not allow this opportunity to slip by, knowing that you are soon to leave Victoria, without attempting to express our admiration for your masterly eloquence and learning, and our thanks for your efforts on our behalf.

We had heard of your zeal for Judaism, of your ability to gain the ears and reach the hearts of your audience, but we could not thoroughly value the influence for good which you possess and exercise to so remarkable a degree.

The great and holy work which you have undertaken with its many difficulties, deserves the support of every Israelite.

The lessons you articulate, that Israel should eradicate dissension from its midsts, and become sensible of its duties as Jews and citizens, so that they may really become examples of Godliness to the rest of the world are precepts,—if taken to heart—calculated to make them proof against the false charges of their enemies.

May the Eternal strengthen you to perform your mission unto Israel! May He establish the work of your hands; and may you be permitted to lay the foundation of a structure imperishable in its parts to the ravages of Time,—an ornament to the Builder,—dedicated to the Most High—the God of Israel! Amen.

Dear Miss Frank:

We say Farewell—if sadly—still buoyed by the strong hope that we may meet again and that we shall have profited by your friendly counsel and solitude, as a community generally.

On behalf of the Congregation

Yours very sincerely

Jacob Isaacs, *President*
Eli Frank, *Vice President*
Gns. Leiser, *Treasurer*
F. Landsbury, *Secretary*

Document 8: Hannah Greenebaum Solomon

In 1890, Hannah Solomon (1858–1942) was asked to organize a nationwide Congress of Jewish Women for the World Parliament of Religions at the World's Columbian Exhibition in Chicago. Through her efforts she brought together leading women from Jewish communities across the nation. At her urging, the congress resolved itself into a permanent organization, the National Council of Jewish Women. The council, with Solomon as its president, became the first national Jewish women's organization in the United States.[35]
The first of the following three excerpts is from The Fabric of My Life: The Autobiography of Hannah G. Solomon. *The second and third are from* A Sheaf of Leaves, *which was printed privately in Chicago in 1911.[36]*

It was 1893 . . . a year when a world's fair was to commemorate the four-hundredth anniversary of the discovery of America, and though many rival cities sought the privilege of being named the Fair site, it was Chicago to which the United States government granted the honor. . . .

I was honored, by those who were planning the women's congresses by being made representative of the Jewish women, and was further authorized to call Jewish women together under whatever division or divisions I thought best. Since I believed then, as I do now, that when we use the word "Jewish" it must have a purely religious connotation, I felt that our place should be with the Parliament of Religions which was to be one of the great features of World's Fair year. A women's board was organized to aid in furthering the Parliament, and I was made chairman for Jewish women's participation.

Today, with our ready telephonic communication, with radio messages flashing across the continent in the twinkling of an eye; when airplane travel permits one to lunch in Chicago and dine in New York; when every organization publishes printed membership lists of easy accessibility, the task confronting me in the early nineties seems, perhaps, a fairly simple one. To me, in 1891, it appeared colossal—and with reason! Somehow, some way, I must gather together America's outstanding Jewish women.

But how could I go about it; how reach the right women? Not only were there no organization lists available ... there was not even a federal organization! The problem of establishing contacts was a poser that gave me the utmost concern. After much thought, however, I determined to write a personal letter to leading rabbis of the larger cities and communities, requesting them to send me the names of the women in their congregations whom they felt would have the most to offer to such a Parliament, in the way of ability, interest and leadership. First, of course, it was necessary to secure the names of these rabbis—a process entailing much time and energy. Then, when I received a response from each of these spiritual leaders, all of whom proved most genuinely interested and cooperative, I wrote ninety letters (all by hand, and each one personal) to the women whose names had been suggested. I began to work toward this end in 1891, and it was almost a year later—a year of planning, conferring and incessant letter-writing—before I was satisfied that we could, indeed, present a Jewish Women's Congress worthy of the stirring Parliament of Religions. The gratifying results and the enthusiasm evidenced at the end of this year's work more than compensated, however, for any effort expended. . . .

How gratifying the day when I could report definite progress and request two places for Jewish women on the general Parliament program. We had selected two remarkable speakers: Henrietta Szold, then secretary of the Jewish Publication Society, who chose as her topic, "What Judaism Has Done for Women," and Josephine Lazarus, a brilliant thinker who wielded a powerful pen, and who elected to discuss "The Outlook for Judaism." Both papers proved scholarly and paved the way for Jewish women, magnificently opening up for them many opportunities to speak on Judaism before women of other faiths.

When the Jewish men of Chicago gathered to make plans for their congress, I was invited to attend the meeting. After some preliminary business, the chairman turned to me, asking, "Mrs. Solomon, will you Jewish women cooperate with us in our sessions?"

"Well," I replied, "our plans are already far advanced, and assignments have been given our representatives in the general Parliament.

We will, however, be very glad to join with you if you will accord us active participation in your program."

The program committee then retired to deliberate, and when they returned, lo and behold! not a single woman's name appeared in their recommendations!

"Mr. Chairman," I inquired, "just where on your program are the women to be placed?"

"Well," hemmed and hawed the chairman, "the program seems complete just as it stands."

"Very well," I replied, "under these circumstances we do not care to cooperate with you, and I request that the fact of our presence at this meeting be expunged from the records."

Does it seem that I spoke hastily in saying, before, that this year of 1893 marked the beginning of women's collaboration with men? Though it is obvious that every forward step met some such stubborn resistance, we really dare not be too critical of these Jewish men, since their attitude was the accepted one of that day. After our Women's Congress proved to be something of a triumph, however, a number of them condescended to acknowledge that we knew better than they the achievements of which Jewish women were capable. . . .

Council of Jewish Women: Its Work and Possibilities
Sinai Temple, February 14, 1897

. . . The position of woman today might have been foretold at the beginning, when, instead of creating her out of dust, the Lord waited until he could build her out of a strong, healthy, germ-proof bone. I would not say that the woman who places herself before the public in any way escapes criticism; yet it is not the persecution our pioneers received, and while it may sting, it is only for a moment. We are prepared to have those dear, good homemakers—the bachelors— mourn over our neglected children, and wonder how our husbands manage without us. But she who now enters any field finds many outstretched hands to lighten the way which once was thorny, friendless, cheerless. One word of encouragement to a strong heart is so powerful an elixir that it counteracts thousands of unkind ones. . . .

We cannot ignore the fact that the generation preceding ours observed so many forms and ceremonies that Judaism was ever present. We are removed but one generation from those who in love, reverence, and fear obeyed every injunction. We can all remember when no Jews would have opened the doors of their business houses from sunset to sunset upon holy days. To many of our own generation the ceremonial and the holiday have lost their appeal, and their hearts must be touched through the intellectual. We are in our day confronted by a question that has over and over troubled Israel: Is Judaism worth saving? To some this question seems heresy. The daughters of Moses Mendelssohn and their friends solved it for themselves, deserting in the time when Israel was emerging from its gloom into the glorious day of religious liberty. From many the religious spirit is departing altogether. The world is asking: Is any religion worth saving? . . .

Women cling to old customs, and love their traditions, and often compel conservatism where radical thought would prevail. That this movement was undertaken by women was therefore natural. That we would have many critics was to be expected. Nothing is more deplorable than the attitude of the rabbis and the Jewish journals toward each other. How should we expect to escape where none, however excellent, are spared? We are criticised for the subjects we attempt to study, or to write upon. In order to stimulate thought and encourage individual effort, we write papers—some of us very bad ones, others very good. But there are worse ways of passing one's leisure moments. It cannot be proven that the sick children are always the unfortunate ones of mothers who write papers. As long as they are not compelled to listen to them, the children are comparatively safe.

Our Problems
Omaha, October, 1898

. . . During the past year the council in its cities had seventy-five study circles varying in membership from five to two hundred, besides many lectures. The classes are led in many cases by rabbis; the interest is growing and we look forward enthusiastically to the coming winter's work. We have established nine mission schools, reaching several thousand children who are being instructed in our religion and ethics, and it is needless to say that their ranks are entirely made up of Jewish children. Many women have been placed upon the school boards of Sabbath-schools through our efforts, and many Sabbath-schools have been established by our members in cities where no synagogues exist. In our philanthropic department but few difficulties have presented themselves. One and all of our sections eagerly discuss philanthropic subjects and without exception they have adopted the newest methods of work. Not a single almsgiving society exists. Our philanthropies take the form of industrial schools—sewing, manual training, kindergarten, crèche, summer outing and personal service. In addition several thousand dollars were raised for the army and navy. If the deed is the supreme test of religion, then does our faith, as exemplified in this branch of our work, reach the highest ideal.

The Struggle for the Right to Preach

BARBARA BROWN ZIKMUND*

As women's lives expanded throughout the nineteenth century there was a growing concern that Christian women ought to have all of the rights and privileges of male leaders in the churches. Whereas some people continued to insist that "woman's work" would always be different from that of man's, increasingly Christians debated: what is the proper role of woman in the church? Can she sing, teach, pray, or preach? What is expressly prohibited and why? Various denominational groups struggled with these questions for different reasons and in different ways, but by the end of the nineteenth century, almost all major Protestant denominations had considered the issue of "preaching women" in some form.

In order to understand the complicated debate that developed over the struggle of women for the right to preach, it is helpful to divide the arguments into two groups. On one side, there were those Christians who responded to pressures for change and felt a personal call to significant new forms and styles of ministry. Women in denominations with free church polity and members of groups upholding the power of the Holy Spirit tended to argue for increased female leadership. On the other side were those persons wishing to preserve the authority of Scripture and to uphold proper order in the church. This conservative position sought to justify historical leadership patterns and maintain the status quo.

There is no simple way to document chronologically the struggle for the right to preach, because various Christian groups resolved this issue at quite different times. The Quakers, Universalists, Unitarians, and Congregationalists resolved it earlier than most Methodists, Presbyterians, Lutherans, and Episcopalians. Part of this discrepancy had to do with

*BARBARA BROWN ZIKMUND is Academic Dean and Associate Professor of Church History at Pacific School of Religion in Berkeley, California. She holds a Ph.D. from Duke University and is an ordained minister in the United Church of Christ. Her research interests include the history of women in the United Church of Christ and patterns of lay and ordained leadership in American church life.

church polity and part of it related to the connection between preaching and priestly functions in ordained ministry. It is possible, however, thematically to isolate and analyze the various positions taken in nineteenth century literature concerning women and the preaching ministry.

During the first third of the century, women were part of an expanding religious landscape deeply influenced by revivalism. Women participated actively in religious meetings, and it was not long before questions of female propriety arose. In the 1830s several church bodies were led to issue "pastoral letters" concerning "the mistaken conduct of those who encourage females to bear an obtrusive and ostentatious part in measures of reform, and countenance any of that sex who so far forget themselves as to itinerate in the character of public lecturers and teachers."[1] It was quite acceptable for pious women to meet by themselves. But the prohibitions of the apostle Paul had to be followed: "To teach and exhort, or to lead in prayer, in public and promiscuous assemblies, is clearly forbidden to women in the Holy Oracles."[2]

The issue was drawn. For the rest of the nineteenth century, two groups of arguments emerged to defend or to reject a woman's right to preach the Gospel.

THE ARGUMENT FOR PREACHING WOMEN

The most pervasive and simplest argument was offered by committed Christian women who claimed that they had received a call from the Lord to preach the Gospel. The right of women to preach was grounded in the work of the Holy Spirit.

Nineteenth century literature resounded with the testimonies of women who had a conviction that God had called them to serve the church in new ways. It was clear that the great temperance leader Francis Willard believed that she had once been called by God to the ordained ministry, but she had been too timid to go without a corresponding call from the Methodist Church. She wrote later in life to encourage "younger women who feel a call, as I once did, to preach the unsearchable riches of Christ." She beseeched "all Christian people, who grieve over the world's great heartache, to encourage every true and capable woman, whose heart God has touched, in her wistful purpose of entering upon that blessed Gospel ministry."[3] (Document 1.)

Women found it difficult to trust their call from the Lord and were ready to discount its power. The great black preacher Jarena Lee remembered how she told the Reverend Richard Allen that she felt it was her duty to preach the Gospel and how he told her that the discipline "did not call for women preachers." She was at first relieved, "because it removed the fear of the cross—but no sooner did this feeling cross my mind, than I found that a love of souls had in a measure departed from me; that holy energy which burned within me, as a fire, began to be smothered." It might appear unseemly for a woman to preach, but she insisted that nothing was impossible with God: "If the man may preach, because the Saviour died for him, why not the woman? seeing he died for her also. Is he not a whole Saviour, instead of a half one?"[4] (Document 2.)

Another woman preacher justified her work as God-given: "Shall women preach? Certainly, if God calls them to preach. He cannot make a mistake. He is not the author of confusion. But will it not subvert the existing social order? If the existing social order is not in harmony with the divine plan, it will have to be subverted."[5]

At the ordination of Antoinette L. Brown to serve the Congregational Church at South Butler, New York, on September 15, 1853, the Reverend Luther Lee followed the same logic: "We are not here to make a minister. It is not to confer on this our sister, a right to preach the gospel. If she has not that right already, we have no power to communicate it to her." Lee argued that all they could do was testify to their belief that Antoinette Brown was "one of the ministers of the New Covenant, authorized, qualified and called of God to preach the gospel of his son Jesus Christ."[6] (Document 3.)

In 1892, Mrs. Josephine Butler wrote, "Give us freedom; refuse us office if you like, though it would be more just in you to share all offices with women. But give us only freedom in the name and in the Spirit of Christ; and then you shall see what God may do with women, in the great work of the world's salvation." She believed that women's gifts in the Spirit went beyond "offices in the church." She looked forward to a new day.[7]

> When the Church or the Churches, become more deeply humble; when they have realized even more than they do now, their desperate need of the help of woman *as man's equal, absolutely,* in her relation to spiritual things, they will grant the freedom we ask; and then good gifts will no longer languish in a prison-house of conventionalities, and women's energies will not have to be folded in napkins and buried under the church floor.[8]

The second argument used to justify changed responsibilities for women in the church was pragmatic. Women were effective in new roles. Women were needed to get the job done. It was a new day.

Writers who took this approach celebrated the results of women's work in the church and argued for their right to preach. The Christian church was confronting new problems and the demands for laborers were urgent. One of the hopeful signs of the times, insisted one author, was that the true position of woman was being recognized more and more. Paul's words to the early church were not meant for women of all times and places—"the very spirit of Christianity has changed all this."[9]

> The women of to-day can enter some of the best universities and graduate with the highest honors; and the time may not be very distant when she will

be admitted to all our theological seminaries, when she may be trained to serve God and humanity by preaching the everlasting Gospel; and then, if she so desires, she can consecrate herself to the Gospel ministry for the glory of God her Saviour; and when that time comes the question about women speaking in churches, like many others of a limited nature, will be settled forever.[10]

Some people did worry that things might get out of hand. If women were permitted in one thing, where would it stop? Even persons who were unwilling to support women preachers and pastors in the present era, however, agreed that practical considerations could change things. "It will not be what the old Greeks judged proper, nor what the customs of the Jews allowed, nor what the Pilgrims of the Mayflower tolerated, nor even what Christians of the nineteenth century may think fitting, that will be standard of propriety for all times. Each age will and must be its own arbiter of what is fitting, deciding according to its own light and surroundings." It followed, therefore, that if it was ever really right and fitting and proper for woman to preach and if she considered it her duty and God blessed her, not even the inspired direction to the Corinthian or Ephesian churches would stand in her way.[11]

A noted male denominational leader supported women in ministry because he believed that they would bring more men to God. "Men ministers are converting the women, as five women in the church to one man indicates; now let us have a woman ministry and we shall see the men converted." And, he added, "there is a profound problem here that we have too long overlooked."[12]

Other authors defended the ministry of women because it enriched the entire church. They noted that many churches were weak in numbers and would languish or die unless all took on the common work. Yet when pastors were constrained "by the law of necessity," to break personal prejudice and the letter of Paul's rule and to allow women to take new responsibilities, they were "amazed at the opening of the mine of spiritual wealth, unknown and unworked before." Many pastors continued to allow these things "not compelled by necessity, but for the richness of the ore." This was a latent power that would never be developed unless Christians recognized another saying of Paul: that there was neither male nor female in Christ Jesus.[13] (Document 4.)

A third argument for preaching women followed the pragmatic position and insisted that women were already engaged in full ministry and therefore should be recognized. Writers of this persuasion wanted change to be celebrated rather than hidden. They pointed out that many female missionaries were unable to share their work in the mixed assemblies of American churches because of Paul's "alleged injunction of silence in the church on the part of women." It was an awkward situation.

For while it is true that many Christians believe that women are enjoined from publicly preaching the Gospel, either at home or abroad, it is certainly true that scores of missionary women are at present doing this very thing. They are telling the good news of salvation to heathen men and women publicly from house to house, to little groups gathered by the wayside, or to larger groups assembled in the zayats [religious meeting houses]. It is not affirmed that a majority of women missionaries are engaged in this kind of work, but that scores are doing it with the approval of the boards under which they are serving. If any one should raise the technical objection that because of its informal and colloquial character this is not preaching, we are ready to affirm that it comes much nearer the preaching enjoined in the great commission than does the reading of a theological disquisition from the pulpit on Sunday morning, or the discussion of some ethical or sociological question before a popular audience on Sunday evening.[14]

The question for the author of this passage was not whether the time was right for women to move into new forms of leadership; instead, the question was whether the church would recognize *existing* ministries and celebrate their power. Just as Peter was unable to accept the universality of the Gospel until his vision of a sheet descending from heaven showed him the oneness of God's people, it was argued that "this extraordinary spectacle of ministering women" was calling the church to recognize life under a new dispensation.[15]

The fourth class of arguments to support the changing circumstances of women reinterpreted the authority of Scripture. For some writers it was especially important to explain how the specific prohibitions of Paul could be interpreted alongside the emerging desires of women for full equity in the church. For others, a general reevaluation of all scriptural authority became necessary. Still others combed the Bible to find new ammunition and specific support *for* the various ministries of women. (Document 5.)

Most liberal thinkers challenged the validity of many scriptural prohibitions for the nineteenth century. They believed that, although Paul did expressly say "let the women keep silence in the churches," it was necessary to look at such scriptural prohibitions in the light of the times in which they were uttered. Scriptural prohibitions could not be explained away by making ridiculous distinctions between social meetings and regular assemblies. Rather, it was important to ask whether Paul wrote these things "for reasons peculiar to those times and places, or for reasons which hold good in all places for all times." Careful examination of the unique circumstances of gentile women in the ancient world made it understandable that women were forbidden to teach in the churches. "But no one can claim that this rule was meant for the women of all time and places."[16]

Furthermore, Protestants have usually argued that the voice of the church must not be followed except as guided by Scripture. However, some also felt that the church must not "ignore the teaching of the deepest spiritual life of the church in forming our conclusions concerning the meaning of Scripture." Every spiritual awakening in the history of Protestantism has honored the witness of Christian women (such as the Quakers, the Wesleyans, and the Salvation Army). It may be that the spiritual intuition of the church has been "far in advance of its exegesis in dealing with this subject."[17]

Another writer emphasized that Paul's understanding of the privilege of speech places responsibility upon both men and women. Paul was neither "an old bachelor" nor a promoter of women. And Paul was not simply setting out rules for the Corinthians, but for all times. Christian women must live under the order of creation and *should* be subordinate to men. However, a woman "need not be shut up in her modest efforts to do good. Let her only keep to her divinely appointed position as the submissive helpmeet of man, and her loving lips, like her tender heart and her gentle hand, shall shed the dew of grace upon the church as well as the home."[18]

> The gospel view of this subject is thus seen to be a plastic one, adaptable to changing times. . . . Scripture left this subject in such shape, that harsher times might keep less cultivated woman in the shade, as they have done; while still the advanced culture of these "last days" should have free scope to receive developed woman's aid in the church, just so fast and so far as developed man himself is ready to accept it as not exhibiting insubordination. The Scripture principle does indeed make women absolutely "keep silence," where the men insist upon this as the only sufficient token of their subjection. But whenever the men give express invitation to utterance, this certainly relieves the women from all risk or hindrance in speaking properly in their presence. When the men of the church themselves come forward, as in many little mission churches, and ask, even entreat women to aid them in their worship, and surely they cannot accuse themselves of the insubordination here condemned, if they kindly and helpfully do their part.[19]

Another tactic used to find a way around Pauline prohibitions against women speaking in the churches was to note that the Greek word used in all of these passages referred to a *wife,* or married woman. In the Greek world this was understandable, for most women were married, but there was reason to doubt whether Paul's words ever applied to unmarried women or widows. Perhaps in the nineteenth century, the ministry of spinsters and widows did not need to abide by Paul's injunctions.[20]

Sometimes the examination of one or two words got very specific. Several writers presented detailed analyses of the Greek verbs *to speak, tell, say, babble, prattle, preach, pray, prophesy,* and *exhort.* They argued that Paul never prohibited women from preaching, praying, or prophesying in a large or small assemblies in the churches. Rather, Paul was concerned that the women at Corinth keep out of all the babble and wrangling in the Corinthian church. Women were instructed to ask questions of their husbands at home, because it was "a shame for a woman to prate and gabble to no profit or education in the assembly."[21]

Another way of interpreting Paul's statements forbidding women to pray or prophesy unveiled was to reason that he was regulating a permissible activity. His concern was not whether women should speak, but how they did it: "why not understand that this was a permission to do it; only she must remember to avoid a scandal by continuing veiled."[22]

All efforts to relate biblical authority to the situation of women in the church examined the usual texts and searched for new passages. Inasmuch as the conservative position grounded its defense of the status quo in biblical material, anyone seeking change also had to do something with the Bible. Most progressive writers argued that certain scriptural passages were not binding—because they were not written for our times, because the Spirit spoke in the church as well as through the Holy Book, because if modern men invited women to speak, women could preach and remain appropriately subordinate, or because Paul's prohibitions were only intended for married women or babbling women or to regulate the manner of female preaching.

Probably the most massive attempt to confront biblical authority occurred with the publication of the *Woman's Bible* in 1898. Under the leadership of Elizabeth Cady Stanton, a committee of female scholars sought to revise all texts and chapters directly referring to women or excluding women. They believed that the Bible continued to have oppressive power over women and they sought, in part, to "translate, transpose and transfigure this mournful objective of piety into an exalted, dignified personage, worthy of our worship."[23] It was a controversial and unpopular book among the church-going public.

Alongside such efforts to counter or modify the power of biblical authority, other writers used Scripture to support the contributions of women in the church. They studied Scripture to lift up those stories and verses that specifically empowered women. These writers celebrated the prophetic work of Miriam, Deborah, Huldah, Hannah, Nodiah, Ruth, and Anna. They remembered the preaching of the Samaritan woman and the company of women that followed Jesus throughout his earthly journeys.[24] They insisted that "there were female laborers in the gospel in the Apostles' day, and that they labored with men, and that they still have a right to continue their labor, and that in a public capacity as well as men." Some of those disciples which Jesus sent forth two by two were women, "for he knew all their hearts and saw that it would be more prudent for her to go with her husband than alone." Such women would leave an example for future generations, "that other women might have the right."[25]

Women must have been very active preachers in the early church, continued this argument, because Paul was always writing to churches giving "his brethren strict charge to help those women who labored with him in the gospel, as he knew they could not labor successfully unless they were assisted." If the work of the men was clearly preaching, why not say the same of the work of women? "No doubt there were more women preachers with him than men." If men were to be allowed to continue in this service, then women should also.[26]

Furthermore, all of the Gospels told of the commissioning of women to preach the Gospel on Easter morning. Jesus met the women and said, "Be not afraid, go and tell my brethren." "This act of the Savior shows that he approved of women preaching, and not only women but also men, and if he had opposed it, he never would have commissioned a woman to preach the first resurrection sermon that was ever delivered in the presence of men."[27]

Finally, those who wished to justify women preaching and prophesying reminded modern Christians that they were living in the age of the dispensation of the Spirit. The day of Pentecost ushered in a new economy captured in the prophecy of Joel as quoted by Peter. One of its most salient characteristics was the promise that "your sons and your daughters shall prophesy." This was "woman's equal warrant with man's for telling out the Gospel of the grace of God."[28] "To prophesy" was not "merely to foretell future events, but to communicate religious truth in general under a Divine inspiration." Prophecy was not special prediction or the miracle of tongues which passed away with the apostles. The Holy Spirit's perpetual presence in the church implied "the equal perpetuity of His gifts and endowments."[29]

THE ARGUMENT AGAINST PREACHING WOMEN

The conservative leadership of the churches responded to the arguments for preaching women in many ways, writing long documents and going to great lengths to defend the status quo. The defense can be divided into three groups.

First, there was the defense from biblical authority. In examining Paul's prohibitions, writers who used this defense refused to make exceptions. They believed that even if we do not understand "the grounds or the propriety of his emphatic prohibition of women praying or speaking in Christian assemblies, certain it is that such is his teaching . . . in the most explicit and didactic terms."[30] Whether or not it can be explained, whatever is clearly scriptural is right and for the best interests of society. (Document 6.)

Moreover, Paul was progressive in many things, "the most liberal of all the Apostles." He vindicated the right of gentile converts to become part of the New Testament church without following Jewish law. If Christianity was going to depart from the established customs with regard to women, "St. Paul would have been preeminently the one to enunciate and emphasize the new departure."[31] However, he did not do so. "Paul did not need to live in our day in order to know the mind of the Spirit, and that the rule he gave is permanent in its nature, because it is based on reasons that are permanent."[32]

There are people who say: If Paul would live today and in America he would speak differently. He wrote his instructions on the background of his age with its conceptions of inferiority of the female sex. Such apostolic teachings, they say, must be taken in an historical sense. Now this interpretation would be all right in the mouth of a champion of modern theology; but one who does not want to give up the formal principle of the Reformation, namely that the Holy Scripture is source and rule of all faith and practice cannot afford to take that view. If we can not believe that in a question like the one here under consideration Paul, under the guidance of the Holy Ghost, said something that is true and binding to-day just as well as at the time of the founding of the church, then we are on dangerous ground.[33]

Those who argued from biblical authority had particular ways of responding to pressures for change. If a woman claimed that she was called by God to be a minister of the Gospel, this was condemned as a perilous perversion of the true doctrine of vocation. "The same Spirit who really calls the true minister also dictated the Holy Scriptures.... [and] the Spirit calls no person to do what the word dictated by him, forbids. The Spirit cannot contradict himself."[34] Indeed, by this argument, the only way anyone can do or teach something contrary to Scripture is to sustain the claim by a miracle. All who claim supernatural inspiration must prove it by supernatural works. And when any of those "preaching women" work a genuine miracle they can "stand on the ground of Deborah or Anna."[35]

Furthermore, all those who are called by the Spirit know that the call is "never complete until the believing choice of the brethren has confirmed it." The brethren must try the spirits to see whether they are of God. But inasmuch as the brethren have no other rule than Scripture, the answer is clear. The word teaches that God does not call a woman, and therefore, the brethren can never confirm her ministry.[36]

Scripture gave two specific reasons why women had to be subordinate. The first was the order of the creation: God did not create man for the woman, but woman for the man. Female subordination was not a passing custom, it was grounded in creation. If a woman insisted upon speaking in public assemblies, "where all stand upon a common level," she thereby denied any subordination to the other sex.[37]

The second reason for woman's subordination was that in paradise the woman, not Adam, was originally deceived and "in the transgression." "Perhaps," wrote one author, "this implies that woman having taken the lead once, and made such bad work of it, there is a special fitness that she hereafter march in the rear. She made a little speech once that was the world's undoing: now let her keep silence."[38]

Building upon the scriptural principle of subordination, it was clear that no woman could ever be a preacher. Within the New Testament, public teaching and ruling in the church went together. All preachers were called by spiritual rule to admonish, command, censure, and even excommunicate in order to conserve the fruits of their labors. But how could a woman do this if one of her male converts included her husband, whom she was bound to obey at home? When women asked for the right to preach as lay persons, they were told that public lay preaching, for men or women, was not legitimate.[39]

Both sides of the debate focused upon particular words and phrases to promote their positions. For example, conservative writers made much of Paul's words about head coverings. Men were supposed to preach in public with their heads uncovered, thereby standing forth as God's heralds and representatives. A covered head was a dishonor to the office and the God it represented. But for women to appear at any public religious assembly unveiled was a glaring impropriety. It was "contrary to the subordination of the position assigned her by her Maker, and to the modesty and reserve suitable to her sex; and even nature settled the point by giving her long hair as her natural veil."[40] Obviously, women could not be preachers.

A second type of argument sought to celebrate the expanding role of women in the churches while denying women the right to preach in large meetings. It was an awkward position, but genuinely defended. Woman was the equal of man and his help. In some ways she was inferior, but in other respects she was superior. She was his counterpart. They were not equal with regard to rule and authority, but they were equal in their respective spheres.[41] (Document 7.)

> A woman should not take such a part in religious meeting, as shall seem to be assuming authority; she should not be a public religious teacher; she should not put herself forward and make herself conspicious. She is then forbidden to lead in any of the exercises of public worship. In all large and promiscuous religious meetings she would be out of her sphere to take part. In the business of the church it is not her place to deliberate, and counsel, and vote, except by courtesy. She is debarred certainly, by the Apostle from the ministry, the duties of which belong to men. Yet in ordinary social religious meetings, the instructions of the Apostle do not forbid her to take part. But they teach her to perform such part, at such times, and in such circumstances as become the subjection and modesty of her sex.[42]

Women, therefore, should share their gifts in the church. Women had unsurpassed social powers that were especially appropriate in the "social, conference exercises of the prayer meeting." "Men are engaged for the livelong day in the distractions and toils and worldliness of business. It is hard for them to leave these for the atmosphere of the prayer meeting. Woman is shielded from many of these withering and chilling influences."[43] The social meeting should benefit from her contributions, not merely her silent worship. She could help as an active, living, speaking disciple. Although a prayer meeting was often thinly attended, it was desirable that women take active parts. "The social meeting is the becoming place for her to testify what the Saviour has done for her."[44]

This important distinction between large promiscuous assemblies and small social or prayer meetings became a much discussed question. When a charge was brought against the Reverend Isaac M. See of Newark, New Jersey, for permitting and encouraging a woman to preach publicly and teach in his church in October, 1876, it was taken before the Presbytery of Newark and the Synod of New Jersey. Reverend See argued that women were allowed to speak and teach in the smaller social meetings of the church and that there was no scriptural authority for the distinction between large and small meetings. Nevertheless, the synod insisted that inviting "women to preach at the regular public services of the Church was irregular and unwise, and contrary to the views of the Scripture and the Church order derived from them." In the same document, however, the synod also recorded its high appreciation of the services of women in other departments of Christian evangelism and benevolence.[45]

The minutes of this case show that there was great effort made to distinguish between the public teaching and preaching of women as ordained leaders, as lay persons in the "social meetings" of the church, and as lay persons invited into a Sunday pulpit.[46] These were difficult distinctions, but ones which those who feared change sought to maintain.

Finally, a third group of arguments rejected the movement of women into new arenas of ministry by citing general social and historical reasons. That is, biblical interpretations notwithstanding, there were other reasons why such new changes should not be allowed.

For one thing, church history upheld the foolishness of allowing women to preach. Women had never been allowed to officiate as ministers in any of the orthodox and historical denominations. Women could only enter the outer court of the Jewish temple and were seated separately in all synagogues. Although there were a few extraordinary and exceptional cases, in "thousands of years among hundreds of millions of God's covenant people" only a few women ever took positions of significant leadership.[47]

Then there was the argument that women dared not accept the tasks of the public preacher or evangelist because of their role as mothers. The great disability of a woman for the work of ministry was "directly connected with her physical constitution, with the fact that she can be a mother, and that motherhood, with all its burdens and blessings, is her divinely appointed destiny."[48] Everyone agreed that celibacy defrauded men and women of their rights to the sanctity of the home. If it was not good for male ministers to be alone, "it must be equally not good for preaching women to be alone." Yet, this raised a delicate point: "A child-bearing woman and a nursing mother is disqualified for the exposure and nervous strain of the pulpit and the exhausting duties of the pastoral office, by a regard for public decency, for her own health and the health of her offspring. To lay this new burden on her soul and body is a refinement of cruelty."[49]

Although this argument could well have been applied to other occupations and professions for women, that was beside the point. Civilization and Christianity ought to remove the obstacles in the way of marriage and teach men how to support the weak.[50]

Women's work was the noblest and most momentous work done on earth. An evangelist might convert thousands, but the worthiness of his public success belonged fully as much to his modest mother as himself. "The instrumentality of the mother's training in the salvation of her children is mighty and decisive; the influence of the minister over his hundreds is slight and non-essential."[51] In essence, ministry was not worth doing when compared to mothering.

Some scholars combined this judgment with Scripture and noted that women were actually "saved through childbearing, if they continued in faith, and love, and holiness with sobriety." It was a promise made to all women on these conditions.[52]

Education created another difficulty for women. If the preaching ministry had any value, it ought not be opened up to the "pastor's wife" or "anyone who knows enough to talk for thirty minutes on religious subjects." We ought to keep the Sabbath ministrations for those who have received training.[53]

Then why not educate women for this work? It was not that simple. Women could not combine household and pastoral duties. Women had to work near their husband's store, or factory, or medical practice. If an unmarried woman sought to prepare for ministry, she would be told that "the education for such a sphere should begin at an age considerably earlier than that at which most women can be considered confirmed spinsters." But even if there was "a moral, healthful helpful woman permanently without family ties or the desire for them," the argument would be that a woman's mind was not suited for ministry.[54] (Document 8.)

> The quality of a woman's mind is different from that of a man. This does not mean necessarily that it is inferior. It simply means that things do not appeal to her from the same side, do not appear to her in the same light, as to man. We are not to be startled any more by saying that reason is the province of the masculine mind, intuition of the feminine. Yet this means that a woman ordinarily cannot convince a man of a thing by argument. In logical presentation of truth, she is usually a failure. Thus arises a serious question: Can a woman's preaching win and hold men in the Church? And when we consider that the great lack of the Church in all ages has been such a virile and logical interpretation of truth as will appeal to *men,* and hold their allegiance, this question assumes large proportions. The church *has* the women—has always had them; she needs the men![55]

One final reason was offered to discredit the movement of women into new responsibilities in the churches. Although the concerns of church women did not spring exclusively from the secular crusade for

"women's rights," the preaching of women and the demand for masculine political rights were so "synchronous" that they had to be viewed as
"two parts of one common impulse." And if the movement for women's
rights was based upon the radical conviction that society ought to disregard all distinctions of sex and allow married women to have independent control of their property, then the logic of this "social contract"
thinking had to be judged totally unacceptable. "The woman is not designed by God, nor entitled to all the franchises in society to which the
male is entitled." Indeed, the consequences of this revolution would be
so terrible that all marriages and children would suffer.[56]

> This common movement for "women's rights", and women's preaching, must
> be regarded, then, as simply infidel. It cannot be candidly upheld without
> attacking the inspiration and authority of the Scriptures. We are convinced
> that there is only one safe attitude for Christians, presbyters, and church
> courts to assume towards it. This is utterly to discountenance it, as they do any
> other assault of fidelity on God's truth and Kingdom.[57]

CONCLUSION

The pressures for recognition of a woman's right to preach in the
church were real. Advocates for change believed that this right was: (1)
grounded in the work of the Holy Spirit, (2) justified by practical considerations, (3) already happening on the mission field, and (4) acceptable
because of new enlightened interpretations of Scripture. Those who
defended the status quo and the subordinate position of women in the
churches did not agree. They argued that: (1) biblical authority prohibited these changes, (2) women's role in the church was expanding enough
under proper limitations, and (3) historical, social, intellectual, and political reasons made any changes in the place of women totally unacceptable.
It was a debate that continued into the twentieth century.

Phoebe Palmer, prominent lay evangelist in the Holiness movement in the
mid-nineteenth century, wrote the
strongest early defense of women's
right to preach the gospel in *The Promise of the Father* (1859). [From Donald
W. and Deane K. Dayton, *Discovering
An Evangelical Heritage* (New York:
Harper & Row, 1976), p. 106.]

Antoinette L. Brown was the first
American woman to be fully ordained
to the Christian ministry. The ordination service was held in the Congregational Church of South Butler, New
York, on September 15, 1853. [From
Donald W. and Deane K. Dayton, *Discovering An Evangelical Heritage* (New
York: Harper & Row, 1976), p. 105.]

Luther Lee, leader and theologian in
the Wesleyan Methodist Church, delivered a strong sermon on the right of
women to preach at the ordination
service of Antoinette Brown. [From
Donald W. and Deane K. Dayton, *Discovering An Evangelical Heritage* (New
York: Harper & Row, 1976), p. 103.]

Frances E. Willard, the founder of
the Women's Christian Temperance
Union, was also a pioneer for the rights
of women—both laity and clergy—in
the church. [From Frances E. Willard,
Glimpses of Fifty Years (Chicago:
Woman's Temperance Publishing Association, 1889), frontispiece.]

Documents: The Struggle for the Right to Preach

ARGUMENTS DEFENDING WOMEN'S RIGHT TO PREACH

Document 1: "Testimony of Women Preachers"

As the arguments over woman's role in the churches became more animated in the late part of the nineteenth century, Frances E. Willard, well-known temperance leader, was asked by the editors of The Homiletic Monthly *to write an article on women and preaching. The article "went beyond prescribed limits" and was finally published as a book,* Woman in the Pulpit *(D. Lathrop, 1888). The book contains several chapters by Miss Willard that defend a woman's right to preach and includes collections of testimonies on the issue by both male and female preachers. The following selections contain the comments of women already in the ministry who responded to Miss Willard's question, "What have these women to say for themselves . . .?"* [58]

Let us now hear from a few "women preachers." It is estimated that there are in the United States five hundred women who have already entered the pulpit as evangelists, and at least a score (exclusive of the 350 Quaker preachers) who are pastors, of whom several have been regularly ordained. The denominations that have ordained women are the Methodist, Baptist, Free Baptist, Congregational, Universalist, and Unitarian. As is well known, the Society of Friends has, from the first, in all things, recognized the equality of men and women in the house of God. What have these women to say for themselves, who, in face of so much prejudice (*i.e.,* their cases being not judged on their merits, but *pre*-judged), have gone forward as ministers of Christ?

First, I give a personal letter from a dear friend, who, for nearly fifteen years, has been preaching in the Methodist Church, with invitations from our leading pulpits in almost every Northern State, enough to occupy all her time for years ahead; with thousands of additions to the church, growing out of her ministry; a woman so gentle that she is beloved by all who meet her, and so eloquent that I have seen doctors of divinity and theological professors deeply moved by her sermons; a woman who always takes a text and stands in the pulpit, pleading, as a mother with her children, "Be ye reconciled to God." Here is what she writes:—

July 13, 1887

MY DEAR FRIEND:—I small find it very difficult to put my views on these questions in writing, for I do not write for the press. If you were only here how gladly I would talk with you. I have felt that the Lord did not wish me to make any defence of my peculiar position, so have never committed my views to writing. You understand; he sent me out simply as an illustration. So I have gone forth, never allowing myself to be drawn into an argument on the subject, and never saying a word in personal defence, but I knew all the time the Lord would send somebody to take care of the defence. One minister in Ohio said to me, "I have my views on these subjects all ready to publish to the world, when you come along, every now and then, with a practical demonstration that confounds me." As to the texts so often quoted, I am not a Greek scholar, but a Greek student told me that in one place where women were forbidden the original word meant "to prattle, to gabble, to make a noise." These formed part of the same church that was drunk at the sacrament, and whose sins were too bad to talk about. And these Corinthian women to-day, our missionaries tell us, are ignorant, prattling, noisy disturbers of their meetings; and yet, even among these, Paul found some whom he allowed to minister, and gave in the very same letter directions regarding how they should dress when preaching; charging them to be more guarded than usual, because of the boldness of the masses of women about them. Paul gives the names of twelve or fourteen women whom he recognized as ordained ministers or deacons. As for me, I shall go on standing as an unwelcome and unanswerable fact before opposers. And, at the end of their profound arguments and fearful prophesying, I will still point to my five blessed boys, and meekly inquire, "Have they gone to ruin?"

The next is from an ordained and settled pastor of the Congregational church. She spoke one Sunday years ago, when the minister of her own church was absent, and has gone on ever since, the church steadily growing not only in spirituality, but in numbers and material resources. This lady writes:—

I am not given to argument on this question, believing in works much more than words. As a question in ethics, I see no controversy. It is surely right for a messenger to give a message of truth. My sainted mother believed that if our Lord gives the word to any of his children to impart, there is no question as to male or female, bond or free; and so do I, gladly receiving it from any.

A third woman preacher, having a regular pastorate, sends this:—

July 15, 1887

MY DEAR FRIEND:—In 1863–4 the Universalist Church ordained two women to the ministry. The success of these women proved the wisdom of the act. The Universalist Register now contains the names of twenty-seven women ministers, most of whom are in charge of active churches. The Unitarian denomination also accords women full ordination, and has a number of eminently successful women in charge of large and growing parishes. Several women have been ordained by councils,—acting not with denominational authority, but independently,—especially Congregationalists and Baptist. Of course, the matter must be set right on Biblical grounds; but with the educated and close Bible student we have no difficulty.

The strongest argument in favor of a woman ministry is found in woman herself, in her sympathetic and intuitional nature, in her high moral sense, in her deep and fervent religious spirit. The mother element in woman's character gives her a peculiar power in religion that is seen very distinctly in her influence over the children and young people of the church, a class that has been most neglected in the regular church administrations, but one that the world is beginning to realize as the most important factor of the people. Then, too, in the parish work, where the best influence is exerted, I think it impossible, from the very nature of the case, for any man to do it as a woman can. I know this is true when I am admitted to the sick-chamber where religious consolation is needed, but where the presence of a man, except the husband or father, I claim, is not in keeping with the best interests of either the sick one or the household. Of course, I think we should have women physicians for such cases.

Then, the confidence of the sorrowing and sinful ones that a pastor holds—I cannot understand how it can be so readily given to a man. Finally, the work needs many laborers. Our young men are being drawn from the ministry through financial attractions, and as the women have gone to the school-room they must go to the pulpit, and the same qualities that have made woman's work a success there will make her a success in the higher capacity of a religious teacher. I do not mean every woman is qualified for the work any more than every man; I only contend that there are women who are particularly adapted to it, and that in the gifts and graces of a woman's nature there is that which so qualifies her for this work that the synod or council that forbids her entrance upon it is acting in opposition to the higher power that ordains through gifts of mind and character, and through deep spiritual aspirations, certain women to this divine work.

I speak out of twelve years' experience; I find the work so natural, so easy in the sense of adjusting myself to its demands, so gratifying, and so much of it to do, that every day seems too short for the sacred ministries vouchsafed to me.

Here is another, from a lady whose pioneer work has made easier the path of every woman who has followed her:—

After twenty-five years' experience as pastor and preacher, I am convinced that there is no work outside the home circle upon which women can so consistently and properly enter as that of the Christian ministry. Although a mother of children born during the years of my ministry, I presume that there are few, if any, clergymen who have lost as little time as I have. That is to say, I doubt not that I have preached more Sundays in the last twenty-five years than the average preacher. I never take vacations, and, excepting a very few Sundays when my children were born, have really lost no time; and yet I think it is conceded by my neighbors that my children are as well cared for as theirs, at any rate. I mention this to show, from actual experience, that the work of the ministry is not necessarily inconsistent with the duties of a wife and mother. The subjects dealt with are those peculiarly interesting to women, and surely none can be so well fitted by nature for understanding the great problems of character and destiny as those whom God has appointed to give birth to new life and to mould the characters of the young.

I believe that it is an accepted rule of interpretation that an author may be allowed to explain himself, that is, that collateral passages may be used in explaining an author's meaning. Thus, when the great apostle says, "It is a shame for a woman to speak in church," I turn back to the eleventh chapter of First Corinthians, and read that he give directions that they should have their heads covered when they speak in a church—that is, prophesy, prophesying, you know, in the New Testament, is not foretelling future events, but preaching,—and I say such a man as Paul has not contradicted himself. He has evidently expected women to speak in a church, when they are properly qualified and the conditions are fitting; but not to speak foolishly, or to babble in a confused meeting where men are speaking, to no purpose, without understanding or order, for "God is not the author of confusion, but of peace."

We must so interpret any statement made by an author that it shall be consistent with his other statements. Paul sent women out to preach, and commended those who labored with him in the Lord. Hence, whatever he said which seems to teach otherwise must be interpreted so as to be consistent with this action and these words.

I might write at great length on this, furnishing many illustrations; but I have given you the principle upon which I proceed. I am in the greatest possible haste, not on account of ministerial or domestic duties,—these would be light and pleasant,—but on account of special work in the campaign which we are carrying forward here.

A leading Quaker preacheress and editor writes as follows:

The prophecy of Joel 2:28–30 settles the question for our dispensation, and the Apostolic Church recognizes this liberty and call to prophesy, and allowed it so far as the prejudices and customs of that Oriental country would permit. I think the equality of men and women under the Gospel was one of the great principles that was to be announced by the apostles, and then left to a slow but sure unfolding.

The truth is, every revolution of the wheel of evangelization brings this truth into fuller recognition. It is very interesting to me to see how

God is providentially making room for us, in spite of the iron-clad prejudices of the churches. For instance, some seventeen years ago, lady medical students were hissed in clinic rooms in Philadelphia, and, if I remember rightly, mobbed. Then the call come from India for female medical missionaries, and Miss Swain went. The demand has sanctified the service in the eyes of the church, and now the lady physician is as honored as she was once despised. Now I notice in my missionary exchanges, and in late missionary literature, that the need of female evangelists for the foreign field is being recognized in conservative circles; not Quakers and Methodists, but Calvinists are saying, "The women of heathen lands must be reached by the ministry of their Christian sisters," and Dr. Thoburn, in an article written for the *Advocate,* goes so far as to say the ordinances will have to be administered by women to the inmates of the zenanas, for one generation at least. And so, you see, I am looking for this problem also to find its solution in the foreign field, and the heathen prejudice against woman's ministry to be relegated back to its cradle, or rather to the land from which it sprung, for its final blow. I believe the preaching of the Gospel by women missionaries will dispel the prejudice against woman's preaching in the home church, much as the services of the medical missionaries have altered the home sentiment about lady physicians.

Document 2: "My Call to Preach the Gospel"

Often called the first female preacher of the First African Methodist Episcopal Church, Jarena Lee was never ordained. Born in New Jersey in 1783, she later felt a call to preach the Gospel within emerging black Methodism. Although at first the Reverend Richard Allen drew the line at female preaching, he later supported her work. She traveled widely and kept a detailed record of her ministry, which was finally published. The following selection gives her description of her call.[59]

Between four and five years after my sanctification, on a certain time, an impressive silence fell upon me, and I stood as if some one was about to speak to me, yet I had no such thought in my heart.—But to my utter surprise there seemed to sound a voice which I thought I distinctly heard, and most certainly understand, which said to me, "Go preach the Gospel!" I immediately replied aloud, "No one will believe me." Again I listened, and again the same voice seemed to say—"Preach the Gospel; I will put words in your mouth, and will turn your enemies to become your friends."

At first I supposed that Satan had spoken to me, for I had read that he could transform himself into an angel of light for the purpose of deception. Immediately I went into a secret place, and called upon the Lord to know if he had called me to preach, and whether I was deceived or not; when there appeared to my view the form and figure of a pulpit, with a Bible lying thereon, the back of which was presented to me as plainly as if it had been a literal fact.

In consequence of this, my mind became so exercised, that during the night following, I took a text and preached in my sleep. I thought there stood before me a great multitude, while I expounded to them the things of religion. So violent were my exertions and so loud were my exclamations, that I awoke from the sound of my own voice, which also awoke the family of the house where I resided. Two days after I went to see the preacher in charge of the African Society, who was the Rev. Richard Allen, the same before named in these pages, to tell him that I felt it my duty to preach the gospel. But as I drew near the street in which his house was, which was in the city of Philadelphia, my courage began to fail me; so terrible did the cross appear, it seemed that I should not be able to bear it. Previous to my setting out to go to see him, so agitated was my mind, that my appetite for my daily food failed me entirely. Several times on my way there, I turned back again; but as often I felt my strength again renewed, and I soon found that the nearer I approached to the house of the minister, the less was my fear. Accordingly, as soon as I came to the door, my fears subsided, the cross was removed, all things appeared pleasant—I was tranquil.

I now told him, that the Lord had revealed it to me, that I must preach the gospel. He replied, by asking, in what sphere I wished to move in? I said, among the Methodists. He then replied, that a Mrs. Cook, a Methodist lady, had also some time before requested the same privilege; who, it was believed, had done much good in the way of exhortation, and holding prayer meetings; and who had been permitted to do so by the verbal license of the preacher in charge at the time. But as to women preaching, he said that our Discipline knew nothing at all about it—that it did not call for women preachers. This I was glad to hear, because it removed the fear of the cross—but no sooner did this feeling cross my mind, than I found that a love of souls had in a measure departed from me; that holy energy which burned within me, as a fire, began to be smothered. This I soon perceived.

O how careful ought we to be, lest through our by-laws of church government and discipline, we bring into disrepute even the word of life. For as unseemly as it may appear now-a-days for a woman to preach, it should be remembered that nothing is impossible with God. And why should it be thought impossible, heterodox, or improper for a woman to preach? seeing the Saviour died for the woman as well as for the man.

If the man may preach, because the Saviour died for him, why not the woman? seeing he died for her also. Is he not a whole Saviour, instead of a half one? as those who hold it wrong for a woman to preach, would seem to make it appear.

Did not Mary *first* preach the risen Saviour, and is not the doctrine of the resurrection the very climax of Christianity—hangs not all our hope on this, argued by St. Paul? Then did not Mary, a woman, preach the gospel? for she preached the resurrection of the crucified Son of God.

But some will say that Mary did not expound the Scripture, therefore, she did not preach, in the proper sense of the term. To this I reply, it may be that the term *preach* in those primitive times, did not mean exactly what it is now *made* to mean; perhaps it was a great deal more simple then than it is now—if it were not, the unlearned fishermen could not have preached the gospel at all, as they had no learning.

To this it may be replied, by those who are determined not to believe that it is right for a woman to preach, that the disciples, though they were fishermen and ignorant of letters too, were inspired so to do. To which I would reply, that though they were inspired, yet that inspiration did not save them from showing their ignorance of letters, and of man's wisdom; this the multitude soon found out, by listening to the remarks of the envious Jewish priests. If then, to preach the gospel, by the gift of heaven, comes by inspiration solely, is God straitened: must he take the man exclusively? May he not, did he not, and can he not inspire a female to preach the simple story of the birth, life, death, and resurrection of our Lord, and accompany it too with power to the sinner's heart. As for me, I am fully persuaded that the Lord called me to labor according to what I have received, in his vineyard. If he has not, how could he consistently bear testimony in favor of my poor labors, in awakening and converting sinners?

In my wanderings up and down among men, preaching according to my ability, I have frequently found families who told me that they had not for several years been to a meeting, and yet, while listening to hear what God would say by his poor female instrument, have believed with trembling—tears rolling down their cheeks, the signs of contrition and repentance towards God. I firmly believe that I have sown seed, in the name of the Lord, which shall appear with its increase at the great day of accounts, when Christ shall come to make up his jewels.

Document 3: Woman's Right to Preach the Gospel

Antoinette Brown became the first fully ordained woman in a recognized American denomination (Congregational) in 1853. She had graduated from Oberlin College and had been allowed to take classes in Oberlin's graduate theological course without a degree. After several years of lecturing and involvement in the abolition and temperance movements, she became the pastor of a small church in

South Butler, New York. The Reverend Luther Lee, a well-known Wesleyan Methodist leader, preached her ordination sermon.

Although the Wesleyan Methodists did not ordain women at that time, Reverend Lee gives a classic statement of the argument for women's rights in the church based upon the prophetic promise of Joel as quoted in the second chapter of Acts. The following selection presents the logic so often used by later Holiness and Pentecostal writers.[60]

There were prophetesses or female prophets in the Primitive Church under the gospel. The fact that there would be, was foretold by the Prophet Joel. "And it shall come to pass afterward, that I will pour out my Spirit upon all flesh; and your sons and your daughters shall prophesy." Joel 2:28.

This text most clearly began to be fulfilled at the day of Pentecost, as we learn from Acts 2:17; where Peter declares the development of that day, to be what was foretold by the prophet. But how was the prediction, that daughters should prophesy, fulfilled on the day of Pentecost? The history of the subject answers this question. It is as follows:

In the first chapter, we are told who constituted the assembled Christians. "Then returned they unto Jerusalem from the mount called Olivet, which is from Jerusalem a sabbath-day's journey. And when they were come in, they went up into an upper room, where abode both Peter, and James, and John, and Andrew, Philip, and Thomas, Bartholomew, and Matthew, James the son of Alpheus, and Simon Zealotes, and Judas the brother of James. These all continued with one accord in prayer and supplication, with the women, and Mary the mother of Jesus, and with his brethren." Verses 12–14.

Here we have named the eleven apostles, then "the women," then Mary the mother of Jesus in particular, and lastly "his brethren." By his brethren is probably meant his near relatives. It is probable that there were a number of women in the company, as they are mentioned as forming one portion of the assembly. In the 15th verse we are told that the whole number present was about one hundred and twenty persons. In the fourth verse of chapter two, we are told that they were all filled with the Holy Ghost, and began to speak with other tongues.

Who were filled with the Holy Ghost, and began to speak with other tongues? Most clearly the hundred and twenty persons, consisting of the apostles, the women, and Mary the mother of Jesus, and his brethren. To deny this would be to falsify the plainest portion of the record. The record declares that there were about one hundred and twenty persons assembled together, that this number embraced the women, and that they were all filled with the Holy Ghost, and began to speak with other tongues. Thus did the Holy Ghost, in his first descent, crown females as well as males, with tongues of fire, to speak the wonderful works of God.

But the remarkable prophecy of Joel did not receive its entire fulfillment on the day of Pentecost, for about twenty-seven years afterwards we read, Acts 21:9, that Phillip of Cesarea, "had four daughters which did prophesy." As this fact is mentioned only incidentally and not as a new or strange thing, it appears probable that female prophets were not unusual in the Primitive Church.

This is the proper place to remark that prophesying is not to be understood in the restricted sense of foretelling. A prophet is not exclusively one who foretells, but who explains prophecies, and teaches; and to prophesy is to explain prophecies and to teach. In this sense every gospel minister is a prophet, and every prophet under the new dispensation is a gospel minister. Here then were four female gospel ministers, daughters of one man. When it is said, "Your sons and your daughters shall prophesy," the meaning is, your sons and your daughters shall become teachers, or gospel ministers.

The Greek word which we translate prophet, is *propheetuo,* and signifies "to foretell, to predict, to explain and apply prophecies." To explain and apply prophecies, was the peculiar work of the first ministers. The Greek word which we translate prophet, is *propheetees,* and signifies "a declarer, a foreteller, a priest, a teacher, and instructor." It was always the work of prophets to labor as religious teachers, and to explain and apply the predictions which had been previously uttered by others, and when we consider that there were whole schools of prophets, we may conclude that but few of the whole number were employed to foretell, and that their principal calling was to labor as religious teachers. That prophets were preachers or religious teachers, is perfectly clear from the use of the words, prophet and prophesy, by the apostles.

The church at Antioch sent Paul and Barnabas to Jerusalem for the settlement of the great question, whether Gentile converts were bound to keep the law of Moses concerning circumcision and other rites. The apostles and the church at Jerusalem, having considered the case, sent back a written answer, and sent also two messengers of their own company, Judas and Silas. "And Judas and Silas being prophets also themselves, exhorted the brethren with many words, and confirmed them." This proves beyond a doubt, that they exhorted, or preached in the common acceptation, by virtue of their prophetic office, and the conclusion is that to be a prophet, is to be a preacher, or public religious teacher. We read again, 1 Corinthians 19:3: "He that prophesieth, speaketh unto men to edification, and exhortation and comfort." Here the entire pulpit work of a gospel preacher is described as the act of prophesying, which renders it certain that prophets were preachers. Again, we read Revelation 2:20,

"Nevertheless, I have a few things against thee, because thou sufferest that woman Jezebel, which calleth herself a prophetess to teach, and to seduce my servants to commit fornication, and to eat things offered to idols." This proves two points; first, that the doctrine must have prevailed that women might rightfully be prophets; and secondly, that being prophets, they taught the people. The complaint is not that she was a *woman,* but that she was a bad woman; not that she was a *prophetess,* but that she called herself one when she was not; not that she *taught,* but that she taught false and corrupting doctrine. It is clear that there would have been no false female teachers, had there been no true ones, and that a false female teacher could not have been sustained in the church, had the doctrine prevailed that the gospel forbade females to preach the gospel.

I have now proved that there were a class of females in the Primitive Church called prophetesses, that is, there were female prophets, and these prophets were preachers or public teachers of religion.

Document 4: "A Supposition"

Probably the most famous female leader in the "Holiness revival," which flourished at mid-century, was Mrs. Phoebe Palmer. After her marriage in 1827 to Dr. Walter C. Palmer, the couple traveled widely and spoke extensively in church meetings. Following the logic that women could receive the gifts of the spirit as readily as men, Mrs. Palmer wrote an important defense of women's ministry. In her book, Promise of the Father: or, A Neglected Specialty of the Last Days *(W. C. Palmer, 1859), she builds an eloquent case that women should finally be allowed to accept the promises of God which have been withheld for centuries. She gives a theological rationale for the practical reality that more and more women are prophesying for the Lord. In this selection she invites women to claim their power and chides men (particularly clergy) for keeping women down.*[61]

Suppose one of the brethren who had received the baptism of fire on the day of Pentecost, now numbered among those who were scattered every where preaching the word, had met a female disciple who had also received the same endowment of power. He finds her proclaiming Jesus to an astonished company of male and female listeners. And now imagine he interferes and withstands her testimony by questioning whether women have a right to testify of Christ before a mixed assembly. Would not such an interference look worse than unmanly? And were her testimony, through this interference, restrained, or rendered less effectual, would it not, in the eye of the Head of the Church, involve guilt? Yet we do not say but a person may err after the same similitude and be sincere, on the same principle that Saul was sincere when he withstood the proclamation of the gospel, and made such cruel havoc of the church. He verily thought he was doing God service. But when his mind was enlightened to see that, in persecuting these men and women, he was withstanding God, and rejecting the divinely-ordained instrumentalities by which the world was to be saved, he could no longer have been sincere unless he had taken every possible pains to make his refusal of error as far reaching as had been his wrong. And how the heart of that beloved disciple of the Saviour would have been grieved, and her hands weakened, by one whom she would have a right to look to for aid against the common enemy, and for sympathy in her work!

A large proportion of the most intelligent, courageous, and self-sacrificing disciples of Christ are females. "Many women followed the saviour" when on earth; and, compared with the fewness of male disciples, many women follow him still. Were the women who followed the incarnate Saviour earnest, intelligently pious, and intrepid, willing to sacrifice that which cost them something, in ministering to him of their substance? In like manner, there are many women in the present day, earnest, intelligent, intrepid, and self-sacrificing, who, were they permitted or encouraged to open their lips in the assemblies of the pious in prayer, or speaking as the Spirit gives utterance, might be instrumental in winning many an erring one to Christ. We say, were they permitted and encouraged; yes, encouragement may now be needful. So long has this endowment of power been withheld from use by the dissuasive sentiments of the pulpit, press, and church officials, that it will need the combined aid of these to give the public mind a proper direction, and undo a wrong introduced by the man of sin centuries ago.

But more especially do we look to the ministry for the correction of this wrong. Few, perhaps, have really intended to do wrong; but little do they know the embarrassment to which they have subjected a large portion of the church of Christ by their unscriptural position in relation to this matter. The Lord our God is one Lord. The same indwelling spirit of might which fell upon Mary and the other women on the glorious day that ushered in the present dispensation still falls upon God's daughters. Not a few of the daughters of the Lord Almighty have, in obedience to the command of the Saviour, tarried at Jerusalem; and, the endowment from on high having fallen upon them, the same impelling power which constrained Mary and the other women to speak as the Spirit gave utterance impels them to testify of Christ.

"The testimony of Jesus is the spirit of prophecy." And how do these divinely-baptized disciples stand ready to obey these impelling influences? Answer, ye thousands of Heaven-touched lips, whose testimonies have so long been repressed in the assemblies of the pious! Yes, answer, ye thousands of female disciples, of every Christian land, whose pent-up voices have so long, under the pressure of these man-made restraints, been uttered in groanings before God.

Document 5: "Objections to Women Speaking"

Women in some of the new denominations on the American fron-
tier did not have to deal with the power of tradition and custom, which
thwarted women in the more historic Protestant churches. The Chris-
tians, Campbellites, or Disciples of Christ accepted the leadership of
women and celebrated new approaches to Scripture and church prac-
tice. Barbara Kellison, a member of the Christian Conference in Des
Moines, Iowa, argues that "if we believe that women have equal rights
in the church with the men, let us manifest it to the world." Practice
should follow our theology. In 1862, therefore, she published a forty-
four page pamphlet entitled Rights of Women in the Church *(printed*
at the Herald and Banner Office, Dayton, Ohio, 1862). The selections
following contain her treatment of the various "Objections of Women
Speaking" in the church and call everyone to "awake to this important
subject."[62]

In this chapter I design noticing some of the frivolous objections
to woman's rights in the church.

Objection 1st—The Saviour did not choose them for Apostles.
True; but only twelve were to be chosen; and the privations and
sufferings were so great as sufficiently to account for her being excused; but among the seventy disciples we find her filling her place.
Disciples signifies learners without distinction of sex.

Objection 2nd—Revelations 2:20. "I have a few things against thee
because thou sufferest that woman Jezebel who calleth herself a
prophetess to teach." This certainty proves that there were true prophetesses, or this false one could not have imposed herself upon the
church. Should this text prove that a religious woman has no right to
preach? On the same ground of reasoning we may say, the men have
no right to preach, as we read of false prophets frequently, and this
is the only false prophetess we read of. Any religious person would
have something against a church that would suffer such a wicked
character as she to teach the servants of God. And John would have
as much against them for admitting a wicked man.

Objection 3d—Paul forbids the female to teach in the church, and
of course if the inspired Apostle will not permit her to teach, it is
wrong. Timothy 2:11, 12—"let the woman (that is the single number)
learn in silence." Who was she, the man's wife? Who was she forbidden to teach? The man, not the church. Now if this teaching means
preaching, it would read thus: "I suffer not a woman to teach in the
church." But this has no reference to that; for Paul never silenced
them, only when he silenced the men, and then he assigns a reason.
But some men are so willing to silence them, they take this Scripture
that proves she should be in subjection to her husband to silence them

in church, when it is not mentioned in this chapter. But the Apostle assigns the reason why she was to be silent, 5:13: For Adam was first formed, then Eve—Now if you take this word teach in the full sense of the word, and do not explain Scripture by Scripture, you will have the woman on a level with the slave—you can teach her, but she dare not teach you, the mother dare not teach her children, and oh! what heathenism we would have, if she was to see any of her fellow creatures in wickedness, she dare not teach them the right way; she would not be permitted to teach school, or teach in the Sabbath School, or college, not yet in the Church. Were she forbidden all these privileges, many that are now rejoicing with the instruction they have received, would be in heathenish darkness. But says the objector, "I am willing she should teach every where except in the Church, for there has been much good done by her teaching in schools and elsewhere. We may thank her for the first Sabbath school that ever was organized among Protestants.

Objection 4th—"It does not look well for her to go into the pulpit with the men." Oh, yes, they are more particular than Jesus Christ, who commissioned them to preach to men, and his apostles that labored with them in the gospel. I suppose they are so nice they will want two heavens, one for the women and one for the men.

Objection 5th—Corinthians 14:34, "Let your women keep silence in the churches." Now, says one, she dare not preach, for Paul has silenced her. 5:28, "Let him keep silence in the Church," and let him speak to himself and to God. He has not the privilege to speak to his wife, and thus we see the man was silenced more particularly than the woman, for she had the privilege to ask her husband. Says the reader, "It is not reasonable to suppose that the man was silent? Oh yes, you can reason when an effort is made to silence the man, but you can silence the woman without reason or judgment. I think sound reason and sense, with the Bible would teach any one that woman has the right to worship God according to the dictates of her conscience, as well as men. Says one, "I never knew the word of God silenced a man." No, for you always read that place with your green spectacles on, i.e., prejudice against woman's preaching. But what is the cause of this? There were so many tongues and languages, the law forbid either male or female speaking in the Church, unless the interpreter was present. But if he was there, all that had the spirit of prophecy might speak, 5:31, "for ye all may prophesy one by one." Here the apostle gives privilege for all to speak. Now if there were women in the Church, you will have to admit they have a right to prophesy or preach. So we find that St. Paul silenced both male and female, and at the proper time gives them all the opportunity to speak, one by one: 5:29, 30—"let the prophets speak two or three and if anything be revealed to another that sitteth by, let the first hold his peace (that is

the men) and if the women are sitting by, silent, then they have a right
to speak if the spirit reveals anything to them, and let the men hold
their peace. But says the objector, 5:35—"if she will learn anything,
let her ask her husband at home," and they take this to prove she had
no right to preach, and there is a great difference between learning
and preaching. Now would any one think a person going to preach
a sermon, was going to Church to learn. No Sir. All say learn first.

Objection 6th—"Paul says it is a shame for a woman to speak in the
Church," and of course it means preaching. No it does not. Webster
says, we never say to speak an argument, a sermon or a story, and if
we wish to tell the story of the cross, it would be preaching, and the
Bible gives the same privilege to the woman as to the man. I admit
with the apostle, that it would be shame for her to rise and speak when
the law silenced both men and women, as the Jews had a law that if
a man was speaking in a public assembly another man sitting by who
did not understand what was said, had a right to ask questions that
he might learn. But this was not allowed to any woman, and this has
no reference to preaching but only asking questions. If they do, they
answer them themselves, and this would not be learning themselves
but teaching the congregation.

Objection 7th—She should not preach, for she is styled the weaker
vessel—1 Peter 3:4. We admit she has not generally as strong a constitution as the man, but there are some women who are more robust
than some men that preach. So this objection will not do for them,
because it would take their right and give it to the women. If she is
weaker, it does not prove she has no right to preach, for if she had
the strength of a Sampson, and no mind, she could not preach. God
never said she had the weaker mind, but he has chosen the weak
things of this world to confound the mighty. Then if she is God's
choice for the promotion of good in the world and the advancement
of his kingdom, no one has any right to say she shall not preach or
pray in the Church, for there are as strong-minded and intelligent
women as men. Then why not give them equal rights in the Church
with the men.

Objection 8th—Some men say the woman has no soul; but I think
no sensible person would say so, if he would consider the difficulty
he runs himself into, for as soon as he says the female has no soul he
will have to admit he has *two;* for eight souls were saved in Noah's Ark;
there were only four men and four women. And if they have two, they
will have to prepare more for the saving of them than they generally
do if they save them both. I think in the effort he would give one to
his wife if he could. God has said we shall work out our own salvation
with fear and trembling before the Lord. But I suppose by the actions
and conversation of some men, they think they can work out the
salvation of their women, for they will not permit them to worship for

themselves. If you wish more proof that a woman has a soul you can read Numbers 30, where her soul is referred to eleven times, and I think you will never say again that she has no soul. Further, when you say that a woman has no right to preach, you limit the spirit of God, and virtually say, that God can not make the impression on her mind that he does on the man's, and say she shall not prophesy, when God says she shall. In this you contradict the inspired word of God in many places, even the teachings of the Savior himself while He was here upon earth, for he commissioned woman to preach his own everlasting gospel.

Objection 9th—It is not right for women to preach to men; this is all a notion, and prejudice is the cause of it, for there is more scripture to prove that women have a right to preach to men, than there is to prove they have a right to preach to women; for the Savior said to the woman: "Go, tell thy Brethren,"—Matthew 28:10. There is no place in the word of God where the men are commanded to preach to the women separate from the men, and we have no such divisions in the word of God, for the inspired Apostle says: "They are all one in Jesus Christ." Then why not worship together as one family, as God designed we should. It would look more like Christianity. In reading the notes of an eminent writer (Barnes), on Galatians, 3:28, he gives the slave the same privilege with his master, in regard to religion. One has no right to rule the other, which is right, for in Christ Jesus they are one; and, further, they are admitted to the favor of God, without respect to their external condition in society. We understand this gives the slave the same right to preach the gospel as his master. He admits the female has a right to salvation, but on what plan he would have them saved I do not know, for he does not grant them the privilege of working out their salvation as the word of God does. But I suppose he would have them die in a state of innocence in order that they might be saved; and he does not grant them the same right to worship God as the slave, for he has the right with his master. I do not presume the gentleman has any wife, or he would grant her the right to worship God according to the dictates of her conscience. It is only where Christianity has been felt, that woman is elevated. It is the Christianity of the Bible that has elevated her to the rights in Church that he has, but not Mr. Barnes' teaching, for he does not permit her the right of the slave. But the Bible says: "Ye are all one." "But," says he, "this does not mean that the sexes are to be regarded, in all respects, equal; it does not prove the duties of the ministry are to be performed by the female; the passage proves only that in regard to salvation they are on a level." But the Bible does not say so, and thus you see he contradicts the word of God, for he says, through his inspired Apostles and prophets, that "the daughters and handmaidens shall prophecy or preach"; and Dr. Clarke, Henry Burkit, Scott, and other learned men, agree with the Bible and say she has a right to preach if God has called her to the work by his spirit. You might as well try to convince me that I have no soul as to persuade me that God never called me to preach his Gospel. He admits she has a right to Heaven. I presume he would prefer a female Heaven, or have them in one corner by themselves, as he will not permit them to worship as men, of course, he would not have them in the same place; but, perhaps he might admit them long enough to sing. If the woman has not the same opportunity to worship as the man of course she can not enjoy the same happiness. He speaks much of the female being elevated where Christianity has its influence; but I presume his teaching would not elevate her very much, not even with the slave. Thus you see how far he is from the word of God. He says, Christianity elevates the female, and has thus made important changes in the world! Yet he will not admit her equality until she arrives in Heaven.

ARGUMENTS REJECTING WOMEN'S RIGHT TO PREACH

Document 6: "Woman's Place in Religious Meetings"

Even though the Congregationalists pioneered in ordaining women, most members of this denomination maintained traditional views of the sexes. Immediately following the Civil War, Victorian values prevailed among upper-class, educated church people. Women were believed to be eternally in subjection to men, although there might be "apparent exceptions." Most women, however, were encouraged to serve within unique and special spheres of activity in the church. The following selection, written by C. Duren and describing "Woman's Place in Religious Meetings" (Congregational Review, January, 1868), is a good example of the "separate but equal" argument that denied women the right to preach.[63]

Man is made the head of the woman. The place of woman, in the family and in society, is one of subjection to man. Man was first formed, and to have dominion of the earth. Woman was formed out of the man, and to be a "helpmeet for him" (Genesis 2:18), a help as over against him, corresponding to him, or the counterpart of him. The scriptural position of woman is one of subjection to man, both in the Jewish and Christian church. The Jewish religion raised the sex far above her rank among the Gentiles; the Christian religion has greatly elevated her. But Christianity has not changed her position in society. The Scriptures very definitely settle the place of woman, and give reasons for it; and we can plainly discern the propriety of the place assigned her. The divine word alone gives us satisfactory and fundamental truth on this point. It proves itself our guide in this, as well as in most matters both pertaining to this life and to the life to come. We find at the present time the "strong-minded" leaving the teachings of Scripture, and trying to reason out the duty and mission of woman; and they are quite confused by the acknowledged fact that she is the equal of man, and the unquestioned fact also that she is differently organized. The inspired word teaches us; and, in both the Jewish and Christian church of the Scriptures, we find her filling beautifully her proper sphere; and we find few, yet sufficient, regulations and admonitions in regard to her duties and work. She is the equal of man, and his help; in some qualities she is his inferior, in other qualities his superior. She is the counterpart of man; this word fitly expresses her place; so that together, and neither alone, they form one whole, one supplying, in many respects, what is wanting in the other. They are not equal, in the sense that they have both equal rule and authority, but equal in their respective spheres.

The Apostle insists that, as compared with man, she must be "in subjection," she must not "usurp authority over the man," she must "learn in silence," "be in silence." There is a seeming harshness, we should say in these days, indelicacy, uncourteousness, in these expressions. But this is according to the truth everywhere taught in Scripture. While the Apostle Paul thus decidedly expresses himself, he always shows his appreciation and honor of women. He associated them with him in his Christian labors. He makes affectionate remembrance of them as his "helpers in Christ." He sends numerous salutations to them in his epistles. He found a most useful place for them in the church. They have always performed with great earnestness and fidelity their duties as members of the church. Though their sphere is more private, they have accomplished at least as great and useful a work as the brethren. Yet the Apostle insists in this passage and elsewhere, that their place in the church is not as public teachers, nor in any way to act as assuming authority.

What is the place of woman in the church; the passage does not call us to discuss. She filled a most useful and necessary place in the primitive church; as the New Testament and the records of the early church show. But the Apostle here teaches what is not her place: "I suffer not a woman to teach nor to usurp authority over the man," but to "learn in silence with all subjection." There can be no doubt that he here refers to her teaching in the church, though it is not expressly stated. He more fully expresses himself, 1 Corinthians 14:34, 35: "Let your women keep silence in the churches; for it is not permitted unto them to speak: but they are commanded to be under obedience, as also saith the law. And if they will learn anything, let them ask their husbands at home; for it is a shame for women to speak in the church." Now these passages most evidently do not forbid females to take any part in religious meeting, for it is evident that they did exercise their spiritual gifts in the early churches. They prayed and prophesied, and exercised perhaps the gifts of faith, and sacred song, and unknown tongues. But we may judge from the instructions of the Apostle that the more manly and assuming spiritual gifts of teaching, government, miracles, healing, were rarely, if ever, bestowed upon them, or exercised by them. Those spiritual gifts that they did exercise in religious meetings, the Apostle teaches, should be used in a modest and unassuming manner, becoming the station of woman. Hence he enjoined that, when they prophesied or prayed, they should not do it with the head uncovered: "Is it comely that a woman pray unto God uncovered?" i.e., in the religious meeting. "Doth not nature herself teach her" this, in giving "her hair for a covering?" "If any man seem to be contentious, we have no such custom, neither the churches of God."

The reason is given why the woman should not teach nor speak in the church. It is because this would be usurping authority over the man; and her place is to "learn in silence in all subjection." It is because "the head of the woman is the man"; and "the woman is the glory of the man."

These reasons, which the Apostle assigns, together with the general teaching of Scripture in regard to woman's place in the church, will teach us, I think, the meaning of the Apostle in "not suffering a woman to teach." A woman should not take such a part in religious meeting, as shall seem to be assuming authority; she should not be a public religious teacher; she should not put herself forward and make herself conspicuous. She is then forbidden to lead in any of the exercises of public worship. In all, large and promiscuous religious meetings, she would be out of her sphere to take part. In the business of the church it is not her place to deliberate, and counsel, and vote, except by courtesy. She is debarred certainly, by the rule of the Apostle, from the ministry, the duties of which belong to men.

Yet in ordinary social religious meetings, the instructions of the Apostle do not forbid her to take part. But they teach her to perform such a part, at such times, and in such circumstances, as become the subjection and modesty of her sex.

In meetings where both sexes are present, a responsibility and duty do not devolve upon women to participate in the services, as upon the men. But the teachings of Scripture do not debar her from taking part for the edification and interest of the meeting. So far as she can contribute to make it spiritual, social and enlivening, there is certainly an obligation resting upon her. Christianity has done much for woman, and it is fitting that she bear witness to its power, and speak of her love to the Saviour. It has cultivated her mental and moral powers, and given her rich inward experience, even superior to man's. She has unsurpassed social powers, a quickness of perception and sympathy, which eminently qualify her for the social, conference exercises of the prayer meeting. She excels in pouring out her heart unto God in prayer, in conversation, in feeling, in nice discrimination, in spiritual experience. Shall she not use these qualities for the enlivening and edification of the social meeting? Shall she not join in the fellowship of Christians with each other and with God? This is not usurping the place of teaching which the Apostle forbids. Her words are certainly more animating and edifying than the stammering, hesitating words of many of the brethren. Men are engaged for the live-long day in the distractions and toils and worldliness of business. It is hard for them to leave these for the atmosphere of the prayer meeting. Woman is shielded from many of these withering and chilling influences. She preserves a more constant communion with God, and a more continual impression of truth. Shall not the social meeting receive the benefit of this? Is it not fitting that she appear there, not merely in silent worship, to help with her inward prayers and feelings, but as an active, living, speaking disciple? May she not communicate, as well as receive? As the Saviour first appeared to woman, after his resurrection, and as they ministered to him during his life, so the Saviour's most precious and intimate manifestations have been to woman. The social meeting is the becoming place for her to testify what the Saviour has done for her.

The prayer meeting is often very thinly attended, is sometimes in the private parlor, or quite as frequently in the kitchen. The church is often very small, especially in its male members. While, too, the brethren are away, engrossed in business, their worldly hearts suggesting that they have no time for the religious meeting, the sisters gather to the place of prayer, as of old they gathered around the cross. The necessity of the case often renders it desirable and proper that the females take part in the exercises of the religious meeting. Many of the small country churches could with difficulty sustain the church meeting and the prayer meeting, without the help of the female member. Many of the neighborhood prayer meetings could with difficulty be sustained without their aid. If their voices be silent the services will at least be very meagre and dragging and uninteresting. Then, in these small and social gatherings, is it right, that, while free and unrestrained religious conversation is indulged, while assembling, it shall suddenly degenerate into a cold and silent and barren service? Shall such a stupifying enchantment be connected with the announcement: "the meeting is begun"?

Yet, while the Scriptures allow a place to woman in the services of the social meeting, and grace and experience beautifully prepare her for that place, let the teachings of the Apostle not be forgotten. Let her not be assuming. Let modesty, the nice sense of female propriety, govern her conduct, and her mode of using her gifts. Let her not undertake the unseemly part to teach, to dictate, to control. Her place is in the social meetings, and not in the promiscuous gathering, or large assembly; in private and not in public worship.

But while the place of woman is private, and in subjection, it is most cheerfully conceded that some women are capable and fitted for what others are not. The Apostle gives the general rule. And while the rule should in all cases be regarded, there may be apparent exceptions. Some special mission may at times be given to woman, as to Deborah and Huldah of old. A very prominent and conspicuous place was filled by Mary Lyon and Fidelia Fisk. Some queens have ruled well; and some women have made extraordinary scientific attainments. The sphere of such rarely qualified women is peculiar, yet, if we should closely examine these cases, we should find that even to them the rule of the Apostle applied and very excellently, too. Among the women of Scripture, who assumed very conspicuous places, are Deborah, Huldah, Anna, Miriam, and the daughters of Philip the evangelist. But Deborah, though she was a wise woman and judged Israel, did not go at the head of the army. Huldah was endowed with the prophetic gift; but she does not stand forth prominent in the civil and religious history of the Jews. Anna, though she devoted herself to the service of God in the temple, did not at all go beyond the bounds of female modesty and propriety. Miriam led the songs of her countrywomen after the triumph at the Red Sea. The daughters of Philip by no means stand forth in any public capacity. The females of the Corinthian church received spiritual gifts; but they appear to have been of a kind befitting their sex; and they were enjoined to use them in a modest and unassuming manner.

The Apostle assigns two reasons why the position of woman is one of subjection.

1. For Adam was first formed, then Eve," verse 13. Adam was made to "have dominion"; Eve, to be a "helpmeet for man." "The man is not of the woman, but the woman of the man. Neither was the man created for the woman, but the woman for the man." 1 Corinthians 11:8, 9. She was created therefore, not to lead and bear authority, but to be subject, to take the subordinate place. There must be a head, an order, in the family and in society; and "the head of the woman is the man." 1 Corinthians 11:3. The organization of woman indicates her sphere. She was so "formed," that she is naturally dependent clinging to the stronger arm of man, controlling by her gentle and winning ways, and her nice discrimination, and her persuasive words, and not by authority and force. She is delicate and beautiful in structure, and not strong; winning, and not commanding, in her bearing. Her place, in the family and in society, is marked by the order of her creation, by the style of her organization, by the kind of her qualities, by the nature of her duties and work.

2. Woman was made to be in subjection, because "Adam was not

deceived; but the woman, being deceived, was in the transgression," i.e., was the first and chief to blame, verse 14. Why did Satan tempt the woman, rather than the man? Because he had reason to suppose that he could more easily prevail. Her nature rendered her more pliable, more easy to be persuaded. She was not formed with those stern and strong qualities that more particularly pertain to man. Therefore she is fitted, not to lead, and command, and reason, and teach, but to be in subjection, to be reliant. Her will is as strong as that of man; but it is controlled by feeling and impulse, rather than by reason. Her emotions are stronger; her understanding is relatively weaker. One suggests the consideration, that she is not a safe teacher, because at first she was deceived, and led man into sin; and she would be very likely to lead others again into error and sin.

But while this is a proper interpretation of the verse, we must also remember that her place of subjection is in punishment for her guilt in being first deceived. God's curse upon woman was, "thy desire shall be to thy husband, and he shall rule over thee." Genesis 3:16.

But, verse 15, though woman is subject to the man, she receives the full benefits of salvation by Christ; yea, she is entitled to, and has received, a larger portion, "notwithstanding she shall be saved in childbearing, if they continue in faith and charity, and holiness, with sobriety." There is no objection to this being received by the pious mother as promise of preservation in the perils of childbirth. But the translation is evidently to be preserved. "She shall be saved through, on account of, child-bearing," δια. She shall be saved, σχθήσεται, not preserved, delivered. It is the appropriate word to signify the salvation wrought by Christ.

"She shall be saved through, on account of, childbearing." The meaning is expressed by Paul in the passage before referred to, 1 Corinthians 11:11, 12: "Nevertheless, neither is the man without the woman, neither the woman without the man, in the Lord. For as the woman is of the man, so is the man also by the woman; but all things of God." Though the woman was created for the man, yet the man is born of the woman. Her honorable office is to introduce man into the world. By her are children nurtured in their tender years. Some consider that τεχνογονίας, in the text, has the meaning of "the nurturing of children"; but "childbearing" is its proper signification; though the word reminds us also of her office in the education of children. It is woman that is earliest and most efficient in forming character. By her is the church increased. Very much does the church owe to pious mothers, to pious teachers, to pious women. Therefore is she equally with man, perhaps we may say, rather than man, entitled to the blessings and privileges of salvation. Together with all the qualities of humanity, she is honored by bearing children, and by giving the first and most permanent impressions to their characters. Therefore she has specially been honored by her Saviour. With exceeding beauty does religion adorn her character.

Together with this interpretation, and included in it, is the idea: "She shall be saved, through bearing him who is the seed of the woman"; through whom man and woman, and all the nations of the earth, are blessed; by whom alone any one can be saved.

There is a noticeable change of number in this verse. "She shall be saved through childbearing, if *they* continue in faith, and love, and holiness, with sobriety." Not only she who bears children, but all women who exercise these graces shall be saved. The promise is to all the sex on these conditions.

Document 7: "Woman's Position and Work in the Church"

Throughout the last several decades of the century, the conservative religious leadership of the nation spent considerable energy explaining why women should not be allowed to preach in the church. The stated reasons were primarily biblical and historical. The selection following is a classic summary of most of the arguments. Written by Samuel J. Niccolls, "Woman's Position and Work in the Church" appeared in the conservative Presbyterian Review *(April, 1889). Here Niccolls tries to put to rest many of the reasons cited for change, while maintaining appreciation for traditional women's work in the church.*[64]

Woman's position in society has come to be regarded as one of the most important tests of true progress in civilization. When we reflect upon her all-powerful influence in the home life, and remember the patent fact that the actual civilization of a people is just that of its average home life, no one can question the appropriateness or justness of this test. Nature and experience teach that the two sexes are joined together in indissoluble wedlock, and neither socially nor morally can one prosper without the other. As in Paradise, so now, they must rise or fall together:

> "The woman's cause is man's; they rise or sink
> Together, dwarfed or God-like, bond or free."

For this reason, a religion or civilization that honors man and dishonors woman, that seeks to exalt one sex and degrade the other, shows itself to be self-contradictory, and proclaims its own ultimate overthrow. It is false to the demands of human nature. It is, then, no unreasonable question to ask of any religion: "What has it to say concerning woman and her relation to man?" Its reply will determine whether it will be a blessing or a curse to the race. The answer which Christianity gives to this question is clear and positive. It is written in a single phrase on the first pages of the inspired record—"an help-meet for man." No definition of woman's position and work is so

comprehensive and exact, and none so honorable to her as this. In
unequivocal terms, it teaches the equality of the sexes. According to
the biblical story of her creation, woman is not man's superior nor
inferior. She is of the same nature with man; made like him in the
Divine image. She was created to be, not his rival or substitute, but his
inspiration, his helpmeet. Since it "was not good for man to be alone,"
she was to give a fulness and glory to his life which were not possible
without her presence and companionship. Matthew Henry's quaint
comment is still true and to the point: "She was not made out of his
head to top him; nor out of his feet to be trampled upon by him, but
out of his side to be equal with him; under his arm to be protected,
and near his heart to be beloved."

The Old Testament Scriptures show, as does the sad experience
of life, how much woman has suffered through sin; but throughout
all their teachings, they consistently maintain the Divine ideal of
woman's mission in her creation. In the New Testament the same
doctrine is clearly unfolded. There, as in Paradise, woman is seen in
the kingdom of grace as man's equal and companion, entitled to all
the blessings of the New Dispensation. Every privilege purchased by
atoning blood is open to her. She equally and as fully as man can "put
on Christ." "There is neither Jew nor Greek; there is neither bond nor
free, there is neither male nor female; for ye are all one in Christ
Jesus." The highest title of honor given her is that old creation-word
—"helper."

But while proclaiming woman's equality with man, the Scriptures
just as plainly affirm her subordination to him. This is not only the
teaching of the story of her creation in Paradise, but also that of an
inspired apostle: "But I would have you know, that the head of every
man is Christ; and the head of the woman is the man; and the head
of Christ is God. Neither was the man created for the woman; but the
woman for the man." This doctrine is in exact harmony with the
ordination of nature. It is written, not primarily in the Christian
documents, and then arbitrarily imposed upon woman; but first in
the constitution of the sexes. Nature proclaims woman's dependence
upon man, and her own heart answers to this law. The terms "subordination" and "dependence" are doubtless hateful to some in these
days, who insist upon woman's emancipation from man's tyranny;
and they must ever be irritating to self-will and pride. Unquestionably
also, man's selfishness and abuse of power have tended to give to them
a meaning akin to slavery and degradation. But in their true Gospel
meaning, they no more imply inferiority or servile subjection than
complete submission to Christ implies dishonor to the believer. On
the contrary, they describe relations in which, paradoxical as it may
seem, woman secures her supremacy over man. The highest degree
of love is reached only through self-abnegation and self-sacrifice.
Humility is love's crown of glory. The noblest love comes not to be

ministered unto, but to minister, and lay down its life for others. It conquers through loving service. Woman's divinely appointed mission is one of love. And it is in exact conformity with the nature of that mission, that the position given her by her Creator, in her relation to man, while not one of inferiority, should still be one of subordination and dependence. In accepting it she acquires her sweet and all-powerful supremacy of love, and in her legitimate empire influences man more powerfully than he controls her.

But whatever may be said for or against this doctrine, we are now concerned only with the fact that it is the doctrine of the Scriptures with reference to woman's position. And, further, it is entitled to stand among the distinctive features of Christianity, by which it is differentiated in its teachings from all other religions. It is well known that in all the religions of heathendom, woman was relegated to an inferior position. In no respect was she considered man's equal. She became his drudge, his slave, or the victim of his lusts. She was not regarded as his God-sent help-meet and true companion. The highest and noblest philosophy of antiquity had no conception of woman's equality with man. The best position it could assign her was one of abject dependence and servile submission to her husband. The ruling class in Greece and Rome looked upon her with mingled mistrust and contempt. But no further proof is needed to show that the degradation of woman is one of the characteristics of a false religion, than to point to her condition to-day in Mohammedan and heathen countries.

The Christian doctrine also stands in equally sharp and distinct contrast with an extreme on the opposite side of the truth. It is the asserted superiority of woman. This fanaticism, less congenial to the sin-perverted nature of man than his desire to keep her in subjection, has never prevailed widely; but it has appeared nevertheless in various forms in the past. Its voice can be heard in some of the anti-Christian doctrines of the present day. It is characteristic of not a few of the arguments which are made to justify woman's appearance in public life, and it is embodied in the latest-born religion of the human intellect, Comptism, with its doctrine of the superior priesthood of woman. It cannot be claimed for the Christian view of woman's position and vocation, that it has always been taught and enforced in the Church. Like other distinctive doctrines of Christianity, it has been obscured by error, thrust into the background, or modified to suit the spirit of the times. From the very first it had to enter into conflict with the all-prevailing notions and practices of heathenism. It was a little leaven cast into a great mass of meal. Nor can it be said that in all Christian lands, woman is enjoying the privileges and rights, either in Church or State, to which she is entitled, according to the teachings of the Gospel of Christ. But this much is undoubtedly true, that all she has already obtained in the way of true liberty and equality with man is owing to the Gospel. It is a matter of history that just in proportion as Christianity gained ascendency in society, the position of woman, legal, social, and religious, improved. It emancipated her from the yoke of oppression under which she had groaned for long centuries. It elevated her to her God-assigned place by man's side. It redeemed her from the curse of polygamy, and restored the marriage relation to its original form. It gave her a new sacredness and a new glory by her connection with the Divine Saviour of the world. The transformation of her position under the influence of the Gospel, though gradual, was permanent; and although her emancipation is not complete, we can confidently point to Christian womanhood as furnishing one of the grandest proofs of the power of the Gospel to elevate and bless our race. The fact, then, that the Gospel has done so much for woman in the past, furnishes an additional reason why her present and future should be controlled by its great and immutable principles. She, more than man, at least in this world, has need of its protecting and fostering care. For her to discard its teachings at this day would not only be base ingratitude to her deliverer, but it would be to invite the return of her old bondage and degradation. She, above all others, ought to reject every doctrine, no matter how plausible or reasonable it may seem, which would lead her to underrate or set aside the distinctive Christian doctrine with reference to her vocation. She cannot afford to let the wisdom of the world, or the so-called spirit of progress, or a plausible liberalism, appealing to self-interest and vanity, teach her. For her to part company with the Bible, is to forsake the only teacher and guide who has insisted upon and defined her rights, and led her to true liberty. And yet in these days, doctrines which attempt to set aside the inspired teachings are proclaimed to woman as defining her Christian duty. A cunning exegesis is called to explain away Apostolic commands. The very apostle whose inspired pen wrote more clearly than any other "the declaration of woman's rights," is designated as "an old fogy," a "crusty old bachelor," and is treated as unworthy of regard in his utterances, because they run counter to the demands of a false liberty.

The true method of inquiry, then, concerning woman's position and work in the Church, is to ask, What does the Word of God teach? What are its principles, and how are they to be applied to this question? A careful study of the New Testament will reveal the following facts: First. Woman has an important position in the Church of the New Dispensation. Women followed our Lord in his public ministry and ministered to him. They watched him with undying love on the cross. They were the earliest at the sepulchre, and were the first to announce with mortal lips, the tidings of his resurrection from the dead. They were present at the organization of the Church, and received with the rest the gift of the Holy Ghost. Nor was this position one of inferiority. Remembering that the Gospels were written in an age when woman was universally regarded as inferior to man, and when even the Levitical law placed certain humiliating restrictions upon her, it is, to say the least, extraordinary that there is not the faintest trace of this spirit in the Gospels. We find it in the Koran, in the sacred books of India, and in the Greek and Roman literature of the Gospel period, but not in the New Testament. Besides this negative testimony, there is positive teaching. Paul's declaration, "There is neither Jew nor Greek, there is neither bond nor free, there is neither male nor female; for ye are one in Christ Jesus," sets forth the great fundamental principle of the New Dispensation, that there is no distinction of persons in it. The artificial or natural distinctions that prevail in the world do not disqualify any from participating in the benefits and blessings of a common salvation. All become sons and daughters of God, and joint heirs with Christ Jesus. A careful perusal also of the New Testament will show that both sexes labored together in the establishment of the Church, and that the work of the one is not more acceptable in the sight of God than the work of the other. Indeed, as if realizing that there would be in that age a tendency to depreciate woman's work in the Church, Paul takes pains to commend those women who had labored with him in the Gospel, and thus holds up their example as worthy of imitation by others. Heartily he commends "Phebe our sister, which is a servant (deacon) of the Church which is at Cenchrea"; "Mary, who bestowed much labor on us"; "Tryphena and Tryphosa, who labor in the Lord"; "the beloved Persis, which labored much in the Lord"; and "those women (of Philippi) which labored with me in the Gospel." He records not only his own thanks, but also those of "all the Churches of the Gentiles," to Priscilla and Aquila his "helpers in Christ Jesus." The ministry of Dorcas is recorded for the instruction and imitation of those who are to come after her, and in the Gospel narrative the names of the Marys, and Martha, and Joanna, and Susanna shine like stars in the firmament. There is enough to show that in the foundation and organization of the Church, woman's work was not exceptional; and that man did not have a monopoly of teaching and preaching the Gospel of Christ.

A second fact plainly appears from the New Testament. It is that a woman's work in the Church was not separated from that of man. It did not run in a line parallel with his; it was co-ordinate; her work was mingled with his. She was a helpmeet at his side. The phrases, "which labored with me in the Gospel," "my helpers in Christ Jesus," and "who bestowed much labor on us," are at once significant and descriptive of the manner in which the service was rendered. These women labored not without man, but with him. The sexes were not segregated in their work, so that woman's work was exclusively for woman, and man's for man.

The third fact clearly seen on the whole face of the narrative is that woman's work was subordinate to that of man. In accordance with the great principles already referred to, man has the leadership. To him is given rule in the Church. There is not a solitary hint of a woman being placed in the position of an apostle, evangelist, pastor, elder, or ruler. There is indeed, good reason to believe that she ministered in the diaconate, and in this sense she occupied an official position on the staff of the Church. If the word in Romans 16:1 had been translated as it is elsewhere in the common version, and as it is rendered in the margin of the Revised Version, the whole passage would read, "I commend unto you Phebe our sister who is a deacon of the Church at Cenchrea." But the Apostolic Church knew of no female bishop or presbyter. Women also shared in the gift of "prophesying" in the Apostolic Church. That gift, according to the Word of God, was to be one of the miraculous signs attending the outpouring of the Spirit upon all flesh. "I will pour out my Spirit upon all flesh; and your sons and your daughters shall prophesy, and your young men shall see visions, and your old men shall dream dreams; and on my servants and on my handmaidens I will pour out in those days of my Spirit; and they shall prophesy." But this gift of prophecy must not be confounded with the preaching and teaching of the Gospel. It was a special utterance or testimony made under the direct inspiration of the Holy Ghost. It was a miraculous endowment of an extraordinary character, and with other like gifts was especially suited to the needs of the Apostolic period. Woman shared in this high honor equally with man; but in the exercise of it, she was under the limitations of the law of subordination which God has established in nature and written in his Word. She was not, even when directly inspired by the Holy Ghost, to prophesy with her head uncovered. The whole direction of the Apostle on this point, translated into our every-day language, is equivalent to saying: "Even when under the power of the Spirit, do not forget your position as a true woman and dishonor your sex by assuming one that does not belong to you. Let not the excitement of a good cause lead you to forget that modesty and humility which are the true glory of your sex." There was then evidently, even under the power of inspiration, a woman's way of prophesying and a man's way—that is, a method suitable to each sex. The wisdom and necessity of the inspired direction in this matter is fully vindicated, when it is remembered how often in times of religious excitement, extreme and unnatural measures have been used for good ends, which afterward were regretted; or else, the subsequent attempt to justify them brought confusion and heresies into the Church.

But apart from this occasional exercise of the miraculous gift of prophecy, we do not find in the New Testament a single case justifying the belief that women in that age engaged in the open, public, and official preaching of the Gospel. There is, indeed, the instance of a certain damsel in Philippi uttering her testimony to the truth of the

Gospel in the streets, but she, alas, was possessed with an evil spirit. When it is written that Anna "spake of Him to all that looked for redemption in Jerusalem," we are not to read into that declaration a meaning derived from modern methods; but it is to be interpreted in view of the customs of that time. In the absence of any proof to the contrary, we must infer that her message was given privately, just as it was to that little family group that heard her testimony in the temple. That woman was a teacher of the Gospel, and a true herald of its glad tidings in the Apostolic Church is undisputed. But requires only a glance to see that her ministry was a household ministry as compared with the public and official proclamation of the Word assigned to man. Even when she fills the office of deacon, as in the case of Phebe, it is of this character. In general, women are exhorted to be "in behavior as becometh holy women, teachers of good things; that they teach the young woman to be sober, to love their husbands, to love their children, to be discreet, chaste, keepers at home, good, obedient to their husbands, that the Word of God be not blasphemed." Indeed, some modern difficulties seem to have troubled the Apostolic Church. St. Paul writes concerning some of the young widows, "They have cast off their first faith. And withal they learn to be idle, wandering about from house to house; and not only idle, but tattlers also and busybodies, speaking things which they ought not." The ambitious and independent woman ready for controversy, and clamorous for her "right" to stand in public places with man, impatient of her own work and eager to demonstrate how well she can do man's special work, is not the woman whom the New Testament crowns with honor and commends as the "helper" of man. The holy women, whose names shine with quenchless lustre on its pages, whose works are recorded for imitation, and whose characters are to be models to their sex, were not those who "usurped authority" or sought to break loose from the more retired yet not less important sphere to which the rule of the Gospel assigned them. Whatever may be said in favor of woman's preaching or exercising rule in the Church, or of training her to share in the ministry now exercised by man, it is a perversion of Scripture to use the language of the New Testament as justifying it. An argument in its favor can be made only by reading into special phrases thoughts utterly foreign to the minds of the inspired writers. When Paul writes of those women "who labored with him in the Gospel," of those who were his "helpers," and of those "who labored much in the Lord," he uses just such terms as scores and hundreds of faithful pastors in these days could use in their truest meaning with reference to many faithful women in their churches. No matter whether they bear official titles or not, they are the pastor's most efficient helpers, and he and the whole Church have reason to thank God in their behalf. But it would be just as preposterous in one

case as in the other, to infer from such expressions that these women
were official and ordained preachers of the Gospel and rulers in the
Church.

Such being the testimony of the Scriptures in regard to woman's
work in the Apostolic Church, the question now comes concerning
her work and position in the Church to-day. Is it to be controlled by
the same principles and move along the same lines? Is the Apostolic
doctrine to be enforced to-day, or do the changed times demand a
new departure? In this woman's age, as it has been called, are we to
reverse or set aside the old view which has prevailed all through the
centuries, and establish a new order of relation between the sexes? Is
there to be, what Dr. Bushnell has aptly called it, "a revolt against
nature," and a change in order of both Church and State? Some
loudly declare that there must be. They say the new day, the day of
woman's complete emancipation, is at hand. In the pulpit, at the polls,
in halls of legislation, in Conference and General Assembly, woman
is to be at man's side, ruling not alone in the household, but directly
and officially in the affairs of Church and State. . . .

But it is now claimed that there must be an enlargement of her
sphere; and that the interests of the Church and humanity demand
that woman shall be ordained to the full work of the Gospel ministry,
and be brought to share in the official rule of the Church equally with
man. It is in the light of Scripture and experience that we should
consider this question. And viewed in that light, the arguments used
in its favor are very far from justifying the proposed change.

1. They are anti-scriptural. They are at best of that negative character which teaches, by artful exegesis, that the Scriptures do
   not mean what they say, and what the whole Church for eighteen centuries believed that they teach.
2. They are contradicted by the testimony of history and experience. Exceptional cases of women possessing special gifts for
   public life, or who have been called to a providential mission,
   do not justify the repeal of laws which are established on general principles. Deborah's career would not warrant the establishment of military schools for the training of women for the
   profession of arms. Neither does the exceptional career of
   some women preachers make it obligatory upon the Church to
   turn the attention of her daughters to the public ministry of the
   Word, and to open her theological seminaries for their instruction. Church legislation, when guided by exceptional cases, will
   result in dire confusion. That there may be some women whose
   minds are fitted for the cares and public duties which primarily
   belong to men, or that there may be situations properly belonging to men which women may be obliged to fill, in default of
   man's presence, is to be admitted; but all this does not overturn
   the Divine rule determining woman's vocation.

3. The argument for woman's preaching, based upon her superior qualifications, if admitted, proves too much. It shows that men are usurpers in the pulpit, ought never to have been there, and ought to leave it as soon as a sufficient number of women can be trained to occupy it. It is also a statement contradicted by history and experience. The fact that the great proportion of the women who have already assumed the office of public teaching in the pulpit have departed from the rule of sound doctrine in their teachings, is not calculated to act in her favor.

4. It is misleading and unwarranted by facts to say that there is an urgent demand for woman's presence in the pulpit. That the world needs woman's ministry in the Gospel, and never more urgently than to-day, is indeed true; but it is such a ministry as she alone can give, and can best give in her peculiar sphere. Without it the full triumph of the Gospel will not be secured. Without it man's ministry falls short of success. But she can best help him in the future, as in the past, not by attempting to do his work, but by exercising her own holy and loving ministry.

The magnificent work which woman is now doing to advance the kingdom of Christ is like any other good movement, exposed to certain perils growing out of its own success. We may be sure that the great adversary of souls and of Christ will seek to pervert it, or poison it with false doctrine, or divert it from scriptural lines. Woman once before yielded to the temptation, "yea, hath God said"; and she is not exempt from man's pride and ambition. It would not, indeed, be surprising if the pendulum which so long hung on the side of her subjection should swing to the opposite extreme for a little while. It is, perhaps, too much to hope that no troubles or strifes, or even divisions will grow out of some of the great organizations she has made for the advancement of philanthropic and Christian aims. A tendency to independence or to make woman man's rival, would be fatal to the success she has already achieved in her great missionary organizations. The Gospel plan of Church work is, that both sexes should labor in harmony. Co-operation, not rivalry, is the Divine method. In a certain sense the phrase, "woman's work for woman" is misleading, for her mission is to man; but woman's work for home life defines exactly the centre and direction of her ministry. Any teaching, then, which would divert her attention from this, her God-assigned sphere, under the notion that she must secure leading power rather than renewing and inspiring influence, is fraught with danger. If true to her mission of love, she will seek to work within rather than without. She will glory in ministering rather than in leadership.

On the other hand the Church cannot afford to take a patronizing attitude toward woman's work in the Church, nor yet one of tacit permission. It ought to have official recognition. The whole Church should heed the Apostolic direction, "Help those women which la-

bored with me in the Gospel." Nor do we see any scriptural reason
why woman should not be placed in the diaconate, and thus have
official position on the staff of the Church. Thousands of noble
women—as missionaries, Bible-readers, and visitors—are virtually exercising that office without the title. Let no man forbid them. But it
might be a help, and it would certainly be an appropriate recognition
of their faithful service, if they were officially set apart for this work
by the authority of the Church. But while we gladly recognize and
emphasize the importance of woman's work in the Church at large,
all this must not lead us to overlook or underrate her still greater and
more important work in the "church in the house." She it is who
makes the family, and out of it are the issues of social and public life.
All honor to the faithful and devoted women who, not counting their
lives dear unto themselves, have gone forth as teachers and missionaries to the ignorant and depraved; who labor among the Indians and
Negroes in our own land, or who live in voluntary exile in far-off
lands among the heathen. God measures the greatness of their sacrifice, and shall write their names in His book of remembrance. All
honor to the kindred spirits of their sex, who labor to support those
who are in the field, and make their holy influence felt in every
department of Church work. But all these, by their labor and calling,
have no sanctity or merit above that which belongs to the Christian
wife and mother. To suppose otherwise, is to fall into the error of the
Church of Rome. Woman reaches her highest glory, not on the platform, nor even in the missionary field as teacher and laborer, but in
the centre of home. There is the throne of her power, and above every
other name that can be given her is that of mother. The world needs
more teachers, and missionaries, and helpers, but not so much as it
needs Christian wives and mothers. We may live without the first class,
but to be without the last is to have the very fountains of life defiled
by sin and poisoned by the curse. Unquestionably, it is in the relation
of mother that the influence of woman is most powerful in the world.
Nor is there a nobler being on the earth than a self-sacrificing Christian mother. "She who rocks the cradle rules the world."

Document 8: "Shall Women Preach?"

*Most of the printed arguments against women preaching were
written by male clergy. However, at the turn of the century, the
Lutheran Quarterly published an interesting series of articles in
which a woman reinforced the biblical arguments presented by a
male. A Professor Neve had made a careful exegetical case that Paul's
prohibitions were binding on all Christians for all times. Margaret R.
Seebach, in "Shall Women Preach?" (Lutheran Quarterly, October,
1903) agreed that women should not preach, but based her case upon*

the practical obstacles and innate differences between men and women. Her article follows.[65]

Are there reasons of practical expediency which justify the position of our Church in not accepting women as preachers? Do the education of women and their altered social standing make it unjust to deny them this privilege? There has been much discussion of this question during the last few years, when the papers have been full of notices of pulpits "supplied in the pastor's absense by his wife." An able and spirited plea has come before our own Church in the form of a story from the pen of one who would be herself richly qualified for such service. Meantime our Lutheran women are doing all but preaching, and often, in connection with their missionary work, addressing audiences larger than many a pastor has before him on Sunday. In these we glory, and even apply to them the words of the conservative Paul in saying "Help those women!" Why, then, do we withhold from the crowning privilege? Why not educate and ordain them as pastors?

Some may reply that it is on account of prejudice, which must be overcome gradually by individual successes. The woman who supplies her husband's pulpit steps imperceptibly, they may say, into work for which she is fitted and opens a door to her sisters. Of all the proposed methods, this seems to us the worst. It is not entering into the fold by the door, but climbing up another way. If an unordained layman of one sex may do this, why not of the other? Yet who would want to see the significance of ordination and the value of ministerial education thus set aside, and our pulpits supplied by anyone who knows enough to talk for thirty minutes on religious subjects? When we define the place of a woman in the Church let us never forget that she is a *layman*—pastor's wife or not. It is no more proper and lawful for her to occupy a pulpit on the Sabbath day as a preacher and spiritual guide than to solemnize marriage or baptism. This is said with no intention to exalt the priesthood of the ordained. The universal priesthood of believers is so great and real an honor that no one need envy the ordained minister as nearer to God or more blest by Him. We have self-government in this country, and every citizen can feel himself the equal of a king. Yet all are not magistrates, and it goes ill when those who are not attempt to take the law into their own hands.

Whatever, then, any other laymen may do in the Church, let us grant, if we will, to women. Let them teach in the schools of the Church, let them pray in prayer meetings, let them conduct mid-week services where it is customary for laymen to do these things. But keep the Sabbath ministrations for those who have received training for this very thing, and whose life-work it is.

Then why not educate women for this work? is the next question we have to meet. The answer is manifold, but it all amounts to this: Because it would involve, on the part of women, the celibacy of the clergy. Without going into details, it is just as impossible for a woman to combine home duties with the work of a pastor and preacher as with any other business or profession. Were it possible for her to leave her household in the hands of others so as to give her time for a work which is supposed to occupy the whole time of a man who adopts it, she would lose in moral influence by such indifference to home and children. Even if she had no one but her husband to consider, his own profession would be an obstacle. Should she receive a call from another charge, would he be expected to leave his medical practice, his store, his factory, and follow her? Or if he were a preacher, would it frequently happen that they could get adjoining charges? Evidently, marriage would mean, for a woman, retirement from the active ministry.

Some one objects that there are many unmarried women who could do this work. It must be remembered, however, that in order to gain the best results, education for such a sphere should begin at an age considerably earlier than that at which most women can be considered confirmed spinsters. Would it not be necessary, especially in the case of beneficiaries, to exact from those who entered on such a course a promise not to marry for an almost prohibitive number of years? The Deaconess is not a case in point. Her training is not so protracted nor so costly, nor is her specialty useless after marriage, as much of the technical theological training would be to a woman.

But even if we can conceive of a moral, healthful, helpful woman permanently without family ties or the desire for them, there is another and a fundamental reason why women should not be taught and ordained as preachers. The quality of a woman's mind is different from that of a man. This does not mean necessarily that it is inferior. It simply means that things do not appeal to her from the same side, do not appear to her in the same light as to man. We are not to be startled any more by the saying that reason is the province of the masculine mind, intuition of the feminine. Yet this means that a woman ordinarily cannot convince a man of a thing by argument. In logical presentation of truth, she is usually a failure. Thus arises a serious question: Can a woman's preaching win and hold men in the Church? And when we consider that the great lack of the Church in all ages has been such a virile and logical interpretation of truth as will appeal to *men,* and hold their allegiance, this question assumes large proportions. The Church *has* the women—has always had them; she needs the men!

Personally, it seems to us that even a limited participation in public speech is a dangerous intoxicant for a woman who has any taste at all for it. A woman can sell her mental and spiritual powers in just as meretricious a desire for admiration and influence as her bodily graces. The aesthetic sense, ever the serpent tempter of woman, would too often gain the ascendency, and we should have lectures on philosophy, art, literature, but not sermons. The mere topics of most of the reported "sermons by a woman" are significant examples of this. Woman in public life is too new to be trusted with this most subtle of temptations. Her intentions are good, but she does not realize what a powerful stimulant success of this kind would prove to spiritual dilettantism. Then the balance would swing to the opposite extreme, and we should have women preaching reactionary dogmas to an extent that would amount to intolerance. Logic would save a man from this, while feeling would drive a woman into it. The very sensationalism of doing a thing so new would be a positive spiritual injury to a sensitive mind. As long as we see in the newspapers such startling headlines as "A Woman Preacher," "Filled Her Husband's Pulpit," and the like, let us stand by St. Paul. The time is not ripe.

Lay Women in the Protestant Tradition

ROSEMARY SKINNER KELLER*

Entrance of women into lay leadership decisively changed the status and role of females in Protestant churches during the nineteenth century. These gains began after the Civil War in the 1870s, when women were being denied ordination in many of the same denominations.

Lay leadership by women did not begin in established church structures. Women were not granted authority on an equal basis with men on national and conference administrative boards devoted to mission and educational work. They were also denied voting privileges in most local churches, as well as in legislative bodies at regional and national levels.

Expanded roles and power for females came through the creation of organizations "for women only," particularly home and foreign missionary societies and deaconess orders. Women raised large sums of money to support mission programs and to send female workers into foreign and national fields. For the first time, they became missionaries in their own right, not because they were married to male missionaries. Through self-created separatist organizations, females enlarged their churches' programs. However, they did not directly challenge the established clergy and lay power structures and leadership of their denominations.

More females became involved in women's missionary society work after the Civil War than in all areas of the social reform and woman's rights movements combined. Between 1861 and 1894, foreign missionary societies were organized by and for women in thirty-three denominations, and home missionary societies in seventeen. They represented

*ROSEMARY SKINNER KELLER is Assistant Professor of Religion and American Culture at Garrett-Evangelical Theological Seminary in Evanston, Illinois. She is a diaconal minister in the United Methodist Church, co-director with Rosemary Ruether of the Institute for the Study of Women in the Church at Garrett-Evangelical, and specializes in the history of women in the Wesleyan tradition. She holds a Ph.D. in American History from the University of Illinois: Chicago Circle and a Master of Religious Education from Yale Divinity School.

white and black churches and most immigrant denominations established in the United States by the late nineteenth century. The ability of females to build grass-roots organizations, and to consolidate those groups into regional and national societies, created a new basis of community among women in the churches. The surprising power of women to raise thousands of dollars from the gleanings of "mite boxes" was a major factor in making missions an identifying mark of late nineteenth century Protestantism.[1]

Women saw in the dedication of deaconesses, who ministered to the neediest and lowliest at home and abroad, a reflection of the ministry of Christ. By 1894, the thirty-three foreign mission societies had sent one thousand female missionaries abroad, most of whom were trained in deaconess homes of Protestant denominations. They served as teachers, evangelists, and physicians in schools, churches, and hospitals on every continent. A major focus of deaconesses' ministry in this country was to Christianize and Americanize the immigrants who crowded the inner cities. They also started schools, industrial homes, agricultural projects, and chapels on Indian reservations, in prairie towns, and in backwood settlements.[2]

THE PURPOSE OF THEIR WORK

The work of women's societies and deaconess orders in the late nineteenth century is best understood through the purposes which they set for their organizations. The women recognized, first, that the primary responsibility of the church was to evangelize the world. Until now, females had left the responsibility to the men, who had not offered to share the work with them. These women believed, too, that their special duty in evangelism was to bring the good news to other women, to the five hundred million females held in forced subjection by false religions and oppressive social customs in non-Christian countries. Education and moral uplift were intrinsic parts of their evangelistic efforts toward other women. (Document 1.)

Though society members concentrated their mission on evangelizing and educating oppressed women, they admitted their self-interest in organizing to expand the roles and opportunities of women in their own churches. The editor of the *Heathen Woman's Friend,* journal of the Woman's Foreign Missionary Society of the Methodist Episcopal Church, forthrightly stated this purpose in the first issue in 1869: "Apart from all considerations of duty to others, it will be profitable to ourselves to unite together in such associations as are contemplated by this Society."[3]

The distinctive feature of the movement, therefore, was "woman's work for woman," a phrase that the Woman's Presbyterian Board of Missions used as the title of their monthly publication. The phrase and theme pervaded the literature of women's religious publications, referring to the service of society members and deaconesses to women of non-Christian lands and urban ghettos. These missionary women sought to liberate oppressed females from the bondage and subordination to which they had been subjected by custom and religion. Further, they strove to enable and channel the energy, ability, and leadership of women in the church, through societies "for women only" and deaconess orders, because similar outlets were not available in existing power structures of their denominations. The founders believed that Christianity promised true womanhood to their sex and that their societies were designed to advance the cause of women, as well as to meet needs of the church.

"Woman's work for woman" in the Protestant churches of late nineteenth century America needs to be examined from the perspectives of three groups of women: first, the senders, those women in cities, villages, and rural areas of the United States who formed societies in local churches and consolidated them into powerful regional and national organizations of their denominations; second, those who were sent, single women deaconesses who consecrated their lives to professional lay service in foreign and home mission fields; and, finally, the receivers, "women of heathendom" in the far reaches of India, China, and Africa, and in the inner-city ghettos of the United States, who were promised elevation and education by their sisters in missionary societies and deaconess orders.

THE SENDERS: FOUNDERS OF WOMEN'S MISSIONARY SOCIETIES

The senders formed the base of "woman's work for woman" through grass-roots missionary societies, which they founded in thousands of churches of every denomination from the eastern seaboard to the Pacific northwest. Within each church, such groups might number as few as three or four women or, occasionally, as many as a hundred or more members.

Antecedents of these organizations went back to the beginning of the century, when the Boston Female Society for Missionary Purposes was created in October 1800. During the next fifteen years, female religious organizations were begun in cities, small towns, and rural areas throughout New England. They espoused a multitude of purposes for prayer, benevolence, missionary work, education, moral reform, and material aid.[4]

Most of these early societies, in contrast to the women's organizations after the Civil War, were local and interdenominational. The first interdenominational organization, on a national scale, was the Women's Union Missionary Society, developed in 1860 by females of six denominations. By 1868 and 1869, the Congregationalists and Methodists withdrew to form their own societies and others followed shortly thereafter.[5]

Among black denominations, the African. Methodist Episcopal women had organized nationally by 1874.

These organizations were a primary source of identification for the women who joined them. They expanded the vision of the world and of their members' lives beyond the roles of wives and mothers. For most women of the day, their lives were defined and encased within the home. Many lived extremely isolated and lonely existences. The societies provided avenues of service for women outside their homes by creating bonds of sisterhood between themselves and the women of "heathen lands" in national and foreign mission stations. Women's missionary journals, recognized as the great "popularizer of missions" to the masses, were the instruments for creating empathetic identification of women with each other and of broadening the horizons of females in their local church societies.[6] (Document 2.)

A common theme ran through the missionary literature: the promise of liberation in Christ bound all women together in religious commitment and special service to each other. The same Lord cared for the unconverted heathen woman as for Christ's faithful followers. Yet, these heathen sisters could not hear this message without a preacher, and no one could preach unless she was sent. The burden of Christian responsibility and the bond of sisterhood demanded that American women see themselves as missionaries. Single women were summoned to enter home or foreign service as deaconesses, and mothers were directed to impress this service upon their daughters. Women who stayed at home organizing societies, raising funds, and sponsoring national and world mission projects were given a new context of identification and purpose for their lives: "Let every lady, who feels that she *would be a missionary,* go to work at home, and she may, by every dollar raised, teach her heathen sisters."[7] (Document 3.)

By elevating women's understanding of themselves as missionaries and channeling their time, energy, and financial resources into the mission cause, societies served their members in a second way. They gave countless thousands of women training and experience to plan, administer, and be responsible for organizations and wide-reaching programs for the first time. This applied to the work of individual societies in the churches, to the interaction of societies at regional and national levels of women's organizations, and to their efforts to maintain favorable working positions and power in relationship to general boards of missions of the denominations.

The goal of national women's organizations was that every church have a women's missionary society in its congregation. The key to the success of national mission programs was the commitment and contributions of women in these local societies. Pages of society journals were filled with detailed instructions for organizing local units and for fundraising. Their goal was to enlist every church woman in the society and

to hold unit meetings often and regularly—every week, month, quarter—
to instill the mission in their members, build commitment, and accomplish their tasks. (Document 4.)

As women in local societies banded together to sponsor regional and
national programs, begin mission stations, and finance workers in these
outposts and institutions, they simultaneously created ties of sisterhood
and unity of purpose among women in widely scattered, remote areas of
the country. The *Missionary Helper,* journal of the Free Baptist Women's
Society, reported that members in Harper's Ferry, West Virginia, on the
basis of "small gleanings" and faith, had committed themselves to send
two or three missionaries to India. In an effort typically employed by
women's societies, the journal writer used their cause to rally loosely knit
auxiliaries together in support:

> The Free Baptist women of Rhode Island have pledged themselves to the
> support of one of these young ladies, and it is confidently expected that some
> part of Maine will assume the support of another. Will not the women of Ohio
> unite in sustaining the third? If each of the two hundred subscribers to the
> *Helper* in Ohio give two cents a week and influence another person to do the
> same, her salary will be secured.[8]

By advancing causes that required widespread cooperation, women
built networks of support across the country and gained their first experience administering programs that they could not oversee locally. The
type of regional or national organization of the societies helped determine how much actual control of their program women could maintain.
Females took the initiative in forming their general organizations in all
denominations except the Congregational Church, first to organize a
women's society in 1869, where impetus was given by male leaders.
Congregational societies provided the incentive for women in other
denominations soon thereafter. Three types of organization were developed, varying from regional to national structures from one denomination to another: first, societies that were incorporated independently to
cooperate as supplemental arms of denominational agencies, such as the
African Methodist Episcopal and the Congregational women's boards;
second, those that were independent and understood themselves as equal
to the general agency, like the Methodist Episcopal society; and, third,
women's groups that were dependent upon and subsidiary to denominational boards, as in the Episcopal Church.[9] (Document 5.)

THOSE WHO WERE SENT: DEACONESSES, THE FIRST LAY
PROFESSIONAL WORKERS

As women gained experience in large-scale voluntary organizations,
deaconesses pioneered as professional female workers in Protestant
churches. This second group of women committed themselves to full-
time lay service in national and foreign mission stations. From 1870 until

the turn of the century, over 140 deaconess homes were opened in the United States. These institutions represented almost every Protestant denomination and some were interdenominational.

Most deaconesses were daughters of ministers or of women's society leaders. Normally, they were young women of strong church background who responded to a call of Christian commitment, just as their brothers might have chosen to be ministers. Many were leaving their families of origin for the first time. Going to inner-city ghettos or to world mission stations across the globe was a radical break with their past, changing the direction of their lives and of the church.

The pattern of deaconess work was set before the Civil War, when the first institutions were established in the Evangelical Alliance of the Lutheran Church by Reverend William Passavant. The primary work of deaconesses was to establish and manage charitable institutions, including settlement houses, hospitals, schools, and churches, for the poor. They interpreted their work as a restoration of the New Testament office of deacon, or servant. Sisters lived together in a Parent or Mother House, modeled on the order of the family. They took no lifetime vows and wore plain, dark dresses as uniforms. (Document 6.)

Reverend Passavant was unable to maintain deaconess work in pre–Civil War America because of public pressure against employment of women and the failure of the church to advocate their rights. Referring to the Lutheran Church, Passavant stated in 1852: "Our attitude so far in this question is neither Scriptural nor just to the female sex or the Church of Christ itself."[10]

Two basic needs, which the churches faced after the Civil War, resulted in greater acceptance of deaconesses. First, middle-class, churchgoing citizens looked to deaconesses to help temper the threat of immigrants pouring into American cities. They branded this newly arrived foreign element as the "unchristian and ignorant masses," who were "revolutionary tinder." Deaconesses were key resources to evangelize and Americanize these masses, to save the cities. (Documents 7 and 8.)

The second need was for single women missionaries in foreign outposts. Most women who had served outside the United States earlier in the nineteenth century were wives of male missionaries. By 1860, general boards of denominations and women's societies called for more women in the mission field to work particularly with native women. They contended that native women had a right to education and elevation and could be of enormous influence in converting their husbands to Christianity. Wives of missionaries were already overburdened in juggling responsibilities as wives and mothers with church duties. Increasing the pool from among single women, notably deaconesses, provided the obvious source. (Document 9.)

The needs for deaconesses in home and foreign mission fields during the late nineteenth century outran the available supply. Their services were welcomed and valued. Controversy regarding deaconesses arose in determining their status. Were they part of the clergy or of the laity?

Those who contended that deaconesses were part of the clergy believed their argument was grounded on strong biblical foundations. They pointed to two offices of ministry prescribed in the New Testament. The diaconate was the office of service, of merciful acts of helpfulness, distinguished from the office of preaching. Deaconesses were more than social workers. Yet, these proponents were careful to spell out the boundaries of women's professional church work as an extension of their roles as wives and mothers: "Wherever helping work is to be done, there woman is in her place . . . [since] the outcasts of society cannot be reached by home influences unless these influences are brought to them and it is only a female hand that can bring them."[11] (Document 10.)

The advocacy of James Thoburn, Bishop of the Methodist Episcopal Church, reveals the tight line that was necessary to win approval of deaconess work. He sought to dispel fears that their work was a stepping stone to ordination, arguing that these women "speak for Jesus" and were not seeking rights for themselves. Because deaconess orders were a sphere "for women only," its members were not crossing over the boundary line acceptable to established leaders of the church.[12]

At the same time that Bishop Thoburn was presenting an acceptable justification of the deaconess movement to authorities of his denomination, he was also strongly supporting the work of the Chicago Training School, the first institution for training deaconesses in the Methodist Episcopal Church. The work of the school demonstrates the difficult position of its members in relating to denominational authorities. While they faithfully fulfilled their basic task of ministering and meeting the daily needs of newly arrived immigrants in the Chicago slums, deaconesses sought to expand opportunities for their sex within and beyond the church.

In editing the *Deaconess Advocate,* journal of the Chicago Training School, Lucy Rider Meyer maintained a distinct policy of patiently and persistently enlarging the vision of readers to wider opportunities for women beyond a sphere designed specifically for them. She interpreted deaconess work as offering liberating choices for females, who could serve in a variety of professional positions. Meyer pressed the church also, to do its part in the women's movement by ordaining women to work alongside men on a basis of equality with them. (Document 11.)

THE RECEIVERS: "WOMEN OF HEATHENDOM"

What did women's society leaders and deaconesses hope to achieve in the lives of females in non-Christian lands and in the inner cities of the United States?

"Woman's work for woman" in the foreign mission field took three primary forms: first, evangelistic efforts among the secluded, upper-class women of the zenanas in India and China and among the poor in cities and villages; second, education of these women, and girls of all classes, in mission schools for academic, domestic, and industrial training; and, third, medical care of women and children, often in hospitals and dispensaries built especially for females.

The work of deaconesses in America's inner cities had distinct parallels. It was directed toward women and children in the slums and focused on the same three thrusts of evangelism, education, and medical assistance. The deaconesses maintained settlement houses that provided practical, academic, and religious training. As the earliest social workers, they did much house-to-house visitation to help meet individual needs of families in the neighborhoods.

Two basic motivations guided the work in home and foreign mission fields. First, deaconesses sought to convert and educate less privileged women to become the base troops for evangelizing the world, whether in distant pagan lands or in America's slums. Second, they hoped to uplift females for their own sakes, because the lives of women were of value in themselves.

"Woman's work for woman" in the inner cities was primarily directed toward conversion. They recognized, however, that the basic needs of food, work, and family had to be met if spiritual change was to follow. Humanitarian uplift was also a characteristic goal of more secular settlement houses of the day, such as Jane Addams' Hull House. Deaconesses went further, however, in teaching the Bible in classes and in seeking religious conversions among the people of the neighborhoods. (Document 12.)

The major justification of "woman's work for woman" was that it made newly converted women agents in this evangelistic enterprise. Females became the crucial power in rehabilitating their families. "Woman's work" was often directed to mothers forced to shoulder full family responsibilities because their husbands were addicted to alcohol and their children were poorly fed and clothed. Mothers were the center of stability and exerted enormous influence within the home. The guideline was to convert and train the women. Then, the salvation of society, through their husbands and sons, would follow.[13]

Work among women in world mission stations was a logical extension of these arguments and values. Amanda Berry Smith elucidated these commitments through her understanding of her work as a missionary. Probably the most famous black female evangelist of the nineteenth century, Smith was a member of the African Methodist Episcopal Church and a missionary to both India and Africa. During her eight years in Africa, she founded missions and schools to uplift the Africans, whom she referred to as "my people." She believed that her "errand in Africa" was to help everyone that she could. Her particular desire to uplift women paralleled that of countless female missionaries. She recognized that "the poor women of Africa, like those of India, have a hard time. As a rule, they have all the hard work to do," such as cutting and carrying wood and planting and sowing rice. She believed Africa was "doomed" unless greater attention was paid to education. Smith particularly stressed the void in the education of girls, with no high schools for females in all of Liberia—"a great shame and a disgrace to the government."[14]

Many foreign missionaries boldly claimed that, if properly educated, women's influence through their homes would be the key to the salvation of Africa, India, and China. Writers in missionary journals appealed for "second mile" giving to women's foreign mission programs and urged their sisters to recognize how many more Christian homes were needed in countries where degradation was beyond conception. Female missionaries were necessary to release the three hundred million women enslaved in India, society members were told. Male missionaries could not reach the native women who were secluded in their homes by husbands and fathers. Isolated from social influences, these females were more superstitious than men and were the main supporters of idolatry. When enlightened, however, women were more zealous in accepting the Gospel. The most promising source of hope, as many missionaries saw it, was to convert the women. In time, they would bring their husbands to Christianity.[15] (Document 13.)

Further, committed native women would take the Christian message to other females and make them strong links in the chain to convert heathen India. Missionaries often wrote of the contagion of faith among native women after their conversions. New converts assisted missionaries as Bible readers to secluded women, leaders of women's prayer groups, practical nurses, and teachers in orphanages and boarding schools.[16]

However, the purpose of "woman's work for woman" was not simply that females become agents of evangelism. Women's society leaders and deaconesses also hoped to create a new woman who would not be confined to a private sphere of the home. They valued their sisters for their own sake.

Deaconesses in the inner cities of America strove to dignify the work that immigrant women had to do for survival. Their work was an expression of their identities as individuals, not as adjuncts of men. Working women could be strong, happy, and independent. (Document 14.)

The efforts of deaconesses in inner-city mission work were directed more toward benevolent aid than toward women's rights. When Lucy Rider Meyer urged women to vote in state elections, however, she was not only seeking to close saloons but also helping females recognize their power through suffrage. She asked each woman who still might feel that her "quiet influence in the home is greater than the influence of her vote at the polls" to reconsider in light of the "dry" vote in Illinois. There women had voted in an election "where what they *did* spoke infinitely more loudly than anything they could possibly *say!*" One thousand saloons had been closed as a result of the election.[17]

In foreign missions, women workers hoped to bring new womanhood to their sisters by destroying the "caste of sex." They rightly pointed out that it was easier to identify the prejudices against women in Eastern countries than in America because social barriers were more blatant and clearly recognizable.

Helen Barrett Montgomery was the most important spokesperson of the women's missionary movement at the turn of the century. She served as president of both the Woman's American Baptist Foreign Mission Society and the interdenominational National Federation of Women's Boards of Foreign Missions. In her book *Western Women in Eastern Lands*, written in 1910, she celebrated the accomplishments of women's missionary work in the preceding fifty years and sharply raised challenges that remain. Her goal for "the New Woman of the Orient" emerges from the core of the Christian faith:

> The Gospel is the most tremendous engine of democracy ever forged. It is destined to break in pieces all castes, privileges, and oppressions. Perhaps the last caste to be destroyed will be that of sex. It is not surprising that, while the main problem of democracy [Negro suffrage] is still undemonstrated, the corollary of women's rights should remain to be grappled with. The surprising thing is that, not only in countries where there is most light and freedom is the impulse felt, but also in the most backward and despotic, so far as women are concerned. This can be accounted for only on the ground that there is a wider adumbration of the spirit of Christ than we dream. He being lifted up, even as He said, is drawing the whole world unto His own perfect charity, justice, friendliness, democracy, to that redeemed humanity in which there shall be neither male nor female, bond nor free, but only free men and free women, whose lives, like His, are given them not to be ministered unto, but to minister.[18]

The daily work of female missionaries was directed toward destroying this "last caste of sex." They pointed with pride to gains made: teaching women to read and write, providing medical care for women, teaching their sisters to be educators and doctors, breaking down child marriage customs, and enabling women to attend public worship services. (Document 15.) Their vision has set a standard even for today.

IN RETROSPECT: AN EVALUATION OF "WOMAN'S WORK FOR WOMAN"

The rise of women into lay leadership brought new dimensions to the mission programs of Protestant churches. More workers and increased funds were channeled into previously untapped areas than would have been possible without their contribution. All this was done by women creating alternative organizations of service outside established power structures.

Nevertheless, responses by bishops, ministers, and general secretaries of church boards to the creation of women's organizations varied from strong support to outright opposition, similar to the acceptance of women into the clergy a century later. In the African Methodist Episcopal Church, women were included in the official structures of the church in 1868, by creation of the position of stewardess, and in 1874, when the Women's Parent Mite Missionary Society was begun. Both moves served to contain the female's functions, however, at a time when preaching women were being denied ordination. The stewardess role was clearly one of helper and assistant to ordained clergymen, and the missionary society limited women's work to a separate sphere outside the official governing bodies of the denomination.[19]

Attitudes within the Methodist Episcopal Church were similar and typical of both black and white denominations. One bishop lauded the "righteous parity" which the late nineteenth century gave to women: "Parity in the churches—parity in the schools—parity in the learned professions—parity wherever her physical and mental conditions fit her to work." Another valued the deaconess movement as a clear alternative to keep women out of the ordained ministry: "Her opportunities for usefulness are now so numerous that she does not *need* to get into the pulpit," he stated with obvious agitation. "There must be no clashing in regard to spheres or rights." Perhaps the most prevalent view was expressed by an eminent minister who wrote of women's missionary societies in a church journal: "Some of the most thoughtful minds are beginning to ask what is to become of this Woman movement in the Church. Let them alone,—all through our history like movements have started. Do not oppose them, and it will die out."[20]

Rather than dying out, however, women's organizations grew and flourished, setting the foundation for wider voluntary and professional activity by lay women in the twentieth century. Helen Barrett Montgomery's 1910 evaluation of women's missionary work was a profound statement of the accomplishments and problems of fifty years of women's service. (Document 16.)

Her recognition of the "caste of sex," within our own country as well as in distant mission fields, established the need for a separate sphere of "woman's work for woman" and provided a challenge for future relationships of men and women in church and society. Montgomery queried whether it would not be better to have one tremendous organization with men and women working side by side. Her hope was that the day would come "in the growth of the kingdom" when this would be possible. But she questioned whether, in her day, men had been "emancipated from the caste of sex so that they can work easily with women, unless they be head and women clearly subordinate. . . . [W]e have still a long stretch of unexplored country to be traversed before the perfect democracy of Jesus is reached."[21]

The senders, who supported women's pioneer mission work throughout the world, were middle- and upper-class women and their young children, trained from an early age to regularly contribute their own "mite for missions." [From *The Missionary Link*, January 1891, p. 12.]

TO-DAY

To-day, these children come from ill-kept, insanitary homes, the homes of the ignorant poor. But also

To-day, they are being trained in right methods of housekeeping by skillful, Christian workers. They are learning to do by doing.

TO-MORROW

To-morrow, we have faith and hope to believe, these same children, older grown, will put into practice the methods they have learned to-day.

To-morrow, we hope to have no *ignorant* poor.

The idealism characteristic of the early deaconess movement is reflected in this cover of the bulletin of the Chicago Training School for Home and Foreign Missions. Through their efforts to raise a new generation of children in the inner cities, deaconesses hoped to eradicate ignorance and poverty. [From *Deaconess Advocate*, May 1914, p.1.]

Black deaconesses performed essential functions as "extensions" of local pastors, just as their sisters in white churches did. These seven deaconesses graduated from the first training school for black deaconesses in the United States, located in Cincinnati, in 1902. [From Rev. Christian Golder, *History of the Deaconess Movement in the Christian Church* (Cincinnati: Jennings & Pye, 1903), p. 411.]

Deaconesses, wearing floor-length black dresses, white collars, and black hats, were familiar and valued figures in American home missionary work, particularly in inner cities. They were concerned that their distinctive costume be recognized as "Protestant, not Romish." [From Frederick A. Norwood, *From Dawn to Midday at Garrett* (Evanston: Garrett-Evangelical Theological Seminary, 1978), p. 80.]

Missionaries, refined, cultured, and well-educated, were sent to foreign mission stations such as this one in North Africa. "Woman's work for woman" focused on teaching native females to improve conditions in their own homes, deemed the most fertile ground for the conversion of men and children to Christianity. [From Ralph E. Diffendorfer, ed., *The World Service of the Methodist Episcopal Church* (Chicago: Methodist Episcopal Church, 1923), p. 629.]

The receivers were females of "heathendom" throughout the world organized into women's societies modeled after those in local churches of the United States. These women belong to a Ladies Aid Society in Africa. Note the Western imperialist supervisor in the background. [From Helen Barrett Montgomery, *Western Women in Eastern Lands* (New York: Macmillan, 1910, p. 268.]

Female missionaries and native converts committed themselves to "woman's work for children," as the tubfull of five little Asian bodies demonstrates. [From Helen Barrett Montgomery, *Western Women in Eastern Lands* (New York: Macmillan, 1910), p. 36.]

Documents: Lay Women in the Protestant Tradition

THE PURPOSE OF THEIR WORK
  1. "Woman's Work for Woman"

THE SENDERS: FOUNDERS OF WOMEN'S MISSIONARY SOCIETIES
  2. "Mass Media" of the Women's Missionary Movements
  3. "Let Every Lady ... Be a Missionary"
  4. Beginnings of Grass-Roots Organization
  5. The Model of a National Women's Society

THOSE WHO WERE SENT: DEACONESSES, FIRST LAY PROFESSIONAL WORKERS
  6. Governance of Deaconess Orders
  7. Deaconess Work among Immigrants in Urban Ghettos
  8. Immigrant Women Enter Deaconess Orders
  9. Single Women Sent to Foreign Mission Stations
  10. Justifying the Deaconess as Clergy or Laity
  11. The "New Woman" of Protestantism

THE RECEIVERS: "WOMEN OF HEATHENDOM"
  12. The Scope of Women's Work in the Inner City
  13. Evangelizing and Educating Women throughout the World
  14. Dignifying the Work of Immigrant Women in America
  15. Destroying the Caste of Sex

IN RETROSPECT: AN EVALUATION OF "WOMAN'S WORK FOR WOMAN"
  16. Accomplishments, Problems, and Prospects for the Work

THE PURPOSE OF THEIR WORK

Document 1: "Woman's Work for Woman"

Two articles in early issues of the Woman's Evangel *graphically illustrate the motivations which bound together women of all denominations in missionary work during the late nineteenth century. The* Evangel *was published by the Women's Missionary Society of the United Brethren Church, a comparatively small denomination.*

"Our Mission," written by Mrs. Lucy Williams, summoned women to their sphere of usefulness alongside men in evangelizing the world for Christ. She treads softly and gently, noting that only now women's "timid feet have crossed the threshold" to assume a duty they had long abrogated to men.[22]

To every intelligent creature God has given capacity for doing some kind of work in the world. As individual Christians we have our distinct duties, our several spheres of usefulness, to be filled by ourselves alone. But to every one who has passed from death unto life comes the command, "Go tell others the story which, while it is every one's distinct duty, is yet a duty common to all. The world's evangelization might have been brought about by other means; but God chose human instrumentality, and so the high honor was conferred upon us. This is the mission of the church and of Christians everywhere. But for long years we as women seemed to have had but limited views of our duty. We were content to save our own souls and let men attend to all the rest. But the door has opened, and at last our timid feet have crossed the threshold. The women of other denominations have begun the work before us; but we are now arousing to our duty, and have even at this early period demonstrated the fact that our work has not been in vain. The mission-work is as grand a one as mortals might desire. How great the blessings are that come to our lives by being born in a land of Christianity,—having the unnumbered advantages and privileges flowing directly and indirectly from this source,—our dull minds may not be fully able to comprehend. But that it *is* an inestimable blessing all may know; and how much will be required in Christian work where so much has been given.

God has given us this work, the work of sending the gospel to those who are without its light and influence, to teach and elevate them mentally and morally, and thus to lead them into the fair light of the gospel and civilization.

In beginning women's missionary society and deaconess work, the early leaders recognized that evangelization of the world was too broad an emphasis for their work. Their special concern was to convert, educate, and raise the status of other women. Leaders under-

stood that women were not being adequately reached under present national and foreign mission programs, and they believed this emphasis was possible only through "woman's work for woman." The purpose of this "woman's work for woman" was presented in an editorial in the first issue of the Woman's Evangel *(January, 1882).*[23]

The glad sound of angel voices ringing over the Judean hills in the stillness of the night-watches, and the "glory of the Lord" shining suddenly about them, struck the simple shepherds with fear. But the angel of the Lord said unto them, "Fear not: behold, I bring you good tidings of great joy, which shall be to all people." . . . This glad announcement was "to all people." To us as women it has come, making the name of wife and mother sacred, which is only true of Christian nations. It has been to women a glad evangel; and because we *love much* do we wish to make our work—as the name of our paper signifies,—an announcement of glad tidings to some of the five hundred millions of women in the degradation and ruin of false religions and oppressive social customs of heathen nations. It will be the earnest purpose of those who have undertaken the work, to make the paper a power in moving hearts to help in the good work of sending the light of life to women and children who are shut out from its blessed influence. Many centuries have passed since the command was given to women, "Go and tell that Jesus has risen," but not till this century (the latter part of it) have Christian women come together with one mind and heart to roll away the stone from the living sepulcher, where her heathen sister sits in total darkness. She has heard that "the Master is here and calleth for thee." . . .

Woman of the nineteenth century, dowered as never women were before,—with gifts, with opportunities, with responsibilities, with all the world open to thy tread and waiting for thy help,—may God help thee to see in these somewhat the measure of thy duty; to discern in the light of thy privilege the weight of thy obligation; to know the blessedness, the grandeur, the awfulness of living now; that

> To serve the present age,
> Thy calling to fulfill,

demands a richer baptism, a fuller consecration, and involves grander possibilities than in all the years past. Christian women of all ranks and denominations, let us join hands in one endeavor—with one thought, one prayer, one motto, one voice,—*The women of all lands for Jesus.*

THE SENDERS: FOUNDERS OF WOMEN'S MISSIONARY SOCIETIES

Document 2: "Mass Media" of the Women's Missionary Movements

Missionary journals were the means of communication for women's societies in the late nineteenth century. "Our Literature Work," an article published in the Lutheran Missionary Journal, *stresses that women must subscribe to journals in order to know the mission's causes and to identify with them. A more subtle effect of the journals was that they brought women into bonds of sisterhood within and beyond their denominations. By the 1890s, sixty thousand women were subscribing to the three largest women's publications in the Presbyterian, Methodist Episcopal, and Baptist churches (see note 6). The writer of the following article, Mrs. Willard Larkin, urged Lutheran women to read literature of other denominations, as well as their own.*[24]

... If there were no literature, how could we carry the glad news of the gospel of peace to lands which were to us unknown and unheard of? So, we must read. It is the duty of every woman in the Missionary Society to know something of what is going on in the present. To know how to give, you must know to whom you are giving. To have the desire to give, you must know something of the wants. To be able to pray, you must know what is needed....

Let us now consider where we may best obtain this knowledge. No Lutheran woman can intelligently understand what the women of her church are doing for the women of heathen lands, unless she reads our Lutheran publications. First, the *Lutheran Missionary Journal* needs and should have the hearty support of every lady in our church. It may be possible that not every woman can afford to pay even the twenty-five cents for the *Journal;* but the woman who can pay can lend it to the woman who cannot, and thereby arouse and secure prayers.

Every leader of a Society needs the *Mission Studies.* Not until they have been used can we understand the help to be derived from, or the inspiration it will give to our work. And to insure the success of this little publication, there should be subscriptions from each one of our Societies. Supplementary to these we can recommend the *Missionary Review of the World, The Gospel in All Lands, The Helping Hand, Life and Light,* and many others of great merit....

Sisters! let us buy missionary literature, let us read it, fill ourselves with it, and then send it forth to bless others. Every woman of every Auxiliary should, for her own sake, for the sake of her Auxiliary, for the sake of society at large, for the heathen's sake and for Jesus' sake, take an earnest, conscientious interest in our literature, and according to her means buy it.

Dear sisters, we are watching a struggle between the forces of life
and death, the life and death of immortal souls.

Do we send out our missionaries, and then forget them? Do we ask
for no tidings of their contest with the mighty forces of heathenism?
Do we leave their messages and appeals unnoticed? Do we carelessly
neglect to know the enemy's strength and numbers? Do not let this
be so. What opportunities we shall miss, what souls will be lost through
our neglect!

Let us read and know, work and pray, and then, and only then,
can we honestly claim the promise, "God giveth the increase."

Document 3: "Let Every Lady . . . Be a Missionary"

*The three documents that follow demonstrate the way in which
journal writers motivated subscribers to support the home and foreign mission programs of their women's societies. In each case, they
sought to develop empathetic identification of women in middle-class
churches of America with their less fortunate sisters. The progression
from one article to the next is important, for their appeals build upon
each other.*

"Our Needs," an essay from the *Missionary Helper* (July, 1878)
published by the Free Baptist Woman's Missionary Society, creates a
picture of female subscribers, isolated in their homes, lacking meaning for their lives. The essay presents a twofold need: first, for money
and the support of women in far-flung heathen countries, and second, for purpose in the lives of women who can supply those resources.[25]

Today, in glancing through our portion of the "vineyard," we cry
out, "Oh! for some divine touch by which the blind eyes of some of
our noblest women may be opened!"

In the sewing-rooms in our cities, in the far-houses of the prairies,
in the kitchens all through our borders, are women who have never
thought of life as anything more than a "bread-winning and bread-
bestowing existence." . . . In blind ignorance of their own individual
capabilities, of their passing opportunities, they are wasting their
substance, their lives, their all, and the golden harvest all around them
are perishing for reapers.

In our denomination are two institutions for the needy. Both, for
years, have needed the very hearts of all our women. Let the grateful
teachers and pupils at Harper's Ferry tell how faithfully, within the
last few months, the needs of the one have been met, and long may
"Myrtle Hall" stand a monument of "woman's work for woman." But
let us stop for a moment and remember the women that have never
heard of the free woman's God, that have never once offered a prayer
to Him to whom the freed-woman, in all her long years of bondage
found her sure and only solace, and whose bare right arm brought

her liberty; women whose cries of agony and death fall upon the dull ears of brass and stone, while the freed-women sing, in loudest and sweetest accents, praises to the "God of their salvation." Christian woman! Stop for a moment and toss a few crumbs to your starving Indian sisters before you prepare the rich *dessert* for the freed-women. Over the waves their needs are coming as they never came before, and *needed* are *all* the Christian women in our denomination to meet them.

The next essay challenges readers even more directly. All women become sisters in Jesus Christ; their degradation by society and their hope for liberation in their Savior bind them together. "Word to our Readers," from the Congregational Woman's Board of Missions journal Life and Light for Heathen Women *(March, 1869), directly appeals to women to volunteer for foreign mission service. Secondarily, the writer is seeking women in their societies to provide financial support to send these early female workers to mission fields.*[26]

We do not profess to be commencing a new work. Others have labored, and we are entering into their labors. And we love to look over the history of the American Board, and of other missionary societies, and gather up examples like those mentioned above, which prove beyond a doubt that Christ meant just what he said when he uttered those blessed words, "The Son of man is come to seek and to save that which was lost." For the Scripture saith, "Whosoever believeth on Him shall not be ashamed. For there is no difference between the Jew and the Greek." No difference, dear sisters, between ourselves and the lowest of heathen women in this respect; "for the same Lord over all is rich unto all that call upon him."

But just here come in those solemn queries: "How, then, shall they call on Him in whom they have not believed? and how shall they believe in Him of whom they have not heard? and how shall they hear without a preacher? and how shall they preach except they be sent?"

"Lift up your eyes and look on the fields, for they are white already to the harvest." We have indeed been praying the Lord of the harvest to send forth more laborers. Now let us heed his voice, saying to each one of us, "Go work to-day in my vineyard."

Christian sisters, to whom among you comes the command,— "Depart; for I will send thee far hence unto the Gentiles?" And to whom is the word put in another form, "Honor the Lord with thy substance, and with the first fruits of all thine increase?" Let us engage in the work of the Lord with faith, with earnestness, and with a humble spirit of prayer and consecration.

Our royal firman reads, "Go teach all nations," with the royal promise annexed, "Lo, I am with you always, even unto the end of the world."

The appeal is capped in "Laborers Wanted," taken from the Hea-
then Woman's Friend (October, 1869), journal of the Foreign Mis-
sionary Society of the Methodist Episcopal Church. Women who
remain at home are given a new status, as well as purpose for their
lives. Their self-understanding is no longer limited by domestic du-
ties. Now they are laborers, missionaries in their own right.[27]

The millions of heathen women will never be saved from their
fearfully lost condition without *laborers*. A *few* must go forth to teach
them, but the *many* must *work* at home. We now especially need the
home laborers, ladies who will go to work earnestly to organize praying bands and working circles to earn and raise money to send missionaries abroad and to support native Bible women to teach heathen
women. How many churches are there in our connection, where the
women would gladly do something, if some one would but take the
lead, and interest and unite them in some plan of earning or saving
a little money. Let every lady, who feels that she *would be a missionary*,
go to work at home, and she may, by every dollar raised, teach her
heathen sisters.

Document 4: Beginnings of Grass-Roots Organization

The following three essays dramatize the ways in which women
learned and disseminated the fundamentals of volunteer local organi-
zation for their causes a century ago.
The first essay, "Suggestions for the Formation of Auxiliaries"
from the Missionary Helper (July, 1878), outlines the detailed,
meticulous instruction which central offices provided local church
women as they organized for the first time.[28]

One of the objects which the Woman's Society aims to accomplish
is to secure, from each woman in the denomination, a pledge of two
cents per week or a dollar a year to carry on our work. To accomplish
this, we do not wish you to withdraw the contributions you are accustomed to give to other branches of Christian work, but we do ask you
to do the following specific things in addition to what you are now
doing:
1. Write on an envelope, "Woman's work for woman," lay it in
some safe place, and deposit in it two cents each week, or more if you
can.
2. Try to persuade each woman in your church to do the same,
using the means that in your judgment will best secure the object,
whether it be by private solicitation or by calling a meeting.
3. As soon as a few—if not more than three or four—will make this
weekly pledge, let them form an auxiliary to the Woman's Missionary
Society, and meet once a month for prayer, reading missionary intelligence, and devising means to interest others. Once a quarter, at a

specified meeting, let all your members bring in the contents of their envelopes and pay to your Treasurer, who shall keep an exact account of all the money she receives and from whom, and forward the same quarterly to Miss DeMeritte.

4. When your society is formed, report it to the district secretary of your Quarterly Meeting or, if you do not know her address, report to the Home Secretary of the Society, and ask for some definite work for which you may become responsible. See that one of the officers is an agent for the *Helper.*

Some of you may not understand that a person in each Quarterly Meeting is appointed a district secretary, or agent, whose duty it is to aid each church to organize an auxiliary. But don't wait for her action. She may be so situated that she can't attend to the work, and if she can, she will be cheered and encouraged to learn that you have moved in the matter.

5. Ask yourself if it is not your privilege to become a life member. The payment of $20, even if made in installments within one or two years, constitutes a life membership.

Excerpts from Life and Light for Heathen Women *provide the response of women in local churches to the directions and steps in beginning their societies given by national or regional organizations.*

The next selection, "How We Formed Our Auxiliary," is a personal account of the way motivation and planning interacted in the initial stages of development.[29]

Having received a Circular of the Woman's Board of Missions, our active Miss L. hastened to the sewing-circle, and made known its message. "Now, ladies," said she, "we must do our part. We are responsible to God, and are bound by the most weighty considerations to do all the good in our power." The ladies, concurring in this thought, at once appointed Miss L. directress of the new society, and her friend Carrie secretary and treasurer.

A list of the female membership of the church was obtained, districts portioned, and the three collectors started on their rounds the ensuing week. At the next meeting of the circle, a favorable report was returned by the collectors; and Carrie, who fills the two-fold offices of secretary and treasurer, promptly wrote the Treasurer of the Woman's Board of Missions at Boston, enclosing the amount obtained. It was agreed that a half-hour should be spent by the circle, quarterly, in listening to the reading of missionary intelligence selected from *Life and Light for Heathen Women,* the *Missionary Herald,* and other authentic sources. It was also voted, that, at the annual meeting of the circle, the above offices be filled for the year; and thus our auxiliary society, in working order, was successfully launched.

The third and final selection, "A Model Auxiliary," expresses the

*pride that women felt in establishing idealistic goals and in taking the
first concrete steps to reach them.*[30]

Our auxiliary, recently formed in B., may truly be said to be a
model. Embracing among its members nearly every female communi-
cant of the church with which it is connected, it is the first to approxi-
mate the standard, we hope ultimately to reach through all our
auxiliaries, when the entire female membership of our churches shall
be so represented. But better even than this, is the fact that, when
these warmhearted sisters formed their society they also agreed to
meet once in every month, to pray for a blessing on the Woman's
Board of Missions, and upon their own contributions in particular,
that thus "their prayers and their alms might come together before
God."

Document 5: The Model of a National Women's Society

*The Women's Parent Mite Missionary Society drew together local
church units of women from the African Methodist Episcopal Church
in one national organization. The following document was written by
Sarah E. Tanner, wife of a prominent bishop of the denomination.
Writing in 1896, Mrs. Tanner recreated the story of the national
society's founding convention in 1874.*

*The essay is important, first, because it describes so graphically the
origins of the earliest missionary society of women in a black denomination. Further, it lifts up essential features of national organizations
by women in all denominations: their pride of accomplishment and
relationship to established male governing authorities, as well as the
careful planning, organization, and content typical of female societies.*[31]

The story of the organization of the Parent Mite Missionary Society has been so often related, that I do not deem it necessary to repeat
again the circumstances that brought this very laudable enterprise
into existence. Suffice it to say, the hearts of our bishops' wives received the inspiration as from God, and like wild fire it spread far and
near among the women of our church. It was in the year 1874, that
the first meeting was held in Washington, D.C., to consider a plan
whereby the women of the church could be brought in line to assist
the Home and Foreign Missionary Society in its efforts to carry the
gospel, not only to those of our own land who are in ignorance of the
atoning blood, but to those in foreign lands also. In furtherance of
this purpose, a convention was called to meet in Philadelphia May 8,
1874, and from this assembly sprang the Parent Mite Missionary
Society of to-day. The sisters of the church rallied to the work, and
with the assistance of both bishops and elders, the society was put on
a firm basis; auxiliary societies in the meantime springing up in all

sections—societies that have greatly assisted in the work, and helped to keep the missionary fire burning. At times it would really seem that only a flicker could be discovered; yet the warmth ever remained, until in all our twenty-one years the treasury, like the widow's oil, has not failed us. On the other hand there has been a steady increase, until the report of the last year shows over eighteen hundred dollars receipts, with an outlay of some fifteen hundred. Seeing the need of more concerted action, the Parent Society thought it wise to call a conference of missionary workers to meet in Philadelphia, Nov. 7, and continue to the 11th inclusive. The purpose was to take a retrospective view of the past, and, if possible, map out plans for more effective work in the future. We are pleased to record the success of the conference. At the opening session there answered to roll call, delegates from Pennsylvania, New Jersey, Delaware, Maryland, Ohio, Indiana, Tennessee, South Carolina and Georgia; with many members of the Parent Mite Society, a number of whom were at the organization, such as Mrs. Mary A. Campbell, Mrs. Harriet Wayman and others.

There were also present Mrs. Sarah J. Early, of Nashville, Tenn., who is numbered among the first graduates of Oberlin, and Mrs. Amanda Smith, known for her evangelistic labors upon four continents, and of whom Bishop Thoburn has said: "During the seventeen years I have lived in Calcutta, I have never known any one who could draw and hold so large an audience as Mrs. Smith." In our conference was the senior, Bishop Wayman, who entered so heartily into whatever seemed to be for the best, that his loving counsel will long be remembered. Bishop Arnett, of the Third Episcopal District, of course, was with us, and greatly assisted in planning for the amendments of our old constitution. Bishop Tanner, who is among the first organizers, was no less enthusiastic than he was twenty-one years ago. . . .

As to the business of the conference, we held three sessions every day, each beginning with devotional exercises. A very excellent paper was read by Mrs. Hannah Jones; "Growth of Missions in the Last Century." The evening service was taken up with welcome addresses, etc.

The second day proved to be a busy one. The first subject for discussion was: "Home Missionary Work." In a masterly way Mrs. Bishop Turner, of Georgia, and Mrs. J. W. Beckett, of Baltimore, did credit, both to the women of the Church and the race. Next came "Caring for the Children," by Mrs. J. P. Sampson, and Miss M. E. Jones. Both of those papers, if put into a balance, would not be found wanting. Following these was read a very well prepared paper, by Miss M. Gant, of Abbeville, S.C., giving useful hints about the "Training of Native Workers."

At the afternoon session of this day, Rev. S. P. Hood read a paper both interesting and instructive on the work in Hayti, he having spent several years on the Island. Mrs. M. A. Cooper spoke on mission work in Bermuda, she having just returned from that sunny little island. . . .

The evening session was devoted to work on the "Dark Continent." A letter was read from our missionary, Rev. J. R. Frederick, by Mrs. M. E. Wilmer. It was full of information in regard to our work in Sierre Leone. Mrs. Sarah J. Early was here introduced and made an address so full of pathos, that the vast audience was stirred to its depth. Mrs. Amanda Smith concluded by one of her happy talks on the many incidents connected with her world-wide missionary work.

Saturday was devoted largely to hearing reports of delegates, and discussions of how to make our auxiliaries more interesting; also to an exceedingly interesting address on "Temperance," by Mrs. F. E. W. Harper. The afternoon was occupied in a visit to the Stephen Smith "Home for Aged and Infirm Colored persons." . . .

Monday came bright and cheery, with the enthusiasm of the delegates plainly visible. Mrs. Bishop Wayman was the first to lead off in an account of her early missionary labors, and was followed by papers on Bands of Hope, Bible reading in large cities, and discussions on topics of general interest. The paper of Mrs. Alice Astwood, on Santo Domingo, read by her husband, owing to her unavoidable absence, was one of rare excellence, and historic value. Last but not least, was the report on Constitutional Amendments. When the report was submitted, Mrs. Fannie J. Coppin, as chairman of the committee made a speech the like of which it is seldom the privilege of one to hear. Strong in every point which goes to make up oratory, it was by far the speech of the day, if not of the Convention.

The closing exercises at 7 P.M., began by Mrs. Amanda Smith. It was simply a Pentecostal shower. Sisters Radcliffe, Aldridge and others led off in singing, after which the Lord's Supper was administered by the Bishops present. . . .

In conclusion, we say: One of the most cheering indications in the Mite Missionary department, and in the conference just adjourned, is the steady activity and increasing interest in the work among our women, both old and young. Especially do we note the enthusiasm of our young women. And what more hopeful sign need we ask than to have our young mothers throwing themselves into the missionary work? Of a necessity the children will be inspired by the example of the mothers; and so we may hope to perpetuate the zeal and devotion to the great cause. Our prayer is that some of these dear little ones now being nestled to sleep by the sweet voice of a mother, singing: "Over the Ocean Wave," or some other missionary song of Zion, will be consecrated to missionary work; and when the years of maturity are theirs, and we mothers who have laid the foundation, be resting

in the "Sweet bye and bye," they will be endowed with the holy fire
to go forth proclaiming the Word.

Sarah E. Tanner

THOSE WHO WERE SENT: DEACONESSES, FIRST LAY PROFESSIONAL WORKERS

Document 6: Governance of Deaconess Orders

*Deaconess work was begun in the United States in the 1840s by
Pastor William Passavant of the Evangelical Alliance of the Lutheran
Church. He patterned the work after European deaconess homes and
institutions of Pastor Theodor Fliedner in Germany. Passavant was
credited with beginning forty-five charitable institutions, such as hospitals, schools, and orphanages in the Lutheran Church.*

*The deaconess work he initiated did not survive the Civil War,
primarily because of prejudice against the employment of women.
Plans for governance, which deaconesses adapted after the Civil War,
however, were based on the principles and regulations of Passavant's
institutions. Their emphasis on the model of family life is notable,
particularly as young women of middle-class backgrounds made a
major transition to life in the inner cities of America's burgeoning
metropolises.[32]*

General Principles

1. The association of Christian females is purely voluntary. The
members unite without persuasion, remain without vows, and retire
without restraint.

2. It is not an order, but the restoration of an office, that of
"Servant" or Deaconess in the primitive church.

3. Its members heartily confess the faith, engage in the worship
and observe the discipline of the Evangelical Lutheran Church.

4. Its object is habitually to engage in works of mercy among the
sick and poor, the ignorant and fatherless, and other suffering members of our Lord's body. In the better attainment of this object, the
association is incorporated and fully empowered to establish and
conduct the necessary charitable institutions.

5. Not earthly reward and honor but the desire for an opportunity
to manifest their gratitude to Jesus Christ in the way revealed in His
word, has influenced the members to associate themselves as servants
of Christ and of His church.

Regulations

1. The members of the Institution shall consist of the deaconnesses
proper and the probationers, both of whom shall be received into the
association in the manner hereinafter provided.

2. They shall alike be subject to the Director and the Directing Sister in regard to the designation of their field of labor and the manner of its performance and shall conscientiously observe both the letter and spirit of its principles and regulations.

3. They shall reside in the Parent House, unless appointed to labor elsewhere by the Board of Managers, in which case they shall still retain their connection with the parent association, continuing subject to its rules, reporting statedly to its Director and Directing Sisters, and holding themselves in readiness to be recalled or to be transferred elsewhere whenever deemed necessary or proper to those in authority.

4. The internal government and regulation of the association shall be vested in the Director and the Directing Sister, both of whom are elected by the joint suffrages of the Sisters and the Board of Directors according to the mode described in the charter. The relation of the Directing Sister towards the other members is, as far as possible, that of a mother or an elder sister, while that of the Director is, as far as possible, that of the Head of the Family and the spiritual guide.

5. The sisters shall wear a plain, economical habit, as much as possible conforming in style, expense and color, which shall be black or gray or blue on week days as they may prefer. In regard to the other articles of dress, the counsel of the Director is first to be sought before being purchased. The wearing of the sister's habit is voluntary to the probations during the probationary year but all display or ornament is to be avoided.

Document 7: Deaconess Work among Immigrants in Urban Ghettos

By the turn of the century, Reverend Christian Golder, Ph.D., became the authoritative writer on deaconess work. His historical research went beyond that of earlier valuable studies, particularly Deaconesses, Biblical, Early Church, European, American, *by Lucy Rider Meyer (1889);* Deaconesses, Ancient and Modern, *by Reverend Henry Wheeler (1889); and* Deaconesses in Europe and America, *by Jane Bancroft Robinson (1890).*

In his history of the deaconess movement, Golder developed a significant case for their work from biblical times until his own day. The excerpt given here vividly describes the need for deaconesses in America's rapidly expanding urban ghettos. Representative of Social Gospel activists, Golder placed considerable responsibility on the churches for the growth of slums. Their membership had moved to the suburbs, leaving the city to saloons, gambling dens, and houses of prostitution.[33]

Never before was the Church called upon to face such giant problems as those of the present day. This is universally acknowledged, and it is the subject matter of discussion at the pastoral conferences, Assemblies, Conventions, and Church gatherings of all kinds. The pulpit and ecclesiastical press have united, and are constantly planning new ways and means. It is clear to everybody that new forces and agencies must be brought into the field. Is it to be wondered at that we have finally rubbed the sleep out of our eyes and entertained the thought of placing the hitherto fallow-lying strength of woman in the service of the kingdom of God in the most comprehensive and liberal manner? Thence we may explain the phenomenal growth of the Deaconess Cause in the United States. Not more than fifteen years ago the institution of deaconess was hardly known. Occasional beginnings failed, and the voices that had been raised died away almost unheard. And now, in a dozen of years, at least one-hundred and forty Deaconess Homes have been established, and among these are a number of Mother Houses, which, in regard to capacity of work and extent, put into the shade many institutions of the Old World. The value of the property amounts to at least five millions of dollars, and the number of deaconesses has grown to nearly two thousand. In the Methodist Episcopal Church alone, within this period of time, from ninety to one hundred Deaconess Institutions, and twenty hospitals in connection with the same, were established. The number of Methodist deaconesses has grown to be over twelve hundred, and the average increase for the past twelve years has been annually twenty-six per cent. The woman's movement, which, in the past decade, has seized upon the public mind more than in the preceding entire century, finds an outlet in the Deaconess Movement, and it is possible that the female diaconate will contribute more to the solution of the woman question than any other factor. The soil for the female diaconate is as thoroughly prepared in the United States to-day as it was sixty years ago in Germany. The young work shows an extraordinary power of life and attraction, and even if here and there the experimental stage has not been passed, it is evident that it is assuming a more definite and certain shape from year to year. Numerous difficulties have been removed, and the leaders have a much more fixed purpose in view. Even the Baptists and Congregationalists have taken up the thread, and the great group of Presbyterians in their annual Assemblies have taken hold of this momentous question, and there are mustard-seed beginnings here and there which promise much good for the future. Farthest in this matter has progressed the German Church of our country. The Methodist Episcopal Church and the Episcopal Church have also accomplished wonderful things. . . .

In another decade there will hardly be one of the larger cities in the United States which will not be able to show at least one of the Deaconess Institutions. Whenever the American has seized upon an idea, he brings it to execution, and that generally on the grandest scale. There is no lack of means, and the necessity is less in doubt. Not less than thirty-three per cent of the population of the United States live in cities with twenty-five thousand population and more, and year after year the influx to the cities is greater. And in this there is a great danger for our Nation. It is a fact that the unchristian and ignorant masses in the great cities are threatening civilization. It would be idle to seek to deceive ourselves in regard to the sad conditions. Everywhere may be found the revolutionary tinder which threatens to be dangerous for the future. The Church of the present has a tremendous mission; she is the light and when the light ceases to give light, how great will the darkness be! Thousands to-day hear the sound of church-bells; but they are indeed far separated from the Church, and there is as broad and deep a chasm between them and the church pews as though they lived in central Africa. . . . The impoverished and degraded masses in the laboring quarters look with envious eyes upon the prosperity of Church members, and accuse them of being confederates of the capitalists. They note the well-being of Christians, without knowing the cause or wishing to know it. They are filled with prejudices, which generally change to bitter hate. Each property-owner is in their eyes an oppressor; they hate the power of riches, and they forget the benefits which they have received, and they recognize the blessings of the Church as little as they do the usefulness of the Government. They hate both, because, in their opinion, they protect capital. But they hate the Church the most because she protects the right of property, and because her members stand socially higher and take a more influential position in society. True, it is to be regretted that to-day there are so many half-hearted Christians who live indifferently and care not in the least for the poor and forsaken. Almost universally the large, wealthy Churches are removed to the suburbs, and the population of the poor in the older city quarters are left to themselves.

Dr. George W. Gray, superintendent of Methodist City Missions in Chicago, has shown that in one district of Chicago, with a population of twenty-two thousand, there are but two Protestant Churches and one Catholic Church; but in the same district there are two hundred and seventy-two saloons, eighty-five wine-houses, seven opium and eight gambling dens, and not less than ninety-two houses of ill-fame. If the Church is indifferent to such conditions, she will sow the wind and reap the whirlwind. . . .

More than ever before are we in need to-day of female power. We need women who will give up the luxuries of life, who will forsake society and friends, and condescend to help this class of men. They must patiently persevere until these people regain confidence and give heed to the Church and the gospel. The only hope and possibility of elevating and saving this class of the population in our great cities lies in the unselfish and devoted activity of such women. The sufferings, cares, and sicknesses of these most abandoned ones can only be reached by ministrations of love that will take a personal interest, nurse, encourage, counsel, and assist; that will give work to the unemployed, gather the children in kindergartens and the infants in day nurseries, and be present everywhere where help is needed. The people need education, not through books on the school bench, but education in the affairs of daily life, in practical economy, in the preparation of food, in sick-nursing, housekeeping, and the training of children. They should also be taught the lessons of morality and practical Christianity, and this can best be done by deaconesses. The spirit and love of Him who "can not to be ministered unto, but to minister, and give His life a ransom for many," must be shown these people in incorporated reality, and for this purpose more than an occasional visit is necessary. Deaconesses who labor in these quarters will come in daily, unsought touch with this class of people; they will develop a relation of friendship, and win them over to confidence. Here is the great and useful field for deaconesses, and the Mother Houses should become central stations whence the most extended ministrations of love might be directed in a systematic manner. The time will come when tens of thousands of deaconesses, in city and country, will sacrifice their lives in Christian love services. We are convinced that the Deaconess Cause has a great future in the United States, and the promising beginning leads to the hope that in this respect even greater things will be accomplished here than up to the present time in Europe.

Document 8: Immigrant Women Enter Deaconess Orders

A majority of the deaconesses came from old-stock Protestant homes and were of rural or small-town, middle-class background. Some, however, were recruited from among the newly arrived immigrant population. They committed themselves to full-time Christian service among their own people in the inner cities.

The following autobiographical sketches of "Two Italian Women Workers," which were published in the Home Mission Monthly *(August, 1905), provide fascinating accounts of such women. The two women who describe their lives here became city missionaries in the First Italian Baptist Church of New York at the beginning of the twentieth century. Conversion of immigrant Catholics to Protestantism must have played a major part in their own daily work—if their personal witnesses are any indication.*[34]

Signorina Eleanora Vaccaneo
A Brief Autobiography

I was born in Busalla, Genoa, Italy, in March, 1888, and came to

America in 1894, at the age of six. There is not very much that is interesting to tell in the life of one not yet seventeen years old, spent part in Italy and part in America.

While in Italy all our family were Catholics, except my grandfather, who prejudiced my mind against the Catholic priests and told me little gospel stories about Jesus Christ, which I did not understand very well on account of being so young.

In 1894 we came to America. Not long after a friend invited us to the Italian mission then not long opened at Mariners' Temple, with Mr. Dassori in charge. He welcomed us warmly, and we have made it our church home ever since. Not long afterward my father, mother, and two older sisters were converted, baptized and united with the church. At the age of eleven I was also converted and baptized, with another sister. My father was a deacon, and our whole family now were baptized believers.

Soon after my conversion I had a desire to be a missionary, so as to work among my own people. In 1902 I began a two year's course at Northfield Seminary, and am now taking daily lectures at Dr. White's Training School, and in the meantime getting my practical experience on our field, teaching the beginner's grade in Sunday school, also in the sewing school, girls' clubs, playing during a number of the services, and making as many calls as I can in the homes. I am glad to have so many opportunities of service, and am thankful to be in America to work among my own people. My prayer is that I may be able to win many of them to Jesus Christ, who alone can save them.

Signora Concetta Pezzano
Bible Reader among the Mothers of the
First Italian Baptist Church, New York
Her Story, written by request

I was born at Polistena, in the Province of Calabria, Italy, in 1874. My parents were Catholics of the strictest kind; every night before retiring more than an hour was spent praying with the rosary and calling upon different saints. The village priest requested me to purchase some white coarse cotton, and on the 25th day of March I was to say "Hail Mary, full of grace, the Lord be with thee, blessed are thou among women," etc., and then make a knot. The second day I was to say the same prayer, once for the first knot, and, after repeating it a second time, make a second knot. Each day I was to repeat the prayer once for every knot, until I had made 365, then I took them to the church; after the priest told me to repeat the same prayer for 365 knots three times, making a total of 1,095, he sprinkled the chain of prayers with holy water and gave it back to me.

As my father was a seafaring man, he came to America, and while in New York heard of the Italian Mission at Mariner's Temple. Mr.

Dassori gave him a Bible, which he brought back with him. The next time I went to confession I took the Bible with me. The priest at once insisted on burning it, and reproved me for even turning its pages over, saying it was wrong to read such books. I told him it belonged to him. In the year 1900 I came to New York, and in company with my father attended the First Italian Baptist Church. I liked the singing, the Lord's Prayer, the testimony of the brethren, and believed what Mr. Dassori said as he preached from God's Word. Soon after I became converted. Before being baptized I burned all the images I had, and prayed to Jesus Christ alone, who forgave my sin and who put a new song in my mouth—"To him be all the praise."

I thank God that he has counted me worthy to be a co-worker with Him, and if my health permitted I would devote my whole life among my own people.

Document 9: Single Women Sent to Foreign Mission Stations

Deaconesses became widely employed in foreign mission work after the Civil War. Their growing presence throughout the world helped to make missions an identifying mark of Protestantism by the turn of the century. Two articles here from early issues of the Heathen Woman's Friend *highlight the justifications employed by mission boards and women's societies for recruitment of single women missionaries.*[35]

Appeal to the Ladies of the Methodist Episcopal Church

The object of this Society is to meet, as far as possible, the great want experienced by our Eastern Missionaries, of Christian women to labor among women of those heathen lands. Few of us have ever realized how complete is the darkness which envelopes them, and how insufficient have been the efforts hitherto made to admit the light of the Gospel to their benighted hearts and homes. Forbidden by the customs of their country to seek for themselves this light, or to receive instruction at the hands of our missionaries, they are accessible only to Christian teachers of their own sex. The wives of our missionaries have done all that they could. Many of them, in addition to their own families, have the care of large Zenana schools, which they have organized and in which they are daily busied; still they have made earnest endeavors to carry the knowledge of Christ to their sisters by personal visits and labors at their homes. What wonder that, in so many instances, physical strength has failed under such constant and great exertions, and the oppressing consciousness of the magnitude of their work. Their labors have been, however, by no means without reward. Many of their heathen sisters are awaking from their ignorance and apathy, and are eagerly asking after the way of life. These calls for help our missionaries are often utterly unable to answer, because they are already over-burdened.

Dear Sisters! shall we not recognize, in this emergency, God's voice as speaking to us—for who can so well do this work as we? Does it not seem as though the responsibility were thus laid directly upon us? And shall we shrink from bearing it?

We well know how close is the relation of the mother to the child, and how important it is that the mother's heart be filled with the love and grace of God if her child is to grow up under Divine influence and be guided by Divine wisdom. How then can we more successfully cooperate with our missionaries, and better insure the rapid extension of the knowledge of the truth as it is in Jesus, than by opening the hearts of the mothers to the purifying and saving influences of God's love? We know too how inestimable is the value, and how incalculable the influence of a pure Christian home; and if the influences of such homes are so indispensable in a Christian land, what must be their importance among a people, the depth of whose degradation is, as we are often assured, altogether beyond our realization?

The Great Motive

Sympathy prompted this help, and this was all right. But after all, the great and permanent basis of our Society is not merely sympathy for woman in her physical suffering or social and mental degradation; for the large majority of heathen women, never having known anything better in these respects, do not feel their want. Physical suffering of course they would avoid, but social and mental elevation they know nothing about. The foundation principle of our Society is the command to give the gospel to every creature. Heathen women are without Christ. This includes everything else; social, mental, and physical degradation. Women without Christ! What is it? We can never take in all that it means of suffering, of sorrow, of social degradation, of mental darkness, and worse than all these, of soul pollution. Woman without Christ! because there *are* such, our Society is in existence and will continue to be, just as long as we remember this. We send her help, not because she is a servant to her husband, and suffers untold cruelties from him, not because she is poor, and wretched and miserable, even when she don't know it, but because she is without Christ. Without Him, she has nothing; with Him she has all things. I firmly believe, and have had the witness of my personal observation, that Christianity does change the whole being. I have rejoiced at the cleaning up outside as well as inside. I have delighted in seeing one layer of dirt after another taken off, and finally, the man clean and clothed and in his right mind, with a face so bright and intelligent that it was hardly possible to recognize in him the stupid, dirty man our eyes first looked upon. Yes, Christianity does refine, cleanse, and elevate every one that comes under its influence.

Document 10: Justifying the Deaconess as Clergy or Laity

While the service of deaconesses was valued, controversy arose over their status as part of the clergy or laity. Proposals to grant full clergy status to deaconesses were threatening to the authority and power that ordained ministers had come to call their own.

The arguments for two orders of ministry, those of preaching and of service, are reasonable and worthy of strong consideration. Even those who favored clergy status for deaconesses, however, were careful to limit their functions to those of the diaconate. These two emphases are expressed in several places in this selection from Christian Golder's The Deaconess Motherhouse.[36]

The Diaconate means service; a service of affectionate helpfulness, which has its origin in the fellowship of Christian love. The term usually signifies the activity of the Church in works of mercy and help. Recent usage confines the word Diaconate to the office of assistant at ecclesiastical functions; nevertheless it should be applied to the special vocation, or rather to the office of helping, as distinguished from the office of preaching. In this sense Luther often translated the word Diaconate (service) with the word office. *Diaconein*—serving, *diaconos* —servant. In as much as the office of helping has been committed to women, we may speak of a Female Diaconate, or Deaconess Cause. . . .

Where a willing service is given for the benefit of a neighbor, without selfish seeking of honor, there we have the original conception of the true Diaconate. "Even as the Son of man came not to be ministered unto, but to minister, and to give his life a ransom for many." (Matthew 20:28). Where there is faith in His Name, service is ennobled and changed into a real control. Augustine says: "Whosoever serves the poor for the sake of the Lord, governs."

"Differences of administrations" are mentioned in the scriptures, (1 Corinthians 12:05), such as the gifts of preaching and teaching, of deeper spiritual knowledge, of administration, of governing, of caring for souls, of discerning of spirits; the gifts of helpfulness, of healing, of languages, etc. All these gifts must be awakened, developed and made to serve the Kingdom of God. Offices of assistant-helpers were created in the Apostolic Church to supplement the spiritual office. Christ Himself did not establish such offices, but they came into existence after the Day of Pentecost, under the direction of the Holy Spirit. Under the stress of their labors the apostles sometimes failed to provide for the widows; therefore seven deacons were ordained for service. (Acts 6:3–6). Until then the apostles had served as ministers to both soul and body. But from now on the spiritual office was separated from the administration of temporal affairs. The Diaconate, therefore, grew out of the Apostolate, as its first offshoot. In this way the needs of soul and body were cared for by separate offices. To the deacon was entrusted the care of the sick and the relief of widows and destitute persons. And they undoubtedly assisted in preaching and teaching, too, as is shown in the case of Stephen and Philip.

But we can trace the idea of the Diaconate to Jesus Himself. We are told that the women followed and "ministered unto him of their substance." (Luke 8). Thus early do we meet with the true Female Diaconate. The Lord is pleased with their service and we are told that the women were the last at the cross and the first at the tomb. This delicate and sympathetic kindness indicates the nature of the true calling of the deaconess. Dean Howson, in his book, entitled "Deaconesses," says: "It would surely be a great mistake to limit the divine law of women's mission on the earth to the mere relation of marriage. The Scripture is far wider than our prejudices. Wherever helping work is to be done, there woman is in her place. Motherly and sisterly care are often most needed, when they cannot be had within the sphere of domestic life. Home is indeed women's highest and most natural sphere; but the outcasts of society cannot be reached by home influences unless these influences are brought to them, and it is only a female hand that can bring them. If the activity of the stronger sex is to penetrate all parts of human life and yet feminine influence is to be restricted within families, the equilibrium of society is not preserved but marred." . . .

The Biblical justification of the Female Diaconate is to be found, however, in Romans 16:1–2. Paul says: "I commend unto you Phebe, our sister, which is a servant of the church which is at Cenchrea: That ye receive her in the Lord, as becometh saints, and that ye assist her in whatsoever business she hath need of you, for she herself also hath been a succorer of many and of mine own self." Therefore, being "a servant of the church that is at Cenchrea," Phebe was a *Diakonos*. The apostle calls her "sister," thereby indicating the community of Christian faith and the relation in which she stood to the Church. Sister Phebe is therefore the first female incumbent of the office of the Diaconate, which was instituted by the apostles, and her work received apostolic approval. Here we find a well regulated female Diaconate. It was, no doubt, introduced quietly, just as the Sabbath was transferred to the first day of the week. In any case this much is certain, that the office existed in a well-regulated form in the Apostolic Church. In his "Church History" Dr. Philip Schaff says: "Deaconesses, or female helpers, had a similar charge of the poor and sick in the female portion of the Church. This office was the more needful on account of the rigid separation of the sexes at that day, especially among the Greeks. It opened to pious women and virgins, and especially to widows, a most suitable field for the regular official exercise of their peculiar gifts of self-denying love and devotion to the welfare of the Church. Through it they could carry the light and comfort of the gospel into the most private and delicate relations of domestic life, without at all overstepping their natural sphere. . . .

The deaconess belonged to the clergy. The Apostolic Constitution is very clear on this point. We are told that the deaconess was consecreted by laying on of hands of the bishop. Her ordination was similar to that of the deacon. Her duties were outlined in the Apostolic Constitution in the following manner: "They guarded the door of the House of God. They were the agents in the dealings of the bishop with the women of his congregation. They directed the latter where to sit in church. They prepared female catechumen for baptism. They nursed the sick, visited and cared for widows and orphans." Three requirements must be met before she could be received: unspotted reputation, vital experience of religion, and practical talent. The requirement of celibacy was added later. Deaconesses must be either maidens or widows. This is necessary in the nature of the case. A married woman can have no regular calling in the exclusive service of the Church. Men are not hindered by marriage in the duties of their office, but if a woman wishes to serve the Lord without restraint, in an ecclesiastical office, she must, under all circumstances, be free from the bonds of wedlock, so long as she holds the office. (1 Corinthians 7:34, 35). . . .

The question has been asked whether the Female Diaconate of the present age should be conceived of as an ecclesiastical office in the apostolic sense. Many are willing to admit it only as the professional practice of charity. In this case there is no difference between it and other professional charity, as practiced by women. It cannot be assumed that only the deaconesses serve as Christians. The Sisters of the Red Cross, the members of Samaritan Societies and other persons, who devote a part or all of their time to benevolent work, do the same. Moreover, it is the duty of all Christians to practice benevolence. But the existence of the Diaconate is seriously jeopardized if we conceive it only as the professional practice of charity, for then it is not an office of the Church. But, according to the Scriptures, it should be an ecclesiastical office distinguished from the general duty of all Christians and all the faithful in the practice of charity. It is a vocation to which a sister may be called and installed in a well-regulated office through special ecclesiastical usage. Unfortunately this is not always done, but the question is an important one, especially for the deaconesses. A sister who feels called of the Lord and compelled by her conscience to devote her life to the service of the Church will find complete security only when she knows that the office is instituted by the Lord, and therefore a part of the organism of the Church. If she is to take upon herself the duties and responsibilities of the office of a deaconess she has a right to claim consideration as a person appointed by the Church.

In the following selection, Bishop John M. Brown of the African Methodist Episcopal Church directly calls for two orders of ordination of women in his denomination, to service as deaconesses and to preaching as presbyters. His position received little support among his fellow clergymen, as did the less radical views of Golder among white clergy.[37]

Let us notice a few evidences of the ordination of women: Says Dr. Schaff in his history of the Apostolic Church, "Besides this class of helpers (referring to Deacons) we find in the Apostolic Church the Order of female deacons or deaconesses which was supplementary to the others." Herzog's Encyclopedia says, "They held among their sex a relation something like the Presbyters."

Calmet, a most celebrated French Scholar and Biblical Critic, says, "Deaconesses served the church in those offices which the Deacons could not themselves exercise, visiting those of their own sex, in sickness or when imprisoned for their faith. They were persons of advanced age, when chosen; and appointed to the office by the imposition of hands." The Critical and Explanatory Commentary says, "That in the earliest churches there were deaconesses to attend to the wants of the female members, there is no good reason to doubt. So early, at least, as the reign of Trajan, we learn from Pliny's celebrated letter to that Emperor, A.D. 110 or 111, that they existed in the Eastern Churches."

Dr. Adam Clarke says of Romans 16:1: "Phoebe is here termed a servant, a deaconess in the church at Cenchrea. There were deaconesses in the Primitive Church, whose business it was to attend the female converts at baptism, to instruct the catechumens, or persons who were candidates for baptism, to visit the sick and those who were in prison, and in short perform those religious offices for the female part of the church which could not with propriety be performed by men. It is evident that they were ordained by the imposition of the hands of a Bishop; and the form of prayers which were used are found in the Apostolical Constitution."

Grotius, on the verse before us (Romans 16:1) remarks, "that in Greece there were female presbyters, as well as deaconesses, for the instruction of their own sex; which female presbyters were ordained by the laying on of hands till the Council of Laodicea." He appeals to the eleventh canon of that council. Dr. Clarke and Grotius proved three things, first, that there were deaconesses, second, that there were female presbyters, and third, that these were ordained by the laying on of hands of the Bishops.

Herzog says, "They were consecrated to their office by the laying on of hands of the Bishop and his blessing." This order is attested by Chrysostom, Epiphanius and Terullian.

Rev. Albert Barnes says, "It is clear from the New Testament that there was an order of women in the church known as deaconesses. Their existence is expressly affirmed in early ecclesiastical history. The Apostolical Constitution book III says, "Ordain a deaconess who is faithful and holy for the ministries toward the women'."

Pliny, in his celebrated letter to Trajan, when trying to find out the opinions and practices of Christians, remarks, "I deemed it necessary to put two female servants, who were called ministrae (that is, deaconesses) to the torture, in order to ascertain, What is truth."

The facts produced from Commentaries, Encyclopaedias and church history show, very clearly, that women were not only ordained deaconesses, but presbyters, by the imposition of the hands of a Bishop. They did much good; as these did so much good, so we find women of the present day who are fully competent to fill the same places in the Church of Christ as regularly ordained deaconesses.

We close with the question, with which we began, "What shall be done with the women?" and answer it. Allow them the largest liberty to exercise their gifts in the Church of God; "There is neither male nor female, for ye are one in Christ Jesus" (Galatians 3:28).Washington, D.C.

Document 11: The "New Woman" of Protestantism

Begun in 1884, the Chicago Training School was the first deaconess home in the Methodist Episcopal Church. It was a model for deaconess institutions of other denominations that followed shortly thereafter.

In the excerpts included here, Lucy Rider Meyer, superintendent of the Chicago Training School and editor of the Message and Deaconess Advocate, *acknowledges the stereotype of the deaconess. Then, she proceeds to shatter it.*[38]

A deaconess is often pictured as a goody-goody kind of woman who goes softly up dirty back stairs, reading the Bible to poor sick women and patting the heads of dirty-faced children. But there is nothing a woman *can* do in the line of Christian work that a deaconess may not do. Her field is as large as the work of woman, and the need of that work. In deaconess ranks to-day may be found physicians, editors, stenographers, teachers, nurses, bookkeepers, superintendents of hospitals and orphanages, kitchen-gardners and kindergartners. In Omaha not only the superintending nurse, but the superintendent of the Methodist Episcopal hospital, an institution that within two years has cared for 1040 patients, are deaconesses.

A cleaner Chicago is what the women voters of the city are working for. What could be more appropriate than that with such an end in view a deaconess should be an election judge? In just that capacity Ida Jordan, superintendent of the Chicago Deaconess Home, has been serving her city. At the polls the white ties stood not for a departure in deaconess work but for a natural and desirable broadening of the deaconess "sphere."

The discussion in regard to the admission of women to the legislative bodies of the church is not confined to the Methodist organization in this country. Our English friends are in the throes of a similar controversy. The brilliant and witty Rev. Mark Guy Pearse, who takes the liberal side of this question, contributes to the *Methodist Times* a bit of history showing that the "new woman" is not an invention of the last decade, but that, in the character of Hilda, Abbess of Whitby, (b. 614, A.D.) she played an important part in the history of the early English church. The town of Whitby is pervaded by her name and influence, for, says the author, "the Abbey made Whitby, and Hilda made the Abbey." But we give the story in his own words:

"Nor is the influence of this noble woman local only. The founder of a double monastery—that is, both for monks and nuns—she became the abbess of each, the head of the training-college from which no less than six bishops went forth, all men of piety—one of whom was the sainted John of Beverley—and to which men came, not only from all parts of England, but even from the Continent. 'The harts and sciences,' says the historian, 'were so well cultivated by her that Whitby was regarded as one of the best seminaries of learning in the then known world. Hence it came to pass that Alcuin, the great philosopher and divine of his age, who was born in Northumberland, and had his education chiefly in the Abbey of Whitby, after founding the University of Paris advised Charles the Great, the Emperor and King of France, to send over some of the young nobility, born in his deminois, to that part of England, where they might receive a more polite, liberal, and learned education than was to be had in France.'

"And more even that this, we find Hilda in the councils and conferences of the church taking part in that Synod of Whitby which determined the form and fate of the church in England. 'Her counsel,' says J. R. Green, 'was sought even by nobles and kings.' ...

"I closed the life of this noble Abbess of Whitby, wondering if God sent a St. Hilda to Methodism *what should we do with her.*"

THE RECEIVERS: "WOMEN OF HEATHENDOM"

Document 12: The Scope of Women's Work in the Inner City

When church workers defined the "heathen world," they pointed to the rapidly expanding urban ghettos of the United States as well

as to the "dark" continents of Asia, Africa, and South America.
"Glimpses of our Field," from the journal of the Kansas City National
Training School, illustrates the wide range of work done by deacon-
esses in the inner cities and supported by women's societies. Almost
all their programs included both relief and rehabilitation of individ-
uals and conversion of the masses to Christianity. Their emphasis on
work with women and children is clearly present in the following
article.[39]

Since the early days of the Training School, Kansas City has afforded many opportunities of service outside the work done in the
Methodist churches. Many of our students and deaconesses receive a
broader vision of the needs of humanity through the experiences
which come from contact with all classes of people in this, our "special
work."

On Monday mornings eight students cross the river and go into
the Packing House district: Aubrey Tyree, Elsie Hill, Mary Wright
and Jeanette Scott go to the Morris Plant; Joy Smith, Ethel Harvey,
Myrtle Gray and Bessie Smith to the plant of Sulzberger & Sons.
There are about fifty girls working in the trimming and head rooms
of each of these plants. When the twelve o'clock whistle blows, work
ceases and girls of many nationalities gather in the lunch rooms for
their noon meal. The Polish, Austrian and Croatian races predominate, though there are also many English speaking girls. The workers
are entitled to only a half hour noon and into this short time once a
week our eight Training School students crowd a share of the good
cheer and joy of living with which their own lives are filled. Songs are
sung; Bible or inspirational stories are told to the American girls; and
brief English classes are conducted for the foreign speaking girl. At
special seasons as Thanksgiving, Christmas or Easter, through the
kindness of the Epworth Leagues of Greater Kansas City, a flower or
spray of holly was given to each, with a message full of love and the
spirit of the season.

On Monday evenings two of our deaconesses conduct classes in the
Kansas City Training School for Sunday School workers held at the
Y.W.C.A.: Miss Garretson teaches Psychology; Miss Mary F. Smith
has a class in story telling and also conducts the work of the Beginners'
Department.

Each Thursday evening Winnogene Penny and two other girls
from the Training School family go to the Crittenden Home. An
entirely new line of work has been undertaken this year. After the
confidence of the girls was won through informal chats, games and
music, a class for the study of the Life of Christ was begun. Each girl
is making a harmony of the Gospels and illustrating her book with
pictures from Christ's life. There has been a real interest in the work
throughout the year and there have been many definite results.

Through this study of the Man of Galilee has come the consciousness of their great need, and a number of the girls have accepted Him as their Friend and Savior.

Saturday afternoon brings an opportunity to do real Settlement work in the Central Italian Mission. This work is under the direction of one of our deaconesses, Miss Hanson. In the Mission there are sewing and cooking classes for the girls and kindergarten games and a story hour for the younger children. Ruth Getty, Hope Wolfe, Maud Randolph and Kezia Hay assist Miss Hanson as teachers.

During the fall and early winter, Myrtle Puckett conducted a story hour at the Kansas City Day Nursery on Saturday afternoons. She was known among the children as the "Bible Teacher." Many stories from the Bible and other helpful sources made the hour a happy one for the little folk and their story teller.

While some of the girls are busy on Saturday afternoon teaching sewing and cooking classes or telling stories, Ruth Murrell and Adah Humfeld are busy in the basement of Fisk Hall. The people come here from the Kensington mission district for warm and comfortable clothing which is distributed either at a low price or without charge, as circumstances demand. During the selection of the desired articles frequent opportunities are afforded for a kind and helpful word.

Each Sunday two members of our family conduct a vesper service at Swope Settlement. It is attended mainly by the Jewish children of the neighborhood who greatly appreciate the story hour and the songs.

The fourth Sunday of each month, Miss Mary F. Smith and Miss Blaschko hold a service at the Parently Home. In this home are placed neglected and delinquent girls. Mrs. Keith, the matron, is a real mother to her family of about fifty girls, ranging in age from four to sixteen years. There is always a helpful song service in which the girls are eager to take part. To hear them sing their favorite, "Keep Sweet," convinces one that the meaning has taken deep root in their hearts. The inspirational talk and earnest prayers which follow, give the girls ideals for true Christian living.

Once a month, also, Miss Curry has charge of a service at the Women's Reformatory. It is heartbreaking to see these delinquent women as the Gospel message is brought to them through the songs, prayers, and lessons. A few sit with hardened faces but in most of them can be seen the conflicting emotions of shame, repentance and determination to begin anew.

And so our days and weeks are full of these extra tasks which only prove that there are still many, many who do not know the Best Friend.

Document 13: Evangelizing and Educating Women Throughout the World

The idealism that pervaded the Social Gospel Movement was as pronounced in foreign mission work as in home fields. Writers in women's journals made their appeals graphic and persuasive to inspire missionary zeal among their contributors. The goal of missionaries to India was the release of the three hundred million women held in bondage by custom and religion.[40]

It is a *fact,* that every Christian woman should bear in mind, that no less than 300,000,000 women are still in the condition of slavery mentioned in the letter of Bro. Scott. It is also a fact, that on account of that social condition, which excludes woman from society, these millions of women can only be reached and taught by Christian women. A missionary may preach to crowds of heathen in the market-places, and at the religious fairs, but no woman will be found in his congregation; and should he preach from house to house, his words would never reach the female members of the household unless they should chance to listen from behind the screen. A Christian woman, however, can go to those villages where the low caste people reside, and can collect in a quiet place a small company of attentive women; she can also go to the private apartments of the women of the higher classes who are kept in seclusion, and be welcomed there; she can open girls' schools among all classes, adapting them to the circumstances of the people, and thus teach Jesus to the women and girls of every caste.

It is evident that we cannot hope for very much permanent success in evangelizing the heathen until the women as well as the men are reached. Rev. J. Walter, an English Wesleyan Missionary, thus speaks of this—

Work in India

"There is an opening which to my mind is the most inviting and the most promising of all. I refer to the great desire in that country for girls' schools. Christian civilization does little for a nation until it has lifted woman from the condition of a thing to the dignity of a sister and a wife. You cannot evangelize a country until you convert the women. Our Indian successes date from the period of our girls' schools. As long as we labored chiefly among the men, we labored almost in vain, but when we reached the women we found the missing link that led us up to the great heart of India. At first there was formidable opposition. . . . When Dr. Caldwell, a very eminent missionary in Tinnevelly, was opening a girls' school the people laughed, and one of them said,—'Why, this missionary will teach the cows next'; and when I was superintending the erection of a school bungalow for the girls and pupils in the village, an old man came and remonstrated with me on my folly. 'Why,' said he, 'if you teach the girls to read and write they will be writing love-letters to the men, and the country will be turned upside down.' I am very glad to say that so far the old man's words have become true—our girls' schools are turning the country upside down."

Document 14: Dignifying the Work of Immigrant Women in America

This curious story of scrubwomen going to work on a downtown night shift praised qualities in women not associated with domesticated genteel females within the home. It was a part of the image of womanhood advanced in the Deaconess Advocate, *which valued females as independent beings with an identity and rights of their own. The stereotype that women's sphere was the home was being questioned by females in the churches as well as by women's rights workers seeking suffrage, education, and legal rights for their sex.[41]*

It was ten o'clock on the downtown streets. They seemed strangely deserted; for the stores were closed, late shoppers and loiterers had gone home and the theater crowds were still housed inside, absorbed in their evening's amusement.

Then in the darkness there came a startling sound—the sound of women's laughter.

A dark mass, like a small army down the street—women. They were blackgarbed, old—past youth at least. They wore queer, small hats, and each carried a bundle loosely wrapped in newspaper,

They cut the corner and scurried—like a flock of sheep, perhaps, that follow a leader; or rats that flee a building—only they were going in—across the street to the great building that loomed on the opposite corner. Some time between the hour of the departure of the last lingering worker and that of the arrival of the morning's first comer, this huge building must be gone over, cleaned, and put in order.

The scrubwomen were going to work—and they went laughing!

Yea, verily, the woman's place is the home! Women must be sheltered, protected! Womanhood is sacred! Woman's hands must be kept unsullied, her shoulders free from burdens!

It was ten o'clock on the downtown streets. The scrubwomen were going to work—and they went laughing!

Document 15: Destroying the Caste of Sex

Writings of women in foreign mission fields demonstrate the new image of womanhood which they sought for their sex. Female missionaries certainly brought much of American culture and standards with them. They valued native women, however, and worked for the dignity, enlightenment, and autonomy of their sex. The concerns for

LAY WOMEN IN THE PROTESTANT TRADITION

evangelism, education, and social rights were interwoven in their
work with native women around the globe. These themes emerge in
the following excerpts from the addresses given by Miss Ellen Parsons
at the Woman's Congress of Missions in Chicago in 1893. The
Woman's Congress followed the World Columbian Exposition held in
that city. It complimented the emphasis at the World's Fair on
women's contributions in all areas of life.[42]

It is more difficult to point to what is distinctively the fruit of
woman's work in missions at home than abroad because the peculiar
barriers of the East are wanting here. Nowhere in our country is the
ordained man prohibited from carrying the gospel into the home or
pressing the claims of religion upon any individual. . . .

But what of those farther shores? Have the toils of all these societies at home and the sacrifices of our countrywomen been also blessed
in the Turkish Empire, in Persia, India, Siam, China, Japan, Korea,
Africa, and the islands of the sea? There, results are farther out of
sight than results at home; we must draw nearer to them. Yes, God
has answered us with his seal of approval. It is imprinted on the
personal transformation from wild, unruly beings, such as met the
first missionaries in Persia, to those dignified ladies who now conduct
Quarterly Meetings on Oroomiah Plain and furnish columns to the
mission paper. Travelers in Syria and Egypt tell us they are often able,
by their faces, to select, out of a casual company whom they see, those
women who have attended mission schools. A visitor in Mexico could
scarce believe that the thoughtful-faced women in the mission congregation were of the same class as those she met on the plaza. Let a
European light down upon any village in Asia Minor, or the China
Empire, and the tidiest house there, with the cleanest tablecloth and
the most inviting bed, is the home of a mission-school graduate. The
transformation appears in the deaths they die; like the old Siamese
woman, a few months ago, whispering "My Saviour" with her last
breath; like the young wife on the Ogowe River, Africa, when heart
and flesh failed, still resisting the witch doctor and charging her
husband to be "faithful to God." These women are transformed by
happiness. Christianity encourages them, wakes their intellect, kin-
dles aspiration, as well as offers peace. Where for thousands of years
they have said, "We are donkeys," a corps of intelligent teachers and
evangelists are now raised up.

As women rise they bring the home up with them. A missionary
of long experience points to the "new affection and respect shown by
husband and children towards Christian wives and mothers, because
their religion has made them worthy of respect and affection which
as heathen women they did not merit."

Without this woman's work for woman, touching life at so many
and such sensitive points, some missions would have been a failure.

The American mother and her babe have bridged the chasm between the dreaded foreigner and the Korean mother's heart. Church membership, which formerly preponderated entirely in favor of men, has in some older missions approached nearly to equalization. Among their tropies are women who have borne persecution, made harder by their traditions for them than for men; and those who zealously prosecute home missions, as among Gilbert Island women, and the Japanese who have been known to sell their dresses for the cause. They have their foreign missionary heroines also, like Yona, the Harriett Newell of Zululand.

Look at woman's work for woman in Japan: prayer unions holding their annual meeting, attended by delegates from different cities, whose travelling expenses were paid by women of their respective churches; a Japanese girl leaving a legacy of $65 to the school where she became a Christian; Bible women in demand beyond the supply, and the Japanese churches paying a part of all of their salary; a boy's school begging for an American woman to teach them. "Such deep Christian experience that," as an Osaka missionary writes, "it seems impossible that they grew to womanhood in ignorance of Christ."

Look at woman's work for women in India. It has found out the class resting under the heaviest curse, the widow, and lifted her to a place of honor. While Christian girls have been passing entrance examinations to the University for twenty years, the first Mohammedan girl has matriculated this year. "Christian women," Miss Thoburn says, "are much more prominent and important than Christian men. If they live in a village they are the only women there who can read and write. No others go to a place of worship with men. Their daughters go away to boarding school and return to be consulted by their own fathers. When the Dufferin medical schools called for students three-fourths of those who came forward were Christian girls." Even indirect results begin to show themselves on the far horizon. The *purdah* is drawn aside for a *fete* day at the Exposition in Calcutta. A class of barbarious midwives study anatomy with a Philadelphia graduate. An appeal against child-marriage is sent to the English Parliament. Brahmo Somaj women gather together into a prayer-meeting at Lahore. "It is your women and doctors that we are afraid of," say the men of India.

In Persia, the respectful term *Khanam* (Lady) is frequently applied to Christian by Persian men, but to Mohammedan women never. A priest asked a missionary lady to offer prayer beside him at the burial of a child. When the American Mission was opened only two women in the whole country could read. At their Jubilee in 1885 the question was put, "How many present can read?" and six hundred women rose to their feet.

Look at woman's work for women in China. A Canton girl, imitating her college sisters in England and America, takes the prize for Bible examination over the heads of all the competing pastors. Up in Shantung several women, without preacher, teacher or sexton, have maintained a house of worship and Sunday service in their community for a period of years. "Direct work for women," says a cautious missionary in that province, "has contributed fully one-half to the improved sentiment towards foreigners." It conveys the idea that they amount to something," says another, "sadly needed for those so near the vanishing point in social life. It is necessary to the stability of the family: when men become Christians and women adhere to heathenism husband and wife are at cross-purposes, and after a year or two of contest the husband surrenders. The family can be won in no other way. There is a kind of fascination about the missionary lady; these heathen women fairly run and troop around her, and when they are won the family becomes a fixed institution in the church. I am of the opinion," continues our missionary from North China, "that for permanent hold of Christianity upon the people, work among women is more important than among men. The request comes from all our stations, 'Send us more ladies'."

Encouraged by such evidences as these, incited by gratitude and the promise of God's Word, and sustained by the Spirit of God, the woman's missionary societies propose to tarry not nor falter, but to hand on their work to children and children's children, enjoining upon them to save America, to save the world, and be found so doing when our Lord shall come.

IN RETROSPECT: AN EVALUATION OF "WOMAN'S WORK FOR WOMAN"

Document 16: Accomplishments, Problems, and Prospects for the Work

Nineteen ten marked the fiftieth anniversary of the first woman's Board of Missions in the United States, the Woman's Union Missionary Society. From this original interdenominational board came the inspiration and impulse for work in home and foreign missions by women in all Protestant denominations.

In 1910, Helen Barrett Montgomery celebrated their contribution by writing Western Women in Eastern Lands: Fifty Years of Woman's Work in Foreign Missions. *Her book is perhaps the most important single piece produced from this era of "woman's work for woman." Its significance is clear from the excerpt included here. Montgomery begins these pages by summarizing the accomplishments of the work. Her purpose, however, is to press women further to understand the problems and policies that still present enormous challenges for continued progress of the work. Finally, Montgomery concludes with a*

*succinct statement of the purpose of woman's work over fifty years,
leaving readers to judge the strengths and limitations of their approach.*[43]

There is a temptation to rest contented in what has already been
accomplished. It is indeed a wonderful story, the growth of the past
fifty years. None of the founders could have dared to expect the great
achievements which, by the grace of God, have been won. We began
in weakness, we stand in power. In 1861 there was a single missionary
in the field, Miss Marston, in Burma; in 1909, there were 4,610 unmarried women in the field, 1,948 of them from the United States. In
1861 there was one organized woman's society in our country; in 1910
there were forty-four. Then the supporters numbered a few hundreds; to-day there are at least two millions. Then the amount contributed was $2000; last year four million dollars was raised. The
development on the field has been as remarkable as that at home.
Beginning with a single teacher, there are at the opening of the
Jubilee year 800 teachers, 140 physicians, 380 evangelists, 79 trained
nurses, 5,783 Bible women and native helpers. Among the 2,100
schools there are 260 boarding and high schools. There are 75 hospitals and 78 dispensaries. In addition to carrying on these large tasks,
the women's missionary organizations have built colleges, hospitals,
dispensaries, nurses' homes, orphanages, leper asylums, homes for
missionaries' children, training schools, and industrial plants. They
have set up printing-presses, translated Bibles, tracts, and school-
books. . . . It is an achievement of which women may well be proud.
But it is only a feeble beginning of what they can do and will do when
the movement is well on its feet. Far better and more wholesome than
for us to form mutual admiration societies, glorying in our past, is it
to turn our attention to the sober study of the task that lies before
us. . . .

[First,] too often we have been playing with our responsibilities.
We have sent out a scout and failed to support her; we have opened
a station and given no buildings and equipment; we have overlapped
sometimes, and sometimes we have scattered. But always and everywhere what we have done has been only the pitiful shadow of what
we ought to do and could do. What are 140 physicians among a
half-billion women? What are 6,000 schools to the 250 million children who ought to be in school? We congratulate ourselves on our
great work. The glory is all God's, the shame ours. He has taken our
scant gifts and multiplied them, but what are they? Let us never think
we are meeting the need of the heathen world; we are only touching
its edges. If physicians were no more frequent in America than they
are in the non-Christian world, we should have but thirty-two all told,
male and female, for the entire United States. Imagine how pleasant
it would be to have but one physician able to perform a simple surgical

operation in the states of Colorado, Montana, and Wyoming; to have only one available for western New York. For we could average no more than one to 2,500,000 of the population if we were no better supplied than is the non-Christian world. Or take the schools. In India less than ten per cent of the men can read, and of women less than one per cent, taking the country as a whole. In China, likewise, ten per cent is a liberal estimate to put on the number of literate men, and one per cent on the women. When we think of the hundreds of millions in ignorance, and realize how dark a prison ignorance really is, we see that educational missions are only beginning.

What a problem it is to get this vision of the whole before our women, so that they shall undertake not merely a work but *the* work; shall see the whole task and their own definite share in that task. . . .

When we speak of the money which is accumulated in Christian countries, the totals are inconceivably great. In the United States alone more wealth has been piled up since the Civil War than in all the centuries since the birth of Christ in the world. If the Protestant *communicants* of the world have only their due proportion of this wealth, they have to-day, $66,000,000, 000. Of this they gave in 1906 less than one one hundred and seventh-fifth of their income. . . .

Let us face the fact that we are amply able to Christianize the world if we care to; that Christian women have their full share in their own hands, to use if they will.

We have the tools, the organization, the machinery. We do not need to create agencies. We have 500 societies already in the field. Buildings are built, languages learned, customs already familiar, the Bible translated. What is needed is simple reinforcement, addition, enlargement. It is as if a railroad were all surveyed, graded, track laid, stations built, trains running, business flourishing, credit sound. It does not need to begin at the beginning, in order to enlarge its capacity and to meet its growing business. All the slow, difficult pioneer tasks have been accomplished. It needs to parallel its tracks, double its rolling-stock, build branch lines, enlarge its working force. . . .

Our second problem is simply the home base of our first. So soon as we attack in earnest the problem of meeting the needs of heathen women and children, we shall be driven to delve into the depths of this second question. We must reach our constituency, or fail in the first undertaking. The women of the Protestant churches of the United States number at least twelve millions. Of these it may be doubted whether we have enlisted in support of foreign missionary work one-fourth. It is not enough to reach a small group of the choice spirits in each church; our business is with all the women of the church. The Problem of reaching them will demand our best thought and endeavor for another generation, as it has for the last two. The point is not that we have not tried, but that we have not yet succeeded. Magnificent pioneer work has been done, many obstacles have been removed, many strong agencies developed; it now remains, as in the case of the work on the field, to advance.

If we are really to reach our constituency, the first requisite is to get the standard clearly set before us. So long as we do not consciously aim for the whole, we shall never reach more than a fraction. The ideal, *every woman member of the church a member of the missionary society,* must be not passively but actively accepted. . . .

One of the problems of the next ten years bids fair to be the adjusting of the relationship which exists between the general denominational Boards and the women. While in general these relations have been of the most amicable nature, at times there has been some slight tension. In the beginning the idea of all the women's societies was frankly auxiliary and supplemental. They were to be "gleaners" or "helping hands in the great field." Their function was to provide an outfit for the missionaries, pay the salaries of unmarried females, or merely to act as collecting agents in the parish for the Board which should spend the money. The exigencies of the situation have led to wide departures from this earlier ideal. The women's Boards have at the solicitation of the general denominational Boards supported stations, built buildings, opened new work, paid for real estate, in fact, done about all that any Board could do in the way of diversified activities. From the beginning the Methodist women have been frankly independent of, though closely associated with, the general Board.

With the very great expansion of women's work for women has come questioning of the organic relations which these organizations sustain to the general Boards. . . .

Would it not be better to have one great organization of the entire church to which both men and women contributed? This is the question that is most agitated to-day. Some of the brethren say: "Let the women collect, they are such splendid collectors. We will spent it far more wisely than they can." Others say, "Let us all work together, have men and women on the Board, men and women in the work."

The first plan will commend itself to few women. The opportunity for self-expression and the development that comes through responsibility are as necessary to women as to men. It is not the united wisdom of the men of the church which would be available for this sacred office of direction, but simply that of some individual secretary or secretaries. The modern educated woman has ideas not only on the way to collect money but on the way to spend it, and the purposes for which it should be spent.

The second plan is very attractive. It looks ideal to have one tremendous organization with men and women working side by side.

Perhaps the day will come in the growth of the kingdom when this can be, but let us look at all sides of the argument before hastening out of organizations which have been so blessed of God.

In the first place, are men ready for it? Are they emancipated from the caste of sex so that they can work easily with women, unless they be head and women clearly subordinate? Certain facts seem to indicate that in spite of the rapid strides undoubtedly made in this direction we have still a long stretch of unexplored country to be traversed before the perfect democracy of Jesus is reached. . . .

The way out from the slight tension which has been traceable during the last few years is not to say: "These women are doing too well, they are raising four million dollars a year, let us absorb them"; but rather, "If the women can do as well with the little left-overs of contribution, let us see what can be done with the men." As one of the delegates wittily put it in the Layman's Conferences at Omaha: "Go to thy aunt, thou sluggard, consider her ways and be wise." The Laymen's Movement is the real answer to the question. Organize, inspire, inform, the men of the church. Bring to bear their splendid, solid, thorough, businesslike study of the whole situation, and such methods will be devised, such systems installed, such enthusiasm roused, that in the thunderous answer of the men to the appeal our little feminine treble will rejoice to find itself submerged. Or to change the figure, when the main lead is uncovered, the brethren will be too busy with their pickaxes mining the glittering veins of gold to grudge women their nuggets picked off the surface.

Let us get down to some principles in the matter. It is good for women to give; their husbands cannot do it for them. It is good for men to give, their wives cannot do it for them. Each has certain interests separate from the other. Both have certain interests together. It is a woman's task to see that the poor, downtrodden, backward women of the non-Christian world have a chance. Let us take care of the kindergartens, orphanages, asylums, and schools that appeal most to us; let us touch the home side of life, believing that in so doing we are aiding the whole great enterprise to which as men and women we are committed.

Women in Social Reform Movements

CAROLYN DE SWARTE GIFFORD*

Elizabeth Cady Stanton, dedicated woman's rights reformer, was fond of declaring: "There is no use in saying what people are ready to hear!"[1] Her statement succinctly sets forth the reformer's task and challenge: how can reformers who are religious most faithfully and effectively say what people are not ready to hear and may never want to accept?

A heated exchange between abolitionist spokeswoman Angelina Grimke and educator Catharine Beecher about the manner in which faithful Christians, and specifically faithful Christian women, ought to pursue reform activity illustrates this dilemma. The controversy in the late 1830s highlighted conflicting attitudes toward abolitionism between conservative and radical reformers. (Documents 1 and 2.)

Both women believed slavery was wrong. Catharine Beecher advocated gradual emancipation and colonization of freed blacks in Africa. This was a cautious program advanced by antislavery advocates to avoid alienating possible supporters. She insisted that female reformers must work within their proper sphere: the private domestic world of women and children. Angelina Grimke, however, championed immediate emancipation. Under this more radical plan, slaves were to be granted unconditional freedom coupled with suffrage and other rights of citizenship. The institution of slavery and the slaveholders themselves were deemed sinful. She maintained that women reformers must step boldly beyond their assigned societal roles to speak the truth effectively.

Miss Grimke wrote to Miss Beecher:

*CAROLYN DE SWARTE GIFFORD received her Ph.D. from Northwestern University in the History and Literature of Religions. She has been a member of a women's ministry team and served as Assistant Chaplain at Northwestern. She has taught courses at Northwestern, McCormick Theological Seminary, Mundelein College, and Northeastern Illinois University.

The efforts of abolitionists have stirred up the *very same spirit* which the efforts of *all thorough-going* reformers have ever done. We consider it a certain proof that the truths we utter are sharper than any two-edged sword, and that they are doing the work of conviction in the hearts of our enemies. If it be not so, I have greatly mistaken the character of Christianity. I consider it to be preeminently aggressive; it waits not to be assaulted, but moves on in all the majesty of Truth to attack the strong holds of the kingdom of darkness, carries the war into the enemy's camp, and throws its fiery darts into the midst of its embattled hosts. Thou seemest to think, on the contrary, that Christianity is just such a weak, dependent, puerile creature as thou hast described woman to be. In my opinion thou hast robbed both the one and the other of all their true glory and dignity. The descriptions may suit the prevailing christianity of this age, and the general character of woman; and if so, we have great cause for shame and confusion of face.[2]

The sharp disagreement between these two female reformers over the nature of Christianity and woman characterized struggles within reform movements through the nineteenth century. The overt issue was differing strategies for change. However, the struggles also included underlying tensions between women reformers and those who were not ready to hear their cries for reform precisely because they came from female voices.

Women reformers were continually forced to justify both the aims of the reforms they sought and their right as women to work for reform in the public sphere. Thus females faced, in ways that male reformers did not, crucial decisions about how to say what people were not ready to hear. With great courage, patience, and steadfastness, women reformers withstood a double assault. Criticisms were directed, first, against their reform efforts and, second, against their understanding of themselves as women. As a result of this second assault, females expended much energy in redefining "true womanhood." The redefinition was, in itself, a profound reform, one that has not yet been completed.

In one important sense, the country was ready to hear the reformers' message. A number of currents of religious and political thought developing in the late eighteenth and early nineteenth centuries provided an atmosphere hospitable to reform ideas. Liberal New England theologians, Enlightenment thinkers, evangelical revivalists, Holiness preachers, Quakers, and transcendentalists differed in many significant respects. Together, however, they infused segments of American society with exciting and optimistic notions about the nature of God and God's relation to creation. They suggested that human beings were essentially good or, at least, that all could be saved who would be saved. These thinkers believed that God was concerned for human well-being and comfort, as well as for salvation, and that America's newly won democratic form of government was God's instrument for carrying out the divine purpose in human society. The urgent duty of God's children was to reform their nation in accord with the God-inspired ideals of liberty and justice so recently enshrined in the documents that were to guide it.[3]

Romantic reformers of a religious orientation believed that if Americans understood their sin and God's will they would eliminate evil and follow the Lord's way. Education, undergirded by strong Christian commitment, became the base upon which reform was grounded. Mary Lyon founded Mt. Holyoke Female Seminary to train young women as schoolteachers, a conscious missionary enterprise to her. She committed herself and the institution that she founded to the Lord's work. (Document 3.) Isabella Graham came to America from England in 1789 believing that the "Church of Christ would eventually flourish" in the United States.[4] She and her daughter, Joanna Bethune, developed schools for infant girls and boys to train them to be good citizens and faithful Christians. (Document 4.) These roles were understood by large numbers of Americans in the nineteenth century as complementary or even synonymous.

During the hundred years inaugurated by this educational and charitable work, American women labored in a variety of reform movements —including moral reform (elimination of prostitution), temperance, prison reform, better treatment of American Indians, and improvement of care for the ill, the insane, and the handicapped. They were also engaged in charitable work among the poor, abolition of slavery, rights for women and freed blacks, and peace and arbitration. They hoped earnestly that through these efforts the United States would become the realization of God's design for human society.

For many women, reform became their religion, a position of faith as much as a cause espoused. In a biographical sketch of her friend and co-worker Susan B. Anthony, Elizabeth Cady Stanton described that stance and suggested that it was appropriate for the era in which they lived:

> Every energy of her soul is centred [sic] upon the needs of the world. To her work is worship. She has not stood aside shivering in the cold shadows of uncertainty; but has moved on with the whirling world, has done the good given her to do, and thus in the darkest hours has been sustained by an unfaltering faith in the final perfection of all things. Her belief is not Orthodox, but it is religious,—based on the high and severe moralities. In ancient Greece she would have been a Stoic; in the era of the Reformation, a Calvinist; in King Charles's time, a Puritan; but in this nineteenth century, by the very laws of her being, she is a Reformer.[5]

Such a description might serve equally well for numerous women who, "by the very laws of their being," supported several reforms during their lifetimes. They believed, with Angelina Grimke, that "moral reformations . . . are bound together in a circle like the sciences; they blend with each other like the colors of the rainbow; they are the parts only of our glorious whole and that whole is Christianity, pure *practical* christianity."[6]

"Pure practical christianity" appealed to most female reformers. Theirs was a faith characterized not by theological subtleties, nor by great attention to liturgical forms, nor by private piety. Rather, it was grounded in basic ethical truths simply stated and lived out in a believer's daily existence. They responded to Christ's call with the resolve to become *useful*: to do God's will by furthering the Lord's purpose for the world. Usefulness meant service, and women reformers dedicated themselves to a life of service.

Margaret Prior, the first missionary hired by the New York Female Moral Reform Society (1837), exemplified a life consecrated to Christian usefulness. Margaret Dye, also active in moral reform work, wrote in a testimonial to her friend Margaret Prior: "Her whole life was regulated upon the principle, 'Ye are *not your own*, ye are *bought with a price; therefore, glorify God in your body and in your spirit, which are his.*'" Mrs. Dye continued, describing the nature of a life which was "not one's own":

> Mrs. Prior's *benevolence*, her active, laborious, untiring, disinterested efforts to *do good*, were what particularly *distinguished her*. She lived not for herself, but to relieve human misery, and win souls to Christ. The world was her field of labor, and every son and daughter of Adam shared in her sympathies. St. Paul's description of a useful woman (1 Timothy 5:10) may with great propriety be applied to her. . . . She was remarkable for devising ways and means of usefulness: her mind was fruitful in *expedients*.[7]

Throughout the century, women continued to speak of themselves as consecrated to lives of usefulness. Over fifty years after Margaret Prior's "walks of usefulness" through New York City, Josephine Shaw Lowell, a tireless worker on behalf of the poor of that city, emphasized that such work "should only be entered into with a feeling of consecration."[8] The methods of charitable visiting had changed greatly from Margaret Prior's earlier work. Mrs. Lowell's "friendly visitors" were instructed not to proselytize, while Mrs. Prior had gone with Bible in hand, eager to win souls for Christ. Still a similar sense of calling motivated their labors.

Some women perceived their call to a particular work or a specific reform. "Mother" Mary Eliza Bickerdyke and Eliza Chappell Porter were among many who developed self-confidence during the Civil War through nursing and organizing civilian supply agencies. (Document 5.) Women in the abolitionist movement felt their usefulness lay in gaining liberty for the slave. (Document 6.) Some, including Laura Haviland, continued to work for the rehabilitation of freed slaves after the Civil War.

The New Testament image of the useful woman, to which Margaret Dye referred in her testimonial, defined the outer boundaries of woman's participation in Christian life in the early decades of the nineteenth century. It set the parameters beyond which woman could not venture in her usefulness. Nineteenth century Americans read biblical passages, such as 1 Timothy 5:9, 10 and 1 Timothy 2:9–15, as guidelines for the activities and qualifications of women's service in the church.[9]

Woman was to be wife and mother; that was her primary role. Indeed, it was her salvation. If she were widowed, unmarried, or especially zealous in doing good, she might perform a diaconal function outside her home, but in a way that acknowledged her subordination to man.

Most women found that they had little time or energy left for service beyond the domestic sphere. A life of broader caring was closed to them, admirable though it may have seemed.

By the beginning of the nineteenth century, however, some upper-middle-class women in the United States found themselves with leisure time. Their fathers' or husbands' wealth allowed them to hire servants and to buy items they had formerly manufactured at home, which shortened the hours necessary for household management. These women had the luxury of choosing how to spend their time. Many, like Margaret Prior, turned to church, charitable, and reform work in conscious opposition to idleness. Amelia Bloomer, a woman's rights reformer, blasted such female idleness in an editorial written in 1854:

> Parents do a great injustice to their daughters when they doom them to a life of idleness or, what is worse, to a life of frivolity and fashionable dissipation. It was said by a distinguished clergyman of one who has passed away from earth, "She ate, she drank, she slept, she dressed, she danced and she died." Such may be truly said to be the history of many women of the present day. They eat, they drink, they sleep, they dress, they dance and at last die, without having accomplished the great purposes of their creation. Can woman be content with this aimless, frivolous life? Is she satisfied to lead a mere butterfly existence, to stifle and crush all aspirations for a nobler destiny, to dwarf the intellect . . . and desecrate all the faculties which the Almighty Father has given her and which He requires her to put to good use and give an account thereof to Him? . . . Shall woman, a being created in God's own image, endowed with reason and intellect, capable of the highest attainments and destined to an immortal existence, alone (among all created beings) be an idler, a drone, and pervert the noble faculties of her being from the great purposes for which they were given?[10]

Mrs. Bloomer's statement reflects ideas about woman that challenged other more dominant attitudes. First, woman was not created by God to be frivolous, useless, ornamental, or doll-like, as upper-middle-class society wished her to be. Second, she advocated an idea with even more radical implications for traditional thinking about woman. Mrs. Bloomer insisted that woman had been created in the image of God. Woman reflected God's image through her reason and intellect. She was morally responsible to her creator for developing her God-given intellectual faculties so that she might use them in God's service.

Mrs. Bloomer's biblically founded thinking about woman's destiny came into direct conflict with prevailing theological and social definitions of woman, especially because she insisted that woman was not an inferior copy of man. Woman had her own high destiny that was not dependent on man's. Woman was accountable to God and not to man—whether the male was her father, her husband, or her clergyman—for what she made of her life. Men were no longer to act as intermediaries between God and woman, nor were they necessarily to be the sole authoritative interpreters of Scripture and theology.

These limitations on men's ability to define women's lives had enormous consequences for women's understanding of their own power. Some women, and a few male supporters, began to oppose scriptural passages condoning the subjection of women (such as the creation account of Genesis 2; 1 Corinthians 2; 1 Timothy 2). They emphasized other texts (such as Genesis 1:27; Acts 2:17, 18; and Galatians 3:28).[11] They proclaimed the moral equality of women and men before God, the "Righteous Judge" who held both sexes to the same duty of pursuing righteousness, justice, and mercy. Woman was not exempt from the demand for righteousness on the grounds of her supposed inferior mental and moral faculties. Nor was she to bear the exclusive burden of being the virtuous, pious sex, while man went about his business unencumbered by morality. This dualistic view of humanity, with woman as heart and man as head, had become increasingly characteristic of nineteenth century culture. The reformers insisted that both sexes were called to righteousness. Both were intellectually equipped to choose the just course of action.

To question these theological presuppositions was also to challenge the social roles they justified. Early in the century, pioneers in education for women began to call for increased opportunities for females to attend school and for curriculum changes reflecting the fact that women had the same intellectual capacity as men. In a pamphlet written in 1819 proposing improvement of female education, Emma Willard raised the question of nature versus nurture. She asked:

> When the youth of the two sexes has been spent so differently, is it strange, or is nature at fault, if more mature age has brought such a difference in character, that our sex have been considered by the other, as pampered, wayward babies of society, who must have some rattle put into our hand to keep us from doing mischief to ourself or others?[12]

Emma Willard perceived that socialization rather than innate qualities accounted for the apparent differences in man's and woman's intellect. She spoke out for equal education for girls so that they would not remain "pampered, wayward babies."

Although Emma Willard knew that most girls would become wives and mothers, she introduced subjects formerly taught only to boys into the curriculum at Troy Female Seminary. She wrote history and geography texts to teach girls about the world beyond their homes, with the expectation that they could and would enter that world. By her example, she encouraged young women to engage in lives of scholarship.

Yet other influential educational reformers held that women, though their minds were not inferior, were fitted for entirely different learning than men. Women such as Catharine Beecher and Mary Lyon, seeing woman's role still primarily as homemaker and teacher of children, prepared their female students to be better mothers or school teachers, capable of raising boys to be moral citizens and girls to be responsible mothers.

Tension between conservative and radical reform existed in educational circles as well as in the movement for abolition of slavery. Again the debate centered around conflicting ideas of woman's sphere. Was she to concentrate her abilities within the home and within the church (which was increasingly viewed in the nineteenth century as an extension of the private, domestic world)? Or was she to exercise her own moral judgment and reason in the larger world beyond the home?

Many women who worked for temperance and moral reform entered into the controversy because they saw consequences of a narrow interpretation of woman's ability and sphere that were even more disturbing than the idleness of upper-middle-class women. They recognized a connection between woman's lack of preparation for anything other than motherhood and domestic duties and her inability to support herself if she were unmarried, widowed, or married to a man who was unemployed due to disability, drunkenness, or economic depression. In the 1830s and 1840s, middle-class women who advocated moral reform saw for themselves the exploitation of their poorer sisters through prostitution. They discovered that very often prostitutes were not "Magdalenes" who lured innocent young men into vice, as society had stereotyped them. Quite the opposite, they were victims of a social system that defined their role narrowly, forced them into dependence upon men, and then labeled them sinners and social outcasts when they sought to support themselves and their children in one of the very few ways open to them. (Document 7.)

In the 1870s, temperance crusaders learned the same lesson that moral reformers had learned earlier when they found themselves continually frustrated in attempts to aid women whose habitally drunken husbands abused them and would not support them. The women were totally dependent on their husbands economically and thus forced to remain in intolerable situations. The legal system to which temperance workers appealed was, for the most part, inaccessible to women and insensitive to women's oppression. "Mother" Eliza Stewart and other Ohio Crusade women received a "spiritual baptism" and experienced a "new Pentecostal power" enabling them to battle for prohibition.[13] In 1874, Eliza Stewart led a band of praying women to confront liquor dealers in Springfield, Ohio. (Document 8.) In the 1890s, Charlton Edholm, a social purity reformer, was still decrying the financial dependence that "forces women to sell their souls."[14]

Female abolitionists contributed to the analysis of woman's oppressive

situation by comparing it with the plight of the slave. As they worked for
the slaves' freedom, they realized that women were also in bondage, a
bondage more subtle, perhaps, but as devastating as that of blacks. They
saw, too, that black women were doubly bound because of their race and
their sex. When the chains of slavery were broken, the bondage of sex
remained. Female reformers saw that sexual bondage cut across racial
and class differences. All women were sisters in bondage.

The "woman question" was no longer simply a subject for parlor
discussion and debate. The phrase stood for an intolerable condition that
demanded thorough-going critique and reform of every institution of
society: politics, law, economy, education, religion, mores. Caroline
Healy Dall, writing in 1867, incorporated into her personal creedal statement an awareness that woman's rights must be sought at many levels.
She began with a statement of her belief in God, the loving father, and
Jesus Christ, the supreme ethical example, which was typical of liberal
Protestant theology of that time. Then she continued:

> I believe in my own work,—the elevation of woman through education, which
> is development; through labor, which is salvation; through legal rights, which
> are only freedom to develop and save,—as part of the mission of Jesus on the
> earth, authorized by him, inspired of God and sure of fulfilment as any
> portion of his law.[15]

Salvation through labor in the work force may seem as questionable
an expression of faith as salvation through bearing children (1 Timothy
2:15). However, Mrs. Dall's commitment to the liberation of her sex is
clear. She was part of a new movement of women after the Civil War.
This was the beginning of a massive effort to win rights for women in
politics, in the legal system, in church hierarchies, and in professional
employment—all areas that women had hardly dared to enter a generation earlier.

This move into formerly forbidden territory can be explained partly
through a general shift in emphasis by reformers from attempts to reform sinful individuals to assaults on the sinful structures of society. At
the same time, the definition of appropriate womanly behavior was being
challenged by conservative and radical women reformers alike. Frances
Willard, leader of the second wave of temperance reform that began in
the 1870s, called for woman's right to vote in her initial speech as president of the Woman's Christian Temperance Union (WCTU) in 1880.
Shortly thereafter, she mobilized her White Ribbon women behind her
suffrage efforts. Less than two decades earlier, the demand for women's
suffrage had been considered outrageous by most Americans.

The WCTU reformers redefined woman's sphere in a conservative
manner. They still believed that there was a proper place and duty for
women. They enlarged the space for woman's activity, however, and
sought to bring the womanly role of housekeeping and childcare to bear

on all institutions. This conservative attitude is reflected in mottoes and slogans of the organization, such as, "The WCTU is organized mother-love." She referred to "the ballot for home protection" in urging woman's right to vote for prohibition. Reformers suggested that woman's political influence through the vote would "clean up" the government, a goal with decidedly domestic overtones. With its consciously conservative image, the WCTU attracted several hundred thousand American women during its heyday and set them to work at many tasks of reform which those same women, a generation earlier, would have thought improper for their sex. (Document 9.)

Assessing the accomplishments of the WCTU at the beginning of its second decade, Miss Willard pointed to an important reason for women's growing ability to enlarge their sphere of action:

> Perhaps the most significant outcome of this movement was the knowledge of their own power gained by the conservative women of the churches.... Now there were women prominent in all church cares and duties eager to clasp hands for a more aggressive work than such women had ever before dreamed of undertaking.[16]

Women felt an increased sense of their own power through "comrade-ship among women."[17] They also gained self-assurance through decades of practicing skills of fund-raising, speaking in public, petitioning governmental bodies, managing their own reform institutions, editing and publishing papers devoted to reform issues, and writing articles, books, and memorials to legislatures and congressional bodies.

By the end of the century, conservative female reformers had caught up with their more radical sisters who had insisted in the early nineteenth century that women could and should do all the things that men do in reform work. In reality, there was no "woman's sphere," but only the world, which needed continual reformation. Though conservatives may have clung to the notion of a special reform work by women, they used this idea to move into an ever-widening arena of public life. Anna Howard Shaw, as she preached a sermon to delegates attending the International Council of Women in 1888, caught the fervor and exhilaration of women who were coming into their own power. Exhorting her audience to keep on with the great works of reform that they had successfully begun, Dr. Shaw exclaimed:

> Now the wisest and best people everywhere feel that if woman enters upon her tasks wielding her own effective armor, if her inspirations are pure and holy, the Spirit Omnipotent, whose influence has held sway in all movements and reforms, whose voice has called into its service the great workmen of every age, shall, in these last days, fall especially upon woman. If she venture to obey, what is man that he should attempt to abrogate her sacred and divine mission? In the presence of what woman has already accomplished, who shall say that a true woman—noble in her humility, strong in her gentleness, rising above all selfishness, gathering up her varied gifts and accomplishments to conse-

crete them to God and humanity—who shall say that such a one is not in a position to do that for which the world will no longer rank her other than among the first in the work of human redemption? Then, influenced by lofty motives, stimulated by the wail of humanity and the glory of God, *woman may go forth and enter into any field of usefulness* which opens up before her.[18]

In Dr. Shaw's sermon, the image of the useful woman from 1 Timothy is endowed with fresher, broader meaning gained from a half-century of struggle. (Document 10.)

By the beginning of the twentieth century, women went forth in rapidly growing numbers into new "fields of usefulness." Many became professional social and settlement workers, reformers laboring under the banner of "Christianity, Science and Philanthropy," seeking to bring expertise as well as good intentions to welfare work.[19] (Document 11.) Some courageously attacked racist attitudes and institutions reemerging in the North and South following the Reconstruction period. (Document 12.) Still others concentrated their efforts on the cause of international peace and arbitration, as the peace movement found new momentum toward the end of the century. (Document 13.) Spurred on by the methods and goals of the labor movement, women formed the Consumer League and the Working Women's Society, organizing shop girls and factory operatives along with their upper-class sisters in action against the oppression of employers.[12] Females also continued in reforms already begun: temperance, women's rights, and education. Multitudes of women at the close of the nineteenth century felt a keen sense of their own power within the larger world. The many fields of reform pioneered by women under religious auspices were increasingly being drawn into the newly developing vocation of "social work." Women responded to the growing needs of secular society, but many continued to act out of the strong theological motives developed by females in nineteenth century social reform.

Female temperance reformers waged an active war against the "liquor crime" in the Ohio Crusade of 1873–74. These crusaders in Hillsboro, Ohio, are praying in front of a saloon, having led a temperance parade down the main street. [From Elizabeth Putnam Gordon, *Women Torch-bearers* (Evanston, Ill.: National Woman's Christian Temperance Union, 1924), frontispiece.]

The earliest infant Sunday school was established in the First Baptist Church of Boston in 1829. Founders envisioned these schools as early training grounds for developing moral and spiritual qualities in future leaders of the young American republic. [From Vergilius Ferm, *Philosophical History of Protestantism* (New York: Philosophical Library, 1957), p. 177.]

*Thine for the oppressed
Laura S. Haviland*

Mary Lyon, one of the earliest and most influential advocates for the education of women in America, in 1836 founded Mt. Holyoke Female Seminary, a model for the training of women as teachers and missionaries. [From Helen Marshall North, ed., *The Mary Lyon Year Book* (Boston and Chicago: Congregational Sunday-School & Publishing Society, 1895), frontispiece.]

Though meek and retiring in appearance, Laura Haviland was a fierce, courageous fighter for the freedom and rehabilitation of blacks in the Civil War and Reconstruction periods. [From Laura S. Haviland, *A Woman's Life-Work: Labors and Experiences of Laura S. Haviland* (Chicago: Publishing Association of Friends, 1889), frontispiece.]

Laura Haviland was an agent of the Underground Railroad, seeking to rescue slaves from bondage before the Civil War. In this etching, she staves off bloodhounds sent out by slaveholders to kill her. [From Laura S. Haviland, *A Woman's Life-Work: Labors and Experiences of Laura S. Haviland* (Chicago: Publishing Association of Friends, 1889), p. 227.]

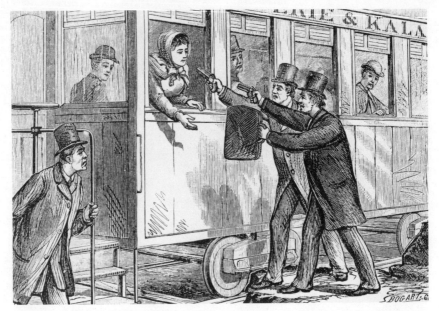

Drawing their pistols, slaveholders attempt to capture Haviland after she smuggled a group of slaves to safety in Michigan. [From Laura S. Haviland, *A Woman's Life-Work: Labors and Experiences of Laura S. Haviland* (Chicago: Publishing Association of Friends, 1889), p. 77.]

Anna Howard Shaw was the first woman ordained in the Methodist Protestant Church in 1880. Later president of the National American Woman's Suffrage Association, Shaw's vision of Christianity underlay her strong advocacy of women's rights. [From Anna Howard Shaw, *The Story of a Pioneer* (New York: Harper Brothers, 1915), frontispiece.]

Ida B. Wells-Barnett, a crusading journalist, lecturer, and clubwoman, campaigned for rights of black people, particularly black women. She fought against lynching and racial segregation and organized the first black women's suffrage organization. [From the University of Chicago Library.]

The early leaders of the Woman's Christian Temperance
Union were sophisticated and genteel, tough-minded and committed to wiping out drunkenness and protecting the American
family. From left to right, seated, Caroline B. Buell, first president Frances E. Willard, and Mary A. Woodbridge; standing,
Esther Pugh and Lillian M. N. Stevens. [From Elizabeth Putnam Gordon, *Women Torch-bearers* (Evanston, Ill.: National
Woman's Christian Temperance Union, 1924), p. 31.]

A New England schoolmarm holds primary classes for freed slaves—women, men, and children—in Vicksburg, Mississippi. Sponsored by the Freedman's Bureau, women came to the South after the Civil War to help educate exslaves just released from bondage. [From Langston Hughes and Milton Meltzer, *A Pictorial History of the American Negro* (New York: Crown Publishers, 1956), p. 190.]

Documents: Women in Social Reform Movements

HOW WOMEN SHOULD PURSUE SOCIAL REFORM: PRE–CIVIL WAR UNDERSTANDINGS

The role that Christian women should play in social reform was debated vigorously by females in these movements in the early nineteenth century. Conflicting views of the nature of Christianity and woman underlie their positions regarding social reform.

Document 1: The Home: Woman's Sphere of Influence

During the antebellum era, Catharine Esther Beecher (1800–1878) established institutions in the Northeast and Midwest to educate young women. She also wrote extensively and persuasively on the need for women to learn their appropriate roles of housewife and teacher, exercising moral influence over fathers and children of the young nation. By her example of peaceable, loving gentleness within the domestic sphere, woman would lead man to activity within the public sphere based on genuine Christian attitudes.[21]

In the arrangement of the duties of life, Heaven has appointed to one sex the superior, and to the other the subordinate station, and this without any reference to the character or conduct of either. It is therefore as much for the dignity as it is for the interest of females, in all respects to conform to the duties of this relation. And it is as much a duty as it is for the child to fulfil similar relations to parents, or subjects to rulers. But while woman holds a subordinate relation in society to the other sex, it is not because it was designed that her duties or her influence should be any the less important, or all-pervading. But it was designed that the mode of gaining influence and of exercising power should be altogether different and peculiar.

It is Christianity that has given to woman her true place in society. And it is the peculiar trait of Christianity alone that can sustain her therein. "Peace on earth and good will to men" is the character of all the rights and privileges, the influence, and the power of woman. A man may act on society by the collision of intellect, in public debate; he may urge his measures by a sense of shame, by fear and by personal interest; he may coerce by the combination of public sentiment; he may drive by physical force, and he does not outstep the boundaries of his sphere. But all the power, and all the conquests that are lawful to woman, are those only which appeal to the kindly, generous, peaceful and benevolent principles.

Woman is to win every thing by peace and love; by making herself so much respected, esteemed and loved, that to yield to her opinions and to gratify her wishes, will be the free-will offering of the heart. But this is to be all accomplished in the domestic and social circle. There let every woman become so cultivated and refined in intellect, that her taste and judgment will be respected; so benevolent in feeling and action, that her motives will be reverenced;—so unassuming and unambitious, that collision and competition will be banished:—so "gentle and easy to be entreated," as that every heart will repose in her presence: then, the fathers, the husbands, and the sons, will find an influence thrown around them, to which they will yield not only willingly but proudly. A man is never ashamed to own such influences, but feels dignified and ennobled in acknowledging them. But the moment woman begins to feel the promptings of ambition, or the thirst for power, her aegis of defence is gone. All the sacred protection of religion, all the generous promptings of chivalry, all the poetry of romantic gallantry, depend upon woman's retaining her place as dependent and defenceless, and making no claims, and maintaining no right but what are the gifts of honour, rectitude and love.

A woman may seek the aid of co-operation and combination among her own sex, to assist her in her appropriate offices of piety, charity, maternal and domestic duty; but whatever, in any measure, throws a woman into the attitude of a combatant, either for herself or others—whatever binds her in a party conflict—whatever obliges her in any way to exert coercive influences, throws her out of her appropriate sphere. If these general principles are correct, they are entirely opposed to the plan of arraying females in any Abolition movement; because it enlists them in an effort to coerce the South by the public sentiment of the North; because it brings them forward as partisans in a conflict that has been begun and carried forward by measures that are any thing rather than peaceful in their tendencies; because it draws them forth from their appropriate retirement, to expose themselves to the ungoverned violence of mobs, and to sneers and ridicule in public places; because it leads them into the arena of political collision, not as peaceful mediators to hush the opposing elements, but as combatants to cheer up and carry forward the measures of strife.

Document 2: Public Advocacy of Causes by Women

Arguments by Angelina and Sarah Grimke advocate a wider function for females in social reform in the name of Christianity. Born and raised in a South Carolina slave-holding family, Sarah (1792–1873) and Angelina (1805–1879) became convinced of the injustice of slavery. After moving to Philadelphia, the sisters wrote and spoke about the sins of slaveholding, first to other women and then to both sexes. In this letter, Angelina Grimke persuasively argues for the right of women to move beyond an acceptable "sphere of influence" to advocate causes of their conviction. The letter was written to Theodore Weld, whom Angelina later married, and to John Greenleaf Whittier, on March 30, 1837.[22]

To Theodore D. Weld and J. G. Whittier
Brethren beloved in the Lord.

As your letters came to hand at the same time and both are devoted mainly to the same subject we have concluded to answer them on one sheet and jointly. You seem greatly alarmed at the idea of our advocating the *rights of woman.* Now we will first tell you *how* we came to begin those letters in the Spectator. Whilst we were at Newburyport we received a note from Mary Parker telling us that Wm. S. Porter had requested her to try to obtain some one to write for his paper in order that it might be better sustained. She asked him whether *she* might choose the subject and named the *province of woman:* he said yes, he would be glad to have such pieces to publish. Just at this time the Pastoral Letter came out, and Mary requested us to write something every week about *Woman* for the Spectator. We consulted together and viewed that unexpected opportunity of throwing our views before the public as providential. As I was writing to C. E. B[eecher], S. M. G. undertook it and as this paper was not an abolition paper we could not see any impropriety in embracing this opening. These letters have not been the means of *arousing* the public attention to the subject of Womans rights, it was the Pastoral Letter which did the mischief. The ministers seemed panic struck at once and commenced a most violent attack upon us. I do not say *absurd* for in truth if it can be fairly established that women *can lecture,* then why may they not preach and if *they* can preach, then woe! woe be unto that Clerical Domination which now rules the whole country to enquire what *right* we had to open our mouths for the dum; the people were continually told "it is a *shame* for a *woman* to speak in the churches." Paul suffered not a *woman* to *teach* but commanded *her* to be in silence. The pulpit is too *sacred a place* for *woman's* foot, etc. Now my dear brothers *this invasion of our rights* was just such an attack upon *us,* as that made upon Abolitionists generally when they were told a few years ago that *they had no right* to discuss the subject of Slavery. Did *you* take no notice of this assertion? Why no! With one heart and one voice you said, *We* will settle *this right before* we go one step further. *The time* to assert a right is *the* time when *that* right is denied. *We must establish this right* for if we do not, it will be impossible for *us* to go *on with the work of Emancipation.*

... And can you not see that women *could* do, and *would* do a hundred times more for the slave if she were not fettered? Why! we are gravely told that we are out of our sphere even when we circulate petitions; out of our "appropriate sphere" when we speak to women only; and out of them when we *sing* in the churches. Silence is *our* province, submission *our* duty. If then we "give *no reason* for the hope that is in us", that we have *equal rights* with our brethren, how can we expect to be permitted *much longer to exercise those rights?* IF I know my

own heart, I am NOT actuated by any selfish considerations (but I do
sincerely thank our dear brother J. G. W[hittier] for the suggestion)
but we are actuated by the full conviction that if we are to do any good
in the Anti Slavery cause, our *right* to labor in it *must* be firmly
established; *not* on the ground of Quakerism, but on the only firm
bases of human rights, the Bible. Indeed I contend brethren that *this*
is not *Quaker* doctrine, it is no more like *their* doctrine on Women than
our Anti Slavery is like their Abolition, just about the same difference.
I will explain myself. Women are regarded as equal to men on the
ground of *spiritual gifts, not* on the broad ground of *humanity.* Woman
may *preach;* this is a *gift;* but woman must *not* make the discipline by
which *she herself* is to be governed.

    ... [W]e say how can we expect to be able to hold meetings much
longer when people are so diligently taught to *despise us* for thus
stepping out of the sphere of woman! Look at this instance: after we
had left Groton the *Abolition* minister there, at a Lyceum meeting
poured out his sarcasm and ridicule upon our heads and among other
things said, he would as soon be caught robbing a hen roost as encouraging a woman to lecture. Now brethren if the leaders of the
people thus speak of our labors, *how long* will we be allowed to prosecute them?

    ... They utterly deny *our right* to interfere with this or any other
moral reform except in the particular way *they* choose to mark out for
us to walk in. If we dare to stand upright and do our duty according
to the dictates of *our own* consciences, why then we are compared to
Fanny Wright and so on. Why, my dear brother can you not see the
deep laid scheme of the clergy against us as lecturers? They know full
well that if they can persuade the people it is a *shame* for us to speak
in public, and that every time we open our mouths for the dumb we
are breaking a divine command, that even if we spoke with the
tongues of *men* or of angels, we should have *no hearers.* They are
springing a deep mine beneath our feet, and we shall *very* soon be
compelled to retreat for we shall have *no* ground to stand on. If we
surrender the right to *speak* to the public this year, we must surrender
the right to petition next year and the right to *write* the year after and
so on. What *then* can *woman* do for the slave when she is herself under
the feet of man and shamed into *silence?* Now we entreat *you* to weigh
candidly the *whole subject,* and then we are sure you will see, this is no
more than an abandonment of our first love than the effort made by
Anti Slavery men to establish the *right* of free discussion. ...

    Anti Slavery men are trying very hard to separate what God hath
joined together. I fully believe that so far from keeping different
moral reformations entirely distinct that no such attempt can ever be
successful. They are bound together in a circle like the sciences; they
blend with each other like the colors of the rainbow; they are the parts

only of our glorious whole and that whole is Christianity, pure *practical* christianity. The fact is *I* believe—but don't be alarmed, for it is only *I*—that Men and Women will have to go out on their own responsibility, just like the prophets of old and declare the *whole* counsel of God to the people. The whole Church Government must come down, the clergy stand right in the way of reform, and I do not know but this stumbling block too must be removed *before* Slavery can be abolished, for the system is supported by *them;* it could not exist without the Church as it is called. This grand principle must be mooted, discussed and established viz. The Ministers of the Gospel are the successors of the *prophets,* not of the *priests.* . . . As there were *prophetesses* as well as prophets, so there *ought* to be now *female* as well as male ministers. Just let this one principle be established and what will become of the power and sacredness of the pastoral office? Is brother Weld frightened at *my ultraism?* Please write us so soon and let us know what you think after reflecting on this letter. . . .

May the Lord bless you my dear brothers is the prayer of your sister in Jesus

A. E. G.

EDUCATING WOMEN AND CHILDREN FOR SERVICE IN THE YOUNG REPUBLIC

Document 3: Mt. Holyoke: The First Female Seminary

Female reformers recognized that education of women was the primary reform upon which all other service by their sex must be grounded. Mary Lyon (1797–1849) was one of the first reformers to advance female education. At Mt. Holyoke, which she founded in 1836, women were trained to be teachers and missionaries. They learned in a Christian environment, where prayer meetings and Miss Lyon's exposition of Scripture were significant parts of their educational experience.

The following document by Mary Lyon is a circular addressed to ladies soliciting funds for the seminary. Her persuasive appeal, written in 1836, contains strong justification of the need for female educators in building a lasting republic.[23]

You would expect that I should feel deeply interested in the success of Mount Holyoke Female Seminary. Had I a thousand lives, I could sacrifice them all in suffering and hardship for its sake. Did I possess the greatest fortune, I could readily relinquish it all, and become poor, and more than poor, if its prosperity should demand it. Its grand object is to furnish the greatest possible number of female teachers of high literary qualifications, and of benevolent, self-denying zeal. The institution is to be only for an older class of young ladies, and every scholar is to board in the establishment. The general course of study, and the general character of the instruction, are to be like those at Ipswich. The institution is to be permanent, continuing onward in its operations from generation to generation. In the thousands of teachers which it will send forth, it will doubtless be an instrument of good, far beyond the present grasp of my feeble comprehension.

But this is not all. This experiment has an important bearing on the great subject of adopting suitable means for supplying our country with well-qualified female teachers, and it is testing the great question of duty on this subject. This constitutes its chief importance. It is like the signing of the Declaration of Independence; the battles were still to be fought, but the question of independence was then settled. It is like fitting out our first little band of missionaries. The great work of evangelizing a world was still before the American churches; but the grand question of duty, and the mode of meeting duty, were then settled, never again to be seriously doubted. Let this enterprise be carried through by the liberality of the Christian community, and it will no longer be doubted whether the work of supplying our country with well-qualified female teachers shall be allowed a standing among the benevolent operations of the day. The work will still be before us, but the principle on which it is to be accomplished will be settled. Another stone in the foundation of our great system of benevolent operations, which are destined, in the hand of God, to convert the world, will then be laid.

The work of bringing this institution into operation has been longer than was anticipated. But the progress of the enterprise in taking an acknowledged standing among the benevolent operations of the day, has exceeded the expectations of its warmest friends. I doubt whether any benevolent object, not excepting even the missionary cause, has ever, within two years from its commencement, made a greater advance in gaining access to the understanding and hearts of the people. Many have rejoiced that so noble a design has been filled with hope, as they have beheld this enterprise go forward in obedience to the great command, "Love thy neighbor as thyself."

Document 4: Molding Future Public Leaders

Infant schools, such as the one begun by Joanna Graham Bethune (1770–1860), were the hope of many educational reformers for molding future Christian leaders of the nation. Joanna Bethune and her mother, Isabella Marshall Graham (1742–1814), had founded the Society for the Relief of Poor Widows with Small Children in 1797. This was one of the earliest charitable associations in the United States and one of the first societies organized by women themselves on behalf of their own sex. They also formed the Orphan Asylum Society

in 1806, prior to the beginning of the infant school by Joanna Be-
thune.

 The following entry was made by Joanna Bethune in her diary in
1827, immediately before the infant school was opened. It emphasizes
the strong Christian commitment underlying the institution.[24]

 Tomorrow I begin the first infant school. It is an important period
of my life, and I now desire to acknowledge the goodness of God in
permitting me to see the work so far. I wished to have others go
forward, and then I would have helped, being averse to appear before
the public in my widowed state; but the Lord has ordered it otherwise.
He has evidently made it my duty to go first in this work; and although
the weather is very hot, and flesh and blood shrink from the labor
before me, yet I dare not to draw back, but go forward trusting, yea,
knowing that my strength shall be equal to my day. Lord, only give
me the consolation of hearing Thee say, "Fear thou not, for I am with
thee; be not dismayed, for I am thy God: I will strengthen thee; yea,
I will help thee, yea, I will uphold thee with the right hand of my
righteousness."

 May all engaged in this new institution have a single eye to Thy
glory. May we go from our knees to every duty, first asking help of
Thee, and then, believing Thy promise, go forward in the work. It
is, again, the weaker vessels that commence this work, as they did the
Sabbath-school; and we have the same promises, the same throne of
grace, the same dear, compassionate Savior, the same Holy Spirit to
influence us, and the same Father, who pities us as His children, and
can as well work by few as by many, by the weak as by the strong, and
who, for His own glory, will bring to pass what we commit to Him.
"That they may see, and know, and consider, and understand together, that the hand of the Lord has done this, and the Holy One
of Israel hath created it." O may the little one become a thousand;
and, like the Sabbath-schools, may infant schools spread over the
land. Oh, is it not a fulfillment of the prophecies, that out of the
mouths of babes and sucklings the Lord will perfect praise? O Lord,
pardon our sins for so long neglecting these children. O let them all
now be gathered into schools. The silver and the gold are Thine, as
well as the cattle upon a thousand hills, and the hearts of all men are
in Thine hand, and Thou canst turn them as rivers of waters. Turn,
then, the attention of the rich to this work. Counsel our counselors.
Give zeal and diligence to our managers; and look in mercy on thy
handmaid, who is again at the head of a new institution, and to whom
many are looking for advice and instruction on this subject. Bless all
the teachers who shall engage in the work. May they indeed be apt
to teach, and may our scholars be apt to learn. O take these lambs in
Thine arms, and may a numerous seed to serve Thee be furnished
by the infant schools. As the garden causeth things that are sown in

it to spring forth, so may the Lord cause righteousness and praise to spring forth before all nations. I now commit this work to Thee, O Lord. Give me all the work. I go forth in Thy strength; may it be perfected in my weakness.

"FIELDS OF USEFULNESS"

Document 5: The Civil War: Nursing and Relief Work

Nursing and organized civilian relief work for soldiers were primary means of service for middle-class women during the Civil War. The following selection describes the work of "Mother" (Mary Ann Ball) Bickerdyke (1817–1901) and Eliza Chappel Porter (1807–1888). They served as volunteer workers for the Northwestern Sanitary Commission, a civilian agency providing food and medical supplies for the Union Army. Mary Livermore, co-organizer of the Chicago office of the Northwestern Sanitary Commission, tells about their work.[25]

After the wounded of Donelson were cared for, Mrs. Bickerdyke left the hospitals, and went back into the army. There was great sickness among our troops at Savannah, Tenn. She had already achieved such a reputation for devotion to the men, for executive ability, and versatility of talent, that the spirits of the sick and wounded revived at the very sound of her voice, and at the sight of her motherly face. While busy here, the battle of Shiloh occurred, nine miles distant by the river, but only six in a direct line. There had been little provision made for the terrible needs of the battle-field in advance of the conflict. The battle occurred unexpectedly, and was a surprise to our men,—who nearly suffered defeat,—and again there was utter destitution and incredible suffering. Three days after the battle, the boats of the Sanitary Commission arrived at the Landing, laden with every species of relief,—condensed food, stimulants, clothing, bedding, medicines, chloroform, surgical instruments, and carefully selected volunteer nurses and surgeons. They were on the ground some days in advance of the government boats.

Here Mother Bickerdyke was found, carrying system, order, and relief wherever she went. One of the surgeons went to the rear with a wounded man, and found her wrapped in the gray overcoat of a rebel officer, for she had disposed of her blanket shawl to some poor fellow who needed it. She was wearing a soft slouch hat, having lost her inevitable Shaker bonnet. Her kettles had been set up, the fire kindled underneath, and she was dispensing hot soup, tea, crackers, panado, whiskey and water, and other refreshments, to the shivering, fainting, wounded men.

"Where did you get these articles?" he inquired; "and under whose authority are you at work?"

She paid no heed to his interrogatories, and indeed, did not hear them, so completely absorbed was she in her work of compassion. Watching her with admiration for her skill, administrative ability, and intelligence,—for she not only fed the wounded men, but temporarily dressed their wounds in some cases,—he approached her again:—

"Madam, you seem to combine in yourself a sick-diet kitchen and a medical staff. May I inquire under whose authority you are working?"

Without pausing in her work, she answered him, "I have received my authority from the Lord God Almighty; have you anything that ranks higher than that?"

. . . During a large part of her army life, Mrs. Bickerdyke was associated with, and most efficiently supplemented by Mrs. Eliza Porter, wife of a Congregationist clergyman of Chicago. She entered the service in the beginning, as did her associate, and turned not from the work until the war ended. Together they worked in the hospitals, enduring cold and hunger, dwelling amid constant alarms, breathing the tainted air of wounds and sickness, and foregoing every species of enjoyment save that which comes from the consciousness of duties well done. Unlike in all respects, they harmonized admirably; and each helped the other. Mrs. Bickerdyke came less frequently into collision with officials when in company with Mrs. Porter; and the obstacles in the way of the latter were more readily overcome when the energy of Mrs. Bickerdyke opposed them. Mrs. Porter patiently won her way, and urged her claims mildly but persistently. Mrs. Bickerdyke was heedless of opposition, which only nerved her to a more invincible energy; and she took what she claimed, no matter who opposed. Both were very dear to the soldiers, from each of whom they expected sympathy and pity, as well as courage and help.

Document 6: Aid to Freed Slaves after the Civil War

Laura Smith Haviland (1808—1898) labored her entire adult life, from before the Civil War through the Reconstruction, on behalf of oppressed black people. She and her husband helped form the first antislavery society in Michigan and opened a preparatory school, the River Raisin Institute, in 1837 to serve both black and white children. After her husband died in 1845, Laura Haviland worked on the Underground Railroad from Cincinnati to Windsor, Canada.

She was an agent for the Michigan Freedman's Aid Commission after the Civil War, aiding freed slaves in the South. In the following account, written in 1879, Laura Haviland describes the plight of freed slaves and relief efforts in Kansas for refugees from the South, work which occupied much of her time during the Reconstruction.[26]

Our investigations have proved to the friends of the former slaves that their emigration from the South was not instituted and put into operation by their own choice, except as the force of circumstances, in their surroundings, pressed them into this remarkable movement. Monthly reports of the Kansas Freedmen's Relief Association have also proved satisfactory to thousands of donors toward their relief. The increasing intelligence among the four millions and a half of slaves, declared free by the nation's pen in the hand of her President, Abraham Lincoln, they found did not bring with it the glorious sunlight of freedom the proclamation promised in its dawn. After fifteen years of patient hoping, waiting, and watching for the shaping of government, they saw clearly that their future condition as a race must be submissive vassalage, a war of races, or emigration. . . .

Is it a wonder the freedmen fled by hundreds and thousands? They are still coming into Kansas. There are many sick and dying among them. Let every man, woman, and child arise and work for the refugees, who are suffering for food, fuel, and clothing. There is great necessity for immediate and vigorous effort, in taking the place of the Good Samaritan in caring for the robbed and bruised stranger, who find many priests and Levites passing by. During the Winter all money and supplies for Kansas refugees should be directed to Elizabeth L. Comstock, North Topeka, Kansas.

Our work is by every possible means aiding these poor people to help themselves, which they are doing wherever work can be found. But Winter season overtaking them on the way to Kansas, and no work to be obtained, the philanthropy of our North will not withhold her liberal hand. It is a debt which we owe to this people. Comparatively few call for assistance who have been in the State a year, and most of these are aged grandparents, the sick, and widows with large families of small children.

Of those who came early in the Spring of 1879, many have raised from one hundred to four hundred bushels of corn each year, but they divide with their friends and relatives who follow them. Some raised a few acres of cotton in their first year, and they are jubilant over their future outlook. . . . In this prospect the door of hope is opening before them, as if by the Almighty hand, which they accept as having led them to the "land of freedom". . . .

On July 12th and 13th two boat-loads more of refugees, numbering four hundred persons, landed in lower Kansas City. I heard it again repeated, "What shall we do? Here in Topeka are two hundred poor people waiting to go somewhere to get work, and only two hundred dollars in our treasury!" Where shall we send them? . . .

While I was still visiting among these people, the steamer Fannie Lewis landed with one hundred and four more refugees from Mississippi. Here they had nothing for their covering except the open sky. We feared that, unless other States should rally to the rescue, nothing but suffering and death would be before them. Again we raise this cry in behalf of this oppressed people, and it will meet a generous response. . . . The lesson is not forgotten, that it is more blessed to give than to receive. He alone who knows the end from the beginning can tell the future of our country, and of the five million of its inhabitants of African descent. Yet eternal right must and will triumph. The debt our nation owes to the ex-slave should be paid. . . .

We must here put in our claim for the sixty thousand emigrants in Kansas from the South. The Freedmen's Relief work in Kansas has been thoroughly organized and officered, and the contributions received for the refugees judiciously distributed. An agricultural and industrial school was established some time ago, and is meeting, so far, with good success. It will, if properly sustained, prove to be a blessing not only to the colored race, but to the State. From a circular issued in June last, by Elizabeth L. Comstock,[27] one of the superintendents of this work, I extract the following paragraphs:

"Our first object is to employ those who come for work or for aid. We are strongly advised by their best friends, and the kind donors both sides the Atlantic, not to give any thing (except in return for labor) to those who are able to work especially during the warm weather. Wages are paid regularly every Saturday, and they come with their money to buy and select from the stock on hand what will suit themselves. Second-hand clothing and bedding have a price affixed almost nominal. . . .

"New shoes and other articles, provisions, etc., that we have to purchase we buy at wholesale, and try to supply them below the market price, some of them at half the retail price. Thus what little is gained on the old clothes makes up in part what we lose on the new. We could employ more laborers if we had more money. The state of the treasury is low now. It seems hard to turn away any poor people who want to work. We should be very glad of help just now in the way of seed for sowing, money to provide food and shelter, and to finish up our buildings. We greatly desire to start several industries before Winter, as blacksmith's shop, carpenter's shop, broom factory, etc., etc., that they may have work during the cold weather. We hope to have our school-house soon ready and to educate the children, and have an evening school for adults.

"An important part of our work will be to train the women and girls in the various branches of household work, and sewing, knitting, etc. Nor do we lose sight of the spiritual garden while providing for the intellectual fields and physical wants. We greatly desire that this long-oppressed race, who have been kept in darkness and ignorance, should have the light of the glorious Gospel, and should have the Bible put into their hands, and be taught to read and understand it.

Of course we meet with some opposition in our work, as many a brave soldier has done before us, in battling for the right and for the colored race."

Document 7: Rescuing Young Women from Prostitution

Exploitation of young women through prostitution became a major cause of female reformers before the middle of the nineteenth century. Margaret Barrett Allen Prior (1773–1842) was the first missionary for the New York Female Moral Reform Society. During her fifteen years of "walks of usefulness" in New York City, she visited the poor and ill in the slums, rescued girls from brothels, and helped them find respectable employment.

In these excerpts from Margaret Prior's journal, she describes a personal effort to rescue a young girl from a house of prostitution and writes of the need for citizens to demand legislation outlawing such "houses of death." [28]

March 20th. A pious lady called and requested me to go with her to E____st., to assist in removing her sick niece from a house of death, to a place where she might with propriety be favored with Christian counsel, and efforts be made for the salvation of her soul. It was a sad errand, but we went together and performed the task. The house was large, and as we passed from room to room the looks of shame and sorrow that met us, were sufficient to draw pity from any heart that had been wont to beat with a mother's or a sister's love. All the inmates were young—some less than 15 years of age. When the misery of their condition was alluded to, several wept, and expressed a wish that they had never been in existence, but said their case was now hopeless. They were told of a way to escape and urged to embrace it; but it was apparently as much in vain as preaching to the spirits in prison. It was a touching fact, that a majority of their number were orphans or fatherless. The poor sufferer whose case had brought us there was wasting away with consumption. To my inquiries respecting how she came here, her aunt replied briefly, that she was the only daughter of a beloved sister, long since laid in the grave; that she had now no near relations but herself, and that in this season of extremity she had desired her aid. When quite young she was extravagantly fond of balls, parties, and other vain amusements, and allowed to go and come as she pleased. Several years since she received the addresses of a young gentleman, and under promise of marriage, she was seduced and ruined. Her downward progress for a time was gradual, but recently it had been more rapid. She supported an infant son for a year or two, by means of her needle, but afterward abandoned herself to vice. This child is now seven years old, has been boarded in a respectable family by his mother, and knows not that she has ever swerved from the path of rectitude. The aunt seemed to be actuated only by Christian principle in her conduct toward this unfortunate relative. In speaking of her own children, she remarked that the fall of their poor cousin had ever been a beacon of warning, and she had only to point to her to produce aversion to the theatre or the ball-room, or to induce a ready compliance with her requirements. How many families may profit by such painful examples, if the will. . . .

Scenes like this are of common occurrence; and yet a heartless world, when requested to consider them, and inquire for the cause and the remedy, turn coldly from us, and perhaps treat our solicitude with derision: and the professed Christian too, when desired by a fellow Christian to feel and act, throws out some stale objection (in common use with the libertine) against the cause of purity; and, with an averted glance, seems disposed to inquire, Cain-like, "Am I my brother's keeper? and some, too, who minister at the sacred altar, and yet are influenced more by the breath of popular favor, than the command to "declare faithfully all the words of the law," when urged to exert their unmeasured influence to prevent the unavailing tears, and sorrow, and anguish of heart, caused by the fall of the innocent! consider, hesitate, and finally exclaim, "Ah! it's a delicate subject, and we don't know how to touch it." The men, too, who make the laws, and those commissioned to enforce them, think the subject so very delicate, that when they know there are fifty houses in a single block, whose inmates, aided by agents in every portion of the city, are con-stantly laboring, with all the assiduity of demons, to destroy, do noth-ing effectual to disturb them, especially if they are careful to keep very still. No matter how many heartbroken fathers, and mothers, and sisters, are sent in sorrow to the grave by their instrumentality. "This is a land of liberty," say they, "and it is a question with us, whether anything can be done." If the public indignation were aroused as it should be, and a correct public sentiment prevailed, methinks the question would soon be settled. . . .

June 1839 [?] I thought, if those who live so remote from this modern Sodom, that they often think and say, "Moral reform may do for the city, but here in the country we don't need it," could have beheld this sacrifice of victims furnished from the country, they would never again repeat the assertion.

June 26. I have visited more or less for fifteen years, and never before have seen so much suffering for want of employment. Many worthy families are left destitute on this account—also many young women who have hitherto maintained themselves by trades.

Numbers of these are now peculiarly exposed to ruin. They are only acquainted with one kind of work, have not friends to teach or assist them, and know not what to do. If they had the good sense to leave the city, or be willing to attempt to do anything and everything that would insure them an honest living, rather than listen to the syren song of those who lie in wait to destroy, there would be less cause to tremble for the fate of many. I have heard during this week of the fall of six, who had sustained a good character until the present state of the times. Three of these were orphan sisters.

Document 8: Waging War against Liquor

Temperance reformers saw drunkenness as a major cause of husbands' abuse and neglect of their wives. Eliza Daniel "Mother" Stewart (1816–1908) was an active temperance worker in Ohio. She lectured throughout the state and testified in court on behalf of oppressed wives. In one notable instance, her testimony led to prosecution of a liquor dealer who had supplied an abused woman's husband.

In this selection from her memoirs, "Mother" Stewart describes a band of praying women, which she led through the streets of Springfield, Ohio, during the Ohio Temperance Crusade of 1873–1874. The women were petitioning tavern owners and druggists to abstain from selling liquor.[29]

We moved out in band and solemn procession the next day. As we reached the door I turned to the brethren who remained in the sanctuary, and begged them to continue in prayer, and gave them our watchword, "I will go in the strength of the Lord God, I will make mention of thy righteousness, Thine only." Ah, who that fell into line and marched out can ever forget that first moving out! The silent uplifting of the heart to God, the cry for strength, for wisdom to say the right words, for grace to meet in the spirit of our blessed Master whatever trial of faith or patience might come to us, the trepidation at the thought of visiting those low and loathsome places that we had always been taught were the haunts of the low, vile and abandoned. It was certainly a new and strange path in which to follow the Friend of sinners. Somehow, we had not before thought that the command, "Take up thy cross and follow me," had meant even into such dark dens of iniquity. What had it meant? In times past we had understood it, deny thyself of some little wordly gratification in the way of amusement or dress. And even in these minor matters we had, with rare exceptions, ceased to be distinguished from the world around us.

But now we had, indeed, taken a solemn advance step. How weak we felt, and how we realized the need of help from on high. Thus we moved out, in great trembling, with bowed head, but with eye of faith steadfastly fixed on the Cross of Calvary, going forth to try to rescue the perishing. Oh! to help bring the world to the foot of the cross!

A holy inspiration filled our souls, and as the bell rang out its peals at the close of each prayer as a message of encouragement sent after us, saying, "Courage, brave hearts, we are praying for you, we are praying for you," we felt a sweet and holy joy come into our souls, a new, glad experience that buoyed us as if treading not upon the earth, but the air. Lo! we were walking with Jesus. To-day, time has brought us thirteen years further on the way, yet thousands will still testify to the blessed joy and peace that they experienced as they entered those haunts of sin, knelt there and cried to God to deliver us from the curse of drink, to save our husbands, to save our boys, to save the liquor-seller himself, from the fearful consequences of his wicked business. Then those sweet songs that many a poor, wretched drunkard had heard his sainted mother sing in the old, far-away home of his child-hood, the gentle word of persuasion to the dealer, to the young man, or the gray-haired frequenter that we found in the grog shop! How many times have I heard the assertion, "I would not exchange that experience for all the rest of my life. . . ."

It had been with many, a fearful struggle to yield up their precon-ceived ideas of what was a lady's place, and what the world might think and say. Not a few carried the subject to their closets, and there on their knees fought the battle with self and pride before the Lord, till He gave them strength and they came forth anointed for the war. As I was passing up street one morning, a little, timid minister's wife met me, and grasping my hand, exclaimed: "Oh Mother Stewart, what shall I do? It seems to me that I can not take up this work." I said, "Never mind, my dear, it will come all right." A short time after, this little woman walked out by the side of Sister C___ at the head of a band; and as they knelt, Sister C___ said: "Pray, Sister H___; yes, you must pray"; and she did, and such a holy baptism came down upon her that as she walked she held to Sister C's arm, exclaiming, "Oh, I am so happy, I am so happy! I am so glad you made me take up my cross!" Thenceforth it was a delight to do whatever work came to her.

EXPANDING WOMEN'S SPHERE OF SOCIAL REFORM: LATE NINETEENTH CENTURY REINTERPRETATIONS

After the Civil War, many women of religious conviction took an active part in enlarging women's role in social reform. Their advocacy was directed, first, toward gaining rights for their sex, through poli-tics, law, religious structures, and professional employment. Second, their emphasis in social reform shifted from attempts to redeem sinful individuals to attacks on unjust institutions of society.

Document 9: The WCTU: "The Ballot for Home Protection"

Basic presuppositions of the female's proper role continued to guide women in broadening the boundaries of their public service. Through the Woman's Christian Temperance Union, Frances Wil-lard (1839–1898) built a powerful organization committed to prohibi-tion and women's suffrage, as well as a wide range of other issues, including social purity, peace, and arbitration. The active participa-

tion of women in cleaning up government and society were the surest means of achieving this end.

Frances Willard, who was president of the WCTU for almost twenty years from 1879 until her death, describes this basic purpose of the organization in her book Woman and Temperance.

[The Woman's Christian Temperance Union] stands as the exponent, not alone of that return to physical sanity which will follow the downfall of the drink habit, but of the reign of a religion of the body which for the first time in history shall correlate with Christ's wholesome, practical, yet blessedly spiritual religion of the soul. "The kingdom of heaven is within you"—shall have a new meaning to the clear-eyed, steady-limbed Christians of the future, from whose brain and blood the taint of alcohol and nicotine has been eliminated by ages of pure habits and noble heredity. "The body is the temple of the Holy Ghost," will not then seem so mystical a statement, nor one indicative of a temple so insalubrious as now. . . .

The women of this land have never had before such training as is furnished by the topical studies of our society, in the laws by which childhood shall set out upon its endless journey with a priceless heritage of powers laid up in store by the tender, sacred foresight of those by whom the young immortal's being was invoked. The laws of health were never studied by so many mothers, or with such immediate results for good on their own lives and those of their children. The deformed waist and foot of the average fashionable American never seemed so hideous and wicked, nor the cumbrous dress of the period so unendurable as now, when from studying one "poison habit," our minds, by the inevitable laws of thought, reach out to wider researches and more varied deductions than we had dreamed at first. The economies of co-operative house-keeping never looked so attractive or so feasible as since the homemakers have learned something about the priceless worth of time and money for the purposes of a Christ-like benevolence. The value of a trained intellect never had such significance as since we have learned what an incalculable saving of words there is in a direct style, what value in the power of classification of fact, what boundless resources for illustrating and enforcing truth come as the sequel of a well-stored memory and a cultivated imagination. The puerility of mere talk for the sake of talk, the unworthiness of "idle words," and vacuous, purposeless gossip, the waste of long and aimless letter-writing, never looked so egregious as to the workers who find every day too short for the glorious and gracious deeds which lie waiting for them on every hand.

But to help forward the coming of Christ into all departments of life, is, in its last analysis, the purpose and aim of the W.C.T.U. For we believe this correlation of New Testament religion with philanthropy, and of the church with civilization, is the perpetual miracle which furnishes the only sufficient antidote to current skepticism. Higher toward the zenith climbs the Sun of Righteousness, making circle after circle of human endeavor and achievement warm and radiant with the healing of its beams. First of all, in our gospel temperance work, this heavenly light penetrated the gloom of the individual, tempted heart (that smallest circle, in which all others are involved), illumined its darkness, melted its hardness, made it a sweet and sunny place—a temple filled with the Holy Ghost.

Having thus come to the heart of the drinking man in the plenitude of his redeeming power, Christ entered the next wider circle, in which two human hearts unite to form a home, and here, by the revelation of her place in His kingdom, He lifted to an equal level with her husband the gentle companion who had supposed herself happy in being the favorite vassal of her liege lord. "There is neither male nor female in Christ Jesus"; this was the "open sesame," a declaration utterly opposed to all custom and tradition, but so steadily the light has shone, and so kindly has it made the heart of man, that without strife of tongues, or edict of soverigns, it is coming now to pass that in proportion as any home is really Christian, the husband and wife are peers in dignity and power. . . .

Beyond this sweet and sacred circle where two hearts grow to be one, where the mystery of birth and the hallowed face of child and mother work their perpetual charm, comes that outer court of home, that third great circle which we call society. Surely and steadily the light of Christ is coming there, through the loving temperance Pentecost, to replace the empty phrase of punctilio by earnest words of cheer and inspiration; to banish the unhealthful tyranny of fashion by enthroning wholesome taste and common sense; to drive out questionable amusements and introduce innocent and delightful pastimes; to exorcise the evil spirit of gossip and domesticate helpful and tolerant speech; nay, more to banish from the social board those false emblems of hospitality and good will,—intoxicating drinks.

Sweep a wider circle still, and behold in that ecclesiastical invention called "denominationalism," Christ coming by the union of His handmaids in work for Him; coming to put away the form outward and visible that He may shed abroad the grace inward and spiritual; to close the theological disquisition of the learned pundit, and open the Bible of the humble saint; to draw away men's thoughts from theories of right living, and centre them upon right living itself; to usher in the priesthood of the people, by pressing upon the conscience of each believer the individual commission, "Go, disciple all nations," and emphasizing the individual promise, "Lo, I am with thee always."

But the modern temperance movement, born of Christ's gospel and cradled at His altars, is rapidly filling one more circle of influence, wide as the widest zone of earthly weal or woe, and that is government. . . . "Thy kingdom come, thy will be done on earth." Christ shall

reign—not visibly, but invisibly; not in form, but in fact; not in substance, but in essence, and the day draws nigh! ... But let it be
remembered that for every Christian man who has a voice in making
and enforcing laws there are at least two Christian women who have
no voice at all. Hence, under such circumstances as now exist, His
militant army must ever be powerless to win those legislative battles
which, more than any others, affect the happiness of aggregate
humanity. But the light gleams already along the sunny hilltops of the
nineteenth century of grace. Upon those who in largest numbers love
Him who has filled their hearts with peace and their homes with
blessing, slowly dawns the consciousness that they may—nay, better
still, they ought to—ask for power to help forward the coming of their
Lord in government—to throw the safeguard of their prohibition
ballots around those who have left the shelter of their arms only to be
entrapped by the saloons that bad men legalize and set along the
streets.

"But some doubted."

This was in our earlier National Conventions. Almost none disputed the value of this added weapon in woman's hand,—indeed, all
deemed it "sure to come." It was only the old, old question of expediency; of "frightening away our sisters among the more conservative."
But later on we asked these questions: Has the policy of silence caused
a great rallying to our camp from the ranks of the conservative? Do
you know an instance in which it has augmented your working force?
Are not all the women upon whose help we can confidently count,
favorable to the "Do everything Policy," as the only one broad enough
to meet our hydra-headed foe? Have not the men of the liquor traffic
said in platform, resolution, and secret circular, "The ballot in
woman's hand will be the death-knell of our trade?"

And so to-day, while each State is free to adopt or disavow the
ballot as a home protection weapon, and although the white-winged
fleet of the W.C.T.U. in a score of States crowds all sail for constitutional prohibition, to be followed up by the "Home Protection," still
though "the silver sails are all out in the West," every ship in the
gleaming line is all the same a Gospel ship—an "old ship Zion—
Hallelujah!"

Document 10: Freedom and Rights for Oppressed People

*Anna Howard Shaw (1847–1915) was the first woman ordained to
the ministry in the Methodist Protestant Church in 1880. She served
pastorates for seven years and obtained a medical degree during that
period. Believing that the key to woman's freedom was the right to
vote, Reverend Shaw resigned her pastorate to lecture and organize
for woman's suffrage. She became superintendent of the Franchise
(Suffrage) Department of the WCTU between 1888 and 1892 and*

*served as president of the National American Woman's Suffrage
Association from 1904 until 1915.*

*In her sermon "The Heavenly Vision," which she preached at the
International Council of Women in 1888, Anna Howard Shaw expressed the growing conviction that woman's work extends "into any
field of usefulness which opens up before her." The realization of her
vision was not protection of the home, as Frances Willard had advocated, but freedom and rights for oppressed people.*[30]

The vision which appeared to David was a world lost in sin. He
heard its cry for deliverance, he saw its uplifted hands. Everywhere
the eyes of good men were turned toward the skies for help. For ages
had they striven against the forces of evil; they had sought by every
device to turn back the flood-tide of base passion and avarice, but to
no purpose. It seemed as if all men were engulfed in one common
ruin. Patient, sphinx-like, sat woman, limited by sin, limited by social
custom, limited by false theories, limited by bigotry and by creeds,
listening to the tramp of the weary millions as they passed on through
the centuries, patiently toiling and waiting, humbly bearing the pain
and weariness which fell to her lot.

Century after century came forth from the divine life only to pass
into the great eternity—and still she toiled and still she waited. At last,
in the mute agony of despair, she lifted her eyes above the earth to
heaven and away from the jarring strifes which surrounded her, and
that which dawned upon her gaze was so full of wonder that her soul
burst its prison-house of bondage as she beheld the vision of true
womanhood. She knew then it was not the purpose of the Divine that
she should crouch beneath the bonds of custom and ignorance. She
learned that she was created not from the side of man, but rather by
the side of man. The world had suffered because she had not kept
her divinely-appointed place. Then she remembered the words of
prophecy, that salvation was to come to the race not through the man,
but through the descendant of the woman. Recognizing her mission
at last, she cried out: "Speak now, Lord, for thy servant heareth thee."
And the answer came: "The Lord giveth the Word, and the women
that publish the tidings are a great host."

To-day the vision is a reality. From every land the voice of woman
is heard proclaiming the word which is given her, and the wondering
world, which for a moment stopped its busy wheel of life that it might
smite and jeer her, has learned at last that wherever the intuitions of
the human mind are called into special exercise, wherever the art of
persuasive eloquence is demanded, wherever heroic conduct is based
upon duty rather than impulse, wherever her efforts in opening the
sacred doors for the benefit of truth can avail—in one and all these
respects woman greatly excels man. Now the wisest and best people
everywhere feel that if woman enters upon her tasks wielding her own

effective armor, if her inspirations are pure and holy, the Spirit Omnipotent, whose influence has held sway in all movements and reforms, whose voice has called into its service the great workmen of every age, shall, in these last days, fall especially upon woman. If she venture to obey, what is man that he should attempt to abrogate her sacred and divine mission? In the presence of what woman has already accomplished, who shall say that a true woman—noble in her humility, strong in her gentleness, rising above all selfishness, gathering up her varied gifts and accomplishments to consecrate them to God and humanity—who shall say that such an one is not in a position to do that for which the world will no longer rank her other than among the first in the work of human redemption? Then, influenced by lofty motives, stimulated by the wail of humanity and the glory of God, woman may go forth and enter into any field of usefulness which opens up before her. . . .

All down through the centuries God has been revealing in visions the great truths which have lifted the race, step by step, until to-day womanhood, in this sunset hour of the nineteenth century, is gathered here from the East and the West, the North and the South, women of every land, of every race, of all religious beliefs. But diverse and varied as are our races, our theories, our religions, yet we come together here with one harmonious purpose—that of lifting humanity into a higher, purer, truer life.

To one has come the vision of political freedom. She saw how the avarice and ambition of one class with power made them forget the rights of another. She saw how the unjust laws embittered both—those who made them and those upon whom the injustice rested. She recognized the great principles of universal equality, seeing that all alike must be free; that humanity everywhere must be lifted out of subjection into the free and full air of divine liberty.

To another was revealed the vision of social freedom. She saw that sin which crushed the lives of one class, rested lightly on the lives of the other. She saw its blighting effect on both, and she lifted up her voice and demanded that there be recognized no sex in sin.

Another has come hither, who, gazing about her, saw men brutalized by the rum fiend, the very life of a nation threatened, and the power of the liquor traffic, with its hand on the helm of the Ship of State, guiding it with sails full spread straight upon the rocks to destruction. Then, looking away from earth, she beheld a vision of what the race and our nation might become, with all its possibility of wealth and power, if freed from this burden, and forth upon her mission of deliverance she sped her way.

Another beheld a vision of what it is to be learned, to explore the great fields of knowledge which the Infinite has spread before the world. And this vision has driven her out from the seclusion of her own quiet life that she might give this great truth to womanhood everywhere. . . .

And so we come, each bearing her torch of living truth, casting over the world the light of the vision that has dawned upon her soul.

But there is still another vision which reaches above earth, beyond time—a vision which has dawned upon many, that they are here not to do their own work, but the will of Him who sent them. And the woman who sees the still higher truth, recognizes the great power to which she belongs and what her life may become when, in submission to that Master, she takes upon herself the nature of Him whom she serves. . . .

This, then, is God's lesson to you and to me. He opens before our eyes the vision of a great truth and for a moment He permits our wondering gaze to rest upon it; then He bids us go forth. Jacob of old saw the vision of God's messengers ascending and descending, but none of them standing still. . . . No man or woman has ever sought to lead his fellows to a higher and better mode of life without learning the power of the world's ingratitude; and though at times popularity may follow in the wake of a reformer, yet the reformer knows popularity is not love. The world will support you when you have compelled it to do so by manifestations of power, but it will shrink from you as soon as power and greatness are no longer on your side. This is the penalty paid by good people who sacrifice themselves for others. They must live without sympathy; their feelings will be misunderstood; their efforts will be uncomprehended. Like Paul, they will be betrayed by friends; like Christ in the agony of Gethsemane, they must bear their struggle alone. . . .

This is the hardest lesson the reformer has to learn. When, with soul aglow with the light of a great truth, she, in obedience to the vision, turns to take it to the needy one, instead of finding a world ready to rise up and receive her, she finds it wrapped in the swaddling clothes of error, eagerly seeking to win others to its conditions of slavery. She longs to make humanity free; she listens to their conflicting creeds, and yearns to save them from the misery they endure. She knows that there is no form of slavery more bitter or arrogant than error, that truth alone can make man free, and she longs to bring the heart of the world and the heart of truth together, that the truth may exercise its transforming power over the life of the world. The greatest test of the reformer's courage comes when, with a warm, earnest longing for humanity, she breaks for it the bread of truth and the world turns from this life-giving power and asks instead of bread a stone.

It is just here that so many of God's workmen fail, and themselves need to turn back to the vision as it appeared to them, and to gather fresh courage and new inspiration for the future. This, my sisters, we all must do if we would succeed. The reformer may be inconsistent, she may be stern or even impatient, but if the world feels that she is in earnest she can not fail. Let the truth which she desires to teach first take possession of herself. Every woman who to-day goes out into the world with a truth, who has not herself become possessed of that truth, had far better stay at home. . . .

Grand as is this vision which meets us here, it is but the dawning of a new day; and as the first beams of morning light give promise of the radiance which shall envelop the earth when the sun, shall have arisen in all its splendor, so there comes to us a prophecy of that glorious day when the vision which we are now beholding, which is beaming in the soul of one, shall enter the hearts and transfigure the lives of all.

WIDENING THE BOUNDARIES OF "FIELDS OF USEFULNESS": MINISTRY TO INSTITUTIONS AND SOCIAL SYSTEMS

Document 11: Reconstructing Charitable Institutions

The work of Josephine Shaw Lowell (1843–1905) exemplified the broadening of reform efforts from individual charity to social change. A Civil War widow at twenty, Lowell devoted her life to serving and reordering charitable institutions in New York State. She lobbied for improvements in jails and almshouses. She helped establish a House of Refuge for Women and also developed the nation's first custodial asylum for feebleminded women. Concerned with eliminating the duplication of charitable efforts, she helped to found the New York Charity Organization Society, a clearinghouse for charity efforts throughout the city. Her philosophy and commitment are expressed graphically in the selection to follow.[31]

The chief value, to my mind, of the colonizing of the more highly educated and, from a worldly standpoint, more favored individuals among those who live in densely crowded neighborhoods, and work hard for a good part of every twenty-four hours, is that they come to know them, to know their lives and to know their needs, and can report them to the people who have the power to supply what is needed.

Experts are required now in every field. Most people have not time to attend to more than their own immediate surroundings and business. So many things press for attention that much which is of the greatest importance is pushed aside, and therefore it is necessary that each part of the public weal should be especially studied by those who devote themselves to personal observation and the collection of facts; and such students and collectors of facts in sociology are, or ought to be, the men and women who take up their residence among the plain people, as Lincoln called them, and observe their daily life near at hand and all day long and every day.

The reason charity, so called, although it is sad to degrade a beautiful word, is so often discredited, and more often so discreditable, is that it has usually worked without any knowledge of this daily life. It has kept out of the way of it, and has tried in a feeble and ineffectual manner to deal with the broken fragments, the failures, thrown out by it. When men and women have broken down because of long hours of overwork and horribly bad surroundings to work in, charity has put them into hospitals, and has either never thought or said anything about the causes of the breakdown, or it has complacently remarked that it was a pity that such conditions were necessary for business reasons.

When charity has found men and women drunken and shiftless and unable to care for their children, charity has taken their children away from them, and has said "That's the way poor people are"; but it has not asked why they are so or tried to prevent their being so.

When girls have gone wrong and boys have stolen, charity has provided refuges for the girls and has put the boys into prison, and has talked as if such ruin of lives, and what looks like ruin of souls, were inevitable, never even wondering what other outlet for the natural love of pleasure and adventure, so carefully provided for in the case of other boys and girls, there was for these boys and girls.

How, that is all changed or is changing; and it is, I believe, because men and women are learning the actual life of the mass of workers who do not break down, but who only die; who are not drunken and shiftless, but who lead lives of such heroic self-sacrifice and devotion as we cannot lead because the demand is not made on us, and of the lives of the boys and girls, who grow up brave and pure through and in the midst of circumstances which, as I have said, seem to us fatal.

But, notwithstanding all the virtues and all the heroism of the mass of the people, they do need and ought to have a great many things they do not have, and the whole community ought to help them to get them; but the first step toward helping them to get them is to know exactly what they need, and this knowledge the residents in college settlements and the individual residents in tenement houses must get for us. They must report the neglect of the city government to do its duty, whether as streetcleaners, as police or as educators. They must report the oppression of employers, whether the oppression be the result of individual carelessness or, as is often the case, the result of trade conditions. They must cry aloud for more air, more space, for a larger and better life in every way for the great masses of men and women in our cities.

Document 12: Exposing Lynching of Her Black People.

Ida B. Wells-Barnett (1862–1931) was a black woman born into a slave family in Holly Springs, Mississippi. Her parents stressed the value of education, and Ida Wells attended Rust University, established as a freedmen's institution in 1866 in her hometown.

Becoming part-owner of the Memphis Free Speech, *Ida Wells-Barnett became a crusader against lynching. She traveled to the scenes of lynchings and riots to discover and publish the truth about events that others, both black and white, were often too frightened to reveal.*

In her speech "Lynch Law in All Its Phases," Ida Wells-Barnett recounts her dismissal as a teacher in the Memphis public schools because of editorials she wrote criticizing inferior conditions in black schools. Her belief that black citizens could better themselves through "character, money-getting and education" was abruptly shattered by a brutal lynching of three young men in Memphis on March 9, 1892.[32]

I am before the American people to-day through no inclination of my own, but because of a deep-seated conviction that the country at large does not know the extent to which lynch law prevails in parts of the Republic, nor the conditions which force into exile those who speak the truth. I cannot believe that the apathy and indifference which so largely obtains regarding mob rule is other than the result of ignorance of the true situation. And yet, the observing and thoughtful must know that in one section, at least, of our common country, a government of the people, by the people, and for the people, means a government by the mob; where the land of the free and home of the brave means a land of lawlessness, murder and outrage; and where liberty of speech means the license of might to destroy the business and drive from home those who exercise this privilege contrary to the will of the mob. . . .

The race problem or negro question, as it has been called, has been omnipresent and all-pervading since long before the Afro-American was raised from the degradation of the slave to the dignity of the citizen. It has never been settled because the right methods have not been employed in the solution. . . . Times without number, since invested with citizenship, the race has been indicted for ignorance, immorality and general worthlessness—declared guilty and executed by its self-constituted judges. The operations of law do not dispose of negroes fast enough, and lynching bees have become the favorite pastime of the South. As excuse for the same, a new cry, as false as it is foul, is raised in an effort to blast race character, a cry which has proclaimed to the world that virtue and innocence are violated by Afro-Americans who must be killed like wild beasts to protect womanhood and childhood.

Born and reared in the South, I had never expected to live else-where. Until this past year I was one among those who believed the condition of the masses gave large excuse for the humiliations and proscriptions under which we labored; that when wealth, education and character became more general among us,—the cause being removed—the effect would cease, and justice be accorded to all alike. I shared the general belief that good newspapers entering regularly the homes of our people in every state could do more to bring about this result than any agency. Preaching the doctrine of self-help, thrift and economy every week, they would be the teachers to those who had been deprived of school advantages, yet were making history every day—and train to think for themselves our mental children of a larger growth. And so, three years ago last June, I became editor and part owner of the *Memphis Free Speech....*

I have no power to describe the feeling of horror that possessed every member of the race in Memphis when the truth dawned upon us that the protection of the law which we had so long enjoyed was no longer ours; all this had been destroyed in a night, and the barriers of the law had been thrown down, and the guardians of the public peace and confidence scoffed away into the shadows, and all authority given into the hands of the mob, and innocent men cut down as if they were brutes—the first feeling was one of utter dismay, then intense indignation. Vengeance was whispered from ear to ear, but sober reflection brought the conviction that it would be extreme folly to seek vengeance when such action meant certain death for the men, and horrible slaughter for the women and children, as one of the evening papers took care to remind us. The power of the State, country and city, the civil authorities and the strong arm of the military power were all on the side of the mob and of lawlessness. Few of our men pos-sessed firearms, our only company's guns were confiscated, and the only white man who would sell a colored man a gun, was himself jailed, and his store closed. We were helpless in our great strength. It was our first object lesson in the doctrine of white supremacy; an illustration of the South's cardinal principle that no matter what the attainments, character or standing of an Afro-American, the laws of the South will not protect him against a white man.

There was only one thing we could do, and a great determination seized upon the people to follow the advice of the martyred Moss and "turn our faces to the West," whose laws protect all alike. The *Free Speech,* supported by our ministers and leading business men, advised the people to leave a community whose laws did not protect them. Hundreds left on foot to walk four hundred miles between Memphis and Oklahoma....

In two months, six thousand persons had left the city and every branch of business began to feel this silent resentment of the outrage, and failure of the authorities to punish the lynchers....

To restore the equilibrium and put a stop to the great financial loss, the next move was to get rid of the *Free Speech*,—the disturbing element which kept the waters troubled; which would not let the people forget, and in obedience to whose advice nearly six thousand persons had left the city. In casting about for an excuse, the mob found it in the following editorial which appeared in the *Memphis Free Speech*,—May 21, 1892: "Eight negroes lynched in one week. Since last issue of the *Free Speech* one was lynched at Little Rock, Ark., where the citizens broke in to the penitentiary and got their man; three near Anniston, Ala., and one in New Orleans, all on the same charge, the new alarm of assaulting white women—and three near Clarksville, Ga., for killing a white man. The same program of hanging—then shooting bullets into the lifeless bodies was carried out to the letter. Nobody in this section of the country believes the old threadbare lie that negro men rape white women. If Southern white men are not careful they will overreach themselves, and public sentiment will have a reaction. A conclusion will then be reached which will be very damaging to the moral reputation of their women." Commenting on this, the *Daily Commercial* of Wednesday following said: "Those negroes who are attempting to make lynching of individuals of their race a means for arousing the worst passions of their kind, are playing with a dangerous sentiment. The negroes may as well understand that there is no mercy for the rapist, and little patience with his defenders. . . ."

I had written that editorial with other matter for the week's paper before leaving home the Friday previous for the General Conference of the A.M.E. Church in Philadelphia. Conference adjourned Tuesday, and Thursday, May 25, at 3 P.M., I landed in New York City for a few days' stay before returning home, and there learned from the papers that my business manager had been driven away and the paper suspended. Telegraphing for news, I received telegrams and letters in return informing me that the trains were being watched, that I was to be dumped into the river and beaten, if not killed; it had been learned that I wrote the editorial and I was to be hanged in front of the court-house and my face bled if I returned, and I was implored by my friends to remain away. The creditors attacked the office in the meantime and the outfit was sold without more ado, thus destroying effectually that which it had taken years to build. One prominent insurance agent publicly declares he will make it his business to shoot me down on sight if I return to Memphis in twenty years, while a leading white lady has remarked that she was opposed to the lynching of those three men in March, but she did wish there was some way by which I could be gotten back and lynched. . . .

The lawlessness here described is not confined to one locality. In the past ten years over a thousand colored men, women and children have been butchered, murdered and burnt in all parts of the South. The details of these horrible outrages seldom reach beyond the narrow world where they occur. Those who commit the murders write the reports, and hence these lasting blots upon the honor of a nation cause but a faint ripple on the outside world. They arouse no great indignation and call forth no adequate demand for justice. The victims were black, and the reports are so written as to make it appear that the helpless creatures deserved the fate which overtook them. . . .

Although the impression has gone abroad that most of the lynchings take place because of assaults on white women only, one-third of the number lynched in the past ten years have been charged with that offense, to say nothing of those who were not guilty of the charge. And according to law none of them were guilty until proven so. But the unsupported word of any white person for any cause is sufficient to cause a lynching. So bold have the lynchers become, masks are laid aside, the temples of justice and strongholds of law are invaded in broad daylight and prisoners taken out and lynched, while governors of states and officers of law stand by and see the work well done.

And yet this Christian nation, the flower of the nineteenth century civilization, says it can do nothing to stop this inhuman slaughter. The general government is willingly powerless to send troops to protect the lives of its black citizens, but the state governments are free to use state troops to shoot them down like cattle, when in desperation the black men attempt to defend themselves, and then tell the world that it was necessary to put down a "race war."

Do you ask the remedy? A public sentiment strong against lawlessness must be aroused. Every individual can contribute to this awakening. When a sentiment against lynch law as strong, deep and mighty as that roused against slavery prevails, I have no fear of the result. It should be already established as a fact and not as a theory, that every human being must have a fair trial for his life and liberty, no matter what the charge against him. When a demand goes up from fearless and persistent reformers from press and pulpit, from industrial and moral associations that this shall be so from Maine to Texas and from ocean to ocean, a way will be found to make it so. . . .

Document 13: Toward Universal Peace

Mary A. Brayton Woodbridge (1830–1894) was one of many Ohio women who received a "baptism of the Holy Spirit" during the Ohio Temperance Crusade in 1873 and 1874.

Through her experiences in the Temperance Crusade, Mary Woodbridge also became a committed worker for world peace and arbitration. The document which follows is from a speech, "Peace and Arbitration in National and International Affairs," given many times by Mary Woodbridge in the last five years of her life.[33]

During the present century, interest in peace and arbitration has been awakened, and has slowly but steadily grown until, under the quickening of conscience, civilized Christian nations are recognizing the fact that individual and national life are so interwoven that what interests one person or one nation, more or less concerns all.

Taking the Scriptures as a standard, we present as a fundamental proposition, that war is contrary to the will and the spirit of Christ; a hindrance to the building of His kingdom upon the earth in withholding "the government from His shoulders". . . .

There is no doctrine of Scripture more self-evident than that peace is God's will for man; that He has ordained it to be the result of right conduct; that perfect peace is the divine gift of those who are stayed on Him. There is no truth more axiomatic than that our homes should be the abiding place of peace, as the result of virtue and justice within its walls. And as the nations are but the aggregation of homes, can any reason be found why they should not be equally pure and righteous?

Let peace depart from the home, let dissension enter and the home life is banished. If this be confined within four walls there is misery to the family, and often to associates; if it be in the nation, its results reach to the limits of its territory, and if international, to the world.

Cast the eye over our land and count if we can the cost of our civil war. Statisticians tell us that 656,000 fathers, brothers and sons were torn from home and home influences to fall upon the battlefield or die in hospital or prison cell. Men made in the image of God, snatched from every holy association, and returned to the earth from whence they came, without apparent thought of that immortality which God has given to every soul! Numberless thousands returned decrepit and unfit for life's duties, physical or moral wrecks. Four long years these and others were consumers of the nation's wealth; and an enfeebled host and their children are consuming still, none the less a fact because such provision has been made in honor and justice to the nation's defenders. Manufacturing interests were depressed and resources diminished by the withdrawal of workmen, while three billion seven hundred million dollars were expended, demanding increased taxation for years.

And these are but few of the many traceable evils resulting from the great war of the rebellion.

"But," you may ask, "what could have been done? Were we not obliged to take such action?" Who would not have answered yes at the moment of our provocation, under the stupefied moral condition of the people, forgetful of the Golden Rule of Christ? But who can affirm that through arbitration the difficulty might not have been amicably settled, even after the boom of that gun at Sumter that rang through the land? This was the belief of President Lincoln, who, in his message of March 2, 1862, exhorted to a settlement of difficulties on the basis of compensation, which, had there been a willing response by Congress, could doubtless have been done. . . .

. . . It is said that Europe began the year 1889 with fifteen million trained soldiers under arms, or on the reserve corps. It is doubtful if any year in the history of the world has had such a showing. For years the nations have been working up to this military climax. As these armies have increased in size the nations have decreased in prosperity. The support of so large an army of non-producers drains their exchequer. Their industrial, educational and moral forces are proportionally weakened, pressing to the alternative of fighting to maintain their life, at the expense of others, or of disbanding their armies that their own life may be preserved. . . . Who would not rejoice in the removal of such questions from the political influences of the present day to a general permanent system of arbitration, or to an international court whose decisions would be received by all governments without demur?

As General Grant said, though the decisions might not suit either nation at the time, it would satisfy the conscience of mankind.

Arbitration is fast becoming a recognized duty. Humanity is loudly calling for its establishment as a permanent and authoritative part of the law of nations. Other forces are also working to the same result. The devotion to material interests which characterizes our age, exerts a powerful opposition to war—the great waster and destroyer of wealth. The growing power of the masses as opposed to the classes, the enlargement of the place and influence of the people in the sphere of government, make it more difficult for sovereigns to array their armies for the settlement of disputes.

The increasing communication between nations, and the establishment of a world's public opinion by which all nations and governments are judged, have thrown a new restraint around the ambitions and resentments of rulers. The glamour which was once over the eyes of men, blinding then to the folly and wickedness of war, is fast passing away.

All these are greatly aided by the quickened forces of Christianity; but there is urgent need and room for more resolute action by the church! Should not the Christian ministry lead public sentiment in this great cause?

The revelations of science are calling a halt to war. At the centennial celebration of the adoption of the constitution of the United States in September, 1887, the late General Philip H. Sheridan, not a private citizen but commander of the United States army, gave his view of the future in these words: "There is one thing you should appreciate, and that is, that improvement in the material of war, in dynamite and other explosives, and in breech-loading guns, is rapidly bringing us to a period when war will be eliminated from history; when we can no longer stand up and fight each other, and when we will have to resort to something else. Now what will that something else be? It will be arbitration. I mean what I say when I express the belief that any of those here present, who may live until the next centennial, will find that arbitration will rule the whole world." . . .

General Philip Sheridan put the day of universal peace and arbitration a century ahead. Did he take into consideration of the great army of women whom the Lord has steadily added to that band of suppliants in whom He fulfilled the prophecy of Joel in 1873–74 [through the Ohio Temperance Crusade]? Did he think of the womanhood of America and of the world, who have been called to take their part in the great movements of the ages that will exalt Christ as Sovereign of the whole world? Nay, he could not have remembered that to them has been opened channel after channel of opportunity which they have readily entered for the glory of God and the salvation of suffering mankind.

. . . From Ohio, where God's first call to woman to enter this great work was heard, this effort came. The spirit moved on in widening sweep of blessing until the nation's heart was stirred. Scarcely had it reached the limits of our own fair land, ere bounding over the deep it went to our sisters on the other side; and back it comes to us in a manifesto of French women against war.

. . . We believe as one nation and another and another shall come under this reign of peace, toward which the thought and the heart of the people are being rapidly turned, there will be real men and women who will do real work for the extension of the Lord's kingdom through arbitration with those governments where His light has not been so clearly seen. When national action shall be subjugated to this principle, Christianity will become dominant, and good will to others will prove that God is Christ and Christ is king.

Yes, it is coming! It may be that in its progress God will, in His wisdom, lay His hand upon nations that will not serve Him, and they shall not be; but the wide world is opening to His gospel and the messengers of peace are ushering in millennial glory.

Notes

Women and Revivalism

1. Reverend Calvin Colton, *History and Character of American Revivals of Religion* (London: Frederick Westley and A. H. Davis, 1832), p. 59.
2. Martha Tomhave Blauvelt, "Society, Religion, and Revivalism: The Second Great Awakening in New Jersey, 1780–1830" (Unpublished ms.), pp. 165–166; Ebenezer Porter, *Letters on the Religious Revivals which Prevailed about the Beginning of the Present Century* (Boston: Congregational Board of Publication, 1858), p. 9; Donald G. Mathews, *Religion in the Old South*, Chicago History of American Religion, ed. Martin E. Marty (Chicago: University of Chicago Press, 1977), p. 47.
3. Gerald Francis Moran, "The Puritan Saint: Religious Experience, Church Membership, and Piety in Connecticut, 1636–1776" (Ph.D. dissertation, Rutgers University, 1973), p. 326. Moran based his statistics on an analysis of the records of forty-nine churches; this is the largest sample any historian has studied in determining the sex ratio of the First Awakening's revival members (see Ibid., pp. 339–340).
4. "On Happiness," *The New-Jersey Magazine, and Monthly Advertiser* (January, 1787): 69–70.
5. James Fordyce, *Sermons to Young Women*, two vols. in one, 3rd Amer. from 12th London ed. (Philadelphia: M. Carey; New York: I. Riley, 1809), 2:5–6.
6. Barbara Welter, "The Cult of True Womanhood, 1802–1860," *American Quarterly* 18 (1966): 151–174.
7. Benjamin Rush, "Thoughts upon Female Education, Accommodated to the Present State of Society, Manners, and Government in the United States of America" [Boston, 1787], in *Essays on Education in the Early Republic*, ed. Frederick Rudolph (Cambridge, Mass.: Howard University Press, 1965), p. 32.
8. Nancy F. Cott, "Young Women in the Second Great Awakening in New England," *Feminist Studies* 3 (1975): 15–29.
9. Phillips Bradley, ed., *Democracy in America by Alexis de Tocqueville*, vol. 2 (New York: A. A. Knopf, 1945), p. 212.
10. Reverend James Fordyce, *Sermons to Young Women*, 2: 56–57, 59–61, 65–66.
11. Anna Maria Smith, Diary 1827–1828 (Unpublished ms., Rutgers University Special Collections, New Brunswick, New Jersey).
12. Amanda Berry Smith, *An Autobiography. The Story of the Lord's Dealings with Mrs. Amanda Smith The Colored Evangelist Containing an Account of Her Life Work of Faith, and Her Travels in America, England, Ireland, Scotland, India and Africa, as an Independent Missionary*, intro. Bishop Thoburn of India (Chicago: Meyer & Brother, 1893).
13. Peter Cartwright, *The Backwoods Preacher. Being the Autobiography of Peter Cartwright, An American Methodist Travelling Preacher* (London: Wesleyan-Methodist Book Room, Hayman Brothers and Lilly, Printers, n.d.), pp. 66–67.
14. Olive Gilbert, *Narrative of Sojourner Truth: A Bondswoman of Olden Time, Emancipated by the New York Legislature in the Early Part of the Present Century: With a History of Her Labors and Correspondence, Drawn from Her "Book of Life"* (Boston: privately printed, 1875), pp. 61–62, 65–68.

15. William C. Conant, *Narratives of Remarkable Conversions and Revival Incidents: including a Review of Revivals, from the Day of Pentecost to the Great Awakening in the Last Century—Conversions of Eminent Persons—Instances of Remarkable Conversions and Answers to Prayer—An Account of the Rise and Progress of the Great Awakening in 1857–'8* (New York: Derby and Jackson, 1858), pp. 163–164.
16. Robert G. Armstrong, *Memoir of Hannah Hobbie: or Christian Activity, and Triumph in Suffering* (New York: American Tract Society, D. Fanshaw, printer, 1837), pp. 239–241.
17. Jane Coombs Greenleaf, to T. C., Esq., of Newburyport, in *Memoir of Mrs. Jane Greenleaf of Newburyport, Mass.* (Newburyport: Moses H. Sargent, 1851), pp. 63–66.
18. C. W. Andrews, *Memoir of Mrs. Ann R. Page*, 2nd ed. (New York: Protestant Episcopal Society for the Promotion of Evangelical Knowledge, 1856), pp. 25–26, 28–29.
19. Reverend Absalom Peters, "Serious Impressions on the Minds of Sinners Vary According to the Variation of the Prayers of Saints," *The Home Missionary, and American Pastor's Journal* 1, no. 5 (September 1, 1828): 87–88.
20. Ashbel Green, "The Christian Duty of Christian Women. A Discourse, Delivered in the Church of Princeton, New Jersey, August 23d, 1825, before the Princeton Female Society, for the Support of a Female School in India," *The Christian Advocate* 4 (Philadelphia: A. Finley, 1826): 1–14.
21. Charles G. Finney, *Lectures on Revivals of Religion*, new ed. rev. and enl. by the author (Oberlin, Ohio: E. J. Goodrich, 1868), pp. 27–29, 109, 110–111.
22. Margaret Van Cott, *The Harvest and the Reaper. Reminiscenses of Revival Work of Mrs. Maggie N. Van Cott. The First Lady Licensed to Preach in the Methodist Episcopal Church in the United States* (New York: N. Tibbals & Sons, 1876), pp. 58–60, 150–157, 213–216.

Women in Utopian Movements

1. There are many standard histories of American utopianism, such as Mark Holloway's *Heavens on Earth: Utopian Communities in America, 1680–1880* (New York: Dover, 1966). For questions on women and sexuality, see Raymond Lee Muncy's *Sex and Marriage in Utopian Communities* (Baltimore, Md.: Penguin, 1974).
2. See Christopher Johnson's *Utopian Communism in France: Cabet and the Icarians, 1839–51* (Ithaca, N.Y.: Cornell University Press, 1974). Robert Owen thought of his movement as a new religion and founded the Society of Rational Religionists. Charles Fourier's socialism was based on a millennialist doctrine of the coming Eighth Epoch of Harmony, when all cosmic contradictions would be resolved.
3. Jacob Boehme, *Mysterium Magnum: An Exposition of the First Book of Moses Called Genesis*, vol. 1, trans. John Sparrow (London: John M. Watkins, 1924), pp. 121–133.
4. Emmanuel Swedenborg (1688–1771), *Arcana Coelestia*, 8 vols. (New York: American Swedenborg Publishing Co., 1870–1874).
5. See Barbara Zikmund, "The Feminist Thrust of Sectarian Christianity," in *Women of Spirit*, ed. McLaughlin and Ruether (New York: Simon and Schuster, 1979), p. 211.
6. Charles Nordhoff, *The Communist Societies of the United States*, reprint of 1875 ed. (New York: Hillary House, 1961), pp. 137–38.
7. Clara Endicott Sears, *Alcott's Fruitlands* (Boston: Houghton Mifflin, 1915), pp. 121–123.
8. See Muncy, *Sex and Marriage in Utopian Communities*, p. 35.
9. Ibid., pp. 122–143.
10. Ibid., pp. 212–213.
11. Adin Ballou, *Practical Christian Socialism* (New York: Fowlers and Wells, 1854), pp. 374–393.
12. See Margaret Lane, *France Wright and the Great Experiment* (Totowa, N.J.: Rowman and Littlefield, 1972).
13. Heinemann's autobiography, *Kurze Erzählung von den Erwickungs Umstanden* (1885), has not been translated. A summary of it is found in Bertha Shambaugh's *The Amana that Was and the Amana that Is* (Iowa State Historical Society, 1932), pp. 37–40.
14. Rene Nooberger, *Ellen White: Prophetess of Destiny* (New Canaan, Conn.: Keats Publishing Company, 1972).
15. On the Eddy-Stetson relation, see Altman K. Swihart's *Since Mrs. Eddy* (New York: Henry Holt and Co., 1931), pp. 3–182.

16. See "Lucy Wright," in *Notable American Women* (Cambridge, Mass.: Belnap Press, 1971).
17. See F. E. Manual and J. Franklin, *Design for Utopia: Selected Works of Charles Fourier* (New York: Schocken, 1971), pp. 76–81.
18. Christina Knoedler, *The Harmony Society: A Nineteenth Century American Utopia* (New York: Vintage, 1954), pp. 76–78, and William Hinds, *American Communities* (Oneida, N.Y.: American Socialist, 1878), pp. 26–28, on women's voting rights in the Rappite and Zoarite communities.
19. For example, see Mary Baker Eddy, *No and Yes* (Boston: E. J. Foster Eddy, 1894), pp. 55–56.
20. Edward Deming and Faith Andrews, *Work and Worship: The Economic Order of the Shakers* (Greenwich, Conn.: New York Graphic Society, 1974), pp. 109–136. A Shaker sister is credited with the invention of the circular saw, cut nails, and a method of making false teeth; see ibid., p. 153.
21. Karl Arndt, *George Rapp's Harmony Society, 1785–1847* (Philadelphia: University of Pennsylvania Press, 1965), p. 583.
22. Hilda Adam King, Hymns to Sophia, nos. 343, 362, 394, 397, 398, trans. from *Harmonisches Gesangbuch* (Economy, 1827), *The Harmonists: A Folk Cultural Approach* (Metuchen, N.J.: Scarecrow Press, 1973), pp. 113–120.
23. W. A. Hinds, Thomas Lake Harris to Hinds, August 22, 1877, *American Communities* (Oneida, N.Y.: Office of the American Socialist, 1878), pp. 143–147.
24. Anna White and Leila Taylor, *Shakerism: Its Meaning and Message* (Columbus, Ohio: Fred J. Meer Press, 1904; reprinted by AMS Press, N.Y.), pp. 255–258.
25. Mary Baker Eddy, *Science and Health, With Key to the Scriptures*, 68th ed. (Boston: E. J. Foster Eddy, 1894), pp. 510, 552–554.
26. John Hymphrey Noyes, *Male Continence* (Oneida, N.Y.: Office of Oneida Circular, 1872), pp. 11–12, 14–16.
27. Joseph Smith, *Doctrine and Covenants*, sec. 132 (Salt Lake City, Utah, 1883; reprint ed. by Greenwood Press, 1971).
28. Henry Edgar, *Modern Times: The Labor Question and the Family* (New York: Calvin Blanchard, 1855), pp. 10–14.
29. Adin Ballou, *History of the Hopedale Community* (Lowell, Mass.: Thompson and Hill, 1897; reprint ed. by Porcupine Press, 1972), pp. 246–249.
30. Frances Wright, *New Harmony Gazette* 1 (October 1, 1825): 4–5.
31. Charles Nordhoff, *Communist Societies of the United States* (New York: Harper & Brothers, 1875), pp. 34–35, 37, 47–48.
32. Ellen Harmon White, *Early Writings* (Washington, D.C.: Review and Herald Press, 1945), pp. 11–13, 32–33.
33. Mary Baker Eddy, "Article XXII: Relation of Members to Pastor Emeritus," *Manual of the Mother Church* (Boston: J. Armstrong, 1906), pp. 63–67; Mrs. Eddy's Christmas letter of 1903 in Archives: *Letters and Miscellany*, vol. 3, p. 325.
34. Augusta Stetson, *Reminiscences, Sermons and Correspondence, Proving Adherence to the Principle of Christian Science as Taught by Mary Baker Eddy* (New York: G. P. Putnam's Sons, 1913), pp. 161–163, 224–228.
35. "Condition of Women in Harmony," *The Phalanx* 1, no. 16 (August 10, 1844): 234–236.
36. Constance Noyes Robertson, *Oneida Community: An Autobiography* (Syracuse University Press, 1970), pp. 297–298, 299, 300, 302, 310.
37. Marianne Dwight, *Letters From Brook Farm* (Poughkeepsie, N.Y.: Vassar College, 1928), pp. 32–33.
38. George Garrison, "The Sanctificationists of Belton," *The Charities Review* 3 (November, 1893): 29–46.

The Leadership of Nuns in Immigrant Catholicism

1. The statistics cited here and elsewhere in this essay are based on research done by the author in the various editions of what is now called the *Official Catholic Directory*, published annually from 1832 on by Sadlier's Kenedy and other publishers under various titles. The results of this research were presented at a meeting of the American Catholic Historical Association at the University of Notre Dame in April, 1979. The author is grateful to the Center for American Catholic Studies at Notre Dame for a travel grant that made this research possible.

2. Statistics regarding nursing from "Nursing in Religious Orders in the United States," *American Journal of Nursing* 30 (July, August, September, 1929), *passim*, and John O'Grady, *Catholic Charities in the United States* (Washington D.C.: National Conference of Catholic Charities, 1930), p. 185, 195.
3. Ray Allen Billington's *The Protestant Crusade* (New York: Macmillan, 1938) is an exhaustive study of the anti-Catholic movement that swept the country in the decades preceding the Civil War. Much of my information is based on his work.
4. I study this complex subject and other topics touched upon in this essay in far greater detail in my book *The Role of the Nun in Nineteenth-century America* (New York: Arno, 1979).
5. Louise Callan, *Philippine Duchesne* (Westminster, Md.: Newman, 1957); Mother Pia Backes, *Her Days Unfolded* (St. Benedict, Oreg.: Benedictine Press, 1953); Mother Theodore Guerin, *Journals and Letters of Mother Theodore Guerin*, ed., Sr. Mary Theodosia Mug (St. Mary-of-the-Woods, Ind.: Providence Press, 1942); Clementine De La Corbiniere, *The Life and Letters of Sister St. Francis Xavier* (St. Mary-of-the-Woods, Ind.: Providence Press, 1934); Mother Theresa Gerhardinger, *The North American Foundations Letters of Mother M. Theresa Gerhardinger*, ed. S. M. Hester Valentine, SSND (Winona, Minn.: St. Mary's College Press, 1977).
6. *The John Carroll Papers*, vol. 3, ed. Thomas O'Brien Hanley, S. J. (Notre Dame University Press, 1976), pp. 155–157.
7. *Journals and Letters of Mother Theodore Guerin*, pp. 1–7; and *History of the Sisters of Providence of St. Mary-of-the-Woods* (New York: Bensiger, 1949), pp. 104–106.
8. *Letters of Mother Theresa Gerhardinger*, pp. 65–77.
9. *Journals and Letters of Mother Theodore Guerin*, pp. 190–194.
10. Sister Mary Hortense Kohler, O.P., *Rooted in Hope* (Milwaukee: Bruce, 1962), pp. 120–122.
11. *The Works of John England, First Bishop of Charleston* (Baltimore: John Murphy, 1849), vol. 5, pp. 244–246.
12. *The Life and Letters of Sister St. Francis Xavier*, pp. 289–292.
13. "Bishop England's Institute of the Sisters of Mercy," *American Ecclesiastical Review* 20, no. 2 (May, 1899), pp. 456–458.
14. "Notes on Satterlee Military Hospital," *American Catholic Historical Society Record* 8 (1897): 404–412.
15. Sister Blandina Segale, *At the End of the Santa Fe Trail* (Milwaukee: Bruce, 1948), pp. 39, 61, 67–69, 97–99, 109–110, 157–159.

The Jewish Woman's Encounter with American Culture

1. For general histories of Jewish women in America, see Rudolf Glanz, *The Jewish Woman in America: Two Female Immigrant Generations, 1820–1929* (New York: KTA, 1976); Anita Lipman Lebeson, *Recall to Life: the Jewish Woman in America* (New York: Thomas Yoselaff, 1970); Charlotte Baum, Paula Hyman, and Sonya Michel, *The Jewish Woman in America* (New York: New American Library, 1977).
2. On the early history of Jews in America, see Nathan Glazer, *American Judaism* (Chicago: University of Chicago Press, 1972), pp. 22–106; and Joseph L. Blau, *Judaism in America: From Curiosity to Third Faith* (Chicago: University of Chicago Press, 1976).
3. Mark Zborowski and Elizabeth Herzog, "The Women's Share," part 2, chapt. 4, *Life Is With People: the Culture of the Shtetl* (New York: Schocken Books, 1962), pp. 124–142.
4. For biographical information on Ray Frank, see Simon Litman, *Ray Frank Litman: A Memoir*, Studies in American Jewish History, vol. 3 (New York: American Jewish Historical Society, 1957).
5. Three Yiddish texts, *Lev Tov*, *Ts'eno Ur'eno*, and the *Techinot*, are mentioned in Baum, Hyman, and Michel, *The Jewish Woman in America*, p. 58. Some prayer books were translated into English for use of American women; see, for example, Reverend M. J. Raphall, ed., *Devotional Exercises for the Daughters of Israel, Intended for Public and Private Worship, on the Various Occasions of Woman's Life* (New York: L. Joachimssen, 1852), and Rabbi Abbraham E. Hirschowitz, ed., *Religious Duties of the Daughters of Israel* (New York: Rabbi A. E. Hirschowitz, 1902). The zogerkeh is described by Zborowski and Herzog, *Life Is With People*, pp. 125, 128.
6. Bella Chagall, *Burning Lights* (New York: Schocken Book, 1947), pp. 179–185.

7. Bernard Martin, *A History of Judaism,* vol. 2 (New York: Basic Books, 1974), p. 204.

8. The most notable "salon Jewess" to forsake Judaism was Dorothea Mendelsohn, daughter of philosopher Moses Mendelsohn and wife of Protestant theologian Friedrich Schlegel. See Baum, Hyman, and Michel, *The Jewish Woman in America,* pp. 19–24.

9. Ibid., p. 27.

10. Martin, *A History of Judaism,* vol. 2, p. 290.

11. Rollin G. Osterweis, *Rebecca Gratz* (New York: G. P. Putnam's Sons, 1935). On the rabbinic controversy over mixed choirs, see Alexander Guttman, *The Struggle Over Reform in Rabbinic Literature* (New York: World Union for Progressive Judaism, 1977), p. 67.

12. Barbara Welter, "The Feminization of American Religion: 1800–1860," in *Problems and Issues in American Social History,* ed. William O'Neill (Minneapolis: Burgess Publishing Co., 1974); Barbara Welter, *Clio's Consciousness Raised: New Perspectives on the History of Women,* ed. Mary Hartman and Louis W. Banner (New York: Harper & Row, 1974); Ann Douglas, *The Feminization of American Culture* (New York: Alfred A. Knopf, 1977).

13. On Penina Moïse, see Lebeson, *Recall to Life,* pp. 68–75. Max I. Dimont has suggested that "one could almost state the phenomenon of the Mikvah as a law: As the mikvah appears, Orthodoxy is in ascendance; as the mikvah vanished, Orthodoxy is in decline" (*The Jews in America,* New York: Simon and Schuster, 1978, p. 91). On Dilah Cohn, see Morris A. Gutstein, *A Priceless Heritage: The Epic Growth of Nineteenth Century Chicago Jewry* (New York: Bloch Publishing Co., 1953), p. 306; and Doctor B. Felsenthal and Herman Eliassof, *Semi-Centennial Celebration* (Chicago: Kehilath Anshe Mayriv, 1897), p. 17.

14. Isaac Leeser, ed., *The Occident and American Jewish Advocate* 1 (1843): 34, 104, 200, 342; 2 (1844): 59, 83, 163; 3 (1845): 163; 4 (1846): 211, 387; 10 (1852): 39, 40, 47, 497.

15. *The Occident* 2 (1844): 163.

16. Ibid.

17. Ibid.

18. Grace Aguilar, *The Women of Israel* (New York: D. Appleton, 1860); Aguilar's *The Spirit of Judaism* (Philadelphia: C. Sherman & Co., 1842) went through several American editions, all edited by Isaac Lesser; George Eliot, *Daniel Deronda* (New York: Harper and Brother, 1876). Emma Lazarus, *Songs of a Semite: The Dance of Death and Other Poems* (New York: Office of the American Hebrew, 1882).

19. For example, see Emma Goldman, *Living My Life* (New York: A. A. Knopf, 1931), chapt. 1–3; Elizabeth Hasanovitch, *One of Them* (Boston: Houghton Mifflin, 1918); Elizabeth G. Stern, *My Mother and I* (New York: Macmillan, 1917); Anzia Yezierska, *The Bread Givers* (New York: Persea Books, 1975), *passim.*

20. Yuri Suhl, "Chapter and Verse," chapt. 15, *Ernestine L. Rose and the Battle for Human Rights* (New York: Reynal and Company, 1959), pp. 124–133.

21. Annie Nathan Meyer, *Barnard Beginnings* (New York: Houghton Mifflin Company, 1935), *passim;* Lloyd P. Gartner, "Temples of Liberty Unpolluted: American Jews and the Public Schools," in B. C. Korn's *A Bicentennial Festscrift for Jacob Radner Marcus* (New York: KTAV, 1976).

22. National Council of Jewish Women, *The First Fifty Years* (New York: National Council of Jewish Women, 1943), pp. 32–38. Sadie American, "Immigration as it Affects Women and Children," *Proceedings* (Council of Jewish Women, 1905), pp. 215–221. Also see the account of Minna Kleeberg's criticism of Jewish schools in Glanz, vol. 2, pp. 119–120.

23. Hannah G. Solomon, "Address," *Papers of the Jewish Women's Congress* (Philadelphia: The Jewish Publication Society of America, 1894), p. 12.

24. For biographical information on Rebecca Gratz, see Rollin G. Osterweis, *Rebecca Gratz* (New York: G. P. Putnam's Sons, 1955).

25. Excerpts from *Letters of Rebecca Gratz,* ed. Rabbi David Philipson, D.D. (Philadelphia: The Jewish Publication Society of America, 1929).

26. Extracts from paper read on February 10, 1895, before the National Council of Jewish Women, New York Branch; published in *The American Jewess* 1 (1895): 153–155.

27. For biographical information on Rosa Sonneschein, see the entry under her name in *The Encyclopedia of Zionism and Israel,* ed. Raphael Patai (New York: McGraw Hill, 1971).

28. Rosa Sonneschein, "Women and Judaism," *The American Jewess* 6 (1897): 205–209.

29. For biographical information on Emma Lazarus, see Heinrich E. Jacob, *The World of*

Emma Lazarus (New York: Schoken Books, 1949); and Beverly Lauderdale and Margaret Shelgren, *Ten Women and God* (New York: A. S. Barnes, 1979).

30. Excerpts from *Emma Lazarus: Selections from her Poetry and Prose,* ed. Morris U. Schappes (New York: Emma Lazarus Federation of Jewish Women's Clubs, 1967).

31. Excerpts from "Epistle to the Hebrews" originally published in the *American Hebrew,* November 3, 1882, to February 23, 1883.

32. Selections from *Bread Givers* by Anzia Yezierska copyright 1925 by Doubleday & Co., Inc., reprinted by permission; for biographical information on Anzia Yezierska, see Alice Kessler Harns' intoduction to *Bread Givers.*

33. Excerpt from *Tomorrow is Beautiful* (New York: Macmillan Co., 1948), pp. 24–26.

34. Ray Frank Litman, "Women in the Synagogue," *Papers of the Jewish Women's Congress* (Philadelphia Jewish Publication Society of America, 1894), pp. 52–65.

35. Biographical material available in the article on Hannah Greenebaum Solomon by Sylvia Johnson in *Notable American Women,* vol. 3, ed. Edward T. James and Janet W. James (Cambridge, Mass.: Belknap Press, 1974), pp. 324–325.

36. Excerpts from *The Fabric of My Life: The Autobiography of Hannah G. Solomon* (New York: Bloch Publishing Co., 1946), pp. 80–83; and *A Sheaf of Leaves* (Chicago: private printing, 1911), pp. 69, 72, 87.

The Struggle for the Right to Preach

1. From a pastoral letter, "The General Association of Massachusetts (Orthodox) to the Churches Under Their Care" [1837]; reprinted in Alice S. Rossi, ed., *The Feminist Papers: From Adams to deBeauvoir* (New York and London: Columbia University, 1973), pp. 305–306.

2. "Pastoral Letter," *Minutes of the General Assembly of the Presbyterian Church in the United States of America* (1832), pp. 346–349, quoted in Lois A. Boyd, "Shall Women Speak? Confrontation in the Church 1876," *Journal of Presbyterian History* (Winter, 1978): 282–283.

3. Frances E. Willard, *Woman in the Pulpit* (Boston: D. Lathrop, 1888), p. 62.

4. Jarena Lee, *Religious Experiences and Journal of Mrs. Jarena Lee, Giving Account of Her Call to Preach the Gospel: Revised and corrected from the Original Manuscript written by Herself* (Philadelphia: printed and published for the author, 1849), p. 15.

5. "One of the best known woman preachers in the United States, who has had experience of over fifteen years," quoted in Willard, *Woman in the Pulpit,* p. 109.

6. Luther Lee, *Woman's Right to Preach the Gospel: A Sermon Preached at the Ordination of the Rev. Miss Antoinette L. Brown at South Butler, Wayne County, N.Y., September 15, 1853* (Syracuse, N.Y.: published by the author, 1853), p. 22.

7. Josephine Butler, "Woman's Place in the Church," *Magazine of Christian Literature* 6 (April, 1892): 32.

8. Ibid.

9. John F. Humphreys, "Women's Work in the Church," *Homiletic Review* 25 (June, 1893): 495–498.

10. Ibid., p. 498.

11. Charles W. Torrey, "Women's Sphere in the Church," *Congregational Quarterly* 9 (April, 1867): 170.

12. Willard, *Woman in the Pulpit,* p. 76.

13. Torrey, "Women's Sphere in the Church," p. 168.

14. A. J. Gordon, "The Ministry of Women," *Missionary Review of the World* (December, 1894): 910.

15. Ibid., p. 921.

16. Humphreys, "Women's Work in the Church," p. 497–498.

17. Gordon, "The Ministry of Women," p. 919.

18. W. S. B. Goodenow, "Woman's Voice in the Church," *New Englander* 36 (January, 1877): 130.

19. Ibid., p. 131.

20. Torrey, "Women's Sphere in the Church," p. 169.

21. H. Loomis, *May A Woman Speak in a Promiscuous Assembly?* (Brooklyn, N.Y.: published by the author, 1874), p. 13. A version of this pamphlet was also published in the *Congregational Quarterly* 16 (1874).

22. Torrey, "Women's Sphere in the Church," ·p. 169. The same reasoning is also found in Gordon, "The Ministry of Women," p. 914.
23. Elizabeth Cady Stanton, et al., *The Woman's Bible,* parts 1 and 2 (New York: European Publishing Company, 1895–1898), pp. 7–8.
24. Barbara Kellison, *The Rights of Women in the Church* (Dayton, Oh.: published by the author, Herald and Banner Office, 1862). This forty-four page pamphlet was written by "a member of the Des Moines Christian Conference, Iowa."
25. Ibid., p. 21.
26. Ibid., pp. 25–26.
27. Ibid., p. 36.
28. Gordon, "The Ministry of Women," p. 911.
29. Ibid., p. 912.
30. Cyrus Cort, "Woman Preaching Viewed in the Light of God's Word and Church History," *Reformed Quarterly Review* 29 (January, 1882): 129.
31. Ibid., p. 124.
32. Stephen Knowlton, "The Silence of Women in the Churches," *Congregational Quarterly* 9 (October, 1867): 334.
33. J. L. Neve, "Shall Women Preach in the Congregation? An Exegetical Treatise," *Lutheran Quarterly* 33 (July, 1903): 412.
34. Robert L. Dabney, "The Public Preaching of Women," in *Discussions: Evangelical,* vol. 2 (Richmond, Va.: Presbyterian Committee of Publication, 1891), p. 100. This article originally appeared in the *Southern Presbyterian Review* (October, 1879).
35. Ibid., p. 97.
36. Ibid., p. 101.
37. Knowlton, "The Silence of Women," pp. 331–332.
38. Ibid., p. 332.
39. Dabney, "The Public Preaching of Women," p. 103.
40. Ibid., p. 104.
41. C. Duren, "Woman's Place in Religious Meetings," *Congregational Review* 8 (January, 1868): 22.
42. Ibid., p. 24.
43. Ibid., p. 25.
44. Ibid.
45. *Case Of The Rev. E. R. Craven against The Rev. I. M. See in the Presbytery of Newark and the Synod of New Jersey* (n.d.); this eighteen-page pamphlet covers a case begun in October, 1876.
46. Ibid., p. 13.
47. Cort, "Woman Preaching Viewed in the Light of God's Word," p. 127.
48. Henry J. Van Dyke, Sr., "Shall Women be Licensed to Preach?" chapter 6 in Willard, *Woman in the Pulpit,* pp. 113–128; this chapter is a reprint of an article that appeared in the *Homiletic Review* (December, 1887).
49. Ibid., p. 123.
50. Ibid.
51. Ibid., p. 114.
52. "Woman's Place in Religious Meetings," p. 29.
53. Margaret R. Seebach, "Shall Women Preach?" *Lutheran Quarterly* 33 (October, 1903): 580–581.
54. Ibid., pp. 581–582.
55. Ibid., pp. 582–583.
56. Dabney, "The Public Preaching of Women," pp. 114–117.
57. Ibid., pp. 117–118.
58. Willard, *Woman in the Pulpit,* pp. 94–101.
59. Lee, *Religious Experiences and Journal,* pp. 14–17.
60. Lee, *Woman's Right to Preach the Gospel.*
61. Phoebe Palmer, *Promise of the Father: or, A Neglected Specialty of the Last Days* (New York: W. C. Palmer, 1859), pp. 28–30.
62. Kellison, *The Rights of Women in the Church,* pp. 14–20.
63. Duren, "Woman's Place in Religious Meetings," pp. 22–29.
64. Samuel J. Niccolls, "Woman's Position and Work in the Church," *Presbyterian Review* 10 (April, 1889): 267–279.

348 NOTES

65. Seebach, "Shall Women Preach?" pp. 579–583.

Lay Women in the Protestant Tradition

1. R. Pierce Beaver, *All Loves Excelling* (Grand Rapids, Mich.: Eerdmans Publishing Co., 1968), p. 85.
2. Ellen C. Parsons, "The History of Woman's Organized Missionary Work as Promoted by American Women," in *Woman in Missions: Papers and Addresses presented at the Woman's Congress of Missions, October 2–4, 1893*, comp. Reverend E. M. Wherry, D.D. (New York: American Tract Society, 1894), pp. 97–104.
3. *Heathen Woman's Friend* 1, no. 1 (May, 1869): 2.
4. Nancy Cott, *The Bonds of Womanhood* (New Haven: Yale, 1977), pp. 132–135; Beaver, *All Loves Excelling*, pp. 14–34; Parsons, "History of Woman's Organized Missionary Work," pp. 84, 85.
5. *Historical Sketches of Woman's Missionary Societies in America and England* (Boston: Mrs. L. H. Daggett, 1879); Parsons, "History of Woman's Organized Missionary Work," pp. 94–96.
6. Parsons, "History of Woman's Organized Missionary Work," p. 97.
7. *The Missionary Helper* 1, no. 4 (July, 1878): 75–77; *Life and Light for Heathen Women* 1, no. 4 (January 1870): 1, 2; *Heathen Woman's Friend* 1, no. 5 (October, 1869): 37.
8. Ibid., p. 74.
9. Beaver, *All Loves Excelling*, chapt. 4.
10. Reverend Christian Golder, *History of the Deaconess Movement in the Christian Church* (Cincinnati: Jennings & Pye, 1903), pp. 255–256.
11. Reverend Christian Golder, *The Deaconess Motherhouse* (Pittsburgh: Pittsburgh Printing Co., 1907), p. 11.
12. James Thoburn, "The Deaconess and Her Vocation," chapt. 4 in *The Deaconess and Her Vocation* (New York: Hunt & Eaton, 1893).
13. *Missionary and Deaconess Advocate* 11, no. 12 (December, 1895): 3.
14. Sylvia M. Jacobs, "A.M.E. Women Missionaries in Africa, 1882–1904," paper presented at "Women in New Worlds: Historical Perspectives on the United Methodist Tradition," Cincinnati, Ohio (February 3, 1980), p. 7; Amanda Berry Smith, *An Autobiography. The Story of the Lord's Dealings with Mrs. Amanda Smith The Colored Evangelist Containing an Account of Her Life Work of Faith, and Her Travels in America, England, Ireland, Scotland, India and Africa, as an Independent Missionary*, intro. Bishop Thoburn of India (Chicago: Meyer & Brothers, 1893), pp. 342, 378, 384, 389, 393, 427, 453; quoted in Jacobs, "A.M.E. Women Missionaries in Africa," p. 7.
15. *Heathen Woman's Friend* 1, no. 1 (May, 1869): 1, 4; 1, no. 2 (July, 1869): 10, 11; 1, no. 4 (September, 1869): 28; 2, no. 8 (February, 1871): 86; 2, no. 9 (March, 1871): 98; 2, no. 12 (June, 1871): 134–139.
16. *Heathen Woman's Friend* 2, no. 9 (March, 1871): 97; 2, no. 10 (April, 1871): 112–114; 2, no. 11 (May, 1871): 123–125.
17. *Deaconess Advocate* 29, no. 5 (May, 1914): 9, 12.
18. Helen Barrett Montgomery, *Western Women in Eastern Lands: Fifty Years of Woman's Work in Foreign Missions* (New York: Macmillan Co., 1910), pp. 206, 207.
19. Jualynne Dodson, "Toward Sanctioning Women's Participation: Preaching Women, The Cutting Edge to Institutionalization of Stewardess and Deaconess in Nineteenth-Century A.M.E. Church"; and David W. Wills, "Womanhood and Domesticity in the A.M.E. Tradition: The Influence of Alexander Payne," unpublished papers presented at "Women in New Worlds," Cincinnati, Ohio (February 3, 1980).
20. Lucy Rider Meyer, *Deaconesses: Biblical, Early Church, European, American* (Chicago: Message Publishing House, 1889), pp. 210–217; *Missionary and Deaconess Advocate* 11, no. 7 (July, 1895): 2; 11, no. 8 (August, 1895): 6; Beaver, *All Loves Excelling*, p. 105.
21. Montgomery, *Western Women in Eastern Lands*, pp. 268–269.
22. Lucy Williams, "Our Mission," *The Woman's Evangel* 1, no. 4 (April, 1882): 54, 55.
23. Editorial, *The Woman's Evangel* 1, no. 1 (January, 1882): 1, 2.
24. Mrs. Willard Larkin, "Our Literature Work," *Lutheran Missionary Journal* 11, no. 2 (February, 1890): 43–45.
25. Mrs. J. L. Phillips, "Our Needs," *The Missionary Helper* 1, no. 4 (July, 1878): 75–77.
26. "Word to our Readers," *Life and Light for Heathen Women* 1, no. 1 (March, 1869): 1, 2.

27. "Laborers Wanted," *The Heathen Woman's Friend* 1, no. 5 (October, 1869): 37.
28. "Suggestions for the Formation of Auxiliaries," *The Missionary Helper* 1, no. 4 (July, 1878): 82, 83.
29. "How We Formed Our Auxiliary," *Life and Light for Heathen Women* 1, no. 1 (March, 1869): 61.
30. "A Model Auxiliary," *Life and Light for Heathen Women* 1, no. 1 (March, 1869): 91, 92.
31. "The Mite Society and Its Convention," *The AME Church Review* 13, no. 3 (January, 1896): 378–382.
32. G. H. Gerberding, *Life and Letters of W. A. Passavant, D.D.* (Greenville, Pa.: The Young Lutheran Co., 1906), pp. 191, 192.
33. Golder, "Mission and Aim of the Female Diaconate in the United States," chapt. 14 in *History of the Deaconess Movement.*
34. "Two Italian Women Workers," *The Home Mission Monthly* 27 (August, 1905): 309, 310.
35. "Appeal to the Ladies of the Methodist Episcopal Church," *The Heathen Woman's Friend* 1, no. 1 (May, 1869): 1, 2; Mrs. E. E. Baldwin, "The Great Motive," *The Heathen Woman's Friend* 2, no. 12 (June, 1871): 135, 316.
36. Golder, "The Scriptural Foundation of the Deaconess Work," chapt. 1 in *The Deaconess Motherhouse.*
37. John M. Brown, "The Ordination of Women: What Is the Authority for It?" in *The AME Church Review* 2, no. 4 (April, 1886): 359–361.
38. *The Message and Deaconess Advocate* 11, no. 12 (December, 1895): 8; *The Deaconess Advocate* 29, no. 4 (April, 1914): 8; "A New Woman of Ye Olden Time," *The Message and Deaconess Advocate* 11, no. 11 (November, 1895): 3, 4.
39. "Glimpses of our Field," *The Shield,* Class of 1915, of the Kansas City National Training School for Deaconesses and Missionaries (private printing, n.d.).
40. "Facts for Christian Women," *The Heathen Woman's Friend* 1, no. 4 (September, 1869): 27, 28.
41. "Women," *The Deaconess Advocate* 29, no. 1 (January, 1914): 7.
42. Excerpts from Parsons, "History of Woman's Organized Missionary Work."
43. Montgomery, excerpts from "Problems and Policies," chapt. 6 in *Western Women in Eastern Lands.*

Women in Social Reform Movements

1. Harriet Beecher Stowe, et al., *Our Famous Women: Comprising the Lives and Deeds of American Women* (Hartford: A. D. Worthington, 1884), p. 622.
2. Angelina E. Grimke, *Letters to Catherine E. Beecher, in Reply to An Essay on Slavery and Abolitionism, Addressed to A. E. Grimke* (Boston: Isaac Knapp, 1838), pp. 30–31.
3. See Conrad Cherry, ed., *God's New Israel: Religious Interpretations of American Destiny* (Englewood Cliffs, N.J.: Prentice-Hall, 1971).
4. Entry on Isabella Marshall Braham by Mary S. Benson in *Notable American Women 1607–1950: A Biographical Dictionary,* ed. Edward T. James (Cambridge: Belknap Press, 1971), p. 71.
5. Stowe, *Our Famous Women,* p. 59.
6. Letter from Angelina E. Grimke to Theodore Weld and John Greenleaf Whittier, August 20, 1837, in *Letters of Theodore Dwight Weld, Angelina Grimke Weld and Sarah Grimke* [1822–1844], ed. Edith H. Barnes and Dwight L. Dumond (Gloucester, Mass.: Peter Smith, 1965), p. 431.
7. S. R. Ingraham, *Walks of Usefulness or, Reminicensces of Mrs. Margaret Prior* (New York: American Female Moral Reform Society, 1844), pp. 61, 63–64. [*Emphasis in quotation added by S. R. Ingraham*]
8. William Rhinelander Stewart, *The Philanthropic Work of Josephine Shaw Lowell* (New York: Macmillan, 1911), p. 139.
9. 1 Timothy 2:9, 10 instructed women to adorn themselves modestly with good works, garb appropriate for Christians, rather than with costly, elaborate fashions.
10. Dexter C. Bloomer, *Life and Writings of Amelia Bloomer* (Boston: Arena, 1895), pp. 153–154.
11. In 1885 the National Woman's Suffrage Association convention considered a resolution calling for the clergy to use the ideas contained in Genesis 1:27 and Galatians 3:28 as the foundation of the church's teaching about woman. See Elizabeth Cady Stanton,

Eighty Years and More: Reminiscences of Elizabeth Cady Stanton (New York: Schocken Books, 1973), p. 381, where the resolution is printed in full.

12. Emma Hart Willard, "An Address to the Public; Particularly of the Members of the Legislature of New York, Proposing a Plan For Improving Female Education" [1819], in *Pioneers of Women's Education in the United States: Emma Willard, Catherine Beecher, Mary Lyon,* ed. Willystine Godsell (New York: McGraw Hill, 1931), p. 55.

13. See Edward Hitchcock, *The Power of Christian Benevolence Illustrated in the Life and Labors of Mary Lyon* (New York: American Tract Society, 1858), esp. pp. 171, 174; Laura S. Haviland, *A Woman's Life-Work: Labors and Experience of Laura S. Haviland* (Chicago: Publishing Association of Friends, 1889), in which Laura Haviland autographs her frontispiece portrait as "Thine for the oppressed"; and Eliza Daniel Stewart, *Memories of the Crusade: A Thrilling Account of the Great Uprising of the Women of Ohio in 1873, Against the Liquor Crime* (Columbus, Ohio: William G. Hubbard, 1889) esp. pp. 31, 40.

14. Charlton Edholm, *Traffic in Girls and Florence Crittenton Missions* (Chicago: Woman's Temperance Publishing Association, 1893), p. 138.

15. Caroline Healy Dall, *The College, the Market and the Court: Woman's Relation to Education, Labor and Law* (New York: Arno Press, 1972), p. xviii.

16. Frances E. Willard, *Glimpses of Fifty Years. The Autobiography of an American Woman* (Chicago: Woman's Temperance Publishing Association, 1892), pp. 470–471.

17. Ibid., p. 477.

18. Anna Howard Shaw, "The Heavenly Vision" [sermon preached at the International Council of Women, Washington D.C., March 24, 1888], in "Report of the International Council of Women," assembled by The National Woman Suffrage Association, Washington, D.C., March 25 to April 1, 1888 (Washington, D.C.; Rufus H. Darby, 1888), p. 25. [Emphasis added]

19. "Christianity, Science and Philanthropy" was the slogan of the State Charities Aid Association of New York.

20. See William Rhinelander Stewart, *The Philanthropic Work of Josephine Shaw Lowell*, p. 340 ff., for Mrs. Lowell's paper read at the first public meeting of the Working Women's Society.

21. Excerpt from Catharine E. Beecher, *An Essay on Slavery and Abolitionism with reference to the Duty of American Females* (Philadelphia: Henry Perkins, 1837), pp. 99–103.

22. *Letters of Theodore Dwight Weld, Angelina Grimke Weld and Sarah Grimke,* pp. 427–432.

23. Mary Lyon, *The Power of Christian Benevolence Illustrated in the Life and Labors of Mary Lyon* (New York: American Tract Society, 1858), pp. 182, 183.

24. George Washington Bethune, *Memoirs of Mrs. Joanna Bethune* (New York: Harper, 1863), pp. 163, 165.

25. Mary A. Livermore, *My Story of the War* (Hartford, Conn.: A. D. Worthington, 1890), pp. 488–490.

26. Haviland, *A Woman's Life-Work,* pp. 482, 492, 498–500, 517–519.

27. Elizabeth Leslie Roux Comstock (1815–1891) was a Quaker and active in abolition work in Michigan, in Temperence speaking, and concerned with the reform of hospitals, prisons, and asylums.

28. Ingraham, *Walks of Usefulness,* pp. 123–125, 176–178, 208, 209.

29. Stewart, *Memories of the Crusade,* pp. 162–165.

30. Excerpts from Shaw, "The Heavenly Vision," pp. 24–29.

31. Josephine Shaw Lowell, "Poverty and its Relief: The Methods Possible in the City of New York," Proceedings of the Twenty-Second Conference of Charities and Correction, New Haven, Ct. (May 24–30, 1895), pp. 44–54.

32. Ida Wells-Barnet, "Lynch Law in All Its Phases," from an address delivered at Tremont Temple for the Boston Monday Lectureship (February 13, 1893) and printed in *Our Day* 11, no. 65 (May, 1893): 333–347.

33. Mary Woodbridge, "Peace and Arbitration in National and International Affairs" (undated ms. written after 1889), reprinted in Reverend A. M. Hills, *Life and Labors of Mrs. Mary A. Woodbridge* (Ravenna, Ohio: F. W. Woodbridge, 1895), pp. 210–220.

Index

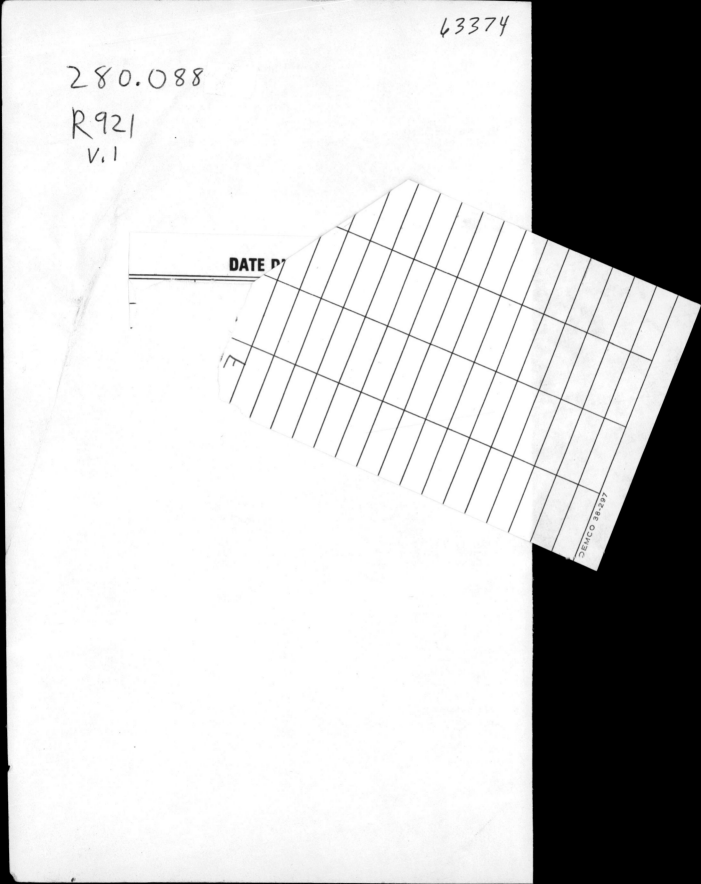